D1709839

MARTIN LUTHER,
THEOLOGIAN OF THE CHURCH

GEORGE WOLFGANG FORELL

WORD&WORLD
Theology for Christian Ministry

Supplement Series, 2

September 1994

Frederick J. Gaiser, Series Editor

Sylvia C. Ruud, Series Managing Editor

Word & World: Theology for Christian Ministry is published quarterly at Luther Seminary, 2481 Como Avenue, St. Paul, Minnesota 55108, U.S.A. Telephone (612) 641-3482.

ISSN 0275-5270
ISBN 0-9632389-1-4

GEORGE WOLFGANG FORELL

MARTIN LUTHER, THEOLOGIAN OF THE CHURCH

COLLECTED ESSAYS

in honor of his seventy-fifth birthday

edited by

William R. Russell

WORD & WORLD

Luther Seminary

St. Paul, Minnesota

Library of Congress Catalog Card Number 94-61151
ISBN 0-9632389-1-4

Printed in the United States of America

CONTENTS

CONTRIBUTORS

Oswald Bayer, Tübingen, Germany

Peter Berger, Brookline, Massachusetts

Dennis Bielfeldt, Des Moines, Iowa

Raymond M. Bost, Newberry, South Carolina

Martin Brecht, Münster, Germany

John and Ellen Buchanan, Iowa City, Iowa

James H. Burtness, St. Paul, Minnesota

Concordia College, Moorhead, Minnesota

Gilbert Doan, Jr., Ardmore, Pennsylvania

Mark U. Edwards, Jr., Northfield, Minnesota

Evangelical Lutheran Church in America, Chicago, Illinois

Robert Fischer, Western Springs, Illinois

Mary Forell-Davis, Jersey City, New Jersey

Edna Franz, Iowa City, Iowa

Melvin D. George, Minneapolis, Minnesota

Gloria Dei Lutheran Church, Iowa City, Iowa

Egil and Lorraine Grislis, Winnipeg, Manitoba

Gustavus Adolphus College, St. Peter, Minnesota

Charles and Anne Hesse, Iowa City, Iowa

Doug Holmgren, Des Moines, Iowa

Masami Ishii, Tokyo, Japan

Tom and Leslie Johnson, Overland Park, Kansas

Helmar Junghans, Leipzig, Germany

Robert Kingdon, Madison, Wisconsin

Georg Kretschmar, Munich, Germany

William H. Lazareth, Princeton, New Jersey

Carter Lindberg, Northboro, Massachusetts

Luther College, Decorah, Iowa

Lutheran Theological Seminary at Philadelphia, Pennsylvania

Lutheran School of Theology at Chicago, Illinois

Carl Mau, Redondo, Washington

Allan R. Negstad, Minneapolis, Minnesota

Heiko Oberman, Tucson, Arizona

Pacific Lutheran Theological Seminary, Berkeley, California

Pacific Lutheran University, Tacoma, Washington

Arthur Puotinen, Des Moines, Iowa

Ruprecht-Karl-Universität, Heidelberg, Germany

Heinz Scheible, Sandhausen, Germany

Richard Schoenleber, Coraopolis, Pennsylvania

Gottfried Seebass, Heidelberg, Germany

Harold Skillrud, Atlanta, Georgia

Trinity Lutheran Seminary, Columbus, Ohio

Richard Trost, Des Moines, Iowa

Wartburg Theological Seminary, Dubuque, Iowa

Paul Werger, Iowa City, Iowa

This book is dedicated to John Amos Russell, the godson of George Wolfgang Forell.

EDITOR'S PREFACE

THIS BOOK WAS DESIGNED AS A GIFT TO GEORGE FORELL ON THE OCCASION OF HIS seventy-fifth birthday (September 19, 1994). It is clear now, however, that the volume is really a gift from George Forell to us. And what a welcome and important gift it is: a most clear and insightful interpretation of Martin Luther and Lutheran theology for our time.

Most of us have been schooled to think that only what is new, modern, and contemporary is relevant. Dr. Forell's gift to us in these pages, gleaned from his prodigious scholarly output of the last fifty years, is a most compelling case that the theological priorities of a historical figure like Martin Luther remain remarkably relevant to the issues of our time.

This has been the theme of Dr. Forell's career, because George Forell, like Martin Luther himself, is a theologian of the church. It might seem a bit surprising, and even contradictory to some, that such an assertion should be made about one who spent some three and a half decades teaching at a large midwestern state university in the United States. For those of us who know the work of Dr. Forell, however, there is no contradiction. Dr. Forell is convinced that religious studies in general and the study of Christian theology in particular are objects worthy of academic inquiry in public or secular contexts, as well as in private or churchly settings. In Dr. Forell's memorable phrase: "Luther should not only be interesting to Lutherans."

For many, such a project would have been enough. Dr. Forell, however, would not be satisfied with merely drawing attention to a dead theologian, however interesting he or she might be. Dr. Forell is a theologian of the church. This means, among other things, that he brings a sense of purpose to his life's work that transcends mere academics. Dr. Forell has not spent his distinguished career investigating Luther simply because Luther was Luther. Dr. Forell has found in Luther a distinctive and clear witness to the gospel of Jesus Christ—for the church of the second half of the twentieth century, and beyond. In fact, Dr. Forell's continuing emphasis on explicating classical Lutheran theology for the modern period explains his ongoing scholarly pursuits and willingness to allow references to the human in these essays, written over a fifty year period, to be rendered into inclusive language, as well as the use, where available and appropriate, of more contemporary translations of Luther's works (in particular, the American edition) and of confessional and biblical texts than were available to him when he first wrote.

Many thanks are due to dozens of people who have made this book possible. Thanks first to Dr. Frederick Gaiser and the *Word & World* editorial board, who approved of and encouraged the idea of a Forell *Festschrift* for their emerging Supplement Series. Dr. Gaiser deserves special commendation for lending his watchful editorial eye to the process that has brought this volume to the light of day. *Word & World* Managing Editor Sylvia Ruud's delightful spirit, organizational skill, and desk-top expertise kept us close to deadlines and sped things along toward their conclusion. Thanks also to Steve Boman, senior student at Luther Seminary, and Leann Freeberg, Augsburg College religion department student assistant, who helped put the essays into readable form. My wife Ann, and our children, Sarah, John, and Mary, have provided their support and encouragement in such proportion that they also deserve a special word of thanks. Thanks to the financial contributors whose support attests to the enduring impact of Dr. Forell's scholarly contributions. Finally, thanks to the inter-library loan librarians at Augsburg College and Luther Seminary, who did such a great job of locating all the necessary materials.

Because the essays collected here span some five decades and were addressed to a wide variety of audiences, some editorial changes have been made for the sake of clarity and continuity. Hopefully, Dr. Forell's original intentions were preserved throughout. Any falsifications are the responsibility of the editor.

As the last graduate student of George Forell, it is a distinct pleasure for me to edit this volume in his honor. Doing so has once again reminded me of the scholarly profundity and eloquence of George Wolfgang Forell, who throughout his career has helped the world see that Martin Luther is indeed a theologian of the church.

George Wolfgang Forell, we, your students and friends, once again salute you with a collection in your honor* and continue to thank God for the gift of your work among us.

Soli Deo gloria.

William R. Russell, Ph.D.
Associate Professor of Religion
Waldorf College
Forest City, Iowa

---

*There was an earlier *Festschrift* on the occasion of Dr. Forell's sixty-fifth birthday: Carter Lindberg, ed., *Piety, Politics, and Ethics: Reformation Studies in Honor of George Wolfgang Forell* (Kirksville, Missouri: Sixteenth Century Journal Publishers, 1984).

ABBREVIATIONS

AC *The Augsburg Confession.*

Ap *The Apology to the Augsburg Confession.*

BC *The Book of Concord: The Confessions of the Evangelical Lutheran Church,* trans. and ed. Theodore G. Tappert et al. (Philadelphia: Fortress, 1959)

EA *Dr. Martin Luthers sämmtliche Werke,* 67 vols. (Erlangen: Heyder & Zimmer, 1826-1857).

FC, Ep *Formula of Concord, Epitome.*

FC, SD *Formula of Concord, Solid Declaration.*

LW *Luther's Works,* ed. Jaroslav Pelikan, Hilton C. Oswald, Helmut T. Lehmann, vols. 1-30 (St. Louis: Concordia, 1955-); vols. 31-55 (Philadelphia: Fortress, 1957-86).

PE *Works of Martin Luther: The Philadelphia Edition,* 6 vols. (1915-1932; reprint, Philadelphia: Muhlenberg, 1930-1943).

WA *D. Martin Luthers Werke: Kritische Gesamtausgabe,* 60 vols. to date (Weimar: Hermann Böhlaus Nachfolger, 1883-).

WA, Br *D. Martin Luthers Werke: Kritische Gesamtausgabe, Briefwechsel,* 15 vols. (Weimar: Hermann Böhlaus Nachfolger, 1930-1978).

WA, TR *D. Martin Luthers Werke: Kritische Gesamtausgabe, Tischreden,* 6 vols. (Weimar: Hermann Böhlaus Nachfolger, 1912-1921).

Word & World
Supplement Series 2
1994

"They Told What Had Happened on the Road"

RAISED IN A PARSONAGE IN MICHELSDORF IN GERMANY, SITUATED IN THE HILLS of Silesia—the son, grandson, and great-grandson of Silesian pastors, I was immersed in the Christian faith and its proclamation. My paternal, non-theological grandparents had died before I was born. My paternal uncles and aunts appeared only rarely in my life. The maternal grandparents who lived in Landeshut, not far from Michelsdorf, were next to my parents the most important influence on me. My grandfather Georg Kretschmar was the superintendent of the district. Two of my mother's siblings were important members of my extended family: an aunt, my god-mother, married to a pastor in Landeshut, and an uncle who was himself a pastor in the same district.

SCHOOL IN SILESIA

In 1925, when my father was called from his rural parish to Breslau, the capital and largest city of the province, to serve as *Sozialpfarrer* for Silesia (and as executive secretary of the Silesian *Frauenhilfe*) I spent six months in Landeshut getting to know my grandparents better and attending a *Volksschule*. Here I soon discovered that while being a pastor's son in the first grade might have given me status in Michelsdorf, it made me subject to hazing and beatings in the rough and tumble environment of this urban school, where most of the other children came from what Karl Marx would have called the proletariat. Before I was six I had learned that class and the dialect associated with class was an inescapable reality. I

This essay, first published in dialog *33/2 (1994) 129-134, is a most appropriate beginning to this book, because here Dr. Forell provides his "theological autobiography." Like the disciples who were met by Jesus "on the road" to Emmaus, Dr. Forell has spent his life telling others of God's gracious presence in Christ. For more information on Dr. Forell's life, see the editor's preface to* Piety, Politics, and Ethics: Reformation Studies in Honor of George Wolfgang Forell, *ed. Carter Lindberg (Kirksville, MO: Sixteenth Century Journal Publishers, 1984) vii-xi.*

learned to speak two languages: the Silesian dialect on the playground, and the High German expected in school and at home.

After the family moved to Breslau, I finished grade school (i.e., the first four years) in a small private school and entered the König Wilhelm Gymnasium to prepare myself to become a pastor. The Gymnasium taught Latin from the first to the last year (*Sexta* to *Ober-Prima*, nine years) and Greek starting at the third year. This emphasis on classical languages and literature—one hour for six days a week for each of these subjects—was eventually very useful to me, though at the time it seemed a meaningless exercise.

THE NAZI THREAT

The routine of my education was interrupted in 1933 when my father was forced into retirement (*zwangspensioniert*) as a result of Hitler's rise to power. At the time 44 years old, he had opposed the rising Nazi tide and was forced to pay the consequences. He decided to leave Germany immediately, convinced that the evil Nazi lunacy would quickly pass. He had to find a job. A Swedish mission society concerned with the fate of the refugees from Germany employed him as pastor and missionary in Vienna. He left Germany in June of 1933. My mother, my younger brother, and I stayed in Breslau until the end of the academic year—which at that time meant until March of 1934—when we also moved to Vienna.

The change from the upper-class environment of the König Wilhelm Gymnasium, attended by the sons of judges, doctors, lawyers, architects, etc.—the *Gebildeten*,[1] in Schleiermacher's phrase—to the Wasa Gymnasium in the ninth district of Vienna was an enormous culture shock. Accustomed to being part of the majority culture I was suddenly a member of a very small minority. In a class of boys and girls who were either Roman Catholics or Jews, the Lutherans had identity problems. (About 18 were Roman Catholics, 17 were Jews, and three were Protestants.) Besides that, I was the only one who spoke with a foreign accent. I was a "*Piefke*," a boy who spoke a different brand of German. As a matter of fact, since I moved to Vienna at the age of thirteen and for the next sixty years I hardly ever opened my mouth on any subject without people asking, "Where are you from?" I did make friends among both the Jews and the Catholics, but I had to ask myself rather early in life what it meant to be "*Evangelisch, A.B.*" (a Protestant committed to the Augsburg Confession).

But while the Christian faith was important in my home, and I went to church and was confirmed, the overwhelming experience in these years was Viennese culture, which I devoured with enthusiasm: from opera to theater, from Austro-Marxism to psychoanalysis. In the background was always the menace of national socialism, which had threatened briefly in 1934. In that summer the

---

[1]F. Schleiermacher, *On Religion: Speeches on Religion to its Cultured Despisers* (Harper Torchbook, New York, 1958). The term "cultured" is a somewhat inadequate translation of the German word "*gebildet*."

Austrian Chancellor Dollfuss was assassinated and the village in Styria where we were on holiday was for a day or so ruled by Austrian Nazi storm-troopers.

While my Catholic and Jewish friends were mostly apolitical, I was aware of the danger especially to me and my Jewish friends. The Austrian government of the time was not devoted to democracy. It practiced its own peculiar brand of Austro-Fascism, claiming to be inspired by the papal encyclicals on social justice. Lutherans were second-class citizens. If a Lutheran and Roman Catholic had married and the marriage failed, the Roman Catholic partner could obtain an annulment from the pope, but since there was no divorce the Lutheran partner remained married to a person who soon might be married to somebody else. The result of all this was a tendency among Protestants to favor liberation from this government through *Anschluß* to the German Reich. They would not believe that the demonic evils of Nazism far outweighed the very real annoyances of Austro-Fascism.

With the exception of one committed social democrat, my friends hardly ever talked politics. We talked about soccer, art, and music, and went to the opera a couple of times a week in the section for people who were willing to stand, either on the main floor or in the gallery. We visited museums and attended professional soccer games, hiked and skied in the Vienna woods, and actually got along with each other amazingly well. I learned a great deal about Catholic and Jewish culture and the peculiar mixture of both which was the genius of Vienna between the first and second World Wars. In 1937 I graduated from the Gymnasium and began to study theology and philosophy at the University of Vienna. By that time I had decided that in the world in which I lived there were only two options.

NIETZSCHE VS. CHRIST

One was the Nietzsche option: The radical rejection of Christianity and with it all the sentimental reductionist alternatives of the enlightenment and liberal protestantism. God is dead and everything is permitted. I gave it some thought. My academic and political environment made it appear attractive. Nietzsche, too, was a Lutheran pastor's son. He wrote better German than any other philosopher I had ever read. He was free from the cloying religious sentimentality that says all the right things and does nothing about it. *Thus Spake Zarathustra* was one of my favorite books.

The other option was to serve Jesus, the Christ, whom I had seen as a stumbling block and foolishness to Jews and gentiles but who was the only person to whom I could be completely committed. The example of my parents, who were so obviously engaged in such service—as counselling, feeding, and clothing refugees—made the first option impossible. God had reached out to me and my efforts to establish autonomy were doomed from the start. I had seen Christ at work through women and men of faith. Anything but discipleship to him would be inconceivable.

FROM VIENNA TO PHILADELPHIA

I knew, of course, that I would have to get out of the doomed city of Vienna as soon as possible. The plan was to go to the Lutheran Theological Seminary at Philadelphia, where a Presbyterian friend of my father had been able to obtain a full scholarship for me. The United Lutheran Church in America still needed pastors who could preach in German and was willing to take a chance on some of us who were trying to escape the Nazi war-machine. While the distinguished Norwegian writer Ronald Fangen, whom I once had given a guided tour of Vienna, had also arranged for a scholarship at Uppsala, Sweden, I decided to go to Philadelphia because my grandfather (who had never been outside the German speaking parts of Europe) had told me, "Wolfgang, you can never become a Swede but you may become an American."

But in March of 1938 Hitler invaded Austria. My plans for an orderly journey to America to begin my studies in the fall of 1938 had to be cancelled. I had to get out immediately. Agents of the Gestapo had been at the office of the mission. My father had not been home; he never went home again but left for Prague. I followed a day later. From there we made our way to Sweden and I tried to obtain my visa to the U.S. My application made months earlier had been lost at the embassy in Vienna. After a short stay in England and France I eventually secured a visa in January of 1939 and began my career as a theological student in Philadelphia.

After Nazi-occupied Vienna, London, and Paris during the Munich crisis of 1938, Philadelphia represented another culture shock. Isolationism was the political mood of the time. The professor who was most kind to me, Dr. Paul Hoh, later president of the seminary, warned me never to make any political comments especially when visiting in congregations with German services. My fellow students, who were extremely kind and supportive to the greenhorn, amused by the way he handled knife and fork, had no interest in foreign policy. Those few fellow-students who were politically engaged were supporters of Roosevelt and the New Deal. Especially my friend and later roommate Morgan Edwards, the son of a Johnstown steelworker who had worked as a butcher in a supermarket before coming to the seminary, introduced me to American politics. He also took me home with him and we visited his father at work in the steel mill.

Theologically I marched to a different drummer from any of my teachers or fellow students. After reading Karl Barth in Europe and especially his small book on the Apostles' Creed, *Credo,* I had become a "Barthian." The theological conflicts at the seminary—and there were very few—were between the "orthodox" and the "liberals," symbolized by Dr. Emil Fischer, who taught systematic theology, and Dr. O. Frederick Nolde, who taught religious education. Both positions seemed irrelevant to me. The emphasis on higher criticism in the interpretation of the Bible, which seemed daring and progressive to some, appeared obvious and obsolete to one who had been influenced by Barth's commentary on Romans. I had read the Old Testament commentaries based on Wellhausen—but they seemed to say nothing to the world that was about to burst into flames. While I had little patience with the question-and-answer orthodoxy of some of my textbooks, I found even that more to the point than the talk about progress and progressive revelation by the very decent and well-meaning Dr. Nolde. The war was starting in Europe, and America was going to be part of it; and progress seemed not to be the category which helped explain the situation during my seminary years.

Even before I graduated from Mt. Airy in 1941 my parents, after having been briefly interned in French concentration camps, had managed to escape to America with the help of the Second Presbyterian Church in New York, and arrived in that city in October of 1940. My brother John Gotthold, who had been shipped on the notorious "Dunera" from England to Australia, was eventually allowed to join the Australian army and later studied theology in Sydney. He came to America after the end of the war and served a number of Episcopal churches in New Jersey until his untimely death in 1961.

Upon my ordination I was called to serve two congregations in New Jersey (Wenonah and Woodbury) of the old Ministerium of Pennsylvania and Adjacent States and to preach every Sunday, twice in English and once in German. The people in my congregations were very good to me and tolerant of my mistakes. They seemed to like my preaching—at least they liked me. They also allowed me to take one day a week—Monday—to drive to Princeton Theological Seminary to do graduate work.

FROM BARTH TO LUTHER

The two most important teachers for me were Otto Pieper and Josef Hromadka. Both were refugees. Pieper had been Barth's successor at the University of Münster, and Hromadka, a Christian socialist, had been the Czech interpreter of Barth's theology in Prague. To him Barth had written his famous letter indicating that the Czechs had the duty to resist the Nazis militarily because of the resurrection of Christ. He allowed me to work with him on Luther's doctrine of the church. I had begun my study of the doctrine of the church at Mt. Airy and had written my B.D. thesis—still required in those days—on Paul's understanding of the church as the people of God, the true Israel. It seemed a good idea to pursue this idea in Luther. This effort produced eventually my Th.M. thesis for Princeton, called *The Reality of the Church as the Communion of Saints*. I claimed that Luther, far from being an individualist, believed that God saves us into a community in which we are "baked together" like the bread in holy communion. Here we share all we own and hold everything in common and do not need the services of an ecclesiastical bureaucracy to sell us shares in salvation. Luther rejected the capitalist notion which undergirded the treasure of merits at the disposal of the papacy. All Christians had free access to this treasure because of the death and resurrection of Christ. Thus it was his doctrine of the church, developed very early in his career, which enabled him to stand up against what he considered the pretensions of the papacy. I published this dissertation myself in 1943. But the importance of this study was that it had forced me to read a lot of Luther. The more I read him the more I liked him. It was the reading of Luther which slowly weaned me from Karl Barth.

UNION, NIEBUHR, AND *FAITH ACTIVE IN LOVE*

In 1943 the United States was at war with Hitler's Germany. The most eloquent theological spokesman for this involvement had been Reinhold Niebuhr. I had volunteered for the chaplaincy, but as an "enemy alien" I did not qualify. I decided to continue my theological studies with Reinhold Niebuhr at Union Theological Seminary. In 1943 this was a daring move, frowned upon by the president of my synod, Dr. Emil Fischer of the Ministerium of Pennsylvania, who had moved from the seminary to this position. But I was not to be discouraged and began my studies at Union in the fall of 1943. I received an assistantship in church history and had the honor of working with Robert Hastings Nichols and John T. McNeill, men of faith and great scholarly achievement.

Reinhold Niebuhr was a controversial figure. Some of my best friends would not take courses from him, considering him a traitor to the pacifist cause. I admired him as a lecturer and as a theologian who had applied his theology to the gigantic problems of the day. I thought his interpretation of Luther was wrong-headed and not based on the sources but on Ernst Troeltsch. I wrote my Th.D. dissertation under him, which dealt with Luther's social ethics and was later published as *Faith Active in Love*.[2] I received much help from John Bennett and John T. McNeill who served on my committee. I took every course Paul Tillich offered and argued with him from my Barthian perspective, to his amusement and my education. He reported to my father, with whom he was associated in anti-Nazi activities, that I questioned his Christianity, but this did not keep him from befriending me, especially in later years when we taught simultaneously in Hamburg, and still later when we both taught in Chicago in the early sixties.

In New York I met my wife, Elizabeth Rossing, a St. Olaf graduate who was then a graduate student at Columbia, and was very intelligent, beautiful, and kind, and shared my religious and political concerns. We met in January and were married in June, 1945.

It is apparent to me now that Niebuhr exerted a great influence on me. My tendency to combine an orthodox Lutheran theology with a liberal political stance was clearly influenced by him. At the time it was a peculiar combination. When, after two years as pastor at a bilingual congregation in the Bronx, I began my teaching career at Gustavus Adolphus College in 1947, this combination struck my colleagues and students as very odd. At the time, the Lutheran church in Minnesota was pretty much the Republican party at prayer. To be an active Democrat was peculiar and to combine this with serious questions concerning the agenda of theological liberalism was unheard-of. I became active in the Democratic-Farmer-Labor Party in Minnesota, had a public controversy with Senator Joseph McCarthy

---

[2]George Wolfgang Forell, *Faith Active in Love* (New York: American, 1954; reprint, Minneapolis: Augsburg, 1959).

on the campus of the college, and served as an alternate delegate to the Democratic convention in 1952. After seven years of teaching philosophy and religion at Gustavus Adolphus College I moved to the school of religion at the University of Iowa in the fall of 1954.

It was the year *Faith Active in Love* was published. In this book I tried to show that Luther was a social activist from the indulgence controversy in Wittenberg to his involvement with the Counts of Mansfeld at the end of his life. The book was well received, especially by Lutherans.

My new position at Iowa meant that I no longer dealt with philosophy but with "religion" and the teaching of religion in a secular university. Iowa had pioneered in this effort and from the beginning had approached it in a multi-religious manner. This was a new experience for me and involved me in the valuable study of non-Christian religions. For years I taught a large course in cooperation with authorities on Judaism, Islam, Hinduism, and Buddhism which opened my eyes to the pluralistic world. While I eventually relinquished this course in order to concentrate on the course dealing with Judaism and Christianity taught jointly with my friend Rabbi Jay Holstein, the Iowa experience gave me a much broader context than my days in the parish and at Gustavus Adolphus College.

But while most of my students heard me in these large introductory courses, I continued to teach undergraduate and graduate students in the area of my graduate work—Christian ethics and reformation studies. I believe it was this combination which involved me in the efforts of the Lutheran church to develop an ethical stance in the controversies of the times flowing from confessional authorities of the church of the reformation.

LUTHERAN THEOLOGY IN AMERICAN CULTURE

It seemed apparent to me that the maintenance of a Lutheran church in North America could not be justified on the same grounds as in Scandinavia or Germany. In those countries the Lutheran church was an aspect of national identity. Practically everybody, including most atheists, would agree that the cultural expressions of the church, the ancient church buildings, the classical music, the rituals marking the stages on life's way from birth to death, were an inescapable component of being a Swede or German. A similar claim cannot be made in this country. Many aspects of Lutheran culture interfere with the acceptance of the Lutheran church as part of our civil religion. Thus efforts are being made to create a Lutheran church more acceptable to the American religious sensibility, to drop the depressing emphasis on the importance of sin and to omit hymns which talk about Jesus' wounded head and the devil as the prince of this world and other gloomy subjects.

But while a Lutheran church without a Lutheran theology may be sociologically viable in Germany or Scandinavia, it is doomed in America. Without a distinctive theology there is no reason to maintain a separate Lutheran church; its disappearance within the mainstream of culture-protestantism of the right or the left is unavoidable and by no means deplorable. There is no need for another version of the UCC or the Episcopal church. For that matter a Southern Baptist church with a slightly German accent is redundant.

That raises the question as to the nature of Lutheran theological identity and its significance for the life of the Christian church in this country. For years I have claimed, in season and out of season—in Lutheran theological journals and Funk and Wagnall's supermarket encyclopedia—that there are certain distinctive aspects of Lutheran theology which if lost would weaken and impoverish the Christian message in our world. Here I shall mention them only as slogans: (1) the distinction of law and gospel; (2) the Christian as righteous and sinner at the same time; (3) the finite as the bearer of the infinite (with its implications for sacrament, scripture, and vocation); and (4) the theology of the cross vs. the theology of glory.

Everything I have ever written has been an attempt to elucidate one or the other aspect of this message, convinced that it might help all Christians to understand their election and the resulting obligation. This proclamation is a debt Lutherans owe to the ecumenical church. It is not a sign of superiority or a reason for isolation, but rather a vocation which should contribute to the wholeness of the people of God. It would be my claim that Quakers and Jesuits, the Salvation Army and the Coptic Church may likewise have obligations to the people of God which, while not equally apparent to me, may be very obvious to them and important to all of us.

THE PROTESTANT FAITH— A POST-DENOMINATIONAL BOOK

This understanding of the Lutheran tradition within the ecumenical context has been the result of my experience as a teacher of theology not only at Iowa but in Tanzania (1960), Japan (1968), India (1978), Hong Kong (1980), and Taiwan (1993), and three years as advisor to the Department of Studies of the LWF (1981-84). I have learned that the theological insights so dear to me and clearly identified with Luther and the church of the reformation are, if freed from the denominational label, of value to people who have no roots in the Europe of the sixteenth century. In Taiwan, my book *The Protestant Faith*[3] has been translated into Chinese, given another title more appropriate to the Chinese setting (*Biblical Systematic Theology*), and published without my knowledge or permission by a non-Lutheran publisher. I understand it is in the third printing and used by Christians of various backgrounds. When, while teaching at the China Evangelical Seminary at Taipei in 1993, I asked for the reason for the book's apparent popularity in a setting so very different from the Iowa students for whom it was originally written, I was told that it summarizes evangelical theology for a post-denominational Christianity in a manner they consider appropriate to their situation. It may be of some significance that while only one of my books is still in print in the U.S.A., three are in print in Chinese.

---

[3]George W. Forell, *The Protestant Faith* (Englewood, Cliffs, NJ: Prentice Hall, 1960; Minneapolis: Augsburg, 1975).

We are, indeed, in a post-denominational age. But this does not imply that we live in a post-theological age. It is our task to express the Christian faith in words that reach people at the turn of the millennium. It is my conviction that the theology developed in the sixteenth century, briefly characterized above, supplies basic resources that can be used for the articulation of the Christian faith in our time. This task should be undertaken in the church for its members as well as for all the people on the outside who are questioning the nature and destiny of humanity.

People inside and outside the church are surrounded by innumerable ideologies soliciting their attention and demanding their loyalty. This situation is inescapable. It was always thus: as Luther observed in the Large Catechism, we trust either God or an idol; for human beings atheism is an impossibility. Thus no other investigation is more significant than that which examines what people believe, which makes theology the queen of the sciences.

But the church is not the only place where this inquiry can be pursued. At the end of my career at Iowa I was invited to give the annual Presidential Lecture which gave me the opportunity to explain what I had been up to for the last thirty-five years. I called it "The Sacred and the Secular: Religion in the State University,"[4] and claimed that (1) the university is a major resource to the study of religion and (2) the study of religion is a valuable resource to the academic task of the university. This is what I had tried to demonstrate while teaching the forty thousand students that had been enrolled in my classes from 1954 to 1990.

Having been brought to America more than half a century ago to preach the gospel in German, I am now apprehensive that the gospel may not be preached at all. If the church abandons its responsibility to theology to devote itself entirely to entertainment, pop-psychology, and social-work, the task of helping people with the big questions will be assumed by others. If that happens, somebody will eventually write a book with the title: *The Treason of the Church*. It was at that point in a very similar condition almost five hundred years ago that Luther entered the picture. At the end of my pilgrimage I am convinced that his relevance to our situation is enormous.

---

[4]George Wolfgang Forell, *The Sacred and the Secular*, Sixth Annual Presidential Lecture (Iowa City, IA: The University of Iowa, 1989).

Part I
ON LUTHER

Word & World
Supplement Series 2
1994

The Reformation and the Modern World

T HERE CAN BE LITTLE DOUBT THAT MARTIN LUTHER IS ONE OF THE BEST KNOWN religious figures in western history. A number of factors have assured him of this lofty position:

1. He appeared at one of the great watersheds of history, the end of the middle ages and the beginning of modern times. This fact alone has kept historians, interested in pigeonholing people, busy assigning him either to the middle ages or modernity.

2. He dealt with issues of universal interest. People are inalienably religious and those who deal creatively and freshly with religious ideas can be sure of an interested audience.

3. He was an extremely prolific and lucid writer. One hundred folio volumes barely contain the results of a lifetime of creative effort. But it is not the bulk of his literary effort which has made him so prominent. Other prolific writers of the past are completely forgotten. He, however, had a gift for finding the colorful phrase, and as Erikson[1] and Osborne[2] have reminded us, he combined some of the theological subtlety of an Augustine with the realism and directness or even crudity of language of his contemporary Rabelais. In fact, some of his more colorful expressions utilized by Osborne in his play seem shocking, even on the hard-boiled

---

[1][Erik Erikson's *Young Man Luther: A Study in Psychoanalysis and History* (New York: Norton, 1962) proposed to analyze Luther's life by means of Erikson's psychoanalytic methodology. Although most serious historians of theology accepted neither Erikson's method nor his conclusions, for a decade and a half *Young Man Luther* was a work against which Luther scholars needed to react. Ed.]

[2][Thomas Osborne wrote the stageplay *Luther*, which ran at the St. James Theatre in New York from September 15, 1963 to March 28, 1974. Ed.]

This essay was published in The Reformation and the Revolution *(Sioux Falls, South Dakota: Augustana College Press, 1970). The volume was a collection of the presentations made at a conference held on the campus of Augustana College, "The Relevance of Martin Luther" (July 5-10, 1969).*

Broadway stage in the second half of the twentieth century. I have been told that the pious Lutheran lady who serves as a copy-editor in one of the Lutheran publishing houses which is preparing to publish Luther's *Table Talks* has been frequently in tears, deeply shocked, while reading the expressions of this man, whom she as a child had learned to venerate and who fits so very poorly into the stereotype of our twentieth-century concept of piety.

4. He was a very human, all too human, being. The very amplitude of his personality makes it possible for almost everybody to identify with some aspect of it. It is indeed possible to show that all through the last four centuries people have in fact identified themselves selectively with certain facets of this vast person. This process has produced a great many "Luthers," none of whom approximates the complexity of the original. Yet it is this amplitude which has enabled every generation to find something in him which brings him closer to them.

It is my claim that this universal fascination exerted by Luther the person has contributed considerably to our misunderstanding of the Protestant reformation as the work of an inspired genius or obsessed madman, as the case may be. Legends which have no basis in fact have been used to interpret the reformation even by people who were completely aware of the legendary character of this material. Two examples must suffice. The distinguished American reformation historian Roland Bainton has written a book called *Here I Stand: A Life of Martin Luther*,[3] fully aware, I am sure, of the fact that Luther never said anything like "Here I stand" at Worms. It was my task as editor of volume 32 of the American edition of *Luther's Works* to sift fact from legend in the proceedings at Worms. Luther's appearance before emperor and empire in 1521 happens to be an event for which we have excellent documentation. Not only the reports of Luther's friends, but also the report of Luther's enemy, the papal nuncio Aleander and the so-called *Reichstag- sakten*, the official minutes of the Imperial Diet, are available. They lead us to believe that Luther said, "May God help me!" (cf. *LW* 32:113) Professor Bainton says, "The earliest printed version added the words: 'Here I stand, I cannot do otherwise.' The words, though not recorded on the spot, may nevertheless be genuine, because the listeners at the moment may have been too moved to write" (Bainton, 185). This is the romantic notion which appeals to our sense of the dramatic and misleads us into misunderstanding the character of the reformation.

Similarly, the much advertised story that Luther had an epileptic seizure while saying his first Mass has been told us only by Cochlaeus, the inveterate enemy of Luther, who also mentions on equally good authority that Martin was the result of sexual intercourse between the devil and Mrs. Luther. Erikson, who is aware of the dubious source of the information concerning the alleged seizure, nevertheless proceeds to build his entire Luther interpretation around this bit of propaganda, and this same fictitious incident becomes one of the most dramatic moments in Osborne's Luther play. Erikson asks ingenuously, "Why did I intro- duce my discussion of Luther with this particular event in the choir, whose inter-

---

[3]Roland Bainton, *Here I Stand: A Life of Martin Luther* (Nashville: Abingdon, 1950).

pretation is subject to so many large and small discrepancies?" (Erikson, 29) and answers, "A man's historical image often depends on which legend temporarily overcomes all others; however, all these ways of viewing a great man's life may be needed to capture the mood of the historical event" (Erikson, 36).

Erikson and Osborne are sympathetic towards Luther, but they like this story because it fits into their understanding of the young genius and his identity crisis—or their vision of Luther as an "angry young man." They want to make a point and are not interested in an understanding of the reformation. But it is the reformation as a major cultural movement that influenced the character of Europe and America which interests us here. And for an understanding of this movement, its character and its influence, it is far more important that Luther was a working university professor than that he made highly dramatic pronouncements at Worms or had seizures in the choir.

I.

Indeed, it is my claim that an important key to the character of the reformation was the University of Wittenberg, namely, the fact that Luther was a member of the faculty of that university and that the reformation was a university movement.

On October 25, 1512, at 7:00 a.m., young man Luther began his lectures in the auditorium of the Black Cloister in Wittenberg. He was then not quite 29 years old. He was one of the five regular professors of theology in a very new university. Indeed, the university had been founded in Wittenberg on the Elbe River, then a town of about 2000 inhabitants and the residence of the electors of Saxony, in 1502, just ten years before Luther gave his first lecture.

The university was patterned after Tübingen, which had opened its doors in 1477 and which had later supplied some of the most distinguished professors for Wittenberg. Besides the faculty of theology there was a faculty of liberal arts, law, and medicine. Liberal arts was the basis for admission to the more advanced work in law, medicine, and theology. At first a university completely in line with the general medieval scholastic tradition, it was changed into the center of the Protestant reformation through the work of Luther and his colleagues.

In brief, I would assert that the reformation can be understood more easily by means of the academic changes that took place in Wittenberg after 1512 and the influence which the professors and students of this university exerted upon their age by means of their academic activities than by any of the subjective experiences in Luther's life, from the thunderstorm near Stotternheim to the so-called "tower experience," whether this tower room was his study or the toilet of the monastery as Denifle, Erikson, Norman O. Brown, and other exponents of the Luther legend want to have it.

What was the prevailing theology at Wittenberg until Luther's arrival? Johann von Staupitz and Martin Polich von Mellerstadt had been the university's most famous teachers. The publicity material of the university referred to them as the "two columns upholding the new school."

Staupitz, the scion of Saxon nobility, was an Augustinian monk who had studied in Tübingen, where he received his doctorate, and had been called by Frederick the Wise to assist him in the organization of his university. Staupitz became the first theological professor at Wittenberg. He was a deeply religious person, yet open to the world—but in no way a reformer. While of great personal significance for Luther's development, he was unable to grasp either the reasons for the need for a reformation or its ultimate direction. By the time of his death in 1524 he had become a Benedictine Abbot and had lost touch with Luther and the reformation. He was a typical sincere medieval Christian theologian, but in no way a precursor of the reformation.

The other "column" upholding the university was Martin Polich, who had studied not only theology but also medicine at Leipzig. The personal physician of the elector, he was brought to Wittenberg as vice chancellor and was universally popular. But while somewhat critical of late medieval scholasticism (he considered the question whether Adam could have become a father if he had not sinned theologically irrelevant and was therefore accused of heresy), he was a Thomist and not in any serious way a humanist, as has sometimes been claimed.

The other theological professors, namely, Nicholaus von Amsdorf and Andreas Bodenstein von Karlstadt, were Scotist and Thomist, respectively. Only later, in 1507, did the appointment of Jodocus Trutfetter, formerly of Erfurt and a teacher of Luther, add a representative of modern theology, the *Via Moderna* of William of Occam, to the faculty. But he lasted only three years and returned in 1510 to Erfurt.

It was in a thoroughly conventional late medieval university, barely touched by humanism, that Luther began to lecture in 1512. Unlike the professors of liberal arts, law, and medicine, he, as a theologian, was allowed to choose his own subjects. Only the time of day was prescribed and also that he was to lecture *a principio usque ad finem horae voce clara et intelligibili* [from the beginning to the end of the hour in a clear and intelligible voice]. He was not obligated to represent any particular school and had to fear no interference from the elector, who believed that "the men whose task it was to interpret the divine law to us" should be completely free to do so. Luther's spiritual superior, Bishop Jerome Schulze of Brandenburg, had in Luther's own words such a deep respect for scholars that it "tended to threaten his episcopal authority."

All this meant that as a properly called university professor and doctor of the Holy Scriptures, whose task was biblical exegesis, Luther had almost complete freedom to study and to teach. The reformation is not the result of his digestive difficulties, however severe they may have been, but of the seriousness of his preparation for his lectures and of these lectures themselves.

As Professor Scheel has pointed out, Luther was the first doctor of theology who only lectured on the scriptures. After his assumption of the chair of biblical exegesis he never gave a lecture on systematic theology or church history, but restricted himself completely to the interpretation of the Bible. It was a change in the character of exegesis, the way in which the Bible was to be read and interpreted, which made the reformation possible and necessary.

Exegesis in the medieval university had been determined by the methodology of hellenistic rationalism. Confronted with the necessity to derive ultimate philosophical truths from the mythology of Homer and Hesiod, they had developed the allegorical method of interpreting these classical epics. Medieval exegesis had adopted this hellenistic approach and adapted it to the study of the Bible. This resulted in the so-called fourfold sense of scripture as described in the Latin jingle: *littera gesta docet, quid credas allegoria, moralis quid agas, quid speres anagogia.* This means: "The letter lets you know what happened and allegory what you must believe; the moral sense what you must do; and the anagogical sense what you may hope for." To illustrate, when the word "Jerusalem" appeared in the Bible it meant, literally, the city in Palestine; allegorically, the church; morally, the human soul; and anagogically, heaven. Or Ishmael and Isaac, the sons of Abraham mentioned in Genesis, would be, literally, the sons of Abraham; allegorically, the two testaments, Old and New, or the synagogue and the church, or law and grace; morally, flesh and spirit; and anagogically, hell and heaven.

It is apparent that with this methodology the authority of the Bible for the church was completely undermined since every passage could mean practically anything the interpreter might want to see in it. The magisterium, the teaching office of the church, was alone able to decide the adequacy and orthodoxy of the many possible interpretations. Thus, the authority of the scripture disappeared behind the authority of the theological teaching office.

Luther inherited this method and used it for a while. We can see this in his early exegesis of the Psalms. He used the various senses of scripture as he had been taught. But some had already objected to this procedure, especially Nicolaus von Lyra (1270-1340), who knew only two senses, the literal and the mystical, and who insisted that the literal sense was fundamental and that a mystical sense might not be present in every passage. Lyra's work had been further developed by Erasmus of Rotterdam, who tried to use the literal sense of the scriptures to criticize the practice of the church. He used allegory only when the literal sense was offensive to him. Erasmus also raised a number of critical questions, suggested that Mark was an excerpt from Matthew, and denied that St. John had written the Book of Revelation.

Luther knew the works of Lyra and Erasmus and used them but found their criteria too non-theological. What Luther substituted for the fourfold sense of scripture was not merely the literal and grammatical sense, but his gradually emerging conviction that there is such a thing as a hermeneutical center which determines the Christian understanding of the Bible. This he expressed very clearly in his prefaces to the September Bible of 1522. He wrote:

> And that is the true test by which to judge all books, when we see whether or not they inculcate Christ. For all the Scriptures show us Christ, Romans 3[:21]; and St. Paul will know nothing but Christ, I Corinthians 2[:2]. Whatever does not teach Christ is not yet apostolic, even though St. Peter or St. Paul does the teaching. Again, whatever preaches Christ would be apostolic, even if Judas, Annas, Pilate, and Herod were doing it.[4]

[4]*Preface to the Epistles of St. James and St. Jude,* LW, 35:396.

The Bible is no longer a law book, consisting of thousands of equally significant verses which can be quoted out of context. Luther abandoned this homogenized view of scripture and insisted that Jesus as the Christ was the center of the
entire scriptural canon and that everything had to be read, understood, and
preached in relation to this central proclamation. Thus he had actually a canon
within the canon as he wrote in 1522.

> From all this you can now judge all the books and decide among them which are
> the best. John's Gospel and St. Paul's epistles, especially that to the Romans, and
> St. Peter's first epistle are the true kernel and marrow of all the books. They ought
> properly to be the foremost books, and it would be advisable for every Christian
> to read them first and most, and by daily reading to make them as much his own
> as his daily bread.[5]

Thus Luther gradually developed, as a result of his daily occupation with the
Bible as a Professor of Bible at the University of Wittenberg, a new way of reading
the Bible which made it authoritative even against the magisterium of the church.
This change can be traced by a careful study of his exegetical work and does not
depend for its validation on unverifiable personal anecdotes. The reformation is
the result of a university professor's concern with doing his work responsibly and
well. This may not be as exciting as the colorful stories of the romantic Luther
legends—but it can be historically substantiated.

But even granted that Luther's breakthrough was primarily theological
rather than psychological, how did this gradually developing insight affect the rest
of the university, his colleagues, and students? Here again the answer is relatively
simple. Luther changed the University of Wittenberg not by any special device
invented by him or by some extraordinary charisma that overpowered his associates, but by means of the available academic resources, especially the required
public disputations.

In the medieval university, higher education consisted of *docere*, "to teach,"
and *disputare*, which means literally "to correct errors." Both the teaching and the
disputations were, of course, carried on in Latin, the official language of the
university, which made any medieval university intellectually accessible to any
teacher or student.

While the teaching tended to be somewhat dogmatic, in the sense that it was
dominated by traditional authority, it was in the disputations that individuals
were given the opportunity to show their intellectual skills.

Indeed, disputations had a double purpose: (1) to establish the truth; (2) to
establish the dialectical skill of the participants. The entire method, however, was
based on what lawyers call the adversary system. In an American court of law,
guilt or innocence is established not through the efforts of impartial commissions
but by means of the partisan presentation of all the evidence on both sides by the
prosecution and the defense. It is the task of the prosecution to collect and present
all the evidence which will convince the judge or jury that the person on trial is

[5]*Preface to the New Testament, LW,* 35:361-362.

guilty; it is the task of the defense to collect and present all the evidence which will convince the judge or jury that the person on trial is innocent.

The theological disputations of the middle ages were similar. The disputants did not give all the facts or even a balanced view of all the evidence; they presented the evidence that supported their position and left it to the opponents to marshal the evidence that would support theirs. It was the magisterium, the official teaching authority of the church, which ultimately decided the issue—or declared the contest a draw.

In the theological school at the University of Wittenberg four types of disputations were part of the prescribed curriculum:

1. Every professor had to hold a public disputation, once a year. This was obviously in order to set an example how this was to be done. The statutes do not say who the opponents were to be.

2. Every Saturday, except for vacation, all professors had to dispute "*circulariter,*" in turn.

3. There were disputations for examination purposes. In order to get a bachelor's degree one had to participate successfully in such a disputation.

4. There were disputations for the doctor's degree.

For certain disputations, the so-called *Disputationes Solemnes,* all members of the faculty and all students had to be present. Absences made one subject to a fine.

It is of special significance for our understanding of Luther's influence upon his colleagues at Wittenberg that it was the professor who generally wrote the theses which the student had to defend in public. As a result, Luther's views were not only presented to his colleagues by means of his own public disputations, but also by means of the disputations of his students.

Thus unlike an American college or university, where the teaching of one professor may never come to the attention of any of his colleagues or only by means of the somewhat garbled version in which a student presents the teachings of one of his instructors to the others, the medieval university forced every professor to present their ideas publicly, and for debate, before colleagues and students.

From the beginning of his tenure at Wittenberg, Luther utilized this procedure with great success in presenting his ideas to his colleagues and students in Wittenberg, as well as in other places of higher learning, as, for example, Heidelberg and Leipzig.

While the significance of the disputations for the development of Luther's theology has not been fully investigated, it is apparent that it was by means of disputation that he created the Wittenberg University theology which carried the reformation from this little Saxon town all over the world. Time does not permit us to analyze or even mention all these disputations. But the so-called *Ninety-five Theses* of 1517 were part of this disputation theology—and so were the disputations against scholastic theology of the same year or the so-called Heidelberg disputation of 1518 or the most famous of all, the Leipzig disputation of 1519, scheduled for Eck and Karlstadt, but finished by Eck and Luther.

And these disputations were continued by the University of Wittenberg long after the initial breakthrough. It was through his disputations against the anti-nomians that Luther corrected some of the excesses of his own followers. But it was through the disputations that Luther convinced his colleagues of the soundness of his theological program. In 1516 Luther wrote three theses which his student Bartholomew Bernhardi had to defend. Professor Amsdorf, Luther's colleague and disciple of Duns Scotus, considered this disputation the turning point in his life. He sent them immediately to his colleagues in Erfurt. He was overwhelmed.

To some interpreters of Luther and the reformation, thunderstorms and lightning, seizures in the choir and tower experiences have been the important aspects of the reformation. It has been my claim that far more impressive than all this is the fact that Luther was able to convince his professional colleagues and his students of the soundness of his position.

In short, the reformation succeeded because Professor Luther prepared his lectures carefully, delivered them persuasively, and used the intellectual life of the university to persuade his colleagues and students of what he considered the truth of the gospel. The key to Luther and the reformation is the medieval university and the fact that Luther took his calling as professor seriously.

II.

We are asking today about the relevance of the sixteenth-century reformation for our time. What, if anything, can we still learn from this movement which once upon a time influenced the course of western civilization in such a decisive manner?

The answer, on the basis of our study, would be that we must learn to use the structures and institutions existing in our time to proclaim our message in the same creative and reasonable manner in which Luther used the structures and institutions of his time.

This presupposes, of course, the conviction that the message of the Christian church, namely, the gospel, has something significant to say in our time and is, therefore, worth proclaiming. But since this may not seem immediately obvious to everybody, let me suggest briefly why I am prepared and even eager to defend this proposition!

The gospel is the "good news" that "God was in Christ reconciling the world unto himself" [2 Cor 5:19]. This is the message that God is love, self-giving, and unconditional love, which once it has been accepted, enables us to love uncondi-tionally. Or, to put it into the basic terms of the New Testament: God forgives our sins, and we are empowered to forgive those who have sinned against us.

Now you may ask, "What has such a 'gospel' possibly to say to our world and the world of the twenty-first century just around the corner? Is not all this an archaic conception of the human predicament, which is utterly out of place in the age of hydrogen bombs, interplanetary space travel, and control of our genetic heritage?"

It is my claim that the relevance of the reformation rests on the fact that the gospel was never more necessary than precisely in our age and because of the unbelievable developments of the last fifty years, which we have not even begun to conceptualize.

Professor Kenneth Boulding has pointed out that we are entering the age of the "developed society."[6] Civilization is, as the term implies, the urbanization of humankind. This process began roughly 5,000 years ago (and not the other day in Chicago, as Professor Harvey Cox seems to think[7]). It meant the development of cities, of politics, metals, the wheel, war, slavery, and exploitation.[8] We are beginning to see the end of this process. The "developed society" we are about to enter is basically the result of the increase in the rate of change of knowledge. We are living in the age of the knowledge explosion, and it is this explosion which is changing our earth into a spaceship. In the words of Professor Boulding:

> We have to visualize the earth as a small, rather crowded spaceship, destination unknown, in which man has to find a slender thread of a way of life in the midst of a continually repeatable cycle of material transformation. In a spaceship, there can be no inputs or outputs. The water must circulate through the kidneys and the algae, the food likewise, the air likewise, and even though there must be inputs of energy, because of the dismal Second Law of Thermodynamics, there can be no inputs and outputs of material, short of the transfer of energy into matter; the ratio of energy to matter is so enormous, however, that this seems implausible. In a spaceship there can be no sewers and no imports.[9]

What has all this to do with Luther and the reformation? To me the answer seems obvious: If we are to live successfully in a spaceship any vision of human relationships short of the vision given us in Jesus Christ seems totally inadequate. An eye for an eye and a tooth for a tooth may have been a pattern adequate to life on the desert—it is totally non-functional in a spaceship. Laissez-faire capitalism or "objectivism" may have had some cogency to people who thought of themselves as lonely pioneers conquering a wilderness. These attitudes are suicidal for people who have to learn to live together within the crowded conditions of spaceship earth. If such life is possible at all short of a concentration camp it will be based on a vision like that of the Christian faith which puts the central emphasis on the cross and forgiveness of sins. Such a vision alone is adequate to these conditions. All forms of mere legalism are obsolete because the laws never keep up with the changes brought about by the rapid increase of knowledge. Only the gospel, which in Luther's words enables us to live simultaneously as "a perfectly free lord of all, subject to none" and as "a perfectly dutiful servant of all, subject to all," is appropriate to the new situation.[10]

Thus we will either recover something like the insight of the reformation and accept our acceptance in spite of the fact that we are not acceptable, and live, or we

---

[6]Kenneth Boulding, *The Wisdom of Man and the Wisdom of God* (New York: National Council of Churches of Christ in the USA, 1966).

[7]Cf., Harvey Cox, *The Secular City: Secularization and Urbanization in Theological Perspective* (New York: MacMillan, 1965).

[8]Boulding, *Wisdom*, 3.

[9]Ibid., 6.

[10]*The Freedom of a Christian* (1520), LW 31:344.

will try to score points against each other in racial, nationalistic, economic, ideological, and military conflicts, which must immediately scuttle the spaceship and the precarious balance on which it depends for survival.

The reformation is relevant to our time because only a vision of human life as Christlike service to the neighbor assures survival of the race under the conditions of the "developed society." Self-righteous boasting, irresponsible aggravation of conflict, the glorification of revolution and chaos are luxuries which the "developed society" of the spaceship cannot afford. It may produce an affluence unthinkable to us today if we learn to live within its limitations. But it will not do so automatically but only if we accept the pattern which life on a spaceship forces upon us. Thus what Luther said 450 years ago in his *Ninety-five Theses* bears repeating against the many voices of an irresponsible utopianism in our time:

> 92. Away then with all those prophets who say to the people of Christ, "Peace, peace," and there is no peace! [Jer. 6:14].
> 93. Blessed be all those prophets who say to the people of Christ, "Cross, cross," and there is no cross!
> 94. Christians should be exhorted to be diligent in following Christ, their head, through penalties, death, and hell;
> 95. And thus be confident of entering into heaven through many tribulations rather than through the false security of peace [Acts 14:22].[11]

---

[11]LW 31:32-33.

Word & World
Supplement Series 2
1994

Faith Active in Love

I. THE METHODOLOGICAL PRINCIPLE

LUTHER REFUSED TO RECOGNIZE ANY PERMANENT AND UNALTERABLE ETHICAL standards as if these existed in a religious vacuum. The ethical standards of the pagan philosophers he considered "lies" and "godless fables." All ethical standards are meaningful only in life. They are good if they serve to reveal God; they are evil if they hide God from people. Actions, faculties, beings, and standards are good or evil according to the function which they fulfill in helping or hindering the establishment of the saving relationship between God and humankind. Thus it is Luther's concern to evaluate everything in relation to God and his revelation in Jesus Christ. And for Luther the center of this revelation of God in Christ is the gospel of the forgiveness of sins. Without this forgiveness of sins, a saving relationship between God and humans would be impossible.

Any ethical assertion implies the existence of certain standards of right and wrong upon which the assertion is based, and any assertion of Christian ethics implies that it is God who has given these standards. Christian ethics is based upon the claim that a saving relationship between God and humanity is possible. Such a claim can only be made on the basis of the gospel of the forgiveness of sins.

As far as Luther is concerned, all ethics is based upon God's forgiveness of sin. This is true of individual ethics as well as social ethics. It is therefore meaningless to say that Luther considered the sermon on the mount the Christian standard

This piece was originally published in 1968 as "The Meaning for Man of Luther's Doctrine of Faith," in Reformation and Authority, *ed. Kyle Sessions (Lexington, MA: Heath and Co., 1968) 83-94. It is a condensed version of* Faith Active in Love: An Investigation of the Principles Underlying Luther's Social Ethics *(Minneapolis: Augsburg Publishing House, 1954).* Faith Active in Love, *which gained general acceptance as the authoritative book in English on Luther's social ethics, grew out of Forell's doctoral work under Reinhold Niebuhr at Union Theological Seminary. Here Forell dispels the charge that Luther had no viable social ethics and Lutheran ethics must, therefore, lead to quietism. The original essay was published without footnotes, though a few have been added here. Curious readers can turn to the book for more complete notes.*

for individual ethics while he suggested the decalogue or some other form of natural law as the standard for social ethics. Neither the sermon on the mount nor the decalogue is the point of reference for Luther's ethics, but always the relationship which God establishes with humankind through the forgiveness of sins in love. The decalogue or the sermon on the mount, if interpreted apart from this point of reference, may become for Luther not the will of God but the will of the devil. Any use of ethical standards divorced from their source perverts these standards from good into evil.

However, Luther's insistence upon this "dynamic" method of referring all ethics to its source in the relationship that God establishes with humankind would seem to make impossible any application of Christian ethics to those outside the Christian church. It would seem that only those who believe in the God-human relationship which God creates through his forgiveness could be reached by the ethical demands which this relationship implies. This would indeed leave the majority of people without any valid ethical standards, and the church without a message for the world.

However, nothing could be further from Luther's thought than to make the validity of God's will dependent upon humankind's subjective assent or rejection. Theology or ethics do not establish the relationship between God and humankind; they are for Luther merely the results of humankind's confrontation with God. What humankind thinks or says about God in theology, or does in response to God in ethical action, is merely the result of what God has done for humankind. Theology and ethics flow from the divine revelation as it confronts humankind in life, but they do not in any way condition the character of this relationship. The relationship to God shapes a person's ethics; one's ethics do not shape one's relationship to God.

The rejection of Christianity, therefore, does not relieve humankind from the responsibility which its confrontation with God entails. People are confronted by God all during their lives through the very fact of their creatureliness and their existence within God's creation. The primacy of the God-human relationship makes theology and ethics not a condition of, but merely a response to, God's revelation. This God-human relationship is simply a fact of human existence and is not at all dependent upon the subjective assent of the individual.

The will of God is valid for human beings whether they like it or not, and therefore the church has a message for all, regardless of their religious predilections.

This is especially obvious in the realm of social ethics. What Luther has to say about the state, the family, and society in general is not based upon a person's faith but is the result of the fact of his or her involvement in these divine orders. By the very fact of one's calling as a father or mother, or as a citizen or as a teacher, one is confronted by the God who has established certain orders of the preservation of society. It is because of this involvement in the divine orders that humankind is at all times aware of and subject to the divine will. Humanity's acceptance or rejection of this divine will does not affect the reality of the confrontation with God in any way.

Here again Luther shows his interest in life, rather than in metaphysical speculation. Life confronts humankind with God: the creator God in the orders of nature established by him to preserve the world, the savior God in the gospel of Christ which addresses humankind in the life-situation. Luther's methodological principle as it applies to social ethics is functional, evaluating all ethical standards in the light of the part they play in relating humankind to God. It is also dynamic, constantly referring all ethics to its source in the revelation of God made possible through the gospel of the forgiveness of sins. And finally it is objective in its application to all people. Social ethics is for Luther not the cause but the result of the confrontation of humankind by God. Since all people are confronted by God as creatures living within the divine creation, God's will was, is, and remains eternally valid for all regardless of their subjective responses to the divine will.

II. THE ETHICAL PRINCIPLE

Luther's ethics received its basic principle not from philosophy but from the word of God. It was a "theological" or "evangelical" ethics, based upon the witness of the gospel. Its basic principle was consequently quite different from all the accepted assumptions of philosophical ethics. Starting with revelation instead of reason, it denied the heretofore sacred assumption of the Christian character of ordered self-love and neglected altogether the motive of all philosophical ethics, namely the desire for happiness. Completely disregarding the secret hedonism and the religious profit motive of the official Roman theologians, Luther suggested an entirely different basic motive for Christian action. Luther took this new principle directly from the Bible, yet it seemed to his contemporaries as if he had discovered something completely new.

Luther said that justification is the basis for all Christian ethics. There is no Christian ethics apart from Christian people; and only people justified by faith are Christian people. It was Luther who insisted that the person precedes the act, that ethics is always the ethics of people, and that one cannot have moral acts apart from moral people. He expressed this thought repeatedly in his book *The Freedom of a Christian*. Here he said:

> The following statements are therefore true: "Good works do not make a good man, but a good man does good works; evil works do not make a wicked man, but a wicked man does evil works." Consequently it is always necessary that the substance or person himself be good before there can be any good works, and that good works follow and proceed from the good person, as Christ also says, "A good tree cannot bear evil fruit, nor can a bad tree bear good fruit" [Matt. 7:18].[1]

But how does a person become pious and a Christian in Luther's sense of the word? From what moment on are one's works good works? The justification which makes a person just in the eyes of God and a doer of good works is a free

[1]*LW* 31:361.

gift. It is a foreign gift that comes to us from the outside. It is sanctity appropriated by faith in the word of God promising forgiveness of sins. Faith is never unethical faith. The one who has faith will be sanctified and do good works. Justification and sanctification are for Luther two aspects of the same process and therefore mutually interdependent.

According to Luther it is quite incorrect to describe justification as the work of God and sanctification as the response of humankind, as if humankind could be justified without being sanctified. On the contrary, "Holy are as many as believe in Christ, be they men or women, slaves or free, etc., not because of their own works but because of the work of God which they receive in faith, as there are the Word, Sacraments, Christ's suffering, death and resurrection, victory, outpouring of the Holy Spirit, etc."[2]

Although Luther had excluded all human merit in his explanation of the motivating principle of Christian ethics, he did not want to imply that this was to exclude good works from the Christian life. Christians were to be free from good works only if these works were understood as producing "works-righteousness." On the other hand, Luther insisted that a living faith expresses itself in works of love. These good works, however, follow spontaneously and not under the compulsion of the law. And although the law itself does not change, the Christian's attitude towards the law is so utterly changed by faith that he or she becomes a lover of the law instead of being merely its slave.

Luther reintroduced an old biblical principle into theology when he insisted upon justification by faith. Furthermore, he insisted that this principle was equally valid in the field of ethics. Here it found a very special expression as "faith active in love." But if "faith active in love" is Luther's ethical principle, it is important to investigate what Luther meant by "love." If faith expresses itself in relation to our fellow human beings in terms of love, how is this love to be defined?

Against this prudential conception of love, which had been developed even further by scholasticism, Luther placed what he considered the "biblical" conception of love. According to Luther, Christian love is diametrically opposed to all human acquisitive desire. Love, insofar as it is truly Christian, is modeled after the love of Christ. It is a love that does not consider self-interest; it is, in fact, the judgment of God over all self-love.

Breaking all precedent and destroying a very practical and comfortable interpretation, Luther said:

> "Love your neighbor as yourself," but not in the sense that you should love yourself; otherwise that would have been commanded. But now it is not commanded in this way, that the commandment is founded on this principle. Thus you do wrong if you love yourself, an evil from which you will not be free unless you love your neighbor in the same way, that is, by ceasing to love yourself.[3]

---

[2]For a similar argument, see *Psalm 2* (1519-20), *LW* 14:327-328.
[3]*Lectures on Romans* (1515-16), *LW* 25:513-514.

It is important to realize that Luther brought about a complete change in the generally accepted definition of love. Up to his time, theologians, guided by the principles of philosophical ethics, had interpreted love in essentially egocentric and eudaemonistic terms, even if these concepts were used in a sublimated sense. Love had been acquisitive love. Now Luther defined Christian love as self-giving, spontaneous, overflowing as the love of God. This love does not ask after the worthiness of the object, it is not concerned with the love-value of humankind, but "makes [the] sun...rise on the evil and on the good, and sends rain on the righteous and on the unrighteous" (Matt 5:45).

It is on the basis of this definition of love as overflowing, spontaneous love that Luther's ethical principle must be understood. If love is really formed by faith, if it is the active tool of faith, then this love must be more than the prudential desire for the highest good. The love which is Christian faith in action must be part of the divine love given to human beings by God in order that they may pass it on to their neighbors. For Luther, the love which is faith active towards the neighbor was a gift of God. He considered humankind merely the tube or channel through which God's love flows. While even Augustine spoke of "using one's neighbor in order to enjoy God," Luther spoke of faith and love as "placing people between God and the neighbor," as a medium which receives from above and gives out again below, and which is like "a vessel or tube through which the stream of divine blessings must flow without intermission to other people." And he continued: "See, those are then truly godlike people, who receive from God all that he has in Christ, and in turn show themselves also by their well-doing to be, as it were, the gods of their neighbors."[4] This clearly shows what Luther meant by faith active in love: in faith a person receives God's love and passes it on to her or his neighbor. The Christian as a child of God is used by God to mediate the divine love to other people.

It is to the needy neighbor that God wants humankind to show its love:

> It is there God is to be found and loved, there he is to be served and ministered to, whoever wishes to minister to God and serve him; so that the commandment of the love of God is brought down in its entirety into the love of the neighbor....For this was the reason why he put off the form of God and took on the form of a servant, that he might draw down our love for him and fasten it in our neighbor.[5]

Whom does it benefit? was the key question concerning any work. It must benefit your neighbor and society, otherwise the work is worthless. "If you find a work in you by which you benefit God or the saints or yourself and not your neighbor, know that such a work is not good."[6] Good works are socially useful, they are works done within the community and for the community.

> A husband is to live, speak, act, hear, suffer, and die for the good of his wife and child, the wife for the husband, the children for the parents, the servants for their

---

[4]*Kirchenpostille, Titus 3:4-7* (1522), WA 10/1:100, line 9.
[5]*Fastenpostille, Romans 13:8* (1525), WA 17/2:99, line 18.
[6]*Adventspostille* (1522), WA 10/1/2:41, line 5..

masters, the masters for their servants, the government for its subjects, the subjects for the government, each one for the neighbor, even for enemies, so that one is the other's hand, mouth, eye, foot, even heart and mind. This is a truly Christian and good work, which can and shall be done at all times, in all places, toward all people.[7]

III. THE PRACTICAL PRINCIPLE

It has been the object of the preceding investigations to show that Luther's theological method demanded that all social ethics be grounded in the confrontation of humankind as the creature with God as the Creator (see "Methodological Principle"). Furthermore, it has been asserted that the principle upon which all ethics rests is the fact of the divine love, which should be apprehended in faith toward God and love toward the neighbor (see "Ethical Principle"). It now becomes necessary to examine Luther's practical principle of social ethics.

It is at this point that Luther has been criticized most severely. There are many who say that Luther's ethics, though theoretically sound, collapses when confronted with practical life, and that Luther, when dealing with the problems of society, gave up all specifically Christian notions, fashioning his social ethics on the basis of "natural law," quite independent from any idea of divine love and grace. Although Luther's champions have refuted these charges, questions concerning the practical principle of his social ethics are at the root of most attacks against him, alleging that he abandoned Christianity when the problems of society confronted him.

What is this controversial practical principle of Luther's social ethics? There can be very little doubt that, according to Luther, social ethics expressed itself in practice within the framework of the "natural orders." A person, as a member of society, is a part of certain orders or collectivities such as the family, the state, the empirical church, and her or his calling. Luther asserted that this membership in the natural orders was part of God's design to preserve the world and to contain the creative forces within humankind which under the influence of sin might lead to disorder and destruction.

He was convinced that sin and the devil had such tremendous power in this world that sinful humankind, left to its own devices in dealing with them, would be utterly destroyed. God in his mercy had, therefore, established the natural orders which counteract the wiles of the devil and guide the destructive forces within humankind into constructive channels, thus making orderly life possible. This civil justice and peace enables Christians to proclaim the gospel in peace, and in this manner participate in the ultimate destruction of the "prince of this world."[8]

He considered one of his important contributions to the ideology of his time that he separated the two realms of existence and yet emphasized the divine origin of both. In his explanation of the eighty-second Psalm, he wrote:

---

[7]Ibid., 41, line 7.
[8]*Zechariah* (1527), LW 20:172-173.

The secular rulers were completely subject to these clerical giants and tyrants....It was not understood or taught what temporal authority was, or how great was the distinction between it and spiritual government....Now, however, the Gospel has come to light. It makes a plain distinction between the temporal and the spiritual estate and teaches, besides, that the temporal estate is an ordinance of God which everyone ought to obey and honor.[9]

Luther subdivides the divinely instituted secular realm into a multitude of "offices," "callings," and "ranks." The three main groups of orders within the secular realm are the family (or society, "family" being used in a wider sense than at the present time), the government, and the empirical church. Luther said:

Three kinds of callings are ordained by God; in them one can live with God and a clear conscience. The first is the family [*Hausstand*], the second political and secular authority, the third the church or the ministry,...after the pattern of the three persons of the Trinity....First of all, you must be a part of a family, a father or mother, a child, servant or maid Secondly, you must live in a city or in the country as a citizen, a subject, or a ruler. For God has created people in order to keep them together in friendship and peace, orderly and honorably. Thirdly, you are part of the church, perhaps a pastor, an assistant, a sexton, or in some other way a servant of the church, if only you have and hear the Word of God.[10]

These orders are ordained by God in order to assure a minimum amount of peace and justice for the world. Without them humans would act worse than animals.

Because the natural orders are divinely instituted, we are not to despise them but rather consider our membership in them an honor and decoration from God.

The divine character of the natural orders explains also Luther's much-publicized attitude towards government or secular authority. This order is also instituted and preserved by God, and is therefore a divine order. Luther emphasizes the emergency character of secular authority as we know it. It is an institution for the days between the times. "For since we are not all believers but the great majority are unbelievers, God has regulated and ordained matters this way in order that the people of the world might not devour one another."[11] Luther says that secular authority, if it fulfills its preserving task, is in fact a "mask of God" behind which God works.[12] No secular authority stands or falls as the result of human endeavor or ingenuity; God alone ordains, upholds, protects, or destroys it.

It is from this point of view that one must understand Luther's position in regard to obedience to the natural orders. Such obedience is not obedience to human beings, but ultimately obedience to God. "For God is giving you the...command and order through your master or parents."[13] And it is God's general procedure, in the secular realm, to rule "not indeed from heaven through angels, but through the constituted authority."[14] Luther could go so far as to say that by

[9]*Psalm 82* (1530), *LW* 13:42.
[10]*WA, TR* 6:266, line 16.
[11]*1 Peter* (1523), *LW* 30:74.
[12]*Exposition of Psalm 127* (1524), *LW* 45:331.
[13]*Lectures on Genesis 21-25* (1535-45), *LW* 4:285.
[14]*Lectures on Genesis 15-20* (1535- 45), *LW* 3:322.

means of the orders God operates through us, so that our words become his words and our actions become his actions.[15]

According to Luther, the natural orders are reasonable orders and have to be interpreted by reason. As a matter of fact, politics and economics are the fields where it is not only proper but imperative to use reason. He said quite plainly that in secular matters it is always advisable to follow the judgment of reason.

Of course, if reason is the standard for the natural orders, it cannot be said that these natural orders are immutable. It has been claimed that Luther insisted upon the general and eternal validity of the social system of his time. However, if he admitted the normative character of reason, he had to make allowances for changes of the established orders from this principle. And he did make provisions for such changes.

Luther was not a great friend of change. He felt, from his eschatological outlook (see below), that there was not much chance for a change for the better. This practical conservatism does not imply a principle of static acceptance of all existing orders. Such a principle has been claimed for Luther, but it contradicts his basic attitude in regard to the reformation of the church. His entire appeal to the Christian nobility is an appeal for change—change in the realm of the church, but change nevertheless. Luther believed that history is made and changed by great individuals and heroes. These heroes, who bring about the changes in history, are the revolutionary antithesis to Luther's basically conservative political thesis. Acting under the influence of special divine guidance, these people are used by God to bring about the necessary changes of the existing political and social conditions. They are the means which God uses to change the concrete expression the natural orders find in any specific historical situation. God, who guides their hearts and gives them courage, also gives success to the work of their hands.

In summary, it can be said that Luther's natural orders were for all practical purposes based on natural law and reason. From these two norms they were constantly redefined. Changes in these orders were possible, but only through the medium of the "miracle-worker." The natural orders are natural and reasonable. Luther used them to describe the existing situation. He felt that they help to explain the world and the forces that preserve it in a semblance of order. However, they do not reveal God, they are not even a part of theology proper, and they do not tell us ultimately what is right and wrong in the sight of God; in short, they have no saving value.

It seems quite clear from the above that Luther's teaching concerning the natural orders does not establish a secular source of ethics for society, but that the natural orders are deeply rooted in God's will for the world. However, so far it would seem as if there were no connection between the ethical principle of the Christian individual, faith active in love, and the divine natural law that governs the orders of nature. But Luther explains that a point of contact between the secular

---

[15]Ibid., 272.

realm and the spiritual realm exists in the person of the individual Christian. At this point, the spiritual realm penetrates the secular, without, however, abolishing it. The gospel itself cannot be used to rule the world, because it is the gospel and demands a voluntary response from humankind. It would cease to be the gospel if it became a new law. But through the believer, who is related to Christ through the gospel and who is at the same time a member of the natural orders, the faith active in love penetrates the social order.

Of the Christians, Luther said: "The citizens of Christ's kingdom are earthly, perishable, mortal men, living in lands scattered hither and yon on earth; and at the same time they are citizens of heaven."[16] Only they truly understand the divine character of the natural orders. And it is for the sake of the Christians that God maintains the world so patiently. "He has indeed created all that the world contains and produces for the sake of pious Christians; he gives and maintains all only for their sake, as long as the world stands, in order that they should richly enjoy these things in this life and have no need."[17] Christians alone maintain both realms through their prayers. Luther asserts:

> But we, as Christians, must know that the whole system of earthly government stands and remains for its allotted time solely through God's order or command and the prayers of Christians. These are the two pillars that support the entire world. When they are gone, everything must crumble. This will become evident as Doomsday approaches; but it can already be seen that all kingdoms and governments are enfeebled and are almost beginning to topple, because the two columns are threatening to drop and to break. The world will not have it otherwise. It will not tolerate God's Word, which, after all, honors and preserves the world; but it persecutes and kills innocent Christians and incessantly storms against the pillars which uphold it.[18]

Yet God desires that Christians take their full responsibility in the world. They may become leaders in secular affairs and even bear the sword. If they attain political power they will at the same time govern their people and serve God. Through Christians in the world, their faith active in love influences the social structure. This Luther stated in the conclusion of his famous *The Freedom of a Christian*. He said:

> The good things we have from God should flow from one to the other and be common to all, so that everyone should "put on" his neighbor and so conduct himself toward him as if he were in the other's place. From Christ the good things have flowed and are flowing into us. He has so "put on" us and acted for us as if he had been what we are. From us they flow on to those who have need of them....We conclude, therefore, that a Christian lives not in himself, but in Christ and in his neighbor. Otherwise he is not a Christian. He lives in Christ through faith, in his neighbor through love. By faith he is caught up beyond himself into God. By love he descends beneath himself into his neighbor. Yet he always remains in God and in his love.[19]

---

[16]*Sermon on Psalm 8* (1529), LW 12:103.

[17]*Kirchenpostille*, WA 22:122, line 30.

[18]*Sermons on the Gospel of St. John 14-16* (1538), LW 24:81-82.

[19]LW 31:371.

Luther, by emphasizing the theoretical separation of the two realms, avoided the identification of the gospel with any specific program of social organization. By placing the individual Christian who alone is the proper object of the "good news" into the social order, he supplied the natural orders with a Christian social impetus that could exert constant pressure regardless of the particular form of social organization Christians might confront. Far from making Christianity irrelevant to the social order, Luther made it possible to make the absolute Christian truth ever available to society, not by means of an hierarchical organization or a legal interpretation of the gospel, but by means of the Christian saint, i.e., the sinner saved by grace, active in the world as the willing tool of God's preserving and saving purpose.

IV. THE LIMITING PRINCIPLE

No study of the principles underlying Luther's social ethics would be realistic if it dealt only with those ideas which according to Luther motivate social action. For an understanding of his thought it is of equal importance to examine that principle which more than anything else restrained Luther from advocating as thorough a reformation of the secular realm as he advocated and carried out in the spiritual realm.

The key to the understanding of Luther's reluctance to press for a complete reformation of society was his firm conviction that it was unbiblical to expect such a change so late in the history of humankind. The social-ethical "quietive" which limits in Luther's thought the social-ethical "motive" of faith active in love is his expectation of the speedily approaching end of this world. Though he was not fanatical on this point and would expressly state that such views were not to be considered articles of faith, he personally believed that history could be divided into six parts. The first part covered the time from Adam to Noah; the second, Noah to Abraham; the third, Abraham to Moses; the fourth, Moses to David; the fifth, David to Christ; the sixth began with the coming of Christ and will last until the end of the world. Luther was convinced that humankind had arrived at the very end of this last period. Against the astrologers, who defended a circular view of history and hoped that soon a new golden age would dawn, he asserted that the papal rule of the Roman empire was the final stage of the last period of history.

Luther believed in social reform, and he tried to do what he could to help in the reorganization of society—but from his eschatological point of view he was unable to take amendments to the constitution of the social order as he found it as seriously as some of his more secular-minded adherents. Whatever Luther taught and did was in his own mind an attempt to prepare people for the coming kingdom of God that would consummate history on the day of judgment. It was at this point that Luther parted ways with the revolutionary minds of his age. The knights and peasants who were being crushed in the death throes of a disintegrating feudal society hoped that Luther would become the leader of a revolution which would restore their ancient privileges. Luther was quite willing to help with word and deed in order to improve their lot. In his *Admonition to Peace*, he said:

We have no one on earth to thank for this disastrous rebellion, except you princes and lords....If it is still possible to give you advice, my lords, give way a little to the will and wrath of God. A cartload of hay must give way to a drunken man—how much more ought you to stop your raging and obstinate tyranny and not deal unreasonably with the peasants, as though they were drunk or out of their minds! Do not start a fight with them, for you do not know how it will end. Try kindness first, for you do not know what God will do to prevent the spark that will kindle all Germany and start a fire that no one can extinguish.[20]

When the historical situation, however, demanded a decision and he had to choose between social revolution and the reformation of the church, Luther's choice was obvious. He was unwilling to sacrifice the reformation of the church and the preaching of the gospel for the sake of a social and political revolution whose outcome at best could benefit humanity only tionionemporarily. As the revolution proceeded without him, he was unable to understand how anybody could have the temerity to use the cloak of the gospel to cover revolutionary designs. And the wrath which Luther poured out so profusely against the revolting peasants was the wrath of a man who felt that here were people who gambled with humanity's chance to have the gospel of Christ freely preached, in order to win temporary material advantage.

Those who criticize Luther's position from the point of view of modern political liberalism or Marxism and attack him as politically reactionary because he chose to be a religious rather than a political leader, accuse him essentially of being Luther rather than Karl Marx. From a completely secular and sensate point of view, Luther's reliance upon the power of God seems nonsensical. But it was this "otherworldly" attitude, this complete reliance on God, which made the reformation possible. Luther succeeded, while the revolutionary heroes, Muenzer and Sickingen, failed.

It has been shown previously that faith was the source of Luther's social ethics; it can now be added that it was also faith that made it impossible for Luther to take any social reform ultimately seriously. Faith was the "motive" and the "quietive" of his social ethics. It was the driving force behind all his attempts to reorganize society and at the same time the reason why all such attempts were in the background of his theological thinking.

It is unfortunate that most attempts to analyze Luther's thought have completely neglected to stress the importance of his eschatology for an understanding of his seeming political and social conservatism. It must also be granted that Luther's unrealized expectations of an immediate end of the world resulted in an unnecessarily superficial repair of the social structure of this world. It does make a difference whether one is going to inhabit a house for another month or another year. Though Luther was justified in not expecting any ultimate solution of the political and social problems that face humankind, a more thorough repair of the mechanisms that govern would have made the position of the church of the

---

[20]*Admonition to Peace* (1525), LW 46:19, 21-22.

reformation a great deal stronger during the great political and social upheavals that confronted it.

Though willing to do anything in his power to help the establishment of the best possible social order in a dying world, he was unable to hope that this society would ever be the kingdom of God. And he rejected every effort to identify any political cause with the interest of this kingdom. Essentially he believed that even the political difficulties of humankind can be solved only through divine intervention. "There is no other help against the Antichrist devil except that the Lord Christ finally address him with the authority of his divine power, 'Get thee behind me, Satan.'"[21] And it is God who eventually brings the tyrants with all their cunning plans to naught. Luther said:

> We have heard of God's great miracles which he does for his own, namely those who trust in him and believe his word and promise. Even if at first he acts as if he might desert them altogether so that they would be swallowed up and perish, he nevertheless comforts them and helps them in all persecution. And finally he upsets the game of the tyrants, throws away their dice, tears up their playing cards, and brings them and all their plans to naught.[22]

This firm belief in God's impending solution of all human problems is the limiting principle of Luther's social ethics. It is brilliantly summarized in a sermon on the Epistle for the Third Sunday after Easter (1 Peter 2:11-20), where Luther says:

> So should Christians in all stations of life—lords and ladies, servants and maids—conduct themselves as guests on earth. Let them, in that capacity, eat and drink, make use of clothing and shoes, houses and lands, as long as God wills, yet be prepared to take up their journey when these things pass, and to move on out of this life as the guest moves on out of the house or the city which is not his home. Let them conduct themselves as does the guest, with civility toward those with whom they come in contact, not infringing on the rights of any. For a visitor may not unrestrainedly follow his own pleasure and inclinations in the house of a stranger. The saying is "If you would be a guest, you must behave civilly; otherwise you may promptly be shown the door or the dungeon." Christians should be aware of their citizenship in a better country, that they may rightly adapt themselves to this world. Let them not occupy the present life as if intending to remain in it; nor as do the monks, who flee responsibility, avoiding civil office and trying to run out of the world. For Peter says rather that we are not to escape our fellows and live each to himself, but to remain in our several callings, united with other mortals as God has bound us and serving one another. At the same time, we are to regard this life as a journey through a country where we have no citizenship—where we are not at home; to think of ourselves as travelers or pilgrims occupying for a night the same inn, eating and drinking there and then leaving the place....
> Let not the occupants of the humbler stations—servants and subjects—grumble. "Why should I vex myself with unpleasant household tasks, with farm work, or heavy labor? This life is not my home anyway, and I may as well have it better.

---

[21]*Sermons* (1537), *WA* 45:47, line 29.

[22]*Sermons on Exodus* (1524-27), *WA* 16:18, line 29.

Therefore, I will abandon my stations and enjoy myself; the monks and priests have in their stations withdrawn themselves from the world and yet drunk deeply, satisfying fleshly lusts." No, this is not the right way. If you are unwilling to put up with your lot, as the guest in a tavern and among strangers must do, you also may not eat and drink. Similarly, they who are favored with loftier positions in life may not, upon this authority, abandon themselves to the idea of living in the sheer idleness and lustful pleasure their more favored station permits, as if they were to be here always. Let them reason thus: "This life, it is true, is transitory—a voyage, a pilgrimage, leading to our actual fatherland. But since it is God's will that everyone should serve his fellows here in his respective calling, in the office committed to him, we will do whatever is enjoined upon us. We will serve our subjects, our neighbors, our wives, and children so long as we can; we would not relax our service even if we knew we had to depart this very hour and leave all earthly things. For, God be praised, had we to die now we would know where we belong, where our home is. While we are here, however, on the way, it is ours to fulfill the obligations of our earthly citizenship. Therefore, we will live with our fellows in obedience to the law of our abiding place, even unto the hour wherein we must cross the threshold, that we may depart in honor, leaving no occasion for complaint.[23]

Thus those who have their homeland in the coming kingdom of God pray expectantly "Thy kingdom come," knowing full well that "the kingdom of God comes of itself, without our prayer, but we pray in this petition that it may also come to us."[24]

V. CONCLUSION

Luther's social ethics can be understood only within the framework of the principles that motivated his life and thought. It does justice neither to Luther nor to history to deal with the reformation as if it were some metaphysical prime mover that can be used to explain the economic and political problems of our age. Luther's social thought must be understood as an integral part of his thinking and in the context of his entire approach to life.

If this road is followed, the following insights about Luther's social ethics can be gained:

1. Luther's approach to ethical problems is existential, not legal. The value of an action depends entirely upon the part it plays in helping or hindering the individual's relationship to God in Christ. All ethical standards are meaningful only in life. They are good if they serve to reveal God, and they are evil if they hide God from humankind. This is true of social ethics as well as individual ethics.

2. The motivating force behind all Christian ethics is God's love. A person receives God's love in faith and passes it on to the neighbor. Faith is active in love toward the neighbor. Faith brings us to Christ and makes him our own with all that he has; then love gives us to our neighbor with all that we have.

---

[23]*WA* 21:342, line 37ff. Trans. J. N. Lenker, *Luther's Complete Works*, vol. 8 (Minneapolis: Luther Press, 1909) 276-278.

[24]*The Small Catechism* (1529) 3:6-7, in *BC*, 346.

3. God confronts all people in his universe and demands from them obedience to the orders that he has ordained for nature. Thus not only Christians but everyone is confronted by his social-ethical demands. Christian social ethics is not the esoteric teaching for the elite, but rather the God-given (i.e., best) practical way for all people to preserve the world from self-destruction until the day of Jesus Christ. Regardless of the world's attitude to the saving gospel of Christ, it must for its own temporal preservation abide by God's natural law. Such obedience does not save humankind, but is conducive to the welfare of the commonwealth.

4. The gospel, as such, cannot be used to rule since it applies only to those who believe. It would cease to be the gospel if it became a new law and were identified with any specific type of social organization. Yet through the person of the individual believer, who is related to Christ through the gospel but is at the same time a member of the natural orders, faith active in love penetrates the social order. Through the Christian individual, whether peasant or prince, the inexhaustible resources of the gospel become available to the social order.

5. All life, of individuals as well as of collectivities, is lived in the shadow of eternity. The social order is merely an interim order valid until the impending end of this world. All the ultimate problems of humankind's individual and social existence can be solved only when the coming kingdom of God ends all human history. Until that time, all human efforts are merely attempts to eliminate proximate evils. The ultimate evils that confront humankind can be overcome only through the parousia of Christ, the coming kingdom of God.

If Luther's social ethics is understood on the basis of the principles upon which it is founded, all specific answers to specific social problems of his time become relatively unimportant. They are primarily of historical rather than theological significance. However, the social-ethical principles derived from Luther's existential understanding of God's revelation are of considerable interest for all those who desire to understand God's plan for the Christian in society.

Though he erred in expecting the end of the world in his time, acceptance of his emphasis upon the finiteness of all human efforts to solve even humankind's social predicament could have saved many an upright and noble person who in our time trusted in human solutions much anguish and despair.

Living his faith in love, Luther tried all during his life to bring his personal Christian witness to bear upon the decisions that confronted his society. From the ninety-five theses of Wittenberg to the quarrel of the counts of Mannsfeld at Eisleben, he never tired of living his social ethics, showing in his own life that through the Christian individual the gospel penetrates the social order. It would have been well for christendom if those who followed Luther's lead had been equally zealous to show their faith active in love.

Word & World
Supplement Series **2**
1994

Justification and Eschatology in Luther's Thought

THE JUXTAPOSITION OF "JUSTIFICATION" AND "ESCHATOLOGY" IN LUTHER'S thought seems at first strikingly inappropriate. Justification is undoubtedly the central concern in Luther's theological effort. It was to Luther

> the master and prince, the lord, the ruler and the judge over all kinds of doctrines; it preserves and governs all church doctrine and raises up our conscience before God. Without this article the world is utter death and darkness. No error is so insignificant, so clumsy, so outworn as not to be supremely pleasing to human reason and to seduce us if we are without the knowledge and the contemplation of this article.[1]

Earlier he had written, "This article is the head and the cornerstone, which alone begets, nourishes, builds, serves and defends the church of God. Without it the church of God cannot exist for even one hour."[2] In his commentary on Galatians he could say about this same article,

> Whoever falls from the doctrine of justification is ignorant of God and is an idolater....For once this doctrine is undermined, nothing more remains but sheer error, hypocrisy, wickedness, and idolatry, regardless of how great the sanctity that appears on the outside. The reason is this: God does not want to be known except through Christ; nor, according to John 1:18, can He be known any other way.[3]

It is this article which in Luther's judgment makes the theologian a judge of this earth and, indeed, of all things. He added, however, that only few people had given this article sufficient attention, had thought it through, and thus were able to teach it correctly.[4]

---

[1]*Promotionsdisputation von Paladius und Tilemann* (June 1, 1537), WA 39/1:205.

[2]*Vorvort zu In prophetam Amos Johannis Brentii epositio* (1530), WA 30/2:650.

[3]*Lectures on Galatians* (1535), LW 26:395-396.

[4]*Isaiah, Scholia* (1532-34), WA 25:375.

This essay first appeared in Church History 38 (1969) 164-174. *Here Dr. Forell outlines Luther's understanding of the importance of eschatological hope for the Christian life, which is made possible through Christ's justifying work on the cross.*

Luther was quite aware of the fact that it was his emphasis on *doctrina* and especially the centrality of justification by faith rather than questions of moral corruption which constituted the central issue of the reformation. He saw the difference between his own efforts and those of Wycliffe and Hus quite clearly. They had attacked the moral decay in the church. Luther knew that,

> Doctrine and life must be distinguished. Life is bad among us, as it is among the papists, but we don't fight about life and condemn the papists on that account. Wycliffe and Hus didn't know this and attacked the papacy for its life. I don't scold myself into becoming good, but I fight over the Word and whether our adversaries teach it in its purity. That doctrine should be attacked—this has never before happened. This is my calling.[5]

For Luther, if only the word remained pure, there was always the hope that the life would also be straightened out through the power of this word. But if the word was missing there was also no hope for a changed life.[6] He said,

> As long as the teaching (*doctrina*) remains pure, there is hope for easily correcting one's life. The rays of the sun remain pure even when they fall and shine on manure. And God keeps something holy in our midst through which we may be sanctified, even if we have fallen. This is His Word, by which we quickly condemn a sin that has been committed. The Lord magnifies this.[7]

In view of the centrality of this doctrine of justification by faith for Luther it is not surprising that it has been both a central object of study for all Luther scholars and the subject of considerable controversy in the history of Luther research, involving practically every scholar in this field up to the present time. This very debate has been an indication of the general awareness of the centrality of the doctrine of justification for all of Luther's thought.

Eschatology, on the other hand, has been a most neglected aspect of Luther's theology. Johannes von Walter pointed out in 1940 that, in spite of the attention given to all the details of Luther's thought, there was then no monograph dealing with Luther's eschatology. And even more significantly, the major efforts of interpreting Luther's theology either avoided the topic entirely (Th. Harnack and E. Seeberg) or dealt with it in a most cursory fashion and more for the sake of completeness than because of any awareness of its significance for an understanding of Luther's theology (J. Köstlin). This, as Walter pointed out, was the more astonishing since Calvin's eschatology had received a great deal of attention. He added that the *meditatio futurae vitae* [meditation on the future life] had seemed to him at least a far more central part of Calvin's theology than of Luther's. Indeed, Walter suggested the reason for the relative neglect of Luther's eschatology himself by saying,

> In the end is not this the deepest and final reason for this state of affairs, that, according to Luther's last utterance, "Heaven and earth have become one in faith," that, therefore, the blessedness of faith cannot be essentially surpassed

---

[5]*Tabletalk* , LW 54:110.
[6]Ibid.
[7]*Lectures on the Minor Prophets* (1524), LW 18:403.

even in the next world, but rather only in so far as the human boundaries to complete communion with God will be lifted?[8]

Since 1940, the significance of Luther's eschatology has received more attention. The way was prepared by Paul Althaus in his seminal work, *Die letzten Dinge,* which focused attention on the problem of eschatology in general and took Luther's own contribution most seriously.[9] Carl Stange entered the discussion of Luther's eschatology by opposing Althaus, especially in his interpretation of Luther's understanding of the immortality of the soul.[10] Walter Koehler insisted in his *Dogmengeschichte als Geschichte des christlichen Selbstbewustseins,* which appeared in 1951, five years after his death, that Luther's eschatology was the mirror of his faith and that Luther's thought was relevant to one of the most acute modern issues since he had bridged the tension between axiological and teleological eschatology. He said,

> Modern dogmatics (E. Troeltsch, P. Althaus) speaks of axiological eschatology and understands by this the experiencing of final, unconditional values here on earth. Luther experienced this in faith; faith is axiological eschatology. One could also say, conscience; out of its terror came the call. But the final values were not immanent but rather transcendent—values "in hope." In this way the bridge was built from axiological to teleological eschatology, which asks about the goal, purpose and end of all being....Thus alongside of the eschatology already completed in principle he knows the drama of the end of history in the succession of scenes, untroubled by the fact that both trains of thought submit to a unification only partially, especially since biblical eschatology itself is not homogeneous.[11]

Since that time there have been a number of studies which have attributed to Luther's eschatology a central place in his theological vision. Wingren showed in 1942 that Luther's eschatology is the key to the ultimate hope that upholds the Christian in vocation.[12] In 1954, this writer tried to show that it is Luther's eschatology which constitutes the limiting principle of his social ethics and the source of

---

[8]Johannes von Walter, *Die Theologie Luthers* (Gütersloh: C. Bertelsmann, 1940) 230.

[9]Paul Althaus, *Die letzten Dinge,* 5th ed. (Gütersloh: C. Bertelsmann, 1949). It is, however, remarkable that the same Althaus gave so little consideration to the central significance of Luther's eschatology in his *Die Theologie Martin Luthers* of 1962 [The Theology of Martin Luther, 1966]. In sixteen pages (339-354) he deals with this issue as the final locus in Luther's theological system.

[10]Carl Stange, "Zur Auslegung des Aussagen Luthers über die Unsterblichkeit der Seele," in *Studien zur Theologie Luthers* (Gütersloh: C. Bertelsmann, 1928) 287f.

[11]Walter Koehler, *Dogmengeschichte, Das Zeitalter der Reformation* (Zürich: Niehans, 1951) 486.

[12]Gustaf Wingren, *Luthers lära om kallelsen* (Lund: Gleerup, 1942); cf., *Luther on Vocation,* (Philadelphia: Muhlenberg, 1957) 248ff. "Summarized in three points, the condition before the resurrection consists of these concepts: We live on earth under the law, even while we believe the gospel. We are always confronted by an unconquered devil, even while we believe in God's victory through Christ.... The final eschatological consummation can be summarized in the following three points: The earthly realm and the sway of the law are past, for Christ's heavenly kingdom, which formerly existed only in the form of the gospel, has now come in power. The devil is conquered and Christ's mastery is revealed. The old man has died completely through the cross, and the entire man has been raised as a spiritual body without sin. These three points correspond exactly with the three points characterizing the condition before the resurrection and supply their resolution. These three, like the first three, constitute a unity, a single truth. For the law ceases where the old being ends; and this abolition of the old being is the same as the victory over the devil. In the divine hour when this occurs, hiddenness is ended and the toil of vocation is terminated. But that day cannot be hastened either by man's effort or his piety."

his efforts to find a temporary and pragmatic solution to the great social problems of his time.[13]

In 1956 T. F. Torrance surveyed the eschatology of the reformation in his *Kingdom and Church* and asserted its crucial significance. He said,

> The Reformation stands for the rediscovery of the living God of the Bible, who actively intervenes in the affairs of men, the Lord and the Judge of history, and with that comes a powerful realization of the historical relevance of eschatology. The Reformation thinks of the ends of the world as having already overtaken humanity, so that even now the Church on earth lives in the last times and even now the last things are being wrought out in history.[14]

Later, in 1960, David Löfgren called attention to the eschatological dimension in Luther's teaching concerning creation. He said,

> The idea of creation and eschatology belong closely together in Luther: Thus when one says that heaven and earth are one creation or work which was made by Him who is called the one and only God, and were made out of nothing, that is an art above all art. That everything, therefore, was brought out of nothing into being and shall again be brought out of being into nothing, until everything will be made anew, more glorious and beautiful—this, I say, we know, and Holy Scripture teaches it and thus pictures it for the children in faith with the words: I believe in God the Father, Creator, etc.[15]

It is because God is the creator that a new creation is possible. And it is because of this new creation that the Christian life in time is possible. Similarly Karl Gerhard Steck, investigating doctrine and church in Luther, asserted that if the eschatological dimension of Luther's understanding of doctrine is lost, the concept "doctrine" is falsified and becomes incomprehensible.[16] Luther's eschatology is seen here as decisive for an understanding of his use of the notion "doctrine," which we have claimed earlier to be so very central for his thought.

---

[13]George W. Forell, *Faith Active in Love* (New York: American, 1954) 156ff. See also, page 188: "All life, of individuals as well as collectivities, is lived in the shadow of eternity. The social order is merely an interim order valid until the impending end of this world. All the ultimate problems of man's individual and social existence can be solved only when the coming kingdom of God ends all human history. Until that time all human efforts are merely attempts to eliminate proximate evils. The ultimate evils that confront man can be overcome only through the parousia of Christ, the coming of the kingdom of God."

[14]T. F. Torrance, *Kingdom and Church: A Study in the Theology of the Reformation* (London: Oliver and Boyd, 1956) 3. He surveyed the theology of the reformation under three headings—The Eschatology of Faith: Martin Luther; The Eschatology of Love: Martin Butzer; The Eschatology of Hope: John Calvin.

[15]David Löfgren, *Die Theologie der Schöpfung bei Luther* (Göttingen: Vandenhoeck & Ruprecht, 1969) 301. See also: "As we have seen, the new creation of man through faith produces not only the right 'image' of God, but also the right perception of things and of the neighbor and thereby gives the believer a greater candour in his life's task, in relation to his calling in the world. And hence the *eschaton* becomes decisive for the life which man lives here and now and includes not only the discovery that God's goodness is proffered here in this life, but also the recognition that the innermost meaning of life lies hidden in death. Man thus obtains his power or obedience finally not from out of himself or any created thing at all, but rather from faith in the resurrection of the dead, which indeed means the end of dying."

[16]Karl Gerhard Steck, *Lehre und Kirche bei Luther* (Munich: C. Kaiser, 1963) 197ff. "Creative power is attributed to doctrine; it creates Christians. In this its eschatological divine power reveals itself. As soon as the eschatological aspect is lost, only an apparently boundless over-estimation of doctrine is left, for which the title 'socratic-idealistic' would be too mild."

Two further monographs dealing with Luther's eschatology have come to my attention. Erich Wittenborn treated *Luthers Predigt vom jüngsten Tag* in his inaugural dissertation at Bonn in 1964.[17] And in 1967 Ulrich Asendorf, who had dealt with Luther's eschatology earlier in his *Der jüngste Tag: Weltende und Gegenwart*,[18] published a comprehensive investigation of Luther's eschatology in which he devoted his attention to our specific topic.[19]

While all these developments since 1940 would indicate a new appreciation for the significance of Luther's eschatology, they would not of themselves warrant the juxtaposition of justification and eschatology. This juxtaposition is justified, however, because we can claim:

1. Luther's justification by faith is an eschatological experience.
2. Luther's view of eschatology makes it the seal of his doctrine of justification.
3. Justification by faith without eschatology is a form of subjectivistic and individualistic self-hypnosis.
4. Eschatology without justification by faith is mere utopianism.

In the contemporary discussion of eschatology it is fashionable to speak of consistent eschatology (*konsequente Eschatologie*), salvation-historical eschatology (*heilsgeschichtliche Eschatologie*), and realized eschatology (*Eschatologie des hic et nunc*).[20] In this context it would be possible to say that Luther's understanding of justification by faith is developed against the background of what we would call realized eschatology. Justification is, indeed, the liberating act of God because humankind is and knows itself to be enslaved. It is this slavery to sin which brings the judgment upon us. Luther can be most colorful in his description of his own personal experience of confrontation with the final judgment here and now. He says,

> I myself "knew a man" [II Cor. 12:2] who claimed that he had often suffered these punishments, in fact over a brief period of time. Yet they were so great and so much like hell that no tongue could adequately express them, no pen could describe them, and one who had not himself experienced them could not believe them. And so great were they that, if they had been sustained or had lasted for half an hour, even for one tenth of an hour, he would have perished completely and all of his bones would have been reduced to ashes. At such a time God seems terribly angry, and with him the whole creation. At such a time there is no flight, no comfort, within or without, but all things accuse. At such a time as that the Psalmist mourns, "I am cut off from thy sight" [Cf. Ps. 31:22], or at least he does not dare to say, "O Lord,...do not chasten me in thy wrath" [Ps. 6:1]. In this moment (strange to say) the soul cannot believe that it can ever be redeemed— other than the fact that the punishment is not yet completely felt....All that remains is the stark-naked desire for help and a terrible groaning, but it does not

[17]Erich Wittenborn, "Luthers Predigt vom Jüngsten Tag" (Th.D. diss., Rheinische Friedrich-Wilhelms-Universität, Bonn, 1964).

[18]Ulrich Asendorf, *Der jüngste Tag: Weltende und Gegenwart* (Hamburg: Furche, 1964).

[19]Ulrich Asendorf, *Eschatologie bei Luther* (Göttingen: Vandenhoeck & Ruprecht, 1967) 36-48.

[20]See Walter Kreck, *Die Zukunft des Gekommenen*, 2nd ed. (Munich: C. Kaiser, 1966) 14-76. See also Helmut Wenz, *Die Ankunft unseres Herrn am Ende der Welt* (Stuttgart: Calwer, 1965) 11-27.

know where to turn for help. In this instance the person is stretched out with Christ so that all his bones may be counted, and every corner of the soul is filled with the greatest bitterness, dread, trembling, and sorrow in such a manner that all these last forever.[21]

This sense of the presence of hell in time is expressed also in Luther's commentary on the prophet Jonah where he describes the anxiety of fate and death most colorfully and asserts: "Those who stand in anxieties appear to enter into hell. For that reason, when someone finds himself in the most extreme misery, this experience is also called the deepest hell. It appears as if they were oppressed by the whole world." And here Luther speaks the language of realized eschatology when he continues in his description of hell: "*Non est certus locus, nihil in scripturis est*" ["It is not a specific place. In Scripture, it is nothingness"].[22] Hell is anxiety:

> I consider the pains of death and of hell to be the same thing. Hell is the terror of death, that is, the sensation of death, in which the damned have a dread of death and nevertheless cannot escape. For the death which is scorned is not felt, but is like sleep.[23]

It is the task of theology to concentrate on the clarification of this issue and not to become side-tracked into other concerns:

> Therefore we are not dealing here with the philosophical knowledge of man, which defines man as a rational animal and so forth. Such things are for science to discuss, not for theology. So a lawyer speaks of a man as an owner and master of property, and a physician speaks of man as healthy or sick. But a theologian discusses man as a sinner. In theology, this is the essence of man. The theologian is concerned that man become aware of this nature of his, corrupted by sins. When this happens, despair follows, casting him into hell.[24]

This, according to Luther, is not intellectual speculation or a mere playing with ideas. It is a true feeling, a real experience, a very serious struggle of the heart.[25]

It was out of this concrete and torturing experience of hell that Luther was freed by the gospel. It is against this background of rejection and condemnation as an eschatological experience that we learn to understand how for Luther justification is the anticipation of the presence of God and of eternal life in time.

This brings us to our second observation: Luther's view of eschatology makes it the seal of his doctrine of justification. It is because God is coming towards us, because the "dear Last Day" is approaching, that we can live here and now as sinners and righteous at the same time. Certainly, "A man is truly justified by faith in the sight of God, even if he finds only disgrace before others and in his own self."[26] Luther rejects clearly what he considers the Erasmian error that

---

[21]*Explanations of the Ninety-five Theses* (1518), LW 31:129.

[22]*Praelectiones in prophetam minores* (1524/26), WA 13:232.

[23]*Operationes in Psalmos* (1519-21), WA 5:463.

[24]*Psalm 51* (1532), LW 12:310-311.

[25]Ibid.

[26]*The Disputation concerning Justification* (1536), LW 34:151.

> Faith alone begins the forgiveness of sins, but works obtain salvation or merit and the kingdom of heaven or eternal life. He [Erasmus] says that faith in this life removes sins and gives remission of sins, afterward he ascribes salvation to works. This is most excellent and plausible, and this argument pleases reason. For reason rushes in blindly and thinks thus: Eternal salvation is something else than Christian righteousness.[27]

For Luther, Christian righteousness is, indeed, salvation, and thus we have salvation now because we are the recipients of this alien righteousness. But Luther also knows that it is because history moves towards a goal which is controlled by God that we are enabled to live in this tension he so colorfully describes as *simul justus et peccator*:

> At this point we say that original sin, although forgiveness has been imputed and thus sin is removed so that it is not imputed, nevertheless, is not substantially or essentially destroyed except in the conflagration of fire by which the whole world and our bodies will be completely purified on the last day. When we have been reduced to dust, then at last sins will be entirely extinguished. In the meantime, while we live, original sin also lives....Therefore sin is only remitted by imputation, but when we die, it is destroyed essentially.[28]

"For original sin is a root and inborn evil, which only comes to an end when this body has been entirely mortified, purged by fire and reformed. Meanwhile, however, it is not imputed to the godly."[29] Luther's use of the Christian hope for a coming kingdom of God, his "teleological" eschatology and the comfort and assurance it provides, is clearly expressed in his discussion of hope in connection with the fifth verse of the fifth chapter of Galatians. He claims that hope can be used in two ways: for the thing hoped for, the object of our hope, and for the feeling of hope, the subjective attitude of hopefulness. And he elaborates this view as follows:

> For as long as we live, sin still clings to our flesh; there remains a law in our flesh and members at war with the law of our mind and making us captive to the law of sin (Rom 7:23). While these passions of the flesh are raging and we, by the Spirit, are struggling against them, the righteousness we hope for remains elsewhere. We have indeed begun to be justified by faith, by which we have also received the first fruits of the Spirit; and the mortification of our flesh has begun. But we are not yet perfectly righteous. Our being justified perfectly still remains to be seen, and this is what we hope for. Thus our righteousness does not yet exist in fact, but it still exists in hope.[30]

It is an eschatological reality.

To those terrified by the wrath of God this knowledge is of the greatest importance. Luther, using his eschatological imagery, says:

> For, as we know from our own experience, in such a conflict of conscience the sense of sin, of the wrath of God, of death, of hell, and of every terror holds powerful sway. Then one must say to him who is distressed: "Brother, you want to have a conscious righteousness; that is, you want to be conscious of righteous-

[27]Ibid., 34:163.
[28]Ibid., 34:164-165.
[29]Ibid., 34:165.
[30]*Lectures on Galatians* (1535), LW 27:21.

43

ness in the same way you are conscious of sin. This will not happen. But your righteousness must transcend your consciousness of sin and you must hope that you are righteous in the sight of God. That is, your righteousness is not visible, and it is not conscious; but it is hoped for as something to be revealed in due time. Therefore you must not judge on the basis of your consciousness of sin, which terrifies and troubles you, but on the basis of the promise and teaching of faith, by which Christ is promised to you as your perfect and eternal righteousness." Thus in the midst of fears and of consciousness of sin, my hope—that is, my feeling of hope—is aroused and strengthened by faith, so that it hopes that I am righteous, and hope—that is, the thing hoped for—hopes that what it does not yet see will be made perfect and will be revealed in due time.[31]

And Luther concludes:

My righteousness is not yet perfect or conscious. Yet I do not despair on that account; but faith shows me Christ, in whom I trust. Then I have taken hold of Him by faith, I struggle against the fiery darts of the devil (Eph. 6:16); and through hope I am encouraged over against my consciousness of sin, since I conclude that perfect righteousness has been prepared for me in heaven. Thus both things are true: that I am righteous here with an incipient righteousness; and that in this hope I am strengthened against sin and look for the consummation of perfect righteousness in heaven.[32]

In the terror which the experience of one's own unrighteousness—remaining after justification by faith—produces, Luther finds hope in the coming consummation of perfect righteousness in heaven. But this is not the result of any human effort; it is not a human process at all. God initiates justification and the same God completes it. Christians must believe in the beginning that God has declared them just. Furthermore, God imputes Christ's righteousness to them.[33] Finally, the same God shall complete what he has begun, and Christians will eventually become what God has declared them to be even now.[34] Perfect righteousness is not a dream. It is a reality coming towards us. It will be revealed in due time. It is for this reason that Christians must pray incessantly for the coming of this day. Luther explains the petition, "Thy kingdom come," by saying:

Help, dear Lord, that the blessed day of your glorious future may come soon, that we be rescued from the wicked world, the devil's kingdom, and be freed from the horrible vexation which we outwardly and inwardly must suffer both from evil people and our own conscience...Therefore they who believe in Christ should become certain and assured of the eternal glory and together with all

[31]Ibid.

[32]Ibid., 22.

[33]Ibid., 26:232: "Then they will find that this is the situation, that Christian righteousness consists in two things: first, in faith, which attributes glory to God; secondly, in God's imputation. For because faith is weak, as I have said, therefore God's imputation had to be added. That is, God does not want to impute the remnant of sin and does not want to punish it or damn us for it. But He wants to cover it and to forgive it, as though it were nothing, not for our sakes or for the sake of our worthiness or works but for the sake of Christ Himself, in whom we believe. Thus a Christian man is righteous and a sinner at the same time, holy and profane, an enemy of God and a child of God."

[34]Ibid., 26:235: "Meanwhile, as long as we are alive, we are supported and nourished at the bosom of divine mercy and forbearance, until the body of sin (Rom. 6:6) is abolished and we are raised up as new beings on that Day. Then there will be new heavens and a new earth, in which righteousness will dwell."

creatures groan and cry out that our Lord God might hasten to bring about the blessed day when such hope will be fulfilled.[35]

The coming day of the Lord is the completion of the work of God begun in our justification. Here eschatology is not so much "realized" as "teleological"; it is an event of the future. Axiological and teleological eschatology were for Luther not mutually exclusive but rather complementary. Thus he could sing:

> Thy kingdom come now here below,
> And after, up there, evermo'.
> The Holy Ghost his temple hold
> In us with graces manifold.
> The devil's wrath and greatness strong
> Crush, that he do thy church no wrong.[36]

The kingdom of God is coming in this time and afterwards in eternity; but it is the very same kingdom:

> The kingdom of faith and the kingdom of future glory are one kingdom, but they are distinguished in that what is offered to us here in the kingdom of faith through the Word and what we receive and grasp by faith will be presented to us there in that revelation. Thus St. Peter says, 1 Peter 1:12, that a Gospel has been preached to us "into which angels long to look." Therefore there is one kingdom, only there is a difference in knowledge. Now we hear it in the Word, then we shall have it in sight. Now we believe and hope for it with all Christians on earth, then we shall possess it with all the holy angels and God's elect in heaven.[37]

On the basis of this summary of the relationship of Luther's doctrine of justification to his eschatology, what can we learn for the contemporary theological situation? As we indicated earlier, Luther teaches us that justification by faith without this eschatological dimension is subjectivistic and individualistic self-hypnosis. Against all those theological efforts in our time which attempt to reduce justification to an essentially subjective psychological experience, Luther insists on an objective event at the end of history: "Meanwhile, as long as we are alive, we are supported and nourished at the bosom of divine mercy and forbearance, until the body of sin (Rom. 6:6) is abolished and we are raised up as new beings *on that Day.* Then there will be new heavens and a new earth, in which righteousness dwell [2 Peter 3:13]."[38] For Luther the solution to the problem of sin remaining after justification is not the "death of God" but rather the "death of humankind." Against those theologians who see the hope for the world in the realization of the death of God and the resulting new freedom for humanity, as for example, the Americans T. J. J. Altizer and William Hamilton,[39] Luther would see the hope for the world in the death and resurrection of humankind—a real death as well as a real resurrec-

---

[35]*Sermons* (1535), *WA* 41:317-318. Cf., *Sermons* (1534), *WA* 37:617; *Sermons* (1531), *WA* 34/2:474-475.

[36]*Our Father in Heaven who Art* (1539), *LW* 53:297.

[37]*Sermon on Psalm 8* (Nov. 1, 1537), *LW* 12:118.

[38]*Lectures on Galatians* (1535), *LW* 26:235, my italics. (The passage from 2 Pet 3:13 is incorrectly identified as Rev 21:1 in *LW*.)

[39]Cf., Thomas J. J. Altizer and William Hamilton, *Radical Theology and the Death of God* (Indianapolis: Bobbs-Merrill, 1966).

tion ushering in a new age, a new heaven and a new earth. This is not merely a psychological transaction within the mind of the believer or unbeliever, but it is an act of God involving not only the individual but also the individual's community and world. Luther reminds us of the reality of the future as the guarantee of our present experience. Justification is not some oriental *satori*, some intuitive flash of insight into the unitary character of reality, no psychological *tour de force*. The guarantee of the reality and absoluteness of justification by faith is the hope that he who came shall come again. This future which is coming towards us is not merely a personal and subjective hope, but a hope for the entire people of the God of Abraham, Isaac, and Jacob, the God of the living and not of the dead. Through the people of God this eschatological hope becomes a hope for all people, indeed, for all of creation. Luther quotes Jesus as saying to the Sadducees who question the resurrection (Matt 22:23ff.):

> You fools, you know nothing of God's word nor anything of his grace and power; you bring only your dreams here, which should prove something. But if you would consider the Holy Scriptures and look at God's omnipotence, then you would see whether God could not raise the dead. He who in creation indeed made everything out of nothing, should he then not also be able to make the dead alive? And from out of what are all people still created everyday? Isn't it true, out of nothing? Since then he can do that which you daily see before your eyes, grasp and feel, should he then not also restore the dead to life? Is that such an unbelievable thing, to raise the dead, when he addresses something that is nothing, and it comes into being? And when he speaks, then it takes place, and when he commands, then it stands before him....I see indeed that you have not studied scripture, from which you should have learned that God's might and power is so great that he can make everything out of nothing. But meanwhile it happens everyday, yet no one pays attention to it; when a young girl is a virgin and a year later a mother, this is common in villages and cities. Therefore nobody calls it a miracle; and if a man would now[40] rise from the dead, I believe the whole world would come running. But that children are born who a year earlier were nothing at all, this we don't ask about, for we do not recognize God's power or understand Holy Scripture.[41]

Finally, eschatology without justification by faith is mere utopianism. For Luther, it is not history which is redemptive but the Christ who came in history. It is because of Christ's justifying deed that we may have hope. This is as valid against the *Schwärmer* [enthusiasts] in Luther's time as against those who today see the historical process itself as the agent of redemption. A certain and prevalent type of evolutionary thinking attributes a moral conscience to the evolutionary process itself. It is almost tragic how rapidly these optimistic theologians of evolution are crushed by the events that were to redeem the world. The same William Hamilton who only yesterday described the great changes taking place in the relationship of the races in the United States of America in terms of what he called the "new optimism" stands today condemned as the typical false prophet by the

---

[40]I am indebted for the correction of the WA reading of *ist* (is) to *itzt* (now) to Professor Ernst Kahler of Greifswald.

[41]*Sermon on Matthew 22:28* (1537/40), WA 47:433.

events he so completely misunderstood. Hamilton quoted the sentimental song of the civil rights movement, "We Shall Overcome," as evidence for the power of the new optimism produced by the "death of God."[42] Today, only a few years later these same young people in America sing "Burn, Baby, Burn," rejecting the naive optimism of the civil rights movement and demanding instead "Black Power."

Without becoming involved in the merits of this complicated issue, we note, however, that it illustrates the total inadequacy of an eschatology without justification by faith. This is also shown by the pathetic new legalism of the so-called situation ethics as presented in England and America under the pretentious title of "The New Morality" by people like J. A. T. Robinson and Joseph Fletcher.[43] Here, too, it is naively assumed that the life of love, the life of discipleship, is a simple human possibility, without the need for justification by faith. The result is, as always, a utopia which enslaves and terrifies people by the very laws devised to free them and make them happy. Here again Luther's warning remains valid:

> For other kingdoms, no matter how happy or well constituted they are, still have innumerable offenses—to such an extent that one cannot find a single civil society in which there are not collected innumerable and glaring sins. They are all shot through with tyranny, stupidity, malfeasance of duty, with all kinds of desires for glory, lust, revenge, avarice. Therefore the person who rules must necessarily dispense injustice to many people.[44]

What was true in Luther's time in Münster can be demonstrated clearly in our time in America and Asia, in Africa and Europe. Luther complained against the *Schwärmer* of his time:

> Their teaching is nothing other than worldly goods, temporal, fleshly, and earthly promise, which the mob gladly hears—namely that they…imagine a kingdom on earth in which all the godless are slain and they alone are to have good days. Who wouldn't want that? That is indeed, however, an open, palpable lie, for Christ has prepared for His own not a worldly kingdom, but rather a heavenly kingdom and says "In the world you will have anxiety and distress" [John 16:33]; likewise, "My kingdom is not of this world" [John 19:36].[45]

We can learn from Luther that history is not redemptive and neither is technology or natural science. The problem with humankind is humankind, and this problem is not solved by avoiding the issue. Luther escaped utopianism because he saw the focus of our problem in us, not in our environment. It is his lasting contribution to have juxtaposed justification and eschatology in such a manner as to avoid both despair and illusion.

---

[42]Altizer and Hamilton, *Radical Theology*, 164.

[43]John A. T. Robinson, *Honest to God* (Philadelphia: Westminster, 1963); and Joseph Fletcher, *Situation Ethics: The New Morality* (Philadelphia: Westminster, 1966).

[44]*Psalm 45* (1532), LW 12:236-237.

[45]*Preface to Menius* (1530), WA 30/2:213.

Word & World
Supplement Series 2
1994

Luther and Christian Liberty

A Focus of Controversy

WHILE LUTHER PROBABLY NEVER SAID "HERE I STAND,"[1] AND WHILE IT IS doubtful that he ever nailed the ninety-five theses on the door of the castle church in Wittenberg,[2] he certainly wrote: "A Christian is a perfectly free lord of all, subject to none. A Christian is a perfectly dutiful servant of all, subject to all."[3] As an Augustinian theologian standing firmly in the western Christian tradition, the issue of freedom and its theological meaning occupied him all his life.

One of his major theological works, and in his own judgment one of his best, was *The Bondage of the Will*,[4] published in 1525, which denies human beings any power to contribute to their own salvation. In their relationship to God, human beings have no freedom at all. Here we find the famous illustration that the human will is placed between God and the devil like a beast of burden, "If God rides it, it wills and goes where God wills....If Satan rides it, it wills and goes where Satan wills; nor can it choose to run to either of the two riders or to seek him out, but the riders contend for the possession and control of it."[5]

This struggle between God and Satan is the key to Luther's understanding of the human predicament so colorfully expressed in his most famous hymn, "A Mighty Fortress is our God." He sings:

The old satanic foe has sworn to work us woe!
With craft and dreadfull might he arms himself to fight.

[1]*LW* 32:113.

[2]Cf. Erwin Iserloh, *The Theses Were Not Posted: Luther between Reform and Reformation* (Boston: Beacon, 1968).

[3]*The Freedom of a Christian* (1520), *LW* 31:344.

[4]*LW* 33:15-295.

[5]*LW* 33:65-66. Note the footnote concerning the history of this illustration and Luther's modification.

This essay first appeared in the Lutheran Theological Seminary Bulletin 68/1 (Winter 1988), 3-11. Dr. Forell delivered it in lecture form at the October, 1987, "Luther Symposium," at Gettysburg, Pennsylvania.

On earth is not his equal.
No strength of ours can match his might!
We would be lost, rejected.
But now a champion comes to fight, Whom God himself elected.
You ask who this may be? The Lord of hosts is he!
Christ Jesus, mighty Lord, God's only Son, adored.
He holds the field victorious.[6]

Because Heiko Oberman has articulated the importance of this battle in Luther's thought so very clearly, his book, *Luther: Man between God and the Devil,*[7] is probably the best book on Luther's theology produced in connection with the celebration of the five-hundredth anniversary of Luther's birth. In this conflict between God and the devil, the issue of freedom is central.

So it is not surprising that Gerhard Ebeling speaks of Luther's understanding of freedom as the "focus (*Brennpunkt*) of the modern controversy about Luther."[8] He observes that while liberty is by no means a very clearly defined concept in our time, it appears to be the "*Grundwort und Grundwert der Neuzeit,*" which means that liberty is seen as the "basic slogan and the basic value of modernity."[9] Our colloquium with its theme "Luther and Liberation Theology" only helps to bear out Ebeling's observation.

It would lead us too far afield to rehearse all the statements about Luther and liberty that have been made by famous and infamous people. The significant point is that those who praise Luther see him as a fighter for freedom, while those who condemn him do so for restricting freedom to the interior of the person and thus contributing to their enslavement more profoundly than even the medieval church had managed to do. Here Karl Marx's observations are paradigmatic. He observed in the context of his critique of Hegel that Luther had freed human beings from the outward fetters the church had forged but put their hearts into chains. He wrote:

> Luther, to be sure, overcame servitude based on devotion, but by replacing it with servitude based on conviction. He shattered faith in authority by restoring the authority of faith. He transformed the priests into laymen by changing the laymen into priests. He liberated man from external religiosity by making religiosity that which is innermost to man. He freed the body of chains by putting the heart in chains.[10]

To obtain some clarity on the subject assigned to us, "Luther and liberty," we shall follow Ebeling and ask first of all about the relationship between freedom and

---

[6]*Lutheran Book of Worship* (Minneapolis: Augsburg; Philadelphia: Board of Publication, LCA, 1978) Hymn 229. Hereafter, *LBW*.

[7]Heiko Oberman, *Luther, Man between God and the Devil* (New Haven: Yale University, 1989).

[8]Gerhard Ebeling, *Lutherstudien*, 3 vols. (Tübingen: Mohr, 1971-1989) 3:375. The chapter is a reprint of Ebeling's Heidelberg lecture of 1982, "*Zum Gegensatz von Luther-Enthusiasmus und Luther-Fremdheit in der Neuzeit.*"

[9]Ibid., 376.

[10]Karl Marx, *Critique of Hegel's "Philosophy of Right,"* ed. Joseph O'Malley (Cambridge: Cambridge University, 1970) 138.

sin, freedom and conscience, and freedom and ethics in Luther's thought.[11] Then we shall look rather closely at Luther's famous pamphlet, *The Freedom of a Christian*, to see what it can teach us about Luther and Christian liberty.

Ebeling observes that all modern talk about liberty negates the notion of sin. Sin, having been moralized and emptied of its religious significance, has been incorporated into freedom. Since the enlightenment, the fall in paradise has been seen as the beginning of human freedom. The great German poet Friedrich Schiller observed:

> If we change the voice of God in Eden, which proscribed the tree of knowledge, into the voice of instinct which kept the human being from this tree, then the alleged disobedience to a divine command is actually the turning against instinct. It is the first expression of self-determination, the first act of daring on the part of human reason, the beginning of humanity's moral existence (*Erster Anfang seines moralischen Daseyns*). This fall of humanity from instinct brought moral evil into creation but only in order to make moral good possible. It is without doubt the happiest and greatest event in human history. Human freedom is born at that moment, the foundation of human morality is laid here.[12]

The sense of sin is the cause of bondage. It is significant that Nietzsche calls Christianity the original sin.[13] And it is obvious that it is Luther's emphasis on sin and the justification of the sinner which is the great obstacle to the acceptance of his theology in modern times.

Luther's modern protestant critics (not to mention the pop-religions of our day, the "new age" cults with their stress on feeling good about oneself) find his emphasis on sin "medieval" and understand it as an extreme form of Augustinianism.[14] But Luther does not really see the human predicament as caused by the actual sins which had troubled medieval casuists, but rather by original sin, the sin against the First Commandment, the root of all other sins, the unwillingness to let God be God. The profound objection to Luther comes from those who understand (correctly, to be sure) that he insists that apart from faith even good works are sin.

It is Luther's emphasis on the utter helplessness of human beings apart from God which is the scandal of his theology for modern men and women. He writes: "Free choice without the grace of God is not free at all, but immutably the captive and slave of evil, since it cannot of itself turn to the good."[15] Again, the *liberum arbitrium*, free will or free choice, "is plainly a divine term (*divinum nomen*), and can be properly applied to none but the Divine Majesty alone; for he alone can do and does...whatever he pleases in heaven and on earth."[16] Christian liberty is not

---

[11]To the following, see Ebeling, *Lutherstudien*, 3:380ff.

[12]Friedrich Schiller, "Etwas über die erste Menschengesellschaft nach dem Leitfaden der mosaischen Urkunde" (1790), as quoted in Ebeling, *Lutherstudien*, 2/1:306-7.

[13]F. Nietzsche, *Der Antichrist* (1888), 61, as quoted in Ebeling, *Lutherstudien*, 3:381.

[14]For appropriate quotations from Dilthey and Troeltsch, see Ebeling, *Lutherstudien*, 3:381-92.

[15]*The Bondage of the Will* (1525), LW 33:67.

[16]Ibid., 68.

freedom of choice or freedom of the will but it means instead to have been justified as a sinner. It means to be freed from the curse of sin, liberated from the obsession with the self, from being turned into the self (*incurvatus in se*), and instead, having become absolutely dependent on God. In Paul's terms, it is having become "a slave of Jesus Christ" (Rom 1:1) which is a phrase utterly abhorrent to contemporary theology and religiosity.

Much of modern religion and contemporary theology has more in common with elements of ancient and medieval religiosity than with Luther. Gnosticism and Pelagianism, not Luther, are the godparents of modern religious thought. One can easily shift from "death of God" to polytheism, pantheism, witchcraft, and devil-worship if one has lost hold of the basic human problem, the sickness unto death, the pervasiveness and power of sin.

But what about freedom and conscience? To quote Ebeling again: "In the long history of the concept of conscience since the days of classical antiquity the phrase 'freedom of conscience' appears first, if I am right, in Luther. It affects as a rallying cry the battle for freedom in the modern world including the idea of human rights."[17]

Of course, Luther was hardly the originator of the quest for individual freedom so basic for the modern world, even though some people have made such assertions. But the reason for their claim is obvious. In his most important political appearance, when he confronted Emperor Charles V at the Diet of Worms, he talked about his absolute commitment to God in the language of conscience saying, "My conscience is captive to the Word of God," and again, "It is neither safe nor right to go against conscience."[18] He expressed eloquently the need to obey his conscience come what may. But there was a difference. As Ebeling puts it: "*Gewissensfreiheit wird hier nicht als ein Recht gefordert, sondern als eine Macht gelebt*"[19] or "Here freedom of conscience is not claimed as a right but lived as power." While in the classical tradition conscience was bound to outside rules, to tradition, if you please (e.g., Antigone and her obligation to bury her brother), and scholastic theology talked about a right conscience, namely, a conscience formed by the law, Luther sees himself as captured by the word of God. In his language this means he must obey because of the gospel rather than the law.

The rule of law is changed into a personal relationship to God in Christ. A clear conscience does not result from obedience to the law, from doing good works, but from the justification of the sinner, in spite of conscience, death, and devil. As Luther wrote in his *Judgment on Monastic Vows* of 1521:

> Christian or evangelical freedom, then, is a freedom of conscience (*libertas conscientiae*) which liberates the conscience from works. Not that no works are done, but no faith is put in them....Christ has freed this conscience from works

[17]Ebeling, *Lutherstudien*, 3:385-86.
[18]*LW* 32:112.
[19]Ebeling, *Lutherstudien*, 3:387.

through the gospel and teaches this conscience not to trust in works, but to rely only on his mercy.[20]

Luther's entire perspective is almost incomprehensible to modern men and women. For them God does not justify; he needs justification. He is justified in the opinion of some because he makes people obey the law. You may actually not believe in God but in order to support certain ethical values, certain just causes, you may become religious, go through religious motions, and join religious institutions. Christianity has become morality. The sequence attributed to Luther that Christian ethics starts with faith which is active in love, has been completely reversed. Today we tend to use God as a traditional fiction to support the many causes in which we have much more confidence than in God. We do believe in our liberty but not as a gift of God, dependent every moment on God's grace, but as a right that makes us into autonomous beings for whom faith in God is an option. This is part of our religious liberty as are atheism, witchcraft, and belief in unidentified flying objects.

THE FREEDOM OF THE CHRISTIAN

Against this background we shall try to learn what Luther means by Christian liberty by carefully looking at one of his most popular writings dealing precisely with this topic. We repeat the basic propositions: "A Christian is a perfectly free lord of all subject to none. A Christian is a perfectly dutiful servant of all, subject to all." As always his indebtedness to Paul is obvious and here especially to 1 Cor 9:19: "For though I am free with respect to all, I have made myself a slave to all, so that I might win more of them."

It appears at first that Luther tries to resolve the apparent contradiction between "free lord" and the "dutiful servant" with the device common to western thought, the distinction between the two aspects of the human being, the spiritual and the bodily. He writes: "According to the spiritual nature, which men refer to as the soul, he is called a spiritual, inner, or new man. According to the bodily nature, which men refer to as flesh, he is called a carnal, outward, or old man."[21] He adds that because of this diversity the scriptures assert contradictory things concerning the same human being, since these two are at odds. As an example he quotes Gal 5:17, "For the desires of the flesh are against the Spirit and the desires of the Spirit against the flesh."

At first glance this may appear to be the same kind of argument that allowed Plato's Socrates to speak of the body as the prison of the soul and to think of human liberation as liberation from the world of shadows, the material world, into the world of ideas, the spiritual world. This is a notion repeated throughout the history of western thought, articulated by mystics and expressed in a multitude of

---

[20]*LW* 44:298.
[21]*LW* 31:344.

versions by idealistic philosophers and gnostic wise men and women (e. g., Mary Baker Eddy).

But nothing could be further from Luther's intention. He never sees the human being in isolation. The Christian who is the subject of this treatise is what he or she is only because of a relationship to Christ. Christian liberty is completely dependent on this relationship and has nothing to do with the sort of questions raised by modern behavioristic psychology and its determinism.[22] The difference is not "matter" and "spirit," in the customary philosophical and religious sense, but the person without Christ and the person with Christ. He writes:

> One thing, and only one thing, is necessary for Christian life, righteousness, and freedom. That one thing is the most holy Word of God, the gospel of Christ, as Christ says, John 11[:25], "I am the resurrection and the life: he who believes in me, though he die yet shall he live"; and John 8[:36], "So if the Son makes you free, you will be free indeed."[23]

For Luther, Christian liberty is a gift given to men and women through the word, which is, as he adds immediately, nothing else but "the gospel of God concerning his Son, who was made flesh, suffered, rose from the dead, and was glorified through the Spirit who sanctifies."[24] To preach Christ means to feed the soul, make it righteous, set it free, and save it, provided it believes the preaching. Faith in the promises of God, trusting God's word, gives the human being everything which God's law demands, but which people cannot produce through their good works. Following the imagery of Ephesians [5:31-32] and less explicitly, Bernard of Clairvaux in his commentary on the Song of Songs, he asserts that faith

> unites the soul with Christ as a bride is united with her bridegroom....Christ and the soul become one flesh. And if they are one flesh and there is between them a true marriage—indeed the most perfect of all marriages...it follows that everything they have they hold in common, the good as well as the evil.[25]

Here occurs the "joyous exchange" (*fröhlicher Wechsel*), that is so much a part of Luther's theology that it has permeated the hymns of the church. Nicolaus Herman (1480-1561) sings:

> Er wechselt mit uns wunderlich, Fleisch und Blut nimmt er an,
> Und giebt uns in seins Vaters Reich Die klare Gottheit dran.
> Er wird ein Knecht und ich ein Herr, Das mag ein Wechsel sein.
> Wie konnt er doch sein freundlicher, Das Herze Jesulein![26]

Luther writes:

> Christ is full of grace, life, and salvation. The soul is full of sins, death, and

---

[22]Cf. B. F. Skinner, *Beyond Freedom and Dignity* (New York: Knopf, 1971).

[23]*The Freedom of a Christian* (1520), LW 31:345.

[24]Ibid., 346.

[25]Ibid., 351.

[26]LBW translation: "He undertakes a great exchange, Puts on our human frame. And in return gives us his realm, His glory and his name. He is a servant I a lord: how great a mystery! How strong the tender Christchild's love! No truer friend then he" (Hymn 47).

damnation. Now let faith come between them and sins, death, and damnation will be Christ's, while grace, life, and salvation will be the soul's; for if Christ is a bridegroom, he must take upon himself the things which are his bride's and bestow upon her things that are his.[27]

He uses the whole armory of christological speech to demonstrate the salvation of human beings.

Christ is God and man in one person. He neither sinned nor died, and is not condemned, and he cannot sin, die, or be condemned; his righteousness, life, and salvation are unconquerable, eternal, omnipotent by the wedding ring of faith he shares in the sins, death, and pains of hell which are his bride's.[28]

Christian liberty is the direct result of this divine intervention: "Thus the believing soul by means of the pledge of its faith is free in Christ, its bridegroom, free from all sins, secure against death and hell, and is endowed with the eternal righteousness, life, and salvation of Christ its bridegroom."[29]

Luther continues in the most colorful language to describe the royal marriage between this "rich and divine bridegroom" and this "poor and wicked harlot." Christian liberty is simply one aspect of the alien righteousness granted to Christians by grace alone. It is the result of having been bound to Christ in this royal marriage. Indeed Christians are free because they are bound to Christ and share in everything he is and has. For this reason, the Christian "needs neither law nor good works but, on the contrary, is injured by them if he believes that he is justified by them."[30]

But he adds immediately that all this is an eschatological reality and applies to the Christian as saint, while he or she is at the same time sinner. To those who have read thus far and now say: "We will take our ease and do no works and be content with faith," Luther answers:

Not so, dear friend, not so. That would indeed be proper if we were wholly inner and perfectly spiritual human beings. But such we shall be only at the last day, the day of the resurrection of the dead. As long as we live in the flesh we only begin to make some progress in that which shall be perfected in the future life.[31]

The ethical consequences of the liberation of the human being resulting from justification by faith and described with the help of the image of the marriage of the soul to Christ are treated in the last part of the booklet. Here Luther deals with the second proposition, "A Christian is a perfectly dutiful servant of all, subject to all." This servanthood of the liberated person has actually two aspects, control of one's own body and major changes in one's dealings with other people.[32] The justified

---

[27]LW 31:351.
[28]Ibid., 351-52.
[29]Ibid., 352.
[30]Ibid., 358.
[31]Ibid.; translation altered. Luther does not write, "you wicked men," but rather, "*Lieber Mensch.*"
[32]Ibid.

person, Luther claims, "meets a contrary will in his own flesh which strives to serve the world and seeks its own advantage."[33]

The Christian life is therefore a life of conflict; one experiences the assaults of the devil, the famous *Anfechtungen* which troubled Luther all his life. Again Paul serves as his resource and he quotes Romans, 1 Corinthians, and Galatians to make his point. He does not rule out some success in this battle. Indeed he claims that the life of the believer is in some ways analogous to the life of Adam and Eve in paradise. "Through his faith he has been restored to Paradise and created anew, he has no need of works that he may become or be righteous; but that he may not be idle and may provide for and keep his body, he must do such works freely only to please God."[34]

ETHICAL CONSEQUENCES

It is apparent that Christian liberty has ethical consequences; it affects the daily life of the Christian. This is particularly true in relation to other human beings, for Christian liberty frees Christians from their obsession with themselves and their own salvation to act in the true interest of the neighbor. Insofar as I act as a justified sinner, I am free to act without any concern for my own self-interest. God has taken care of me so that I might be empowered to care for my neighbor.

Again Christ is the model. And here Luther comes to the most daring assertions of this little book. The Christian ought to think, he says,

> Although I am an unworthy and condemned person, my God has given me in Christ all the riches of righteousness and salvation without any merit on my part, out of pure, free mercy, so that from now on I need nothing except faith which believes that this is true. Why should I not therefore freely, joyfully with all my heart, and with an eager will do all things which I know are pleasing and acceptable to such a Father who has overwhelmed me with his inestimable riches? *I will therefore give myself as a Christ to my neighbor, just as Christ offered himself to me;* I will do nothing in this life except what I see is necessary, profitable, and salutary to my neighbor, since through faith I have an abundance of all good things in Christ.[35]

We have received freedom in order to serve those in need.

> Just as our neighbor is in need and lacks that in which we abound, so we were in need before God and lacked his mercy. Hence, as our heavenly Father has in Christ freely come to our aid, we also ought freely to help our neighbor through our body and its works and *each one should become as it were a Christ to the other that we may be Christs to one another and Christ may be the same in all*, that is, that we may be truly Christians.[36]

If we ask how this might be accomplished, Luther suggests as the prominent example of liberation the blessed Virgin Mary, who "out of free and willing

---

[33]Ibid., 359.

[34]Ibid., 360.

[35]Ibid., 367 (emphasis added).

[36]Ibid., 367-68 (emphasis added).

love...submitted to the law like other women that she might not offend or despise them. She was not justified by this work, but being righteous she did it freely and willingly."[37]

For Luther, Christian liberty is not a human achievement but a gift of God's grace. But it is an empowering gift because it enables the recipient to be freed from self-concern, the obsession with his or her own interest, for the real needs of others. Christian ethics in the more restricted sense is only possible on the basis of this liberation. There are all kinds of good works that people can do. They are works of the law which may contribute to the earthly welfare of human beings. But the life that makes a woman or a man into a Christ to others is only possible for those who have been made one with him and thus can say with Paul: "It is no longer I who live, but Christ who lives in me" (Gal 2:20). For Luther this alone is Christian liberty.

[37]Ibid., 368.

Word & World
Supplement Series 2
1994

Luther and Conscience

IT IS PART OF THE CONVENTIONAL WISDOM THAT THE REFORMATION WAS BASED
upon the assertion of freedom of conscience, the autonomous human conscience
against the heteronomy of church and state. The illustration generally used in
order to support this claim is Luther's celebrated appearance at the Diet of Worms.
Standing before emperor and pope's representative he said:

> Since then your serene majesty and your lordships seek a simple answer, I will
> give it in this manner, neither horned nor toothed: Unless I am convinced by the
> testimony of the Scriptures or by clear reason (for I do not trust either in the pope
> or in councils alone, since it is well known that they have often erred and
> contradicted themselves) I am bound by the Scriptures I have quoted and my
> conscience is captive to the Word of God. I cannot and will not retract anything,
> since it is neither safe nor right to go against conscience (*Cum contra conscientiam
> agere neque tutum neque integrum sit*).[1]

Even if Luther never said, "*Ich kan nicht anders, hie stehe Ich, Got helff mir,
amen,*"[2] the emphasis upon conscience in his defense has never been questioned.
But while there is considerable agreement on the significance of conscience for
Luther's theology and ethics, the character of this significance is the focus of a
major debate. One of the most important Luther scholars of the twentieth century,
Karl Holl, claimed in his seminal essay, "What Did Luther Understand by 'Religion'?":

> Luther's religion is a "religion of conscience" in the most pronounced sense of
> the word, with all the urgency and the personal character belonging to it. It issues

[1] *Luther at the Diet of Worms* (1521), LW 32:112.
[2] Ibid., 32:113.

This essay first appeared in The Lutheran Theological Seminary at Gettysburg Bulletin *55/1
(1975) 3-11, and was delivered first at the 1974 Martin Luther Colloquium. Here Dr. Forell uses
Luther's distinction between law and gospel to explicate the reformer's understanding of "conscience."*

from a particular kind of conscientious experience—namely, his unique experience of the conflict between a keen sense of responsibility and the unconditional, absolute validity of the divine will—and rests on the conviction that in the sense of obligation (*sollen*), which impresses its demands so irresistibly upon the human will, divinity reveals itself most clearly.[3]

This meant that the "voice of conscience" was seen as the point of contact between God's revelation and the human being. This gave conscience an essentially positive meaning in line with the scholastic tradition of synteresis, the divine spark in the human being after the fall. Emmanuel Hirsch has pointed out that it was Peter Abelard who had first called attention to the importance of conscience for ethics and who saw Paul's struggle for justification by grace through faith essentially as a struggle for the *lex naturalis* against the *lex scripta*, for rationalism against legalism. Abelard's natural law rationalism was summarized in the sentence, "The words of the natural law are those who command love of God and love of the neighbor."[4] For the development of Christian ethics it is significant that Abelard discovered the natural law written into the human heart in the conscience. To sin is to act against conscience. And this became the accepted opinion in the schools. But this insight, which might have led to the advocacy of freedom of conscience, resulted in the opposite by its subordination to the law. Biel said: "Conscience is the herald of the law."[5] Hirsch summarizes the medieval development which Luther eventually confronted under two headings: (1) Conscience is always subject to law. It binds conscience and is never independent of it. (2) Conscience is not an originally religious experience. Rather it is the experience of oneself. "The ultimate height and depth of the encounter with God are independent of the conscience."[6]

It is against this background that we must understand Luther's appeal to conscience in Worms and also the disregard of this appeal by the secretary to the archbishop of Trier who shouted: "Lay aside your conscience, Martin; you must lay it aside because it is in error."[7] By Luther's time a conscience which opposes the law of God out of ignorance or error must simply be put aside. Unlike Abelard, who had daringly asserted that if the Jews followed their conscience in crucifying Jesus they did not sin, properly speaking,[8] later scholastics deny the possibility of a conscience which through error involves of necessity in sin. The priest who speaks within the limits of the pastoral office overrules the erring conscience.[9]

For Thomas, synteresis is the guarding or keeping of the natural principles of

---

[3]K. Holl, *What Did Luther Understand by Religion?* (Philadelphia: Fortress, 1977) 48.

[4]"Verba autem legis naturalis ea sunt, quae dei et proximi charitatem commendant." Abelard, in Migne, *Patrologia Latina*, 178, 814c, as quoted in E. Hirsch, *Lutherstudien*, vol. 1 (Gütersloh: C Bertelsmann, 1954) 13.

[5]"Conscientia vero est quasi praeco legis," as quoted in Hirsch, 17.

[6]Hirsch, 107.

[7]*LW* 32:130.

[8]Hirsch, *Lutherstudien*, 16.

[9]Ibid., 25.

the moral law, the habit of understanding these primary principles or precepts.[10] Conscience is then the ability (*habitus*) to act according to law. It can be used almost in the same sense as reason (*ratio vel conscientia*). A command of conscience and a command of reason can be the same thing. Thomas Aquinas proposes that in matters of faith the synteresis is inapplicable since the light of reason does not suffice for the comprehension of matters of faith.[11]

It was this tradition which Luther reflected in his earliest comments on conscience. In 1509 he wrote in the margin of St. Augustine's *De Trinitate*, where Augustine reflects on John 1:4, on the light which shines in human beings and enables them to live and move and have their being in God, "It appears that this light is our synteresis."[12] Here Luther clearly affirms synteresis as a valuable gift of God to human beings. And similarly in a 1516 comment on Tauler's fifty-second sermon he sees a reference to synteresis in Tauler's description of the word of God speaking to the soul. Synteresis reveals that God is closer to the soul than it is to itself.[13]

In a sermon of 1514 Luther distinguished two kinds of synteresis, the *synteresis voluntatis* and the *synteresis rationis*,[14] but as Hirsch has observed, he uses synteresis in order to understand the contradiction in human beings between the will and reason designed to enable them to serve God, and the factual opposition between human will and reason and God. This aptitude is not able to determine the human will and understanding. As early as his Romans commentary he questions the general aptitude as well and writes:

> The common saying that human nature in a general and universal way knows and wills the good but errs and does not will it in particular cases would be better stated if we were to say that in particular cases human nature knows and wills what is good but in general neither knows nor wills it. The reason is that it knows nothing but its own good, or what is good and honorable and useful for itself, but not what is good for God and other people. Therefore it knows and wills more what is particular, yes, only what is an individual good. And this is in agreement with Scripture, which describes man as so turned in on himself that he uses not only physical but even spiritual goods for his own purposes and in all things seeks only himself.[15]

The significant difference between Luther's view of synteresis and conscience from the tradition which he had inherited is the essentially accusing function of both. While *conscientia* was traditionally understood in relation to specific actions and could be either accusing or excusing, synteresis, as we have observed above, was the natural inclination of the soul towards the good, an inextinguishable spark

[10]Roy J. Deferrari, *A Latin-English Dictionary of St. Thomas Aquinas* (Boston: St. Paul Editions, 1960) 1025.

[11]Hirsch, *Lutherstudien*, 33.

[12]*Randbemerkungen Luthers zu Augustins Schrift de trinitate* (1509), WA 9:18.

[13]*Zu Taulers Predigten* (c. 1516), WA 9:103.

[14]*Sermo, De Propria Sapientia et Voluntate* (1514), WA 1:36.

[15]*Lectures on Romans* (1515), LW 25:345.

(*scintilla*) of reason. For Luther even the effect of synteresis could best be described as "the worm" (*vermis*), and "murmuring" of a guilty conscience.[16] It is therefore dubious whether for Luther synteresis or conscience are ever the thoroughly positive force, that, for example Erich Seeberg describes in Luther, "the unformed instinct of the soul for God, to be formed by the will and intellect."[17]

Against this conscience interpretation of Karl Holl and his disciples, Ernst Wolf[18] is correct in his insistence that (1) Luther denies any formation of a constant, essential core of the human being through God's word. On the contrary he says,

> this word "formed" (*formatum*) is under a curse, for it forces us to think of the soul as being the same after as before the outpouring of love and as if the form were merely added to it at the time of the action, although it is necessary that it be wholly put to death and be changed before putting on love and working in love.[19]

Continuity would deny that the Christian is a new creature. (2) Luther rejects the notion that there is a constant core of the human being which constitutes the connection between the unformed and the newly formed conscience. (3)Finally, he refused to consider this alleged core as the instrument by which the human being encounters the divine demand. The encounter with Christ, not the experience of an irresistible divine demand, results in the presence of God, existence *coram deo*. Friedrich Gogarten states this point forcefully when he writes:

> Conscience, as Luther understands it and as it occupies a central place in his theology, is precisely where faith must take up the struggle against ethics as the attempt to bring the relationship to God under the control of the human being. In dealing with conscience we deal with the human being as he really is. But not as he is lord over himself through his ethical self-understanding and thus autonomously confronts the world, but as he is delivered into the power of the authorities which rule the world.[20]

Who are these authorities? For Luther they are law, death, and devil, and his understanding of conscience must be seen in relationship to these authorities which it serves.[21] As he wrote in *De Votis Monasticis* in 1521:

> For conscience is not the power to do works, but to judge them. The proper work of conscience (as Paul says in Romans 2 [:15]), is to accuse or excuse, to make guilty or guiltless, uncertain or certain. Its purpose is not to do, but to pass judgment on what has been done and what should be done, and this judgment makes us stand accused or saved in God's sight.[22]

---

[16]*First Psalm Lectures* (1513-16), LW 11:389.

[17]Erich Seeberg, *Luthers Theologie*, vol. 2 (Stuttgart: W. Kohlhammer, 1937) 85.

[18]To the following, see Ernst Wolf, *Peregrinatio* (Munich: C. Kaiser, 1962) 88ff.

[19]*Lectures on Romans* (1515), LW 25:325.

[20]Friedrich Gogarten, *Die Verkundigung Jesu Christi*, 2nd ed. (Tübingen: Mohr, 1965) 295.

[21]To the following, see G. Jacob, *Der Gewissensbegriff in der Theologie Luthers* (Tübingen: Mohr, 1929).

[22]*The Judgment of Martin Luther on Monastic Vows* (1521), LW 44:298.

I. CONSCIENCE AND LAW

For Luther the proper use of the law is "to make guilty those who are smug and at peace, so that they may see that they are in danger of sin, wrath, and death, so that they may be terrified and despairing, blanching, and quaking at the rustling of a leaf (Lev 26:6)."[23] The place where the law encounters the human being is in the conscience:

> For the law does nothing but accuse consciences and manifest sin, which is dead without the law. The knowledge of sin—I am not speaking about the speculative knowledge which hypocrites have, but I am speaking about the knowledge in which the wrath of God against sin is perceived and a true taste of death is sensed—this knowledge terrifies hearts, drives them to despair and kills them.[24]

The result of the encounter of conscience and law is *Angst,* what Tillich has called the moral and ethical anxiety of guilt and condemnation.[24b] For Luther the law is not something artificial, something contrived by church or state, family or peer group, in order to socialize a human being. Rather it is a reality which confronts people in their utter loneliness even after church and state, family and peer group have given him a clean bill of health. It is the devastating abyss that opens up between our actuality and our potentiality which condemns us even if others might acquit us. This was Luther's experience, and neither the good will of his father nor the approval of his superior in the monastic order, nor the respect of his peer group which elected him to high office in the monastery was able to bridge the abyss which terrified his heart.

II. CONSCIENCE AND DEATH

The horizon against which this terror is experienced is death. In a sermon on Matt 26:36-46 Luther said:

> At times sin rages and raves in the heart to such a degree that poor miserable people put themselves to death because of it, in an effort to get rid of this torture of conscience....These poor people consider death a means to free themselves from such anxiety (*Angst*).[25]

And again preaching on 1 Cor 15:56 in 1533 he said: "For it is impossible for man to endure a bad conscience when it really lays hold of him and he begins to feel God's wrath. Thus we see some people dying suddenly or committing suicide because of such terror and despair."[26]

As it is Luther's custom, he personalizes the powers which meet human beings. While we—until recently, at least—tended to depersonalize the devil, Luther personalizes not only the devil but also the law and death. They are not

---

[23]*Lectures on Galatians* (1535), LW 26:148.

[24]Ibid., 148-149.

[24b][Dr. Forell refers to Paul Tillich, *The Courage to Be* (New Haven: Yale University, 1952) 32f. Ed.]

[25]*Hauspostille* (1545), WA 52:736, line 30.

[26]*1 Corinthians 15* (1534), LW 28:208.

abstract impersonal forces but concrete, personal, even tangible enemies which meet us face to face in our life. In this approach Luther does not stand alone. His contemporary Albrecht Dürer, in his famous woodcut of the knight, death, and the devil, does the same thing. And two hundred years later Bach can sing "*Komm süsser Tod*" ["Come sweet death"], personalizing the power in a similar way.

And death meets the individual in her or his conscience. The emphasis is here quite properly on the "individual." For Luther, death accentuates the loneliness of the person confronted by the ultimate threat to personal being. In *On Temporal Authority* he wrote, "every man runs his own risk in believing as he does, and he must see to it himself that he believes rightly. As nobody else can go to heaven or hell for me, so nobody else can believe or disbelieve for me."[27] Even pastoral support and the comfort of fellow Christians is finally cut off. As he wrote in 1522: "Therefore, imagine that you are facing death or persecution. I cannot be with you then, nor you with me, but each one of us must then struggle for himself to overcome the devil and death and the world."[28]

As Luther reminded the people when he returned from the Wartburg in 1522 to restore a semblance of order in Wittenberg:

> The summons of death comes to us all and no one can die for another. Everyone must fight his own battle with death by himself, alone. We can shout into another's ears, but everyone must himself be prepared for the time of death, for I will not be with you then, nor you with me.[29]

Because I must die and must die alone, the accusing power of conscience is ultimately threatening, indeed because I must die, I fear the accusing conscience, and because I fear the accusing conscience, I want to die. Death and the wrath of God confront us together. Death is an enemy who threatens to devour us, not an objective phenomenon which can be observed and studied. It may be that also—but then it is the death of others. I meet it, Luther says, like the disciples in the storm-tossed boat.[30] Or as the lonely Peter, when, confronted by the high priest's servant, he denies Christ three times out of fear of death. But his conscience makes him aware of his hopeless situation and drives his sin into his heart. Luther observes: "If Peter was not grey and bald before, in these three days he became grey and bald."[31]

III. CONSCIENCE AND THE DEVIL

"Such an evil beast and wicked devil is conscience. For all authors, sacred and profane, have depicted this monster in horrible fashion."[32] This illustrates the close connection Luther sees between conscience and devil. In the discussion of

---

[27]LW 45:108.

[28]*Receiving Both Kinds in the Sacrament* (1522), LW 36:248.

[29]*Sermon* (1522), LW 51:70.

[30]*Fastenpostille* (1525), WA 17/2:104.

[31]*Sermons* (1528), WA 27:110, line 24.

[32]*Lectures on Genesis* (1535/45), LW 7:271.

Luther's demonology his personification of the devil is generally taken out of the context of his personification of all the powers surrounding the human being and attacking him in his conscience and driving him to despair. The devil is part of this conspiracy.

For Luther the conscience can be an instrument of the devil, the device to make his assaults, his *Anfechtungen*, real. Here law and death become allies of the devil trying to make the sinner rely on his or her own good works and accomplishments. But relying on their own righteousness human beings are lost and driven into sadness. He writes:

> Therefore we should be on our guard, lest the amazing skill and infinite wiles of Satan deceive us into mistaking the accuser and condemner for the Comforter and Savior, and thus losing the true Christ behind the mask of the false Christ, that is, of the devil, and making Him of no advantage to us.[33]

Or later, "You soon lose your red lips and red cheeks, forget to dance and leap, because the devil is a spirit of sadness (*spiritus tristitiae*)."[34] Indeed, death and devil sometimes tend to merge, and Luther can say that we must "battle with death and death's prince or chief, the devil."[35] And the devil promotes the *justitia personalis*, and then calls into question our alleged purity and holiness. Luther wrote: "That is the devil's art which he frequently tries on me. He asks me how godly or how evil are you, and uses masterfully Scripture and law in this interrogation...and he brings people to such anxiety that one wants to despair."[36]

> Therefore you must make thorough preparations not only for the time of temptation but also for the time and struggle of death. Then your conscience will be terrified by the recollection of your past sins. The devil will attack you vigorously and will try to swamp you with piles, floods, and whole oceans of sins, in order to frighten you, draw you away from Christ, and plunge you into despair.[37]

The devil uses the conscience to drive human beings into despair, thus making the guilty conscience a "fierce and savage beast."[38]

For Luther, conscience is the place where the law, death, and the devil encounter the human being and drive him into despair. The guilty conscience is one of the most terrifying human experiences. But this is not Luther's final word on conscience. As early as his Romans commentary, he could also say "He who believes in Christ is secure in his conscience and righteous and, as the Scripture says, 'bold as a lion' (Prov. 28:1)."[39] In 1513 in an exposition of Psalm 118 he wrote: "Where could there be a higher or greater joy than in a happy, secure, and fearless

---

[33]*Lectures on Galatians* (1535), LW 27:12.

[34]*20 Sermons* (1533), WA 37:185.

[35]*Psalm 118* (1530), LW 14:85.

[36]*Sermons* (1532), WA 36:20ff.

[37]*Lectures on Galatians* (1535), LW 26:35.

[38]*Lectures on Genesis* (1535-45), LW 1:287.

[39]*Lectures on Romans* (1515), LW 25:400.

conscience, a conscience that trusts in God and fears neither the world nor the devil?"[40] In a sermon preached at Leipzig in 1519 Luther had said:

> One must know how one stands with God, if the conscience is to be joyful and be able to stand. For when a person doubts this and does not steadfastly believe that he has a gracious God, then he actually does not have a gracious God. As he believes so he has. Therefore no one can know that he is in grace and that God is gracious toward him except through faith. If he believes it, he is saved; if he does not believe it, he is damned. For this confidence (*zuvorsicht*) and good conscience is the real, basically good faith, which the grace of God works in us.[41]

The secret for Luther is to look to Christ and not to Moses, the gospel not the law. In a sermon of 1532 he said:

> Christ offers us such freedom that we must simply tolerate no master over our conscience but insist on our baptism and as people called to Christ and made righteous and holy through him say, "This is my right, my treasure, my work and my defense against all sin and unrighteousness (which the law can produce and lay upon me)"....Thus a person can defend himself against the suggestions and assaults of the devil, whether these concern present or former sins. The point is to keep Moses and Christ, works and faith, external life and conscience apart. When the law would get to me and terrify my heart it is time to give the dear law a vacation, and if it does not want a vacation confidently drive it away and say, "I shall gladly do and demand good works in due season wherever I can when I am among people. But here in my conscience I want to know nothing of such matters. Leave me here untroubled and tell me nothing of it. Here I listen neither to Moses nor the Pharisees. Here baptism and Christ must rule alone and be everything."[42]

The traditional teaching concerning conscience which Luther had inherited had insisted that conscience is always subject to law. Law binds conscience; also conscience is not an originally religious experience, rather it is the experience of oneself.[43] Luther claimed that the conscience is only secure if it is free from the law and totally subject to Christ, and that only an encounter with Christ can free our conscience from its fatal involvement with law, death, and devil. As long as we operate with an independent conscience it will only produce anxiety and despair. Paul Tillich in his description of the various anxieties which human beings experience—fate and death, guilt and condemnation, emptiness and meaningless—seems very close to Luther's description of the effect of conscience on humanity.[44]

Indeed, conscience produces *Angst*. But *Angst* does not provide a sound basis for responsible Christian ethics. Luther is aware of this and suggests ways in which human beings might find guidance for the individual and social ethical decisions that they must make. He says: "When I am among people I shall gladly do and demand good works" (see note 42). Here the law in its political use is an important

---

[40]*LW* 14:100-101.
[41]*LW* 51:59.
[42]*WA* 36:279.
[43]Cf. Hirsch, *Lutherstudien*, 107.
[44]Tillich, *The Courage to Be*, 32 ff.

positive instrument. And this law is essentially the law of love. For Luther, faith is active in love, and love is active in justice. The structures which must be developed and cultivated for this are the varieties of human vocations which enable all human beings to be at least moderately useful to each other, in spite of selfishness and sin. And ultimately it is human reason, much maligned by Luther, which, while impotent and even dangerous when attempting to attain God, serves human beings well in their necessary and inescapable attempts to construct a humane society. Indeed, as he wrote in his Galatians commentary of 1535:

> "Our *politeuma* is in heaven," not in a local sense, but to the extent that a Christian believes, to that extent he is in heaven; and to the extent that he does his duty in faith, to that extent he is doing it in heaven....Therefore the spiritual and heavenly blessings must be distinguished from the earthly blessings, which is to have a good government (*politiam*) and household (*oeconomiam*), to have children, peace, wealth, food and other physical advantages. But the heavenly blessing is to be set free from the law, sin, and death; to be justified and made alive; to have a gracious God; to have a confident heart, *a joyful conscience* (*conscientiam hilarem*) [italics mine], and spiritual comfort; to have knowledge of Christ, the gift of prophecy, and the revelation of the Scriptures; to have the gifts of the Holy Spirit; to rejoice in God, etc.—these are the heavenly blessings of the church of Christ.[45]

A joyful conscience is a gift, not an achievement. It belongs with freedom from the law, sin, and death. A wonderful, unpredictable, and undeserved gift, it cannot be used as the basis of ethics. And Luther refused to do so. He built his ethics on law interpreted by love, as illustrated in his explanation to the Ten Commandments in the *Small Catechism*, and on justice and equity as administered by human beings serving in the structures which God has allowed people to develop for their protection and peace. It is not because conscience is necessarily a reliable guide to the moral life that we must respect every person's conscience, but because it is an essential aspect of humanity. We are not saved by obeying the dictates of our conscience, but we must obey them nevertheless. In obeying them we might eventually learn that we are saved by grace through faith—in spite of our conscience.

[45]*LW* 26:439-440.

Word & World
Supplement Series 2
1994

Luther's Conception of "Natural Orders"

THERE IS HARDLY A SUBJECT IN THE FIELD OF THEOLOGY WHICH LIES CLOSER TO THE center of all important contemporary theological discussion than a study dealing with the "natural orders." Some of the most heated theological arguments revolved around this problem. Those who inquire into this problem immediately finds themselves face to face with the famous "Troeltsch-Holl" discussion in regard to the importance of the natural law for Luther. They find themselves confronted with the "Barth-Brunner" discussion concerning nature and grace. And what is more important, they find themselves at the edge of the abyss which separates Roman Catholic theology from the theology of the evangelical reformers. And here we can also find the dividing line between all forms of modernistic protestantism and the reformation's faith in the absolute revelation in Christ Jesus.

THE PROBLEM

It can therefore be said that the main problems of modern theological thinking are involved in a study of Luther's conception of the "natural orders." But the question becomes even more acute in view of the numerous recent attacks upon Luther. These attacks are generally leveled against Luther's concept of "secular authority." Here his doctrine of the natural orders plays an important part. And it is here that Luther is most misunderstood and misrepresented. This fact has been demonstrated by some recent comments by British and American theologians. It causes little surprise when the somewhat senile Dean Inge puts Luther in the same

---

This essay first appeared in Lutheran Church Quarterly 18 (1945) 160-177. *Here Dr. Forell shows how Luther understood the "natural orders" of creation as the spheres in which the Christian, guided by law and reason, lives out her or his vocation in the world.*

class with Machiavelli and Hobbes.[1] But if even Reinhold Niebuhr[2] follows the general pattern, and mentions Luther in the same breath with the notorious English totalitarian, it is a sign of the great success of the anti-Luther propaganda.[3]

And the situation becomes almost pathetic when we realize that Luther, when writing of these problems, was not at all aware of their importance for the future of evangelical Christianity. When Luther dealt with the problem of "natural law" and the "natural orders" he did not feel that he was dealing with anything close to the nerve-center and very life of the church of Christ. He considered these problems quite removed from the main articles of the Christian faith, removed from the articles upon which the church stands or falls.

But if that is the case, how did it happen that this question of Luther's conception of the "natural orders" became of such vital importance for the church? When did theologians begin to discuss the issues involved?

A short historical review may help us to answer this question. In 1901 Eugene Ehrhardt published a small booklet, *La notion du droit naturel chez Luther* ["The Understanding of Natural Law in Luther"]. Here he tried to demonstrate that, according to Luther, natural law was the source of all positive law and of all human morality. He further claimed that for Luther the gospel and the kingdom of Christ are entirely spiritual conceptions and have no fundamental importance for the situation in the world. Ehrhardt differentiated between a "general revelation" which gives humankind the natural law and its orders, and a "special revelation" which has no importance whatsoever for the actual social orders.[4]

Ehrhardt's interpretation of Luther's conception of the natural law and the natural orders was later taken up by Ernst Troeltsch. In his monumental work dealing with the social teachings of the Christian churches, Troeltsch tried to explain all social teachings of Luther and Lutheranism on the basis of Luther's concept of the natural law. Troeltsch speaks of Luther's "double morality," claims that Luther went so far as to glorify power for power's sake, and asserts that, in glorifying power, Luther made no allowance for any change in the structure of society as it existed in the sixteenth century.[5]

This dualistic conception of ethics, as claimed for Luther by Troeltsch, has been sharply criticized by Karl Holl. Holl insisted against Troeltsch that natural

---

[1]W. R. Inge, in *The Churchman* (October 15, 1941): "This is very much like the notorious doctrine of Machiavelli, and (an Englishman may add) of Hobbes....There is very little to be said for this coarse and foul-mouthed leader of a revolution. It is a real misfortune for humanity that he appeared just at the crisis in the Christian world."

[2][Niebuhr was Dr. Forell's doctoral advisor. Ed.]

[3]Reinhold Niebuhr, *The Children of Light and the Children of Darkness* (New York: Scribner, 1944) 28f: "Human intelligence is never as pure an instrument of the universal perspective as the liberal democratic theory assumes, though neither is it as purely the instrument of the ego, as is assumed by the anti-democratic theory, derived from the pessimism of such men as Thomas Hobbes and Martin Luther." Cf. Lewis Mumford, *The Condition of Man* (New York: Harcourt, Brace, 1944) 184ff.

[4]Cf. Franz Lau, *"Äusserliche Ordnung" und "weltlich Ding" in Luthers Theologie* (Göttingen: Vandenhoeck & Ruprecht, 1933) 33f.

[5]Ernst Troeltsch, *The Social Teachings of the Christian Churches*, 2 vols. (New York: Macmillan, 1931) 2:508, 529, 509.

law or natural orders are of no importance whatsoever, as far as Luther's ethics are concerned. All Christian ethics and all "ranks" or "offices" are derived not from some "natural law" but directly from the Christian law of love.[6]

Since the appearance of Holl's investigations, the problem has been to moderate and correct Holl's criticism of Troeltsch. This problem has been attacked in various ways. Some scholars have attempted to understand Luther's conception of the "natural law" and the "natural orders" from his principle of the "two realms" and the separation of the spiritual realm from the secular realm.[7] Others again have tried to solve the problem from Luther's medieval conception of the *Corpus Christianum*.[8] They have insisted that Luther did not speak of two completely independent realms, but actually knew only one, namely the Christian commonwealth; only within this commonwealth could there be a problem in regard to the relation of the spiritual power to the secular power.[9]

Recently Franz Lau has tried to develop Luther's conception of the natural orders. He begins by investigating Luther's "wrestling with the theology of the natural orders." He bases his interpretation upon Luther's conception of the "divine ordination" of the natural orders. And he insists that to a certain extent, and to all practical purposes, rationality is the criterion of the natural orders for Luther.[10] In this country J. T. McNeill analyzed Luther's concept of the natural law and the literature on the subject in a recent article in *Church History*.[11]

But none of these discussions of the problem of natural law and the natural orders and their importance for a theological system has evoked so much attention as the famous discussion between Brunner and Barth. Here the same issue was involved. Barth accused Brunner of an unevangelical emphasis upon the natural orders and Brunner accused Barth of departure from the theological conceptions of Luther and Calvin. Brunner claimed that Barth failed to appreciate the importance of a "natural theology," in the sense of the reformers, for the life of the church.[12]

But this heated discussion between Barth and Brunner is not the only modern theological discussion arising from the problem of the natural orders. The entire theological school which attempted to find theological foundations for a national

---

[6]Karl Holl, *Gesammelte Aufsätze zur Kirchengeschichte*, vol. I, *Luther* (Tübingen: Mohr, 1923) 224, 243, 250.

[7]Hermann Jordan, *Luthers Staatauffassung* (Munich: Müller & Fröhlich, 1917) 11: "The basis for the position from which Luther slowly learned to view the state is the knowledge of the separation of the spiritual and the secular spheres. This separation became constantly clearer to him."

[8]Rudolph Sohm, *Kirchenrecht*, 2 vols. (Leipzig: Duncker & Humbolt, 1892-1923). Karl Rieker, *Die rechtliche Stellung der evangelishchen Kirche Deutschlands* (Leipzig: Hirschfeld, 1893).

[9]Rieker, *Die rechtliche Stellung*, 53: "The Reformers are not concerned with the relation of two social bodies to each other. They only know one such body and that is 'Christendom,' the Christian community of the Holy Roman Empire of the German Nation. This is divided into territories and domains. Within this social body, i.e., within its individual parts, the Reformers are concerned with the relationship of the two 'regiments' or 'powers' with each other."

[10]Lau, *Äusserliche Ordnung*, 10-17.

[11]John T. McNeill, "Natural Law in the Thought of Luther," *Church History* 10/3 (1941) 211-227.

[12]Emil Brunner, *Natur und Gnade, zum Gespräch mit Karl Barth* (Tübingen: Mohr, 1935); Karl Barth, *Nein, Antwort an Emil Brunner* (Munich: Kaiser, 1934).

socialist interpretation of the gospel leaned heavily upon Luther's teachings about the natural orders and natural law. Not only E. Hirsch and F. Gogarten, but also the national socialist legal philosophers, tried to justify their law, as conditioned by "blood" and "race," on the basis of a natural law.[13] And especially those popular Nazi-religionists who tried to reduce the gospel of Christ to some general pagan morality have frequently appealed to Luther.[14]

However, the most important issue involved in the discussion of Luther's conception of the natural orders and of natural law is where our problem throws light upon the gulf which separates Roman Catholicism and evangelical Christianity. A certain evaluation of Luther's conception of the natural orders will lead to the conclusion that this gulf is not nearly so wide as has been claimed, and that it has actually been bridged. It was one of the claims of Karl Barth that Brunner, in his evaluation of the natural orders, betrayed the evangelical position and played into the hands of Roman Catholic theology. Barth insisted that this "appreciation" of natural theology and of the *analogia entis* played into the hands of Roman Catholic theologians like Przywara and could eventually lead to an outright betrayal of the message of the reformation.[15] Against this position of Karl Barth, Brunner insisted that there is an essential difference between his conception of natural theology and the official teachings of the Roman Catholic Church.

However, a recent book by a Roman Catholic theologian,[16] dealing with the question of natural law in Luther's theology, demonstrates that Barth's fears were not completely unfounded. This book, which appeared with the "imprimatur" of the bishop of Rothenburg, has as its stated aim to help to find a common ground upon which Roman Catholics and evangelical Christians alike can justify their agreement with the Nazi state. It throws some light on our problem, for this common ground is, according to a competent Roman Catholic theologian, exactly Luther's teaching concerning the natural law.

Troeltsch versus Holl, Barth versus Brunner, Nazis versus Christians, Roman Catholics versus evangelical Christians—the confusion is appalling. Before we enter upon an investigation of the subject itself, however, we realize its extraordi-

---

[13]Helmut Nicolai, *Die Rassengesetzliche Rechtslehre* (Munich: F. Eher, 1934); cf. Franz-Xaver Arnold, *Zur Frage des Naturrechts bei Martin Luther* (Munich: M. Hueber, 1937) 3; Ulrich Scheuner, *Gesetz und Einzelordnung.*

[14]Wehrkreispfarrer Mueller, *Neue Kirche im neuen Staat* (June 1933) 74: "God does not ask more than that we should admit our faults and the next time attempt to do better. On the day of judgment God will ask every individual if he has tried to be a decent fellow." Cf. E. Wolf, *Martin Luther* (Munich: Kaiser, 1934) 27, and H. W. Beyer, "Luthers Wort in unserer Zeit," *Luther* 15/3 (1933) 68.

[15]Barth, *Nein*, 32: "The place where I am writing these lines is very suited to stimulate the imagination in regard to the perspectives that would open up if Brunner were right. I am sitting before an open window on the Monte Pinci in Rome. Over there I see, unmistakably, St. Peter's. Shouldn't I ask tomorrow (still taking for granted that Brunner's doctrine is right) for an interview with the *Analogia Entis* itself, or at least with one of the scholars over there? Shouldn't I tell him that a deplorable misunderstanding of one of the cardinal points has complicated the relationship between Roman Catholic and evangelical theology? Shouldn't I tell him that the time has come to remove this misunderstanding?"

[16]F.-X. Arnold, *Zur Frage des Naturrechts.*

nary complexity, its many serious pitfalls, and its tragic importance for the theology of the church of the reformation.

LUTHER AND THE POSSIBILITY OF A GENERAL KNOWLEDGE OF GOD

According to Luther there cannot be any doubt that human beings are by nature religious. Luther is willing to say that it is natural that we should call upon God. For him this fact is proven by the pagans. There has never been any pagan who did not pray to idols. However, in their idol-worship they missed the true God. But, according to Luther, the Jews were also given to idolatry. The only difference was that the Jews had the Mosaic law while the pagans had merely the law which was written in their hearts. But essentially there was no difference. Jews and gentiles are by nature religious. Even moral behavior is a part of this natural religion. Luther said: "It is natural to honor God, not to steal, not to commit adultery, not to bear false witness, not to kill."[17]

For Luther it is even a part of natural and reasonable religion that there should be one divine being, that this being is eternal and has numerous other divine attributes. Luther considers monotheism a reasonable, logical conclusion of natural religion. Nor does he hesitate to quote the "pagan" Aristotle in order to show that anybody can know about the existence of one deity.[18] The belief in the existence of a god is in all human hearts and cannot be extinguished. Luther will grant that there have at times been people who denied the existence of a god. But, according to him, we must consider such a denial an attempt to close one's ears and eyes by force in order to avoid knowing about the existence of a god.[19]

Reason can tell us that God is, and it is almost impossible to deny the existence of a god. Natural religion is therefore not a theological abstraction, but a reality that confronts us every day. This natural religion is the very source of all religion.[20] But just for this reason natural religion is nothing else than idolatry. Even if we can derive from our reason that there is a god, even if we can find that this divine being is powerful, invisible, just, immortal, and good, what we have found is still merely an idol. As a matter of fact, this natural knowledge about the existence of a god is the basis for all idolatry. This knowledge does not bring us one step closer to the reality of God as revealed in Jesus Christ. On the contrary, it leads us into our most terrible sin, even the sin against the First Commandment. Natural religion is the necessary premise for idolatry. Luther said:

[17]*Sermons on Genesis* (1527), WA 24:920.

[18]*Sommerpostille* (1544), WA 21:510, line 30: "[Monotheism] is only a very small part of the knowledge which one ought to have of God, if one does not know any more. For even the pagans see that by means of their reason and deduce it from reasonable causes. Even the pagan Aristotle deduces it in his best book from a saying of their wisest poet Homer, and says that that would not be a good regime where there is more than one Lord, even as it is not a good home if there is more than one master or one mistress to rule and to give orders to the servants. Therefore there must be in everything only one Lord and Regent."

[19]*Jonah* (1526), LW 19:53-54.

[20]Ernst Wolf, *Martin Luther*, 9.

> [Reason] knows that there is a God, but it does not know who or which is the true God. It shares the experience of the Jews during Christ's sojourn on earth....They were aware that Christ was among them and that He was moving about among them; but they did not know which person it was....Thus reason also plays blindman's buff with God; it consistently gropes in the dark and misses the mark. It calls that God which is not God and fails to call Him God who really is God. Reason would do neither the one nor the other if it were not conscious of the existence of God or if it really knew who and what God is. Therefore it rushes in clumsily and assigns the name God and ascribes divine honor to its own idea of God. Thus reason never finds the true God, but it finds the devil or its own concept of God, ruled by the devil.[21]

In other words, natural religion is having a god, but this god can never be anything else than an idol for it is always the creature of our own human wishes and desires. Luther said: "This man has a god who is called Mammon...and so he who trusts in his ability, in his wisdom, in his power, in his friends, and in his honor, he also has a god."[22]

All these idols we can know on the basis of our natural religious faculties. We can know idols through reason or through law. However, we can never know God apart from the revelation in Jesus Christ as we have it in the word. Although, according to Luther, God is everywhere, in every creature, in every stone, in fire and water, he does not want to be found anywhere apart from the word. God is everywhere, but since he does not want to be found anywhere but in the word, we cannot find him anywhere else.[23] "[God] has set down for us a definite way to show us how and where to find him, namely the Word."[24] "It is one thing if God is present, and another if he is present for you. He is there for you when he adds his Word and binds himself, saying, 'Here you are to find me.'"[25]

According to Luther this word of God judges all religion, and from this word of God all human knowledge about a divine being actually becomes utter ignorance. Therefore Luther could say:

> This [trust in works] is the height of wisdom, righteousness, and religion about which reason is able to judge; it is common to all the heathen, the papists, the Jews, the Mohammedans, and the sectarians. They cannot rise higher than that Pharisee in Luke (18:11-12). They do not know the righteousness of faith or Christian righteousness....Therefore there is no difference at all between a papist, a Jew, a Turk, or a sectarian. Their persons, locations, rituals, religions, works, and forms of worship are, of course, diverse; but they all have the same reason, the same heart, the same opinion and idea. The Turk thinks the very same as the Carthusian, namely, "If I do this or that, I have a God who is favorably disposed toward me; if I do not, I have a God who is wrathful. There is no middle ground between human working and the knowledge of Christ; if this knowledge is obscured, it does not matter whether you become a monk or a heathen afterwards.[26]

[21]*Jonah* (1526), *LW* 19:54-55.

[22]Cf. E. Wolf, *Martin Luther*, 11.

[23]*The Sacrament of the Body and Blood of Christ* (1526), *LW* 36:342.

[24]Ibid.

[25]*That These Words of Christ, "This is My Body," Still Stand Firm Against the Fanatics* (1527), *LW* 37:68.

[26]*Lectures on Galatians* (1535), *LW* 26:396.

"It does not matter," that is Luther's last word about the results of all natural theology. One can have some sense of the divine by means of reason, but in the light of the word of God, the revelation in Christ, this sense becomes utter nonsense. It is doubtless true that Luther believed that reason can give us a general knowledge of a divine being. But the reason which supplies us with our knowledge is, according to Luther, "by nature an evil whore."[27] Therefore reason's religion and piety are in reality utter blasphemy.[28]

We shall have to keep this in mind as we enter upon the investigation of the natural and divine aspects of the orders of nature. Any doctrine of the orders of nature is an integral part of a natural knowledge of God. If Luther is so very skeptical toward all theological results of reason, why and how does he use the conception of natural orders? What are their norms, and what do they explain ?

THE DIVINE CHARACTER OF THE "NATURAL ORDERS," ACCORDING TO LUTHER

According to Luther, one is always a member of two realms simultaneously. Everyone is a member of a secular realm and of a spiritual realm. It is important to realize the difference between these two realms and to keep them separate. Luther claimed that Jesus (Matt 22:21) had emphasized the separation of the two realms when he said: "Render therefore unto Caesar the things which are Caesar's; and unto God the things that are God's." Luther himself pointed frequently to the difference between the two and reiterated the need for a clear separation.[29] But although the spiritual realm is separated from the secular realm, ultimately they are both God's realms.

Luther considered it one of his important contributions to the ideology of his time that he had separated the two realms of existence, and yet had emphasized the divine origin of both.[30] In his explanation of Psalm 82 he wrote that "the secular rulers were completely subject to these clerical giants and tyrants....It was not understood or taught what temporal authority was, or how great was the distinction between it and spiritual government." And he continued: "Now, however, the Gospel has come to light. It makes a plain distinction between the temporal and the spiritual estate and teaches, besides, that the temporal estate is an ordinance of God which everyone ought to obey and honor."[31]

Although Luther had separated "temporal" and "spiritual" authorities, he claimed divine institution for the secular realm. This secular realm is subdivided into a multitude of "offices," "vocations," and "ranks." The three main groups of

---

[27]*The Last Sermon in Wittenberg* (1546), LW 51:375-376: "Therefore, just as the Jews set up all over the land their own self-chosen shrines, as if Jerusalem were too narrow, so we also have done. As a young man must resist lust and an old man avarice, so reason is by nature a harmful whore."

[28]*I Peter* (c. 1522), LW 30:36f: "The pagans have committed a far greater sin by their worship of the Sun and the Moon (which they considered the true worship of God) than by any of their other sins. Human piety is therefore pure blasphemy and the greatest sin that man commits."

[29]*An Open Letter on the Harsh Book against the Peasants* (1525), LW 46:70.

[30]*Whether Soldiers, Too, Can Be Saved* (1526), LW 46:95

[31]*Psalm 82* (1530), LW 13:42.

orders within the secular realm are the family or society (family is used in a wider sense than at the present time), the government, and the church. These orders are divinely instituted. "All ranks and professions of society are instituted by God to serve him."[32] Luther insisted upon the divine institution of marriage against the "popish heresy" of celibacy.[33] And his repeated and vehement insistence upon the divine character of the order of government is generally known.[34]

But for Luther the divine character of the natural orders was proven further by the constant attack of Satan against these orders. Not only that Satan attacks God in the spiritual realm, but Satan is constantly trying to destroy the divine order in the natural realm. For Luther it seemed obvious that the attack of the Roman Church against matrimony and the accompanying false emphasis upon celibacy were in reality attacks of the devil against the divinely ordained natural orders. Concerning the enemies of matrimony Luther said: "Those blind fools consider the institution of marriage as some superfluous human affair. They think one can get along without marriage, as one can get along without a second coat or an overcoat." Such an attitude is blasphemous, for natural orders are divine orders.

It is from this point of view that one must understand Luther's position in regard to obedience to the natural orders. Such obedience is not merely obedience to other human beings, but ultimately obedience to God. It is God who orders us, "through [our] master or parents."[35] And it is God's general procedure, in the secular realm, to rule "not indeed from heaven through angels, but through the constituted authority."[36]

Luther could go as far as to say that by means of these "orders," God operates through us so that our words become his word and our actions become his action.[37]

But in order to fully understand this divine aspect of the natural orders, we must see it in the light of Luther's general conceptions of the immanence of God.

---

[32]*Psalm 119* (1529), WA 31/1:22. See also, *Psalm 117*, LW 14:15: "At the same time He confirms all crafts, classes, and trades existing under such secular governments, regardless of name, insofar as they are honest and praiseworthy according to their own law. They may be citizens, farmers, shoemakers, tailors, clerks, knights, masters, servants, etc.; for without such, as Ecclesiasticus says, no city or country could exist (38:36). One must recognize that in themselves such occupations are not contrary to God, one should not turn up one's nose at them and creep away into a monastery or set up some other sect. Yes, these are all estates established by God to serve Him according to the words of Gen. 3:19: 'In the sweat of your face you shall eat bread.' This is the way He intended it to be."

[33]*Genesis 15-20* (c. 1538), LW 3:97: "The Holy Spirit forestalls the heresy of the papists concerning celibacy, inasmuch as He points out that Adam was joined in marriage with Eve by God's ordinance."

[34]*Deudsch Katechismus* (1529), WA 30/1:192: "Since authority does not grow out of the human will or plan, but is instituted and preserved by God himself (and if he did not preserve it, it would fall even if all the world tried to preserve it), therefore it is rightly called a 'divine thing,' a 'divine order,' and such persons are rightly called 'divine,' or 'gods,' especially if to the institution is added the divine word and commandment."

[35]*Genesis 21-25* (1540), LW 4:285.

[36]*Genesis 15-20* (1538), LW 3:322.

[37]Ibid., 272: "This, then, is the great glory with which the Divine Majesty honors us: It works through us in such a manner that It says that our words are Its words and that our actions are Its actions, so that one can truthfully say that the mouth of a godly teacher is God's mouth and that the hand which you extend to alleviate the want of a brother is God's hand."

The God who is present in stone and fire is also present in the orders of nature. But as little as we can find God revealed in any stone or in any fire, just as little can we find him revealed in the natural orders. "It is one thing if God is present, and another if he is present for you."[38] We must keep this word of Luther in mind when we consider the divine character of the natural orders. The natural orders, apart from the word of God, are meaningless; it is only through the word that they become divine orders for us. Luther knows nothing of any immediate, natural laws which can guide us in our conduct. He knows nothing of "natural orders" which are the voice of the "blood" or the "race" and speak to us with some magic immediacy. The natural orders are not simply nature. They are nature under the divine command. It is an utter distortion of Luther's thought if one says that nature reveals God's command. The obedience of children to their parents, of citizens to their magistrates, of pupils to their teachers, and of Christians to their pastors is not immediately meaningful or valuable. It receives its meaning from the word of God. "Apart from this Word all life is condemned."[39] Only through the word is the divine character of the natural order revealed.

The Natural and Reasonable Character of the Natural Orders According to Luther

Because of his belief in the immanence of God, Luther had spoken of the divine character of the natural orders.

Because of his belief in the separation of the spiritual and secular realms, Luther spoke also of the natural and reasonable character of the natural orders. Luther said in regard to the "ranks" of society that they were called "human orders, because they rule without the word of God, but not without God's providence."[40]

But now the question arises, what is for Luther the immediate source and norm of these natural orders? In spite of Holl's vehement denial[41] it seems established by all the evidence that Luther considered natural and positive law the norms for the natural orders. According to Luther, natural law is the basis for all positive law. And he believed that there were some general laws which were accepted almost universally. He said: "There are some common laws that are

---

[38]*That These Words, "This is my Body," Still Stand Firm Against the Fanatics* (1527), LW 37:68.

[39]*Genesis 26-30,* LW 5:71: "Consequently, I give this warning diligently and frequently—and it must always be impressed—lest we be carried away by our own opinions or thoughts, however godly, angelic, an heavenly they may be. Thus Paul also warns in Col. 2:18: "Let no one disqualify you, insisting on self-abasement and worship of angels, taking his stand on visions." For they are without the Word. For God speaks with us and deals with us through the ministers of the Word, through parents, and through the government, in order that we may not be carried about with any wind of doctrine (Eph. 4:14). Children should listen to their parents, citizens to the government, a Christian to the pastor and the ministers of the Word, a pupil to his teacher. Apart from this Word all life is condemned, and all sects are lost. But if the Word is there, then I have sure comfort, whether I am a father or a mother or a child. Then I hear the Word, and I know what I should believe and what I should do; for God speaks with me, too, in the very station of life in which I live."

[40]*On the Papacy in Rome* (1520), LW 39:97.

[41]K. Holl, *Gesammelte Aufsätze,* 243ff.

accepted everywhere, e. g., to honor parents, not to commit murder, not to commit adultery, to serve God, etc." However, the ceremonial law of Moses was considered by Luther the "*Sachsenspiegel*" [early thirteenth-century German lawbook] of the Jews, and he claimed that it does not concern the gentiles, "just as the *Sachsenspiegel* is not observed by France, though the natural law there is in agreement with it."[42]

Luther refused to define this "natural law." But it was for him not a codex of laws that can be placed beside the existing positive law. On the contrary, it is the source of all positive law.[43] Positive law always "pertained to a definite people, definite persons, a definited place, and to a definite time."[44] In this sense Luther considered the ceremonial law of the Old Testament the "positive law" of the Jews. As such it was of value at a certain time and in certain places. However, the time of its validity passed.[45] In contrast to the Mosaic ceremonial law, the Decalogue is, according to Luther, a very good representation of the kernel of the general natural law that underlies all positive law, and as such it is of unlimited validity. Luther said about this decalogue that "the natural laws were never so orderly and well written as by Moses."[46]

Now this natural law, as found in the Ten Commandments, is the basis of all ranks and orders in society. It is the norm for all life within the orders of nature. And this natural law has always to be considered as a corrective to the positive law. Luther was full of skepticism in regard to written laws and lawyers. He felt that written laws must always be moderated and redefined on the basis of the unwritten natural law. Moreover, Luther thought that justice would be served far better if good judges would rule without being "chained" by the regulations of the written law. But Luther realized also that such good judges who could judge justly without the written law are "pretty rare birds."[47] Therefore he considered the written law indispensable for general use. However, it had to be constantly corrected.

But if one norm of all natural orders is natural law, the other norm is, according to Luther, reason. It may sound peculiar to hear Luther advocate the use of reason as the criterion for the natural orders in view of all his criticism of the reliability of human reason. But one must always keep in mind that Luther's criticism of reason is directed at the reason that considers itself a substitute for

[42]*Against the Heavenly Prophets* (1525), LW 40:98.

[43]*Genesis 21-25* (1540), LW 4:219: "For elsewhere, of course, there is no lack of the authority of laws, not only of those that are divine but also of those that are drawn by sound inference from the fountainhead of natural right, as laws and civil rights are. On our side are the examples of Scripture, the written laws and the rights."

[44]*Genesis 26-30*, LW 5:20.

[45]*On Marriage Matters* (1530), LW 46:291: "This is why Moses' law cannot be valid simply and completely in all respects with us. We have to take into consideration the character and ways of our land when we want to make or apply laws and rules, because our rules and laws are based on the character of our land and its ways and not on those of the land of Moses, just as Moses' laws are based on the ways and character of his people and not those of ours."

[46]*Against the Heavenly Prophets* (1525), LW 40:98.

[47]*A Sermon on Keeping Children in School* (1530), LW 46:239.

revelation. In all questions of the everyday life, Luther advocates the use of reason for the achievement of reasonable results. Luther said: "Judges and overlords must be *intelligent* and pious and measure justice according to *reason* and interpret the law accordingly."[48] Here his attitude is similar to his position in respect to the free will of humankind. In the same sense in which Luther denied a theological and granted a psychological free will, he denied the theological validity of reason (versus revelation) and granted its psychological and practical validity. According to Luther, the natural orders are reasonable orders and have to be interpreted by reason. As a matter of fact, politics and economics are the fields where it is not only proper but imperative to use reason.[49] Luther said quite plainly that in secular matters it is always advisable to follow the judgement of reason.

But now, if it is reason which is normative for the natural orders, it cannot be said that these natural orders are immutable. It has been claimed that Luther insisted upon the general and eternal validity of the social system of his time.[50] However, if Luther admitted the normative character of reason, he had to make allowances for changes of the established orders from this principle. And Luther did make provisions for such changes. It is Franz Lau's great contribution to have called attention to Luther's provisions for the change of an existing situation.[51]

Luther was not a great friend of change. He felt, from his eschatological outlook (which has been almost completely overlooked by all investigations), that there was not much chance for a change for the better. He said: "Because there is no hope of getting another government in the Roman Empire, as Daniel also indicates (Dan. 2:40), it is not advisable to change it. Rather, let him who is able darn and patch it up as long as we live."[52]

But this practical conservatism, which had its source in Luther's almost apocalyptic eschatological expectations, does not imply a principle of static acceptance of all existing orders. This principle has been claimed for Luther.[53] But it contradicts the very basic attitude of Luther in regard to the reformation of the church. His entire appeal to the Christian nobility is such an appeal for change. Of course it is change in the realm of the church, but change nevertheless.[54]

---

[48]WA 19:637; cf., *Temporal Authority*, LW 45:119: "Therefore, a prince must have the law as firmly in hand as the sword, and determine in his own mind when and where the law is to be applied strictly or with moderation, so that law may prevail at all times and in all cases, and reason may be the highest law and the master of all administration of law."

[49]*Genesis 15-20* (1538), LW 3:322: "Moreover, in harmony with the testimony of Scripture, we praise civil works; for God wanted us to bear the common hardships and misfortunes of human nature, and He tells us not to despair in them but to be confident that He will be with us. Indeed, He has provided us with natural reason, by means of which we are to exercise control over those civil works, lest we tempt God, who makes the earth subject to us."

[50]Boehmer, Troeltsch, Wunsch, and Gogarten, according to Lau, *Äusserliche Ordnung*, 53.

[51]Ibid., 50ff.

[52]*Psalm 101*, LW 13:217.

[53]Georg Wünsch, *Der Zusammenbruch des Luthertums als Sozialgestaltung* (Tübingen: Mohr, 1921).

[54]*Address to the Christian Nobility*, LW 44:183: "Did not God set aside his own law, which he had given from heaven, when it was perverted and abused? And does he not daily overturn what he has set up and destroy what he has made because of the same perversion and abuse?"

Luther believed that history is made and changed by great individuals and heroes.[55] Luther mentions people like Alexander, Scipio, and Augustus as such heroes of history. These heroes of history, who bring about the changes in history, are the revolutionary antithesis to Luther's basically conservative political thesis. According to Luther, these people act under the influence of an "heroic inspiration" and therefore are placed outside the generally valid moral standards. But their moral standards are not examples for imitation.[56] Yet, even if their standards are different, they are not outside the realm of ethics. They are still subject to the natural orders, in this case the "orders of exception." Luther provided for the reality of change in the social order by these "orders of exception," which pertain to the hero only, but which nevertheless are orders.[57]

In conclusion it can be said that Luther's natural orders were for all practical purposes based on natural law and reason. On the basis of these two norms they were constantly redefined. Changes in these orders were possible, but only through the medium of the hero. The natural orders are "natural" and "reasonable," and they are important as far as they go. Luther used his conception of the natural orders to describe an existing situation. They explained the world and the forces that preserve it in a semblance of order. They do not reveal God, they are not even a part of theology, and they do not tell us ultimately what is right and wrong in the sight of God. Of course, God is in the natural orders by virtue of the divine ubiquity. But in this sense even the devil is a servant of God, and nothing that is, is outside the realm of God's power. But the fact that there are general, reasonable, and provable laws, which are accepted by almost all people, does not in an way constitute an ability of humankind to know God. The fact of the natural orders does not constitute a point of contact for revelation.

SIN AND THE NATURAL ORDERS

In order to understand Luther's skepticism in regard to the natural orders, they have to be examined in their relation to sin. According to Luther, the norms of the natural orders, as well as the orders themselves, are affected by sin. Luther was

---

[55]Lau, *Äusserliche Ordnung*, 52.

[56]*Genesis 26-30* (1535-45), LW 5:326: "If you want to be like Joshua and Samson, see to it that all the circumstances impel you to change the civil administration and slay the magistrate, just as those heroes were moved by a special call. Otherwise the example has no validity. For you have more and greater examples which testify that one should not slay a magistrate, should not change the civil administration....

Accordingly, this is handed down not as an example but in order that we may abstain from the example and from imitating it. We should admire but not imitate it. For there are some things which we should imitate and some things which we should admire. Hope, believe, pray, just as Leah did. But you should not marry four wives, as Jacob did. For this pertains only to Jacob and to those whom God wanted to be exempted from the rule."

[57]Ibid., 312: "It is necessary for him to be so heroic in order that he may not break the customs. Indeed, he should rather preserve, defend, and guide them. Even though he himself for his own person has been excepted in a special manner, yet he must descend to the first declension and the rule....Thus although heroic men break the laws, they do not tear states apart."

aware of the fact that all "offices" and positions of power are misused.[58] And yet he wanted people to stay in their "offices," to do their duty as parents, rulers, soldiers, or whatever their "rank" may be. A Christian is always a member of the natural orders, and these orders cannot be anything but sinful orders. Luther said: "Contrary to God's command, [the world] misuses every secular ordinance and law."[59] And in writing of the princes in this world he said: "There are very few princes who are not regarded as fools or scoundrels; that is because they show themselves to be so."[60] "There is no kingdom in which conditions are so good that there is no tyranny at all."[61] Luther went so far as to say:

> Therefore it is no wonder that worldly kings, princes, and lords are enemies of God and persecute His Word. This is the natural thing for them; they are born that way. It is a natural and innate characteristic of reason that it has neither grace nor intelligence to think or to act otherwise. Therefore Psalm 2 paints that kind of color on their helmets and shields, calling them adversaries of God and of His Christ.[62]

These few passages from Luther's writings point out clearly how thoroughly he thought the natural orders are infected by sin. The main reason for this situation is that they are administered by sinful human beings. And as long as the world stands, this fact will have to be kept in mind.

But besides the fact that the natural orders are poorly administered by sinful humans, they also lend themselves to idolatry. These orders give people the opportunity to express their pride, vanity, and presumption. Those who administer the natural orders forget too easily the source of all their power, and they claim to be gods themselves.[63] Luther emphasized again and again that it is idolatry to put one's trust in princes and authorities.[64] Only in humility can a person administer the "orders," but since pride invariably creeps in, all orders become idols.

There is still another way in which sin is involved in the question of the natural orders. They are orders by reason of sin. There is not one of the natural orders that has not its meaning in its relation to sin. For Luther the authority of the princes was justified just by reason of human sin. Parallel to Romans 13, Luther defined the task of the government as punishment of evil doers.[65] If people were

---

[58]*Introduction to The Babylonian Captivity of the Church* (1520), WA 6:486: "Everybody does as he pleases, and some authorities are just as useful as if they did not exist at all."

[59]*The Sermon on the Mount* (1532), LW 21:113.

[60]*Temporal Authority* (1523), LW 45:116.

[61]*Genesis 6-14* (1535), LW 2:306. See also, ibid., 365: "'As it was in the beginning, so it is now and ever shall be, world without end.' Princes who are not satisfied with what they have endeavor to get the possessions of others if they are better."

[62]*Commentary on Psalm 101* (1534), LW 13:168.

[63]*Genesis 6-14* (1535), LW 2:119: "Even though we do not condemn civil and political activities, the human heart nevertheless taints these good works when it uses them for vainglory, gain, and oppression either against its neighbor or against God."

[64]*Sermons on Exodus* (1524-1527), WA 16:49, line 34.

[65]Introduction to *An die Herren deutschs Ordens* (1523), WA 12:229: "It is the will of God that those who do evil be punished and that those who do well be protected, so that concord might be maintained in the world....For since we do not all believe, and since the great majority consists of unbelievers, God

actually Christians the need for a government with the power of the sword would disappear.[66] And what is true about this natural order is true also of the order of marriage. For Luther marriage is, among other things, a medicine against sexual license.[67] In that sense all natural orders exist by reason of sin and, to a certain degree also, for the punishment of sin. All who are involved in the natural orders are also involved in all the difficulties, hard work, and troubles that are connected with them.[68] Even the most important and most outstanding of all natural orders imply for those who administer them a great deal of punishment and trouble.[69] The natural orders are not only administered by sinners and directed against sinners, but they are also punishment for sinners. For Luther the natural orders are most thoroughly involved in sin.

But this fact of the actual involvement of the natural orders in the reality of sin is not their only contact with sin. They are further involved in sin through their norms, namely, nature and reason. Nature is for Luther always the fallen nature. The world is always the sinful world. As such it is always against Christ, full of sin, and the enemy of God.[70] Luther said quite frankly: "The kingdom of the world remains the kingdom of Satan."[71] And again: "God has thrown us into the world, under the power of the devil."[72] Nature itself is always found as corrupt nature. Natural law is therefore always subject to the perversions of sin.

And what is true about one norm of the natural orders is not less true about the other norm. Reason like nature is always corrupt reason. And reason proves its sinful corruption not only in regard to the achievement of a knowledge of God; reason is even in its limited realm subject to sin. That means that although the natural orders are reasonable orders, reason cannot give us a knowledge of that which makes the natural orders important. Luther can say: "The heathen and other godless men do not understand this glory of marriage."[73] Human reason is not

---

has created and ordered things in such a manner that the people of the world do not devour one another; He has instituted the secular authority to carry the sword and to keep evil in check so that the people who don't want to have peace are forced to keep peace."

[66]Ibid., 330: "If we all were Christians and would follow the Gospel, the secular sword and power would not be necessary or useful. For if there were no evildoers there would be no punishment."

[67]*The Sermon on the Mount* (1532), LW 21:86: "That is why God has ordained for every person to have his own wife or husband, to control and channel his lust and his appetites. If you do not go any further than this, He approves it, He even pronounces His blessing upon it, and He is pleased with it as His ordinance and creature."

[68]*Genesis 1-5* (1536), LW 1:203: "But his position is burdened with a definite punishment, since it is the husband's duty to support his family, to rule, to direct, and to instruct; and these things cannot be done without extraordinary trouble and very great effort."

[69]Ibid., 204: "But these very important duties have their own punishment added to them, namely, that they cannot be carried on without the utmost difficulties, as is shown by examples all around us."

[70]*Temporal Authority* (1523), LW 45:112f.: "For such tyrants are acting as worldly princes are supposed to act, and worldly princes they surely are. But the world is God's enemy; hence, they too have to do what is antagonistic to God and agreeable to the world, that they may not be bereft of honor, but remain worldly princes."

[71]*Genesis 45-50* (1545), LW 8:93.

[72]*Whether Soldiers, Too, Can Be Saved* (1526), LW 46:117.

[73]*Genesis 1-5* (1536), LW 1:240.

only unable to know God, but also unable to appreciate the works of God.[74] Although Luther granted reason the power to administer and correct the natural orders, he knew that because of its connection with sin, this very action is involved in sin. It is sinful reason which is the norm for the natural orders.[75] And ultimately reason can be so distorted by sin that it destroys the orders it is supposed to correct. In this connection Luther referred to the monastic institutions of the Roman Church. Although God created marriage, and although it is a reasonable institution, "when that clever harlot, our natural reason..., takes a look at married life, she turns up her nose" and goes into the monastery.[76] Although the natural orders are subject to reason, reason proves a very unreliable criterion. Both natural law and reason are completely immersed in sin.

CONCLUSIONS

If we try to examine the results of our study of Luther's conception of the natural orders, we can easily understand the confusion caused by his teachings. Luther is truly dialectical in his utterances. What can we say in regard to the complicated discussions that have arisen in reference to Luther's doctrine of the natural orders? Who is right according to Luther—Troeltsch or Holl, Barth, or Brunner, the Roman Catholic defenders of natural law or the evangelical Christian attackers?

As far as Luther's central motive is concerned we can say: Holl is more right than Troeltsch. Even if Holl denied statements of Luther that cannot be denied, he was right in the emphasis. Luther is really not interested in natural law as such. Natural law is not basic for his ethics. Luther works with the concept of natural law but never from a theological point of view. Natural law and its natural orders are reasonable, and reason has no understanding when matters of God are concerned.[77] And all human consideration of divine affairs is error.[78] In that sense the natural orders are merely a sinful means to preserve a sinful world; they are not the norms for Christian ethics; on the contrary, they bring an element of constant tension into Christian ethics. Holl was right when he said Luther's ethics receives its impulse from the gospel.

And Barth is right against Brunner. Luther's conception of the natural orders never tries to give humankind the claim to be a worthy object of revelation. They

---

[74]Cf. Lau, *Äusserliche Ordnung*, 104.

[75]*The Sermon on the Mount* (1532), LW 21:198: "Thus this is an excellent illustration that puts us all to shame. We, who are rational people and who have the Scriptures in addition, do not have enough wisdom to imitate the birds. When we listen to the little birds singing every day, we are listening to our own embarrassment before God and the people. But after his fall from the word and the commandment of God, man became crazy and foolish; and there is no creature alive which is not wiser than he. A little finch, which can neither speak nor read, is his theologian and master in the Scriptures, even though he has the whole Bible and his reason to help him."

[76]*The Estate of Marriage* (1522), LW 45:39.

[77]*Sermons on Genesis* (1527), WA 24:18.

[78]*Die Disputation contra missam privatum* (1536), WA 39/1:138.

have nothing whatsoever to do with God's revelation in Jesus Christ.[79] Luther never said that the fact of the natural orders gives human beings in any way an ability to be reached by revelation. On the contrary, it reveals how much more perverted we are by sin than, for example, the birds.[80] According to Luther, the fact that we are human and not birds does not bring us one step closer to the revelation of God. From Luther's perspective, Barth has the right emphasis and not Brunner. As far as salvation is concerned, it is one of the most uninteresting things in the world that humans are humans and not turtles. Revelation is a miracle, not anything that can be expected on the basis of some imaginary human point of contact. At least the natural orders do not furnish such a point of contact.

And this also answers the Roman Catholic attempt to prove, on the basis of Luther's teachings concerning natural law, that he really held to the Roman teaching concerning natural law. He did not. The will of God is revealed to us in God's word; we do not even know what is right or wrong apart from this word. For Luther nothing is right except the working of Christ in us. Luther said: "They are all flesh, because they all savor of the flesh, that is, of the things that are their own, and they are devoid of the glory of God and the Spirit of God."[81] "Flesh means the entire nature of man, with reason and all his powers."[82]

Nobody described the immense gulf that separates Roman Catholicism and evangelical Christianity more clearly than did Martin Luther. He said:

> This divine power they have attributed to our own works, saying: 'If you do this or that work, you will conquer sin, death, and the wrath of God.' In this way they have made us true God by nature! Here the papists, under the Christian name, have shown themselves to be seven times greater idolaters than the Gentiles.[83]

---

[79]*John 17* (1528), *WA* 28:91: "Let him who wants to fare safely be on guard against the advice of reason and human thought in regard to this article. For it is quite impossible to comprehend even the smallest article of faith by means of human sense or reason. Therefore, no man on earth has ever been able to discover one correct thought or any sure knowledge of God; to this fact the pagans themselves bear witness. This shows that the higher human reason climbs in order to investigate and explore the being, work, will, and counsel of God, the further it goes astray and finally ends by denying God....This must happen to all who try to live without the Word and to ask the counsel of reason in regard to the articles of faith, and try to square them with this reason."

[80]*Sermon on the Mount* (1532), *LW* 21:197: "You see, He is making the birds our schoolmasters and teachers. It is a great and abiding disgrace to us that in the Gospel a helpless sparrow should become a theologian and a preacher to the wisest of men, and daily should emphasize this to our eyes and ears, as if he were saying to us: 'Look, you miserable man! You have house and home, money and property. Every year you have a field full of grain and other plants of all sorts, more than you ever need. Yet you cannot find peace, and you are always worried about starving. If you do not know that you have supplies and cannot see them before your very eyes, you cannot trust God to give you food for one day. Though we are innumerable, none of us spends his living days worrying. Still God feeds us every day.' In other words, we have as many teachers and preachers as there are little birds in the air. Their living example is an embarrassment to us. Whenever we hear a bird singing toward heaven and proclaiming God's praises and our disgrace, we should feel ashamed and not even dare to lift up our eyes. But we are as hard as stone, and we pay no attention even though we hear the great multitude preaching and singing every day."

[81]*The Bondage of the Will* (1525), *LW* 33:225.

[82]*Lectures on Galatians* (1535), *LW* 26:139.

[83]Ibid., 283.

Yes, indeed, the gulf is tremendous and it cannot be bridged by a false interpretation of Luther's teachings concerning the natural orders.

For Luther the natural orders are real, they are administered by sinful people, they exist for the sake of sinful people, and they punish sinful people. Within these orders human reason rules. But this reason is itself sinful. Christians, too, stand within this realm of the natural orders. As far as they are members of these orders, they have to obey their rules. Therefore they may be forced by the sinful situation and orders to do things that are not Christian. However, this fact does not in any way lessen the demands of Christ upon the individual Christian. These ethical demands are eternal and directed to humankind in a sinful situation. They do not, in some miraculous manner, change the sinful character of the natural orders. But the ethical norms of Christ and his word must enlighten the reason of the Christian. This believing reason then becomes a beautiful and mighty instrument and tool in the hands of God.[84] In that manner Christ transforms the natural orders through the medium of the Christian individual. The natural orders will never extricate themselves from sin; however, used by people who know what is right and wrong through the revelation of Christ, they may be used to preserve the world from chaos and self-destruction until the day of Jesus Christ.

[84]*Tabletalk,* EA 58:366.

Word & World
Supplement Series 2
1994

The Political Use of the Law

A NY DISCUSSION OF THE SUBJECT OF LUTHER AND POLITICS MUST BE GUARDED against a number of quite obvious pitfalls. First of all, it should be kept in mind that Luther was not a professional politician. When he abandoned the study of the law and entered the monastery he had given up the primary concern with politics. As far as he was concerned, the political life was the special responsibility of the lawyers. The government of the world was one of the most important responsibilities which God had entrusted to humankind, but it was not the direct responsibility of the church. In his *Sermon on Keeping Children in School* of 1530 he showed how important he considered both the political task of the lawyer and the theological task of the pastor. Excoriating the greed of his compatriots, which made them satisfied with only the rudiments of an education for their children, Luther said,

> And do not be disturbed because the run-of-the-mill miser despises learning so deeply and says, "Ha, if my son can read and write German and do arithmetic, that is enough. I am going to make a businessman of him." They will soon quiet down; indeed, they will be glad to dig twenty feet into the earth with their bare hands just to get a scholar. For if preaching and law should fail, the businessman will not be a businessman for long; that I know for sure. We theologians and jurists must remain or everything else will go down to destruction with us; you can be sure of that.[1]

The work of the jurist as well as the work of the theologian is vital to the life of the community, yet each is also clearly different, and Luther knew himself to be called to serve God in the church.

---

[1]LW 46:251.

This essay first appeared as a lecture presented in the context of the 1959 "Luther Lectures," held at Luther College, Decorah, Iowa. Here Dr. Forell outlines the principles underlying Luther's view of the law in politics. This essay lays the theoretical bases for Luther's responses to the concrete foreign and domestic issues facing Europe in the 16th century. The essay was published in Luther and Culture, *ed. George Forell, Harold Grimm, and Theodore Hoelty-Nickel (Decorah, Iowa: Luther College Press, 1960).*

In spite of this distinction it must be remembered that Luther did become constantly involved in politics. No Christian has ever been more of a political football than Luther. From the beginning Luther and the reformation were inextricably involved in the maelstrom of sixteenth-century politics. Politics was at the bottom of the sale of the indulgences which became the occasion for the reformation, and thirty years later when Luther died in Eisleben, he had just exhausted himself in the successful attempt to find a settlement to a complicated legal dispute of the counts of Mansfeld. Never during his eventful life was he allowed to lose sight of politics. From the domestic crisis of the Peasant War to the international conflict with the Turks, Luther was always in the center of the political controversies of his time, forced by the exigencies of the situation to choose sides and to express his position in public.

It would, therefore, lead nowhere if one would discuss "Luther and Politics" in the light of his theoretical advocacy of the separation of church and state without reference to his actual involvement in the political ferment of his time. But, conversely, to discuss only this political participation without regard to his effort to distinguish the two realms and keep them separate would be equally fruitless.

Luther became willingly involved in politics if one of two circumstances were given. Sometimes he felt that the political issue could not really be understood without explaining its theological implications. Here Luther, who knew himself called by God to be a doctor, a teacher of the church, would try to instruct the Christian people on the basis of God's word in respect to their responsibilities in the great political decisions which confronted them. This form of political participation brought about his writings in the Peasant War and in regard to the conflict of the empire with the Turks. Of course, in many of these struggles he did not merely volunteer his counsel but was asked for his opinion by rulers who respected his judgment and his influence.

The second situation which might involve Luther in politics arose when he believed that the respect which he enjoyed among some of the great of this world might enable him to influence for peace and justice people who would not listen to anyone else. Here he acted as an individual Christian citizen. He might deal with questions of inheritance and property not because he felt that he possessed any special legal competence, but rather because he knew that some people would listen to him who would reject the judgment of the most competent lawyer. This is the reason why as an old and sick man he went to Eisleben to settle the complicated dispute among the counts of Mansfeld. Luther was too much concerned with living persons rather than written propositions to let ever-so-valid theories about the separation of the functions of the lawyer and the pastor stop him from helping people if he seemed to be the one who could do it. It was never an attempt to vindicate his theological theories which motivated Luther's life but rather the readiness to serve the word of God, be that as a doctor of the church or as a Christian individual for some reason able to help where others might not have the same opportunity.

As a result, Luther's life supplies us with a multitude of political acts, some wise and some foolish, some of great international significance and some of no public consequence at all. It would be of little use to us in the twentieth century to study each of these acts. Whether they were at one time wise or foolish, significant or inconsequential, after more than four hundred years they have obviously no longer any political significance for us. Luther's views on the east-west struggle of his time are historically interesting but they do not immediately shed light on the east-west struggle which confronts us in our time. Similarly his writings on the political problems of the farmers of his time do not help us solve our own very real and very political farm problems.

Should we grant, however, that Luther was one of the great prophetic minds which God has been pleased to give the church, we might still be able to learn something for our own political decisions from the principles which guided Luther in his. In order to discover the principles which undergirded Luther's political action we shall look at some of his writings for what they may reveal about Luther and politics.

THE POLITICAL USE OF THE LAW

The well-known methodological device which characterizes Luther's Christian proclamation is the distinction between God's demand and God's gift, the law and the gospel. This distinction is a constant feature of his theological thought. As early as the *Heidelberg Disputation* of 1518 Luther insisted that "the law humbles, grace exalts. The law effects fear and wrath, grace effects hope and mercy."[2] In a sermon preached on September 14, 1522, he illustrated the distinction by using the example of an illness. "The law," he said, "reveals the illness, the gospel offers the medicine."[3]

But it is in his great commentary on St. Paul's epistle to the Galatians that he deals with the question of law and gospel most thoroughly. This commentary is of special significance for our study since it is based on lectures which Luther delivered in 1531. By that time he was in a position to speak not only against the perversion of the Christian understanding of politics as he saw it among the followers of Rome, but also against the equally serious distortion of the political task by those whom Luther called the "enthusiasts," but whom we shall call more politely if less accurately the "left wing" of the reformation.

His main concern in this commentary is the clearest possible distinction between law and gospel, but in order to make this distinction as intelligible as possible he deals parenthetically also with the law as a resource for the political life. Commenting on Gal 3:2 (where St. Paul writes, "Let me ask you only this: Did you receive the Spirit by doing the works of the law or by believing what you heard?") Luther adds:

> Therefore the Law and the Gospel are two altogether different doctrines....For the Law is a taskmaster; it demands that we work and that we give. In short, it

[2]*LW* 31:51.
[3]*WA* 10/3:333.

wants to have something from us. The Gospel, on the contrary, does not demand; it grants freely; it commands us to hold out our hands and to receive what is being offered. Now demanding and granting, receiving and offering, are exact opposites and cannot exist together....Therefore, if the Gospel is a gift and offers a gift, it does not demand anything. On the other hand, the Law does not grant anything; it makes demands on us, and impossible ones at that.[4]

The fundamental concern which motivates Luther's sharp distinction between law and gospel is the reformer's eagerness to make sure that salvation is proclaimed as the free gift of God's grace and not as humankind's achievement. Even the slightest concession to the law as a means to establish a human claim upon God completely falsifies the relationship and endangers one's salvation.

While this distinction of law and gospel is crucial for Luther, he has no illusions that it is easily accomplished. In the same commentary he says in another place: "Therefore whoever knows well how to distinguish the Gospel from the Law should give thanks to God and know that he is a real theologian. I admit that in the time of temptation I myself do not know how to do this as I should."[5] And this is the method he proposes,

> The way to distinguish the one from the other is to locate the Gospel in heaven and the Law on earth, to call the righteousness of the Gospel heavenly and divine and the righteousness of the Law earthly and human, and to distinguish as sharply between [them]...as God distinguishes between heaven and earth or between light and darkness or between day and night....Therefore, if the issue is faith, heavenly righteousness, or conscience, let us leave the Law out of consideration altogether and let it remain on the earth. But if the issue is works, then let us light the lamp of works and of the righteousness of the Law in the night.[6]

The gospel determines our relationship to God in Christ, while the law guides our life in relationship to the social order. Lest we ascribe no theological significance to the law at all, Luther insists that the law, while not making us God's children, does reveal our estrangement from God and thus makes us aware of our need for the gospel. Luther distinguishes two functions of the law. Its theological function is to make us aware of our need of salvation, to reveal our desperate plight. The gospel is the good news, but it would not really be good news unless humankind were in fact in a bad way. It is liberation from the bonds of sin and death, but only because people are in fact chained by these bonds. The law reveals this bondage. Luther describes this function as follows:

> Therefore the proper use and aim of the Law is to make guilty those who are smug and at peace, so that they may see that they are in danger of sin, wrath, and death, so that they may be terrified and despairing, blanching and quaking at the rustling of a leaf.[7]

It is the function of the law, "to render us naked and guilty";[8] "to lead us forth from

---

[4]*Lectures on Galatians* (1535), LW 26:208-209.
[5]Ibid., 115.
[6]Ibid., 115-116.
[7]Ibid., 148.
[8]Ibid., 149.

our tabernacles, that is, from our peace and self-confidence, to set us into the sight of God, and to reveal the wrath of God to us."[9] The Law produces worry (*perturbatio*) and anxiety (*anxietas*). This is, indeed, the mental prison from which only Christ can make us free.[10]

We note that the law is not some specific legal code but rather the demand of the living God which confronts all people at all times in some way and produces the fearful captivity from which Christ alone can save.

While this "theological" or "proper" use of the law is from the point of view of the Christian proclamation its most significant function, it is by no means its only function. Luther clearly teaches a second use of the law, a civil or political use. It is this use which is crucial for his understanding of politics. This is how he states it:

> Here one must know that there is a double use of the Law. One is the civic use. God has ordained civic laws, indeed all laws, to restrain transgressions. Therefore every law was given to hinder sins. Does this mean then when the Law restrains sins, it justifies? Not at all. When I refrain from killing of from committing adultery or from stealing, or when I abstain from other sins, I do not do this voluntarily or from the love of virtue but because I am afraid of the sword and of the executioner. This prevents me, as the ropes or the chains prevent a lion or a bear from ravaging something that comes along.[11]

This political use is an essential function of the law,

> For the devil reigns in the whole world and drives men to all sorts of shameful deeds. This is why God has ordained magistrates, parents, teachers, laws, shackles, and all civic ordinances, so that, if they cannot do any more, they will at least bind the hands of the devil and keep him from raging at will.[12]

It is apparent to Luther that were it not for the law sinful human beings would act like wild animals. The law, therefore, must be strictly enforced by the political powers. "In society (*politia*)...obedience to the Law must be strictly (*saeverissime*) required."[13] For,

> If there were no worldly government, one man could not stand before another; each would necessarily devour the other, as irrational beasts devour one another. Therefore as it is the function and honor of the office of preaching to make sinners saints, dead men live, damned men saved, and the devil's children God's children, so it is the function and honor of worldly government (*weltlichen Regiments*) to make men out of wild beasts and to prevent men from becoming wild beasts.[14]

In view of this pessimistic description of humanity and of the destructive forces released by sin, it is not surprising that some of Luther's critics have claimed

[9]Ibid., 150.
[10]Ibid., 338-339.
[11]Ibid., 308.
[12]Ibid., 308-309.
[13]Ibid., 116.
[14]*A Sermon On Keeping Children in School*, LW 46:237.

that he underestimates the human possibilities for justice and equity and that his "political use of the law" is actually a call for the ruthless exercise of power by a tyrannical government. Luther has been compared to the British philosopher Thomas Hobbes who, starting with a similarly realistic analysis of the human situation as a war of all against all, came to the conclusion that only an absolute, powerful government could guarantee a measure of peace and justice in the world. Hobbes said,

> The Sovereign Power, whether placed in One Man, as in Monarchy, or in one Assembly of men as in Popular and Aristocraticall Commonwealths, is as great, as possibly men can be imagined to make it. And though of so unlimited a Power, men may fancy many evill consequences, yet the consequences of the want of it, which is perpetuall warre of every man against his neighbour are much worse.[15]

Lumping Luther and Hobbes together, Professor Reinhold Niebuhr has said,

> Human intelligence is never as pure an instrument of the universal perspective as the liberal democratic theory assumes, though neither is it as purely the instrument of the ego, as is assumed by the anti-democratic theory, derived from the pessimism of such men as Thomas Hobbes and Martin Luther.[16]

A very important distinction has here been overlooked. While for Hobbes it is the ruler of the absolute state who restrains others from giving free reign to their self-destructive sinful desires, Luther's understanding is quite different. For him it is God who, by establishing the structures of this world to which humans respond with their codes of law, who has created the possibility for a life of relative peace and justice. For Hobbes and Machiavelli before him, only the subjects are under the law while the ruler is not bound by it. Machiavelli said,

> A prudent ruler cannot and should not observe faith when such observance is to his disadvantage and the causes that made him give his promise have vanished. If men were all good, this advice would not be good, but since men are wicked and do not keep their promises to you, you likewise do not have to keep yours to them.[17]

Less cynically but to the same effect, Hobbes said, "A fourth opinion, repugnant to the nature of a Commonwealth is this, That he that hath the Sovereign Power, is subject to the civill Lawes."[18] Against this "absolutism" Luther insists that rulers are indeed bound by their word. He said,

> If it should happen that we sign a treaty or pact with our enemies or the Turks, then the emperor and the princes could both give and receive an oath—even though the Turk swears by the devil or Mohammed, whom he regards and worships as his god, the way we worshp our Lord Christ and swear by him.[19]

---

[15]Thomas Hobbes, *Leviathan*, ed. A. R. Waller (Cambridge: Cambridge University, 1935) 146.

[16]Reinhold Niebuhr, *The Children of Light and the Children of Darkness* (New York: Charles Scribner's Sons, 1946) 45.

[17]N. Machiavelli, *The Prince and Other Works* (New York: Farrar, Straus, 1941) 148.

[18]Hobbes, *Leviathan*, 235.

[19]*The Sermon on the Mount* (1530-1532), LW 21:102.

He opposed the notion that anybody, even the pope, had the right to free a ruler from a treaty. And he was convinced that God through judgments in history would punish the ruler as well as the subjects for their disobedience to law. God uses the princes to punish the subjects and uses other rulers to punish faithless princes. Thus Luther saw in the defeat and death of King Ladislas of Hungary in the battle of Varna (November 10, 1444) a judgment of God over this ruler for the breach of a peace treaty which he had signed in 1443 and which he had broken upon the advice of the papacy, with tragic results for himself and his people.[20] The law is binding for rulers as well as the ruled because even in its political use it is ultimately rooted in God's will. Thus it has an inherent validity quite apart from the sanctions with which the government enforces it. It is, indeed, the task of the government to enforce the law, but should it fail to do so, such a failure would ultimately not destroy the neglected law but the neglectful government. Luther said, "For every kingdom (*Reich*) must have its own laws and statutes; without law no kingdom or government can survive, as everyday experience amply shows."[21]

It is apparent that Luther has a great deal of respect for the political function of the law. But what specifically does he mean by this law as it operates in the area of politics? Obviously it is not a code which could be substituted for the positive laws as they are part of the social structure of every civilized nation. Luther never claimed that he had at his disposal some superior legal code which could be substituted for the existing statutes and thus bring about political improvement. He suggested rather that God had revealed the law to all people and that "what the law requires is written on their hearts" (Rom 2:15) and thus undergirds all positive laws and is their permanent criterion.

When he attempted to define this underlying law he used the so-called "golden rule." He said,

> All men have a certain natural knowledge implanted in their minds (Rom. 2:14-15), by which they know naturally that one should do to others what he wants done to himself (Matt. 7:12). This principle and others like it, which we call the law of nature, are the foundations of human law and of all good works.[22]

Another form in which this basic demand which undergirds all human society can be expressed is the command "You shall love your neighbor as yourself." Luther commented:

> It is a brief statement, expressed beautifully and forcefully: "You shall love your neighbor as yourself." No one can find a better, surer, or more available pattern than himself; nor can there be a nobler or more profound attitude of the mind than love; nor is there a more excellent object than one's neighbor....Thus if you want to know how the neighbor is to be loved and want to have an outstanding pattern of this, consider carefully how you love yourself. In need or danger you would certainly want desperately to be loved and assisted with all the counsels, resources, and powers not only of all men but of all creation. And so you do not

[20]*Defense and Explanation of All the Articles* (1521), LW 32:90.

[21]*Temporal Authority* (1523), LW 45:105.

[22]*Lectures on Galatians*, LW 27:53.

need any book to instruct and admonish you how you should love your neighbor, for you have the loveliest and best of books about all laws right in your own heart.[23]

To Luther all this is not a particularly Christian insight but actually available to all people. I do not have to be a Christian in order to understand the "golden rule." Neither do I have to be a believer to be impressed by the inherent logic of evaluating my responsibility for others in the light of my obvious and demonstrable concern for myself. This is a better and more universal standard than any ever-so-detailed code of laws, which of necessity will sooner or later be out of date. Luther says, "For if you seek to take an advantage of your neighbor which you would not want him to take of you, then love is gone and natural law broken."[24]

The existing statutory laws must be evaluated with the help of the underlying standards here described and in view of the needs of the contemporary situation. This re-examination involves the law of Moses as well as the ethical teachings and codes of law that come to us from pagan writers. Luther stated that we are free from the political laws of the Mosaic code but subject to the laws of the government under which we happen to live. But he added that the German monarchs could, if they so desired, utilize some of these Mosaic political laws for the administration of their empire. They would then become binding for the citizens of the empire.[25] Of course, he said,

> Moses' law cannot be valid simply and completely in all respects with us. We have to take into consideration the character and ways of our land when we want to make or apply laws and rules, because our rules and laws are based on the character of our land and its ways and not on those of the land of Moses, just as Moses' laws are based on the ways and character or his people and not those of ours.[26]

His judgment concerning the pagan laws was quite similar. Luther said:

> Before justification many good men even among the pagans—such as Xenophon, Aristides, Fabius, Cicero, Pomponius Atticus, etc.—performed the works of the Law and accomplished great things. Cicero suffered death courageously in a righteous and good cause. Pomponius was a man of integrity and veracity; for he himself never lied, and he could not bear it if others did.[27]

These people were gifted with heroic virtues, ruled their countries well and in the interest of the common good.[28] Obviously, even the pagan law expressed the undergirding structure of the divine will for the preservation of humankind. But while Luther could say, "The [books of the pagans] teach virtue, laws, and wisdom with respect to temporal goods, honor, and peace on earth,"[29] he never advocated

[23]Ibid., 57.
[24]*Trade and Usury*, LW 45:307.
[25]*Lectures on Galatians*, LW 26:447.
[26]*On Marriage Matters* (1530), LW 46:291.
[27]*Lectures on Galatians*, LW 26:123-124.
[28]Ibid., 354.
[29]*Psalm 101* (1534-1535), LW 13:199.

merely a return to these books. The political use of the law implies that the statutes must be adjusted to present needs. It is not sufficient for laws to be old; they must also meet the contemporary situation.

In order to achieve this goal Luther made suggestions which always shock those who know only his great theological concerns. It is well-known that in the relationship of human beings to God Luther considered "reason" the very enemy of salvation. Yet while reason is incompetent in our relationship to God and cannot reach him, Luther is convinced that this very same reason is an essential tool in the ordering of human affairs.

> In the human affairs of this world man's reason suffices. He needs no other light than reason. God does not teach in scripture how to build houses and to make clothes, marry, make war and similar things. For these the natural light [of reason] is sufficient.[30]

For Luther the area of law is the area of reason, "Human reason has the Law as its object."[31] The same person who is

> drowned in wickedness and is a slave of the devil has a will, reason, free choice, and power to build a house, to carry on a governmental office, to steer a ship, and to do other tasks that have been made subject to man according to Gen. 1:28; these have not been taken away from man. Procreation, government, and the home have not been abolished.[32]

> In the worldly kingdom (*weltlichen Reich*) men must act on the basis of reason— wherein the laws have their origin—for God has subjected temporal rule and all of physical life to reason.[33]

And the careful use of reason will produce some success in its proper sphere. Luther says, "To some extent reason is able to perform [civil righteousness]."[34] Here is room even for the efforts of the much-maligned Aristotle. Luther's sharp criticism of the complete dependence upon Aristotle of the scholastic theologians has often been quoted. He considered the rule of Aristotle at the universities one of the reasons for the sorry state of Christendom. But he was prepared to admit that it is really the misuse of Aristotle for theological purposes which is at fault.

> The sophists [Luther's term for scholastic theologians]...do not know of any other righteousness than civil righteousness or the righteousness of the Law, which is known in some measure even to the heathen. Therefore they snatch the words "do," "work," and the like, from moral philosophy and from the Law, and transfer them to theology, where they act in a way that is not only evil but ungodly. Philosophy and theology must be carefully distinguished.[35]

'To do' means one thing in philosophy and something else again in theology. In moral philosophy 'to do' requires a good will (*bonam voluntatem*) and right

[30]*Christmas Postil* (1522), WA 10/1/1:531.
[31]*Lectures on Galatians*, LW 26:88.
[32]Ibid., 174.
[33]*A Sermon on Keeping Children in School*, LW 46:242.
[34]*Lectures on Galatians*, LW 26:183.
[35]Ibid., 261.

reason (*rectam rationem*). This is as far as philosophy can go. Thus it will help the welfare and peace of the commonwealth. But it is important to note that the pagan philosophers do not claim that with their "right reason" and "good will" they can achieve the remission of sins and everlasting life. But, Luther says, this is exactly what the sophist and the monk hope to achieve with their works. "Therefore a heathen philosopher is much better than a self-righteous person."[36] "In civil life...one becomes a doer on the basis of deeds, just as one becomes a lutenist by often playing the lute, as Aristotle says."[37]

In the realm of politics it is perfectly proper to establish good habits by law. People may not become better before God if they do not steal or murder in fear of the police and the law, but their communities will become safer nevertheless. And as the result of their restraint certain behavior patterns may become established which will cover men and women with a thin coat of civic decency. Here Aristotle's advice can be taken quite seriously. Luther was aware how thin this veneer of civic justice is at best and how difficult it is to maintain. Here wisdom and courage are needed, and Luther can sound like a Greek philosopher when he says,

> In the political realm (*politia*) prudence and fortitude are different....And yet they stick together so closely that they cannot be easily separated. Now fortitude is a steadiness of mind, which does not despair in the midst of adversity but endures bravely and looks for better things. But unless fortitude is directed by prudence, it becomes rashness; on the other hand, unless fortitude is added to prudence, prudence is useless.[38]

In view of this prudential approach to matters political we cannot be surprised that Luther wrote:

> A prince must have the law as firmly in hand as the sword, and determine in his own mind when and where the law is to be applied strictly or with moderation, so that the law may prevail at all times and in all cases, and reason may be the highest law and the master of all administration of law.[39]

And in another book he wrote:

> In Greek this virtue, or wisdom, which can and must guide and moderate the severity of law according to cases, and which judges the same deed to be good or evil according to the difference of the motives and intentions of the heart, is called *epieikeia*; in Latin it is *aequitas*, and *Billichkeit* [justice] in German. Now because law must be framed simply and briefly, it cannot possibly embrace all the cases and problems. This is why the judges and lords must be wise and pious in this matter and mete out reasonable justice, and let the law take its course, or set it aside, accordingly....All laws that regulate men's actions must be subject to justice [*Billichkeit*], their mistress, because of the innumerable and varied circumstances which no one can anticipate or set down.[40]

---

[36]Ibid., 262.
[37]Ibid., 256.
[38]*Lectures on Galatians*, LW 27:23.
[39]*Temporal Authority*, LW 45:119.
[40]*Whether Soldiers, Too, Can Be Saved* (1526), LW 46:102-103.

We have discovered that Luther identifies the law in its political use rather broadly with the golden rule. It must be used in this world with the help of reason, prudence, and equity. And it is sound policy in dealing with it to take into account the wisdom of the ages, be it the Mosaic law or the political philosophy of the ancient Greeks and Romans. The question arises, "How does the Christian fit into this 'political use' of the law?" In order to find an answer to this question it has to be remembered that for Luther nobody is ever a Christian in a static sense. The Christian life is actually the process of becoming Christian. As such it is an ongoing process completely dominated by the initiative of God. Luther says,

> This life, therefore, is not godliness but the process of becoming godly, not health but getting well, not being but becoming, not rest but exercise. We are not now what we shall be, but we are on the way. The process is not finished, but it is actively going on. This is not the goal but it is the right road. At present, everything does not gleam and sparkle, but everything is being cleansed.[41]

In other words, it must be remembered that the Christian remains all during her or his life *simul justus et peccator*. Thus the Christian (*homo Christianus*) is righteous and sinner at the same time, holy and profane, an enemy of God and a child of God."[42]

Luther suggested that the historical sequence of the age of law and the age of grace is experienced by each individual Christian simultaneously. Believers live at the same time in the age of law and in the age of grace.

> For what happened historically and temporally when Christ came—namely, that He abrogated the Law and brought liberty and eternal life to light—this happens personally and spiritually every day in any Christian, in whom there are found the time of Law and the time of grace in constant alteration....In the experience of the Christian, therefore, both are found, the time of Law and the time of grace.[43]

Insofar as they are sinners, Christians are subject to the law with all its restraining power and everything that Luther has said about the political use of the law applies to Christians as well. It is true, of course, that Luther did occasionally suggest that no government would be necessary if all people were altogether Christian.[44] But since it is a fundamental assertion of his theology that all Christians are still in the process of becoming Christians, the law is obviously valid for them also. As a result all special exemptions from the political law for the clergy, so much a part of the political pattern of the medieval world, were rejected by Luther. As early as the *Open Letter to the Christian Nobility* of 1520 Luther wrote:

> I say therefore that since the temporal power is ordained of God to punish the wicked and protect the good, it should be left free to perform its office in the

---

[41]*Defense and Explanation*, LW 32:24.
[42]*Lectures on Galatians*, LW 26:232.
[43]Ibid., 340-341.
[44]*Temporal Authority*, LW 45:89.

whole body of Christendom without restrction and without respect to persons, whether it affect pope, bishops, priests, monks, nuns, or anyone else.[45]

All people, Christians and non-Christians alike, are subject to the political use of the law.

But Luther did believe that the Christians as Christians had a special relationship to the law. Believers know that God is at work through the law. They will understand, praise, and support the law in its political function as an instrument of God's preserving grace. Thus Luther says,

> When I have this righteousness within me, I descend from heaven like the rain that makes the earth fertile. That is, I come forth into another kingdom, and I perform good works whenever the opportunity arises. If I am a minister of the Word, I preach, I comfort the saddened, I administer the sacraments. If I am a father, I rule my household and family, I train my children in piety and honesty. If I am a magistrate, I perform the office which I have received by divine command. If I am a servant, I faithfully tend to my master's affairs. In short, whoever knows for sure Christ is his righteousness not only cheerfully and gladly works in his calling but also submits himself for the sake of love (per charitatem) to magistrates, also to their wicked laws, and to everything else in this present life—even, if need be, to burden and danger. For he knows that God wants this and that this obedience pleases Him.[46]

Thus Christians are indeed under the law in its political use, but knowing God in Jesus Christ they accept their political duties in the light of their knowledge of God. Even these political duties are then opportunities for greater service, not in order to attain justification but rather because justification has been granted.

> Since a true Christian lives and labors on earth not for himself alone but for his neighbor, he does by the very nature of his spirit even what he himself has no need of, but is needful and useful to his neighbor. Because the sword is most beneficial and necessary for the whole world in order to preserve peace, punish sin, and restrain the wicked, the Christian submits most willingly to the rule of the sword, pays his taxes, honors those in authority, serves, helps, and does all he can to assist the governing authority, that it may continue to function and be held in honor and fear. Although he has no need of these things for himself—to him they are not essential—nevertheless, he concerns himself about what is serviceable and of benefit to others, as Paul teaches in Ephesians 5 [:21-6:9].[47]

A Christian person does her or his political duty as all other works of love: "He does not visit the sick in order that he himself may be made well, or feed others because he himself needs food—so he serves the governing authority not because he needs it but for the sake of others, that they may be protected and that the wicked may not become worse."[48]

---

[45]To the Christian Nobility (1520), LW 44:130. For the Roman Catholic claims for special privileges for the clergy see Karl Mirbt, Quellen zur Geschichte des Papsttums und des römischen Katholizismus, 3rd ed. (Tübingen: Mohr, 1911) 161 and 285 (exemption from taxes); 112, 149, 285, 350, 54 (exemption from trial in secular courts).

[46]Lectures on Galatians, LW 26:11-12.

[47]Temporal Authority, LW 45:94.

[48]Ibid., 94.

Luther believed that being a Christian will make a person a better citizen, more alert and willing to do political duties as a service to God and the neighbor. For the person saved by the gospel, all the real and remaining obligations of the law are suffused and redeemed by a new relationship to God. But Luther realized also that his polemics against justification by the works of the law might easily lead some of his listeners to claim that the law did not apply to them at all. His claim that works do not save might easily be misunderstood to mean that those who were saved should do no works. No wonder he said,

> It is difficult and dangerous to teach that we are justified by faith without works and yet to require works at the same time. Unless the ministers of Christ are faithful and prudent here and are "stewards of the mysteries of God" (1 Cor. 4:1), who rightly divide the Word of truth (2 Tim. 2:15), they will immediately confuse faith and love at this point. Both topics, faith and works, must be carefully taught and emphasized, but in such a way that they both remain within their limits. Otherwise, if works alone are taught, as happened under the papacy, faith is lost. If faith alone is taught, unspiritual men will immediately suppose that works are not necessary.[49]

Luther taught both faith and works. But he considered the area of politics preeminently the area of law and of works. Human beings' responsibility in the field of politics must be seen in the light of their obligations under the law. Because no one can escape the law, no one can escape political duties. A *homo sapiens* under the law is *homo politicus*, the political person. As such, persons are called to do their duty in foreign[50] and domestic[51] politics.

[49]*Lectures on Galatians*, LW 27:62-63.
[50][See below, "Luther's Theology and Foreign Policy," 96-107. Ed.]
[51][See below, "Luther's Theology and Domestic Politics," 108-122. Ed.]

Word & World
Supplement Series 2
1994

Luther's Theology and Foreign Policy

MARTIN LUTHER LIVED IN AN AGE OF PROFOUND INTERNATIONAL TENSIONS. Europe's political situation was in a state of flux. The reasons for the unrest were numerous. In 1519 Emperor Maximilian had died. Shortly before his death he had attempted to make sure that the empire would be passed on to his grandson Charles, who had recently inherited the Spanish crown. But Maximilian had died before he could achieve this ambition. Nevertheless, with the help of complicated international negotiations, expensive bribes, and the pressure of the early version of what one would call today "public opinion," the election of Charles V as emperor was finally brought about in June 1519. Because of the new emperor's considerable military and political resources as ruler of Spain he was in a position to try to be emperor in fact as well as name. For the last time the idea of a universal European empire had the chance of being realized. Charles V almost accomplished the feat, but the effort caused tremendous tensions, and Luther was often unwittingly in the very center of these international political maneuvers.

A second factor which contributed greatly to the international conflicts of Luther's time was the pressure which the Turks exerted upon the eastern frontiers of the empire. Large parts of southeastern Europe were under Turkish rule. During the early years of the reformation the Turkish threat constantly increased. In 1521 Suleiman II captured Belgrade. In the battle of Mohacz of 1526 he routed the Hungarian army and struck terror into the hearts of Christendom. While this danger from the Turks abated temporarily during some periods of Luther's ministry it increased again towards the end of his life. Thus all during his ministry

---

Here Dr. Forell traces the practical implications of Luther's understanding of "The Political Use of the Law" in the arena of sixteenth-century international relations. This essay was the second in a series presented in the context of the 1959 "Luther Lectures" at Luther College, Decorah, Iowa and published under the title, "Foreign Policy," in Luther and Culture *(Decorah, Iowa: Luther College Press, 1960) 24-43.*

Luther was forced to comment on the meaning of this threat and counsel his followers in regard to their responsibilities in this conflict.

A third element contributing to international tensions was the papacy, which in the sixteenth century was still a major political power. The papacy made alliances, fought wars, and acted like any other political kingdom. As a matter of fact, the actions of the papacy in the international conflicts of the first half of the sixteenth century were inspired almost exclusively by political and economic considerations. Luther knew that and was bound to use this obvious political partisanship of the papacy as material for his criticism. Because of the deep involvement of the papacy in the international intrigues of the time any criticism of the papacy was bound to have political overtones.

Fourthly, one of the major political power-blocks which eventually came into being in Germany was the so-called Smalcald League. The participants in this confederation were joined together for the defense of their right to reformation. They were followers of Luther and forced into this defensive alliance because their stand at the Diet of Augsburg had made them into outlaws in the eyes of the majority of their princely neighbors. Only by standing together could they hope to be allowed to worship God according to the faith expressed in the Augsburg Confession. We cannot be surprised that among these confederates the judgments of Luther, even on matters of foreign policy, were sought and respected.

What then was Luther's counsel in these many international conflicts? What was his attitude towards Emperor and Turks, Pope and Smalcald confederates? We must begin by stating the theological presuppositions of his advice in matters of foreign policy. First of all, international conflicts are ways in which God shows ultimate lordship over history. Secondly, they are ways in which the devil shows his provisional power in this age to obstruct the advance of God's word. But it is essential to understand that nothing the devil does can ultimately frustrate God's plan. The sovereign power of God over all history is a basic element of Luther's theology. It is clearly expressed in one of his major theological works, the powerful attack against Erasmus of Rotterdam which he called *On the Bondage of the Will*. Here he quotes the 115th Psalm, "Our God is in the heavens; he does whatever he pleases."[1] And he cites Jer 18:6: "Can I not do with you, O house of Israel, just as this potter has done? says the Lord. Just like the clay in the potter's hand, so are you in my hand, O house of Israel."[2] "The Lord has made everything for its purpose, even the wicked for the day of trouble" (Prov 16:4)[3]

In his exposition of the Second Psalm of 1532 Luther describes this sovereign power of God most eloquently. The judgments of God are not hidden. The wrath of God, whom the godless consider asleep and unwilling to bother with their deeds, will finally overwhelm them.

The examples are before our eyes. The empire of the Romans was indeed most

[1]LW 33:68.
[2]Ibid., 203.
[3]Ibid., 174.

powerful and yet this empire, which contemplated the destruction of Christ's kingdom, was itself destroyed and perished. The church, however, which kept the faith in the promises, remained intact, even though gravely afflicted.[4]

And Luther continues,

The prophet says here that God will speak in his wrath. For it is certain that at this word entire nations will collapse and will in no way be able to protect themselves against this fall. Thus God spoke in his wrath when he sent forth the Romans against the holy city Jerusalem and later when he sent the Vandals and the Goths against Rome. These were powerful and overwhelming words and a voice of iron which overthrew the mightiest ruler.[5]

We see here that for Luther the kingdoms of this world and their rulers are tools in the hands of a sovereign God who through them accomplishes a sovereign purpose. But Luther does add that conflicts may also be the result of the demonic powers which try vainly to obstruct God's holy purpose. Thus when the gospel is being preached Satan will use every device at his disposal in order to create national and international chaos and drown out the good news of Christ. This is why Luther can say:

Here you can learn why in our age seditions and godless opinions emerged in the church. Satan cannot tolerate the word. Christ thunders now through his gospel in the whole world and reveals the papal idolatry and abomination. Do you expect Satan to keep silent and accept such damage to his empire lying down? Didn't we see how terribly he raved when some moral questions (*moralia*) were corrected by that holy man John Hus? For unlike us he did not condemn the sacrifice of the mass and merits and other religious observances but only doubted the primacy of the pope, contested the sale of indulgences and denied purgatory. And yet he so affected Satan that he involved Germany and Bohemia in a long and terrible war. [6]

International conflict is here seen as a demonic device of the devil to obstruct the path of the gospel. Yet, to Luther it is evident that such interference, however terrible, can only be provisionally successful. Ultimately it is doomed with its originator the devil. The sovereignty of God over the nations is the fundamental premise which undergirds all of Luther's statements on foreign policy.

But once this basic *theological* premise has been stated it is apparent that the basic *political* premise for Luther's participation in foreign policy is a great and astonishing readiness to accept the facts of political life. In this practical area Luther's thought is characterized by an unexpected combination of realism, conservatism, and pragmatism. His analysis of the political situation is singularly free from the common sentimental illusions of amateur politicians. His advice is a lively combination of caution, courage, and prudence.

Of course, politics in general and foreign policy in particular belong for Luther in the realm of the law. It is, therefore, proper that reason should rule and

---

[4]WA 40/2:228.
[5]Ibid., 231.
[6]Ibid., 201-202.

guide people in these decisions. It is not even necessary that a ruler in order to rule competently should be a Christian. Luther says, "Caesar does not need to be a saint."[7] For the ruler it suffices that he uses reason; in this way God maintains all government, even that of the Tartars and Turks.[8]

Luther writes to the Christians in Riga:

> You have just heard that those in authority should be watchful and diligent, and perform all the duties of their office: bar the gates, defend the towers and walls, put on armor, and procure supplies, In general, they should proceed as if there were no God and they had to rescue themselves and manage their own affairs.[9]

Of course, God rules even the international affairs of nations, but for Luther this does not excuse the political leaders and the individual citizens from taking their proper responsibility in these matters. For Luther insists that God has chosen to exercise authority through human beings. All the preparations and activities of humankind are ways in which God accomplishes his purpose. "Indeed," Luther states, "one could very well say that the course of the world, and especially the doing of his saints, are God's mask, under which he conceals himself and so marvelously exercises dominion."[10]

Those who exercise the function of government should, according to Luther, face the complexities of the political life realistically. This is not at all easy. Most people have no idea how complicated the decisions in the realm of politics actually are. Yet Luther observes that as a matter of fact,

> Nobody thinks he is too clumsy or inept. If he were the government, he would really do splendidly; and he is dissatisfied with anything done by others in the government....Those are the Master Smart Alecks who are so clever that they can bridle a steed in its hind end. All they can do is to condemn other people and to improve upon them. When they do get control of things, they ruin everything. It is as the saying goes: "Whoever watches the game knows best how to do it."[11]

Luther is convinced that spectators who see the clash of political interests from the outside and who have to assume no responsibility are never aware of the intricacies of international relations. Such people think that all these problems can be figured out logically. They say: "How can it fail? It is as certain as the fact that seven plus three make ten." And indeed, this is good mathematics, here seven and three do make ten. But in real life this may happen: God may melt seven pieces into one and thus make out of seven one or divide three into thirty and it turns out that the result which was supposed to be ten and was so certain in theory is quite different in actuality.[12] And then Luther continues to illustrate this point with examples taken from the international scene as he observed it. In 1525 Pope

---

[7]*Sermons* (1528), WA 27:418.
[8]Ibid.
[9]*Exposition of Psalm 127* (1524), LW 45:331.
[10]Ibid.
[11]*Psalm 101* (1534-1535), LW 13:147-148.
[12]Ibid., 149.

Clement and the King of France had been sure that they had the emperor in their power. Yet at the battle of Pavia France was defeated and the king became a prisoner. Luther observes that pope and king certainly learned then that in international politics three and seven do not necessarily add up to ten.

Luther was especially sceptical about the specific political advice which the clergy might give in such international questions. He felt that they tended to add mostly pomp and ceremony and little expert information and opinion to such international consultations.[13] Furthermore, there was always the danger that political and international tensions would be merely complicated by the injection of ideological considerations. In the *Magnificat*, dedicated to John Frederick, Duke of Saxony, Luther described this problem as follows:

> Oh, this is a thing that ought to be known to all princes and rulers who, not content with confessing the right, immediately want to obtain it and win the victory, without the fear of God; they fill the world with bloodshed and misery, and think what they do is right and well done because they have, or think they have, a just cause. What else is that but proud and haughty Moab, which calls itself worthy to possess the right...while if it regards itself right in the sight of God, it is not worthy to live on earth or eat a crust of bread, because of its sins.[14]

Luther has little patience with those defenders of ideological warfare who try to camouflage their attitude by saying: "I am not doing this out of hostility to the person but out of love for righteousness. I am a friend to the person but an enemy to the cause." He quotes such phrases and adds that they seem so gentle and beautiful that they obscure the beam in one's own eye and see only the splinter in the brother's eye.[15]

Luther was a realist when examining the actual causes of international tensions and war. He cautioned against the false pretense which is always at the bottom of ideological warfare. He proclaimed the involvement of all participants in sin and preferred that if wars had to be fought they be fought for the defense of a city or the preservation of a border rather than in defense of the Christian faith or of the Holy Trinity. From this point of view he wrote in his book *On War Against the Turks*:

> Therefore the urging and inciting with which the emperor and the princes have been stirred up to fight against the Turk ought to cease. He has been urged, as head of Christendom and as protector of the church and defender of the faith, to wipe out the Turk's religion, and the urging and exhorting have been based on the wickedness and vice of the Turks. Not so! The emperor is not the head of Christendom or defender of the gospel or the faith. The church and the faith must have a defender other than emperor and kings. They are usually the worst enemies of Christendom and of the faith....That kind of urging and exhorting only makes things worse and angers God deeply because it interferes with his honor and his work and would ascribe it to men, which is idolatry and blasphemy. And if the emperor were supposed to destroy the unbelievers and

---

[13]Ibid., 150.

[14]*LW* 21:336-337.

[15]*The Sermon on the Mount* (1530-1532), *LW* 21:223.

non-Christians, he would have to begin with the pope, bishops, and clergy, and perhaps not spare us or himself; for there is enough horrible idolatry in his own empire to make it unnecessary for him to fight the Turks for this reason. There are entirely too make Turks, Jews, heathen, and non-Christians among us with open false doctrine and with offensive, shameful lives. Let the Turk believe and live as he will, just as one lets the papacy and other false Christians live. The emperor's sword has nothing to do with the faith; it belongs to physical, worldly things.[16]

Added to this sober realism of Luther in questions of international politics was a cautious conservatism which made it impossible for him to identify change and improvement. Concerning rulers in general he would say that "There is as great a difference between changing a government and improving it as the distance from heaven to earth. It is easy to change a government, but it is difficult to get one that is better, and the danger is that you will not. Why? Because it is not in our will or power, but only in the will and the hand of God."[17] In matters of politics and international relations experience and precedent are most important. After all, the existing laws represent the distillation of the wisdom of the ages. It would be foolish to discard them without having the assurance that something better would be put in their place. Luther said,

> The imperial law, according to which the Roman Empire still rules today and will continue to rule until the Last Day, is nothing more than heathen wisdom, established and set down before Rome had ever heard a thing about Christians or even about God Himself. Yet I dare say that if all the wise men were brewed into one drink, they would not only leave all the cases and disputes unresolved but would even be unable to speak or think this well about them. Those who set down the law had to be experienced in big deals and to be familiar with the thinking of many people; for this they had been endowed with a high degree of intelligence and brains. In other words, those who had such wisdom in secular government lived once and will never live again.[18]

All utopian political hopes were alien to Luther. In view of his frequently expressed hope that the end of the world was at hand he was convinced that only the most urgent changes should be made in the political structure and in the relationship of the nations to each other. He said:

> Because there is no hope of getting another government in the Roman Empire, as Daniel also indicates (Dan. 2:40), it is not advisable to change it. Rather, let him who is able darn and patch it up as long as we live; let him punish the abuse and put bandages and ointment on the smallpox. But if someone is going to tear out the pox unmercifully, then no one will feel the pain and the damage more than those clever barbers who would rather tear out the sores than heal them.[19]

No victory or defeat could ultimately affect the destiny of nations unless God had so ordained it. For this reason Luther did not feel that the decisions for change or

---

[16]LW 46:185-186.

[17]*Whether Soldiers, Too, Can Be Saved* (1526), LW 46:111-112.

[18]*Psalm 101*, LW 13:198.

[19]Ibid., 217; cf. also George W. Forell, *Faith Active in Love* (Minneapolis: Augsburg, 1959) 154ff.

reform of the international pattern were as significant as those affecting the procla-mation of the gospel. As radical as he was in his insistence that the word of God be preached in its purity, whatever the cost, so conservative was he in his political views. Since no change in the area of foreign politics would affect the ultimate destiny of humankind these changes were to be made cautiously. An existing international situation might present great problems, yet these problems are known. When advocating change we are dealing with an unknown situation. What might at first appear as an improvement could turn out to be the very opposite. By recklessly promoting changes we may actually be jumping from the frying pan into the fire. So Luther could say:

> Temporal power is in duty bound to defend its subjects, as I have frequently said, for it bears the sword in order to keep in fear those who do not heed such divine teaching and to compel them to leave others in peace....Yet this defense of its subjects should not be accompanied by still greater harm; that would be to leap from the frying pan into the fire. It is a poor defense to expose a whole city to danger for the sake of one person, or to risk the entire country for a single village or castle, unless God enjoined this by a special command as He did in former times. If a robber knight robs a citizen of his property and you, my lord, lead your army against him to punish this injustice, and in so doing lay waste the whole land, who will have wrought the greater harm, the knight or the lord? David overlooked many things when he was unable to punish without bringing harm upon others. All rulers must do the same. On the other hand a citizen must endure a certain measure of suffering for the sake of the community, and not demand that all other men undergo the greater injury for his sake. Christ did not want the weeds to be gathered up, lest the wheat also be rooted up with them. (Matt. 13:29). If men went to war on every provocation and passed by no insult, we should never be at peace and have nothing but destruction. Therefore, right or wrong is never a sufficient reason indiscriminately to punish or make war. It is a sufficient cause to punish within bounds and without destroying another. The lord or ruler must always look to what will profit the whole mass of his subjects rather than any one portion. That householder will never grow rich who, because someone has plucked a feather from his goose, flings the whole goose after him.[20]

This long quotation shows also that hand in hand with Luther's conservatism goes an attitude in political questions which could best be described as pragma-tism. This is here not a philosophy but a common sense approach to life which judges political action not according to theories but according to its effect on the welfare of the citizens. Luther's counsel in questions of foreign policy always expresses this concern for the practical political results of an action. In the *Treatise on Good Works* of 1520 he wrote:

> A prince must also be very wise and not always try to impose his own will, even if he has the right and the best of all reasons to do so. For it is a far nobler virtue to put up with a slight to one's own rights than [it is to risk damage] to life and property, where this is to the advantage of the subjects. As we know, worldly rights are valid only with respect to the things of this world.[21]

[20]*Magnificat*, LW 21:337-338.
[21]LW 44:94.

He called the slogan, *fiat justitia et pereat mundus*,[22] which happened to be the motto of Ferdinand of Austria, "absolutely foolish."[23]

And he praised the Roman Emperor Augustus because of the Roman historian Suetonius' report that he did not wish to wage war, however just his cause might be, unless there were sure indications that the result would produce greater benefit than harm, or at least that the damage would be bearable. The saying of Augustus which Luther liked particularly well and which he quoted repeatedly with approval was: "War can be likened to fishing with a golden net—you never catch as much as you risk losing."[24]

About those who hold responsible positions in government Luther said:

> He who drives a cart must act differently than if he were walking alone. When he is on his own he can walk, jump, and do what he likes, but when he is driving he must control and guide so that the horse and cart can follow. He has to pay greater regard to the horse and cart than to himself. A prince is in the same position. He stands at the head and leads the multitude, and must not go or do as he wants but as the multitude are able. He has to pay more regard to their needs and necessities than to his own will and pleasure.[25]

Any other behavior on the part of those who govern is bound to lead to disaster both for those who rule and those under their care.

> When a prince rules according to his own mad will and follows his own opinion he is like a mad driver who rushes straight ahead with his horse and cart through bushes, hedges, ditches, streams, uphill and downdale, regardless of road and bridges. He will not drive for very long. He is bound to smash up.[26]

It was Luther's concern with the practical results of statecraft as they affect people in their daily life which led him to suggest that it might actually be better, politically speaking, to have a competent and intelligent ruler who is personally evil than to have a ruler who, though personally a model of virtue, is politically incompetent and stupid. Indeed, Luther insists that a good and wise ruler is the ideal head of government, but if this ideal is not available it may turn out to be in the long-range interest of the commonwealth if a personally evil person rules the state intelligently and with skill than if someone who is personally virtuous rules without intelligence and competence. This is how he puts it:

> The question has been properly raised whether a prince is better if he is good and imprudent or prudent yet also evil. Here Moses certainly demands both. Nevertheless, if one cannot have both, it is better for him to be prudent and not good than good and not prudent; for the good man would actually rule nothing but would be ruled only by others, and at that only by the worst people.[27]

22["Do justice and the world is vanquished." Ed.]

23*LW* 44:94.

24Ibid., cf. *Psalm 82* (1530), *LW* 13:56-57.

25*LW* 44:94.

26Ibid., 94-95.

27*Lectures on Deuteronomy* (1525), *LW* 45:120.

Luther had too much respect for the technical demands of competent government to believe that good intentions were all that a ruler needed.

In view of this political pragmatism with its concern for the practical consequences of all political thoughts, words, and deeds, how does Luther conceive of the possibility of international order? International order should be the result of wise decisions by peaceloving princes. If the rulers were virtuous they would avoid war and work for peace. But Luther has no illusions about the sincerity of their desire for peace. He said, "Who is not aware that a prince is a rare prize in heaven."[28]

He was sure that there would not be many rulers present "when the roll is called up yonder." Yet God had made provisions for peace, not through the moral excellency of princes but rather through the balance of power which is the result of the multitude of peoples and interests in this world. He said,

> But if a lord or prince does not recognize this duty and God's commandment and allows himself to think that he is prince, not for his subjects' sake, but because of his handsome, blond hair as though God had made him a prince to rejoice in his power and wealth and honor, take pleasure in these things, and rely on them. If he is that kind of prince, he belongs among the heathen; indeed, he is a fool....God restrains such princes by giving fists to other people, too. There are also people on the other side of the mountain. Thus one sword keeps the other in the scabbard.[29]

Thus peace is the result of the multiplicity of forces and interests which tend to check each other and prevent even a wicked and foolish ruler from dominating everybody else. Not in the goodness of an individual, who wants peace, but in the goodness of God, who has created this variety of interests and pressures which require compromise and make war risky, rests our hope for peace. Luther carries his basic ideas through with amazing consistency. The powers of this world have to play God's masquerade. Through them he punishes evil-doers and presses towards peace. Even in the international relationships of the nations God rules and accomplishes his own ultimate purpose.

It is in the light of these basic insights that we must try to understand Luther's specific counsel in the international conflicts of his time. He warned the emperor against crusades, yet encouraged him to defend the borders of Germany and protect the life and property of its citizens against the Turkish attacks.[30] He condemned the military machinations and the international intrigues of the pope and saw in them further proof for the fact that the papacy is in truth the Antichrist proclaimed in the prophecies of the Bible. By allying himself with the pope the king of France fell under the same condemnation.[31] In Luther's relationship to the

---

[28]*Temporal Authority* (1523), LW 45:120.

[29]*Whether Soldiers, Too, Can Be Saved,* LW 46:122.

[30]Cf. George W. Forell, "Luther's View Concerning the Imperial Foreign Policy," *Lutheran Quarterly* 4/2 (May 1952) 153-169. [Reprinted in the present volume, pp. 135-146.]

[31]Cf. George W. Forell, "Luther and the War Against the Turks," *Church History* 14/4 (December 1945). [Reprinted in the present volume, pp. 123-134.]

League of Smalcald it was the gradual attainment of greater technical knowledge of the legal problems here involved which eventually led him to the position that the defense against the attacks of the emperor and the Roman Catholic princes was not only a right but also a duty for those princes who were loyal to the gospel.[32] But in all these specific questions of foreign policy Luther was guided by the principles which we have here observed.

A final question may now be asked. Is there anything in Luther's utterances on foreign policy which might give us some counsel in our own complex foreign-political decisions? Is this merely ancient history, of interest to us because of Luther's significance for the Evangelical Church of the Augsburg Confession, but without relevance to the political life in the second half of the twentieth century? Or did Luther in wrestling with the political questions of his revolutionary age with the help of biblical revelation come upon answers which may have something to say to our time?

It seems that a number of Luther's insights are as helpful and correct today as they were in the sixteenth century. First of all, international conflicts are ways in which God shows ultimate lordship over history in our time as in the days of Luther. In an age which tends to understand all events as governed only by chance, Luther reminds us that the God who once used the Persian ruler Cyrus may today use the Chinese ruler Mao Tse Tung. World history is not the "tale told by an idiot, full of sound and fury, signifying nothing." For those who believe in God's revelation in Jesus Christ it is within history that God executes judgment. As one great secular historian of our time has said,

> If men put their faith in science and make it the be-all and end-all of life, as though it were not to be subdued to any higher ethical end, there is something in the very composition of the universe that will make it execute judgment on itself, if only in the shape of the atomic bomb.[33]

Luther never lost sight of this ultimate judgment of God. He can remind us not to lose sight of it either. No view of foreign politics which does not keep in mind the ultimate lordship of God over history is truly realistic.

Secondly, Luther sought, and we should learn from him, to heed the biblical warning: "Like a roaring lion your adversary the devil prowls around, looking for someone to devour" (1 Pet 5:8). The reality of the demonic powers as they affect the relationships of nations has been demonstrated with terrifying force in the twentieth century. We have seen whole cities incinerated by the command of relatively moral leaders. Can we doubt the power of the devil? We have seen millions dying in gas-chambers upon the order of people possessed by the devil! We know that even today we live every minute at the brink of total disaster. Can we question the power of him whom Luther calls "the prince of this world"? In an age in which we are tempted to explain international conflicts and tensions with the aid of some

[32]Cf. Johannes Heckel, *Lex Charitatis: Eine juristische Untersuchung über das Recht in der Theologie Martin Luthers* (Munich: Verlag der Bayrischen Akademie der Wissenschaften, 1953) 184 ff.

[33]Herbert Butterfield, *Christianity and History* (London: Fontana, 1957) 82f.

individual villain, allegedly responsible for all our difficulties, whose removal will usher in the reign of peace, Luther reminds us that there are principalities and powers in the service of evil which utilize individuals but which are hardly affected by their removal. If we take this biblical insight of Luther seriously we will judge international conflicts with greater realism and become aware of a dimension of our existence which has been obscured by the superficial rationalism of our age.

Thirdly, Luther made some very practical suggestions for the day-to-day conduct of foreign policy. They are especially important for those who desire the responsible participation of church people in the formulation and execution of a nation's foreign policy. Luther advocated a sober realism in regard to human beings and their possibilities. He had no illusions about their innate goodness. He had no utopian hopes that humans could through their efforts establish God's kingdom on earth. While some Christians have added great confusion to the conduct of foreign politics with their attempts to use the state as an instrument of the gospel, Luther finally rejected ideological warfare and crusades as blasphemous efforts on the part of humankind to usurp the work of God. The sobriety with which Luther judged the international conflicts of his time could well be imitated by Christians today. When Herbert Butterfield says, "It is essential not to have faith in human nature. Such faith is a recent heresy and a very disastrous one,"[34] he is enunciating an insight which was part and parcel of Luther's counsel in foreign politics. It is an insight which when ignored by christendom has led to *Schwärmerei*, the enthusiastic confusion of law and gospel. This confusion is an obvious and unfortunate aspect of some of the pronouncements on international questions made by Christians in our time. Here, too, Luther's counsel is certainly very much to the point in our own discussions.

And this evaluation applies certainly also to his conservatism. Here, again, Herbert Butterfield has made a very "Lutheran" observation. He says,

> Somewhere or other there exists a point at which our ambitions, however well-meaning, do become a defiance of the providential order. At that point there would be better hope for the world if we would try to see rather how to make the best of it, and accept some of our limitations and discomforts as the decree of Providence, lest by too feverish an activity we only make matters worse.[35]

Luther said, "To change is easy, to improve is troublesome and dangerous." This piece of practical advice could be of special benefit to an age which has shown a fantastic talent for bringing about changes in the map of the world without demonstrating any talent to bring about substantial improvements for the people of the world. The naive assumption that any change is an improvement is as false in the overthrow of governments as in the change of borders and the relocation of peoples. Here, too, Luther's conservatism might supply some counterbalance to the prevailing naive identification of change and betterment.

---

[34]Ibid., 66.
[35]Ibid., 135.

And finally, Luther seems to have suggested that politics in general and international politics in particular is the area where we ought to ask concerning every policy, "Does it work?" While absolute trust in God is basic to the Christian faith such absolute trust in international schemes and political panaceas is blasphemous and an offense against the First Commandment. "When a prince rules according to his own mad will...he is like a mad driver who rushes straight ahead with his horse and cart through bushes, hedges, ditches, streams, uphill and downdale, regardless of road and bridges."[36] In politics bushes and hedges, ditches and water, hills and valleys ought to be most carefully and patiently studied. Foreign policy in particular should concern itself most attentively with the building of roads and bridges. Here the questions, "What will work? What will reduce conflict? What is in the interest of all concerned?" are most important. They ought to be answered using all the resources of intelligence and imagination at our command. If we participate in this effort as actively and intelligently as we are able we will have the privilege to know that we are dancing in God's masquerade and that God uses us and others to guide the nations of the world to the goal which his providence has destined for them.

---

[36]*Treatise on Good Works,* LW 44:94-95.

Word & World
Supplement Series 2
1994

Luther's Theology and Domestic Politics

T HE AGE IN WHICH LUTHER LIVED AND WORKED WAS NOT ONLY A PERIOD OF far-reaching international conflicts but also vast domestic upheavals. This was especially true of Germany. In France or England the government of the country was in the hands of a king whose territory coincided with a region of considerable national and cultural homogeneity. In Germany, however, the effective rule was in the hands of princes whose territories were essentially the result of the accidents of inheritance. The frontiers of the territorial states of sixteenth-century Germany had little to do with language and culture or—at the beginning of the century—even with religion. They had come about by prudent marriages and sudden deaths and were more often the result of the fertility and resistance to disease of the ruling family than the economic and cultural interests of the people under its rule. Of the house of Habsburg, which had been particularly fertile and successful in its marital alliances it was said: *Bella gerant alii, tu felice Austria nube!*—Let the others fight wars, thou fortunate Austria get married! The purpose of the governments thus established, as far as the prince was concerned, was the maintenance and extension of his power. As far as the people were concerned a good government was one which guaranteed public safety and maintained law and order. None of these territorial princes represented the cultural and social reality of Germany. Thus the actual focus of political power in Luther's Germany was not some German Reich but rather units like Saxony and Württemberg, Bavaria and Austria, Brandenburg and the Palatinate. It cannot surprise us that the princes who governed these

---

The essay (originally titled, "Domestic Politics") is the third in a series from Luther and Culture *(Decorah, Iowa: Luther College Press, 1960), the published form of the 1959 "Luther Lectures." Here Dr. Forell investigates both Luther's views of Christian participation in political affairs (with particular reference to the "Peasants' War") and how Luther's insights might apply to life in the modern world.*

territories would attempt to benefit politically from the reformation and would try to use it for the extension and strengthening of their territorial power.

But while these territorial princes became increasingly the true power centers of the political life of Germany there remained other groups who did not want to recognize this development. Particularly the members of the lower nobility, the knights, felt that they had no political obligation towards the territorial princes. They dreamed nostalgically of the days of the Hohenstauffen emperors when the noble knights had been the support of the Holy Roman Empire. But the empire of the Hohenstauffen had vanished. The power of an emperor like Charles V rested on the fact of his own extensive territorial possessions. With the decline of the medieval empire the knights had become obsolete, without, however, fully realizing this fact. Unwilling to face the profound changes in their status they felt betrayed and in a mood of revolt. No wonder that they saw in the reformation with its revolt against the ecclesiastical status quo a movement which might be used for their political ends. It is not surprising that men like Ulrich von Hutten and Franz von Sickingen supported the reformation for political reasons.

A third group which had considerable political interests in the reformation were the free cities of Germany. Involved in a constant struggle for independence at first against the nobility, the robber barons who threatened the public safety necessary for successful trade, later against the territorial princes who jeopardized the political existence of the cities and attempted to incorporate them into their territories, they saw in the reformation a movement which might be used to support their claims for freedom. Among the burghers of these precariously free cities there were many adherents of Luther whose support was not entirely grounded in theology.

A fourth group which placed political as well as religious hopes in the reformation were some of the craftspeople, the weavers and miners, who found insufficient protection in the ancient guild system and whose prosperity was subject to extreme fluctuations in a rising capitalist society. They, too, hoped for some improvement of their fate through the victory of the reformation.

But the people who still made up the majority of Luther's contemporaries were the peasants. Restless for more than a hundred years, expressing their grievances in sporadic and abortive revolts, they now pinned all their hopes on political changes which the reformation would bring about. They expected that Luther's movement would free them from excessive taxes, end their serfdom, and give them all sorts of other rights ranging from the right to choose their own pastors to the right to fish and hunt.[1] All these hopes they connected with the open and free proclamation of the gospel. The reformation was for them as much a political as a religious movement.

It was against this background of complex political pressures which threatened to engulf the reformation that Luther was forced to develop and express his political views. He did this all during his life, but with particular clarity in his book

---

[1]Cf. *Admonition to Peace, A Reply to the Twelve Articles of the Peasants in Swabia* (1525), LW 46:8-43.

Temporal Authority: To What Extent it Should be Obeyed of 1523;[2] his writings in the Peasant War of 1525,[3] and the book *Whether Soldiers, Too, Can Be Saved* of 1526.[4] In all these writings he operates consistently with the distinction of the two ways of ruling which God has ordained, "the spiritual, by which the Holy Spirit produces Christians and righteous people under Christ," and the secular, "which restrains the un-Christians and wicked so that—no thanks to them—they are obliged to keep still and to maintain an outward peace."[5] Politics is obviously the realm of the law. It is the area in which God creates order through the sword. Even if people do not want to do what is right, and Luther was singularly free from illusions concerning the innate goodness of human beings, they are forced to it even against their will by the restraining arm of the law. Of course Luther knew as well as anybody that such law, even if rigidly enforced, does not make people good. He denounced all claims that through obedience to the law people could become Christians and be saved. But this did not mean that in the political life of the state such laws could not be of great usefulness. Even if people abstained from murder, raping, and robbing only because they were afraid of punishment, the ensuing situation was politically, if not morally, better than if people were allowed to show their hostility and agreed to their heart's content. We know that when we drive along the highway at considerable speed and a police car enters the stream of traffic we usually drive more slowly and with greater concern for the traffic laws. To be sure, the arrival of the police car has not made us morally better; nevertheless it has made our behavior safer both for ourselves and all other drivers on the road. It was this distinction between politically safer and morally better behavior which Luther saw so very clearly.

It is the task of political government to concern itself with order and law rather than with faith and salvation. While it is well equipped to attain a moderate success in achieving the former for its citizens, it is bound to fail utterly in the effort to secure faith and salvation for them.

Luther said,

> If anyone attempted to rule the world by the gospel and to abolish all temporal law and sword on the plea that all are baptized and Christian, and that, according to the gospel, there shall be among them no law or sword—or need for either— pray tell me, friend, what would he be doing? He would be loosing the ropes and chains of the savage wild beasts and letting them bite and mangle everyone, meanwhile insisting that they were harmless, tame, and gentle creatures.[6]

And a little later he continued:

> It is out of the question that there should be a common Christian government over the whole world, or indeed over a single country or any considerable body of people, for the wicked always outnumber the good. Hence, a man who would

[2]*LW* 45:81-129.
[3]*LW* 46:8-85.
[4]*LW* 46:93-137.
[5]*Temporal Authority, LW* 45:91.
[6]Ibid.

venture to govern an entire country or the world with the gospel would be like a shepherd who should put together in one fold wolves, lions, eagles, and sheep, and let them mingle freely wi th one another, saying, "Help yourselves, and be good and peaceful toward one another. The fold is open, there is plenty of food. You need have no fear of dogs and clubs." The sheep would doubtless keep the peace and allow themselves to be fed and governed peacefully, but they would not live long, nor would one beast survive another.[7]

Luther, therefore, is convinced that the secular government must be retained until the end of this world. In this world, "Christ's government does not extend over all men."[8] The great majority of people can only be kept in line by sanctions. Yet it is evident that

where temporal government or law alone prevails, there sheer hypocrisy is inevitable, even though the commandments be God's very own. For without the Holy Spirit in the heart no one becomes truly righteous, no matter how fine the work he does. On the other hand, where the spiritual government alone prevails over land and people, there wickedness is given free rein and the door is open for all manner of rascality, for the world as a whole cannot receive or comprehend it.[9]

Since the majority of people are not servants of Christ but rather serve the devil, even the very commandments of God will only serve to widen the gulf between them and their creator. Yet, even though these commandments will have no saving value for the unbeliever they will contribute to political order and peace. It is for the unbelievers that political rule is established. Christians, insofar as they are sinners and under the law, will also be under the restraining force of the political authorities. But insofar as they are Christians and under the gospel they do not need it. Nevertheless they will support and uphold government in order to aid those who depend upon it. Christians should do everything in their power to uphold the government, and this is as true for the Christian prince as for the Christian subject. To the ruler, Luther said:

A prince's duty is fourfold: First, toward God there must be true confidence and earnest prayer; second, toward his subjects there must be love and Christian service; third, with respect to his counselors and officials he must maintain an untrammeled reason and unfettered judgment; fourth, with respect to evildoers he must manifest a restrained severity and firmness.[10]

If a prince does his duty in this manner his life and work will be pleasing to God and to his subjects. But Luther does not promise the ruler that such obedience to God's will produces peace of mind and an easy life. On the contrary, it is the good ruler who "will have to expect much envy and sorrow on account of it; the cross will soon rest on the shoulders of such a prince."[11]

But what about the political duties of the subject? To them Luther said,

[7]Ibid., 91-92.
[8]Ibid., 92.
[9]Ibid.
[10]Ibid., 126.
[11]Ibid.

> You are under obligation to serve and assist the sword by whatever means you can, with body, goods, honor, and soul....Therefore, if you see that there is a lack of hangmen, constables, judges, lords, or princes, and you find that you are qualified, you should offer your services and seek the position, that the essential governmental authority may not be despised and become enfeebled or perish. The world cannot and dare not dispense with it.[12]

To those Christians who wanted to shirk their political responsibilities because Christ and the apostles did apparently not engage in political activities Luther said: "You tell me, why did Christ not take a wife, or become a cobbler or a tailor? If an office or vocation were to be regarded as disreputable on the ground that Christ did not pursue it himself, what would become of all the offices and vocations other the ministry, the one occupation he did follow?"[13] Politics is a legitimate occupation in which good people are needed. Luther was so keenly aware of the need for the most competent people available to serve God in politics that he said to the parents of gifted children:

> Indeed, there is need in this office for abler people than are needed in the office of preaching, so it is necessary to get the best boys for this work; for in the preaching office Christ does the whole thing, by his Spirit, but in the worldly kingdom men must act on the basis of reason—wherein the laws also have their origin—for God has subjected temporal rule and all of physical life to reason (Genesis 2 [:15]). He has not sent the Holy Spirit from heaven for this purpose.[14]

To the parents who refuse to give their youngsters an education which would qualify them for government service Luther says,

> You would have to be a gross, ungrateful clod, worthy of being numbered among the beasts, if you should see that your son could become a man to help the emperor preserve his empire, sword, and crown; to help protect so many men's bodies, wives, children, property, and honor—and yet would not risk enough on it to let him study and come to such a position.[15]

Again Luther's political realism is obvious. Sound government is the result of competent, well-trained people in key positions. Luther had as little patience with inspired enthusiasts in politics as in theology. What politics needs is expertly trained people who know what they are doing. Commenting on Deut 1:13 ff. he said,

> You see, therefore, that in divine Law no account is taken of the rich, powerful, noble, strong, and friendly, for handling public office, as is the custom of the world; but of the wise, understanding, and experienced, even if they are poor, lowly, weak, etc.[16]

He quoted the Emperor Maximilian with approval who when his nobles complained that he used so many commoners as negotiators in international

---

[12]Ibid., 95.

[13]Ibid., 100.

[14]*A Sermon on Keeping Children in School* (1530), LW 46:242.

[15]Ibid., 241.

[16]*Lectures on Deuteronomy* (1525), LW 9:19.

affairs, said, "What else can I do? You [lords] cannot be used, so I have to take writers." And the same emperor said, according to Luther, "I can make knights, but I can't make doctors."[17]

Because the art of government demands experts Luther advocated careful education for those who would assume political responsibility. He praised a nobleman who had once said to him, "I want my son to study. It takes no great skill to hang two legs over a horse and become a knight; in fact I taught him that myself already."[18] Yet even if occasionally a nobleman might feel like that, Luther was sure that in the long run the effective administration of government would be in the hands of the poor and the commoners, for they alone would furnish the trained people to fill these offices.[19] He arrived at this conclusion not because he believed in the superiority of this particular class of human beings but because his analysis of the situation led him to believe that the rich were too much interested in wealth to give their children the necessary education to qualify them for a profession in which there was little financial reward. It was not the hope for a revolution of the lower classes but his realism concerning human nature which led him to the prediction that the common people would eventually rule.

Indeed, nothing could be further from Luther's thought than the advocacy of any kind of revolution. Even before he had some depressing first-hand experiences with the nature of revolution during the Peasant War he rejected the notion that a revolution could ever be justified. In 1522 he wrote *A Sincere Admonition to All Christians, to Guard against Insurrection and Rebellion.*[20] Here he said that insurrection

> is still an unprofitable method of procedure. It never brings about the desired result. For insurrection lacks discernment; it generally harms the innocent more than the guilty. Hence, no insurrection is ever right, no matter how right the cause it seeks to promote. It always results in more damage than improvement, and verifies the saying, "Things go from bad to worse."[21]

This is perhaps the most widely advertised aspect of Luther's political thought, and it is certainly incontrovertible that he was rigid in his rejection of any kind of political rebellion. The reasons which he gave were many.

First, and according to Luther, sufficient reason for all Christians, government is divinely ordained. He repeatedly quoted Rom 13:1 ff. and 1 Pet 2:13 to make it very clear that, "The authority (*Gewalt*) which everywhere exists has been ordained by God. He then who resists the governing authority resists the ordinance of God."[22] But while Luther felt that this divine command should be sufficient reason for Christians to obey the government and to cooperate with it to the best of their ability, he also realized that if a government was tyrannical and the

[17]*On Keeping Children in School* (1530), LW 46:249.
[18]Ibid.
[19]Ibid., 251.
[20]LW 45:57-74.
[21]Ibid., 62.
[22]*Temporal Authority*, LW 45:85-86.

ruler a truly evil person, the subjects might feel justified in revolting on the grounds of reason and natural law. But Luther grants this right to revolt only in one case. He says,

> It is only right that if a prince, king, or lord becomes insane, he should be deposed and put under restraint, for he is not to be considered a man since his reason is gone. "That is true," you say, "and a raving tyrant is also insane; he is to be considered as even worse than an insane man, for he does much more harm." It will be a little difficult for me to respond to that statement, for that argument seems very impressive and seems to be in agreement with justice and equity. Nevertheless, it is my opinion that madmen and tyrants are not the same. A madman can neither do nor tolerate anything reasonable, and there is no hope for him because the light of reason has gone out. A tyrant, however, may do things that are far worse than the insane man does, but he still knows that he is doing wrong. He still has a conscience and his faculties. There is also hope that he may improve and permit someone to talk to him and instruct him and follow this advice. We can never hope that an insane man will do this for he is like a clod or a stone.[23]

Luther claims that as long as a legitimate ruler is essentially a human being, which he defines as those who know the difference between right and wrong, even if they actually do wrong, revolution is not a proper remedy against tyranny. And in addition to this basic theological reason for rejecting revolution he offers a number of non-theological considerations. Once we grant the right of tyrannicide, he says, who is going to decide who is a tyrant? Human beings tend to call anybody who does not please them a tyrant. Does that mean that we can kill any ruler we do not like? The history of the Roman Empire furnishes Luther with numerous illustrations for the debilitating effects of such political murder. It shows that the Romans "killed many a fine emperor simply because they did not like him or he did not do what they wanted, that is, let them be lords and make him their fool."[24]

> If injustice is to be suffered, then it is better for subjects to suffer it from their rulers than for the rulers to suffer it from their subjects. The mob neither has any moderation nor even knows what moderation is. And every person in it has more than five tyrants hiding in him. Now it is better to suffer wrong from one tyrant, that is, from the ruler, than from unnumbered tyrants, that is, from the mob.[25]

Luther does not deny that revolts against rulers have been successful in the past. He says,

> I know well enough...of subjects deposing and exiling or killing their rulers. The Jews, the Greeks, and the Romans all did this and God permitted it and even let these nations grow and prosper in spite of it. However, the final outcome was always tragic....I feel there can be no stable government unless a nation respects and honors its rulers.[26]

If rulers are tyrannical—and Luther is convinced that they usually are unfair

---

[23]*Whether Soldiers, Too, Can Be Saved*, LW 46:105.
[24]Ibid.
[25]Ibid., 106.
[26]Ibid., 106-107.

and unjust—the punishment rests in God's hand. No punishment human beings devise can possibly equal God's punishment.[27] God can kill an evil ruler in an instant, if that is his will: "He has fire, water, iron, stone, and countless ways of killing. How quickly he can kill a tyrant!"[28] If he chooses not to do it, Luther claims, that may be because of our sins. Quoting Job 4:30, he says, "'He permits a knave to rule because of the people's sins.' We have no trouble seeing that a scoundrel is ruling. However, no one wants to see that he is ruling not because he is a scoundrel, but because of the people's sin."[29] Indeed, Luther is prepared to grant that God may even use a revolution to overthrow and punish a ruler. But while such a revolution may actually accomplish God's purpose, those who engage in it are personally disobeying God. Yet Luther warns that rulers should not rest at ease in their tyrannical ways because of his teaching. It is not Luther's teaching but only God's will which still upholds them. "The lords are just as secure because of our teaching," he says, "as they are without it...since most of the crowd does not listen to us. The preservation of the rulers whom God has appointed is a matter that rests with God and in his hands alone."[30]

Nothing, perhaps, illustrates Luther's matter-of-fact conservatism towards government better than a story which he tells in his book *Whether Soldiers, Too, Can Be Saved.*

> We read of a widow who stood and prayed for her tyrant most devoutly, asking God to give him long life, etc. The tyrant heard it and was astonished because he knew very well that he had done her much harm, and that this was not the usual prayer for tyrants. People do not ordinarily pray such prayers for tyrants, so he asked her why she prayed thus for him. She answered, "I had ten cows when your grandfather lived and ruled. He took two of them and I prayed that he might die and that your father might become lord. This is what happened, and your father took three cows. I prayed again that you might become lord, and that your father might die. Now you have taken four cows, and so I am praying for you, for now I am afraid that your successor will take the last cow and everything I have."[31]

This is not an ideological conservatism which praises the good old days. Neither the old days nor the new days are good in themselves. Luther is politically conservative because he is sure that change does not imply improvement. Things can get worse as well as better. His own political experience tempted him to believe that changes promoted by enthusiastic political dreamers will make things worse rather than better. What he had seen in the Peasant War had convinced him that nothing could cause more damage in the political life of a people than the wild ranting of agitators of the type of Thomas Müntzer. Not only had they spilled much blood, but when it was all over the situation of the people whose interests these revolutionaries claimed to promote was much worse than it had ever been

[27]Ibid.
[28]Ibid., 109.
[29]Ibid.
[30]Ibid., 110.
[31]Ibid., 111.

before. While blasphemously claiming the sword of Gideon for their cause they had not led their followers into any promised land but rather into a captivity from which they were not to escape for centuries.

It cannot be denied that Luther's experience in the Peasant War played an important part in the final shape of his political thinking. Furthermore, Luther's political thought has often been interpreted exclusively in the light of his utterances in connection with this revolutionary upheaval. Thus no examination of his views on domestic politics would be complete without an examination of his position in this greatest political crisis of his lifetime. It appears that in the three successive periods of this conflict Luther tried to apply his political principles with admirable consistency. He spoke to the peasants before the hostilities really began.[32] He spoke again while the conflict seemed to go the peasants' way and threatened to bring about the complete destruction of the established order.[33] And he spoke once more when the revolt had suddenly and utterly collapsed and the peasants were suffering cruel and inhuman punishment from their victorious lords.[34]

From the beginning Luther objected strenuously to the claim of the peasants that they were fighting for the freedom of the gospel. He insisted that they were confusing God's kingdom and their own doubtful utopia. Against their article, "There shall be no serfs, for Christ has made all men free," Luther wrote,

> That is making Christian freedom a completely physical matter....A slave can be a Christian, and have Christian freedom, in the same way that a prisoner or a sick man is a Christian and yet not free. This article would make all men equal, and turn the spiritual kingdom of Christ into a worldly, external kingdom; and that is impossible.[35]

He warned them even then,

> You speak in this article as though you were already lords in the land and had taken all the property of the rulers for your own and would be no one's subjects, and would give nothing. This shows what your intention really is. Stop it, dear sirs, stop it! It will not be you who puts an end to it! The chapters of Scripture which your lying preacher and false prophet has smeared on the margin do not help you at all; they are against you.[36]

But this warning probably did not even reach the peasants. The printing presses of the sixteenth century could not keep up with the rush of revolutionary events. On a journey from Eisleben Luther came in personal contact with the rebellion and became convinced that unless the government would act with authority complete chaos and anarchy would destroy all political order. This reaction of Luther becomes understandable if one remembers the almost complete loss of nerve on the part of most of the political authorities. The rulers were in a state of shock. Especially

---

[32]*Admonition to Peace* (April 20 [?], 1525), *LW* 46:8-43.

[33]*Against the Robbing and Murdering Hordes of Peasants* (May 4 [?], 1525), *LW* 46:49-55.

[34]*An Open Letter on the Harsh Book against the Peasants* (July, 1525), *LW* 46:63-85.

[35]*Admonition to Peace*, *LW* 46:39.

[36]Ibid., 38.

Luther's own prince, Frederick the Wise, suggested shortly before his death that negotiations with the peasants would be the only possible solution. Many were thinking of yielding to the increasing size of the peasant armies. Leonhard von Eck, a Bavarian counselor, observed that the peasants might indeed succeed because of the complete despondency of the forces of law and order. In April of 1525 he wrote: "So far I have seen nothing more terrifying than the unbelievable faint-heartedness of all authorities."[37] It was into this situation that Luther wrote his call to arms *Against the Robbing and Murdering Hordes of Peasants.* This is no longer an admonition to peace, it is a call to the government to use its God-given sword. The revolting peasants are perjurers who have broken their oath of loyalty, they are rebels, and rebellion is the worst of all crimes.

> For rebellion is not just simple murder; it is like a great fire, which attacks and devastates a whole land. Thus rebellion brings with it a land filled with murder and bloodshed; it makes widows and orphans, and turns everything upside down, like the worst disaster. Therefore let everyone who can, smite, slay, and stab, secretly or openly, remembering that nothing can be more poisonous, hurtful, or devilish than a rebel. It is just as when one must kill a mad dog; if you do not strike him, he will strike you, and a whole land with you.[38]

And what is worst these peasants blaspheme Christ.

> They cloak this terrible and horrible sin with the gospel....Thus, they become the worst blasphemers of God and slanderers of his holy name. Under the outward appearance of the gospel, they honor and serve the devil, thus deserving death in body and soul ten times over.[39]

Luther had little hope that his call would be heard. He knew that should the rebellious peasants be victorious he would have to pay for his book with his life. On May 4, 1525, he wrote to John Rühel, the counselor of Count Albert of Mansfeld, from Seeburg, while on the way back from Eisleben to Wittenberg,

> Well, if I get home I shall prepare for death with God's help, and await my new lords, the murderers and robbers, who tell me they will not harm anyone. They are like the highway robber who said to the good coachman: "I shall do you no harm, but give me all you have and drive where I tell you; and if you don't you will die!" Beautiful innocence! How magnificently the devil decorates himself and his murderers! But I would rather lose my neck a hundred times than approve of and justify the peasants' actions; may God help me with his grace to do this....I am writing this so that you may be comforted and can comfort others, especially my gracious lord, Count Albrecht. Encourage His Grace to continue courageously, to entrust this matter to God, and to act according to God's divine command in using the sword for as long as he can. For the conscience is on firm ground in this case, even if one has to perish for it. On the other hand, even if the peasants served God's wrath in punishing and destroying the sovereigns, God would nevertheless reward them with the fire of hell.[40]

---

[37]Karl Brandi, *Deutsche Geschichte im Zeitalter der Reformation und Gegenreformation*, 2nd ed. (Leipzig: Koehler and Amelang, 1941) 160f.

[38]*LW* 46:50.

[39]Ibid., 50-51.

[40]*Luther to John Rühel* (May 4, 1525), *LW* 49:111.

Luther considered the extirpation of the princes and his own execution by the victorious peasants a distinct possibility. In this situation he wrote his angry pamphlet. Not because it would win him favor with the princes did he speak up, but because he firmly believed that it was his duty to speak up even should it cost him his life. It is the same Luther who stood against pope and emperor, who when the power of the rebellious peasants was at its peak defied them fearlessly. His language may have been overly sharp, but so was his language in all other controversies. While we may not agree with his sentiments and especially with the aggressive way in which he expressed them, they were consistent with everything he had said before and was to say afterwards. In the light of what happened to the peasants later it is easy for us to say that Luther should have known that the peasants never had a chance. With his call to war against the peasants he was beating a dead horse. Perhaps this is correct. Probably the peasants never did have a real chance. But for the evaluation of Luther's part in the Peasant War such an observation is irrelevant. He obviously believed that the rebels might win and so did some of the best informed politicians in Saxony. Because he believed this, Luther made every effort to make sure that they would not. But before Luther's angry appeal could be widely distributed the tide had turned and the peasants were in full flight. In April the revolutionary leader Thomas Müntzer had written to the members of his former congregation in Allstedt, "Attack, Attack, Attack! The time has come. The evildoers are cowed like dogs....Pay no attention to the misery of the godless! Indeed they will humbly plead and snivel and implore you like children. Show no mercy....Do not let your swords grow cold!"[41] On May 14, he stood with about 8000 peasants at Frankenhausen. In a few hours the peasants were utterly routed by a princely army of about 1000 calvary and 3000 footsoldiers. After the battle Müntzer was captured hiding in bed in the attic of a house in Frankenhausen. A few days later he was dead. By the end of May 1525 the Peasant War in the neighborhood of Wittenberg was over. But the bloodbath among the defeated peasants had only begun. As cowardly as the nobility and the princes had been as long as the peasants were armed, so courageous they became once they were defeated. They made up in the cruelty of the punishment of their defenseless foes what they had lacked in wisdom and foresight. In view of these excesses of the rulers many of Luther's friends turned to him to speak against this abuse of their victory. For Luther's sharp attack against the peasants, written while the rebellion threatened to succeed, was receiving wide circulation after the peasants were defeated and helpless.

Luther responded to these requests in his *An Open Letter on the Harsh Book Against the Peasants* of 1525. Here he reiterates his utter rejection of all rebellion. He does not apologize for what he has previously written. "The peasants would not listen," he says; "they would not let anyone tell them anything, so their ears must now be unbuttoned with musket balls till their heads jump off their shoulders.

---

[41]Otto H. Brandt, *Thomas Müntzer, Sein Leben und seine Schriften* (Jena, 1933) 74f.

Such pupils need such a rod."[42] He attributes the entire revolt and its tragic consequences to the confusion of law and gospel, of the kingdom of wrath and severity and the kingdom of grace and mercy.[43]

> Now he who would confuse these two kingdoms—as our false fanatics do— would put wrath into God's kingdom and mercy into the world's kingdom; and that is the same as putting the devil in heaven and God in hell. These sympathiz- ers with the peasants would like to do both of these things. First they wanted to go to work with the sword, fight for the gospel as "Christian brethren," and kill other people, who were supposed to be merciful and patient. Now that the kingdom of the world has overcome them, they want to have mercy in it.[44]

Luther rejects this confusion of the two kingdoms categorically. Indeed, he says, the severity of the world's kingdom is one of God's blessings.

> Suppose I have a wife and children, a house, servants, and property, and a thief or murderer fell upon me, killed me in my own house, ravished my wife and children, took all that I had, and went unpunished so that he could do the same thing again, when he wished. Tell me, who would be more in need of mercy in such a case, I or the thief and murderer? Without doubt it would be I who would need most that people should have mercy on me. But how can this mercy be shown to me and my poor, miserable wife and children, except by restraining such a scoundrel, and by protecting me and maintaining my rights, or, if he will not be restrained and keeps it up, by giving him what he deserves and punishing him, so that he must stop it? What a fine mercy to me it would be, to have mercy on the thief and murderer, and let him kill, abuse, and rob me![45]

This story illustrates that Luther is concerned that a false sentimentality in regard to the function of the political order will prevent it from its primary responsibility, the maintenance of law and order. Mercy to murderers is cruelty to those they are about to murder. It will only lead to more crimes and create chaos in the kingdom of this world.

But what about the excesses of the princes? Here Luther does not mince words either. If the princes are abusing their power, "they have not learned it from me; and they will have their reward. For the Supreme Judge, who is using them to punish the self-willed peasants, has not forgotten them either, and they will not escape Him."[46] Luther asserted that he had written his book against the peasants for princes who wanted to be instructed concerning their God-given duties from the word of God. They were to fight courageously as long as the rebellion was going on. "Afterward, however, if they won, they were to show grace, not only to those whom they considered innocent, but to the guilty as well."[47]

And Luther shows the same toughness of mind towards the victorious princes that he had shown towards the victorious peasants. He says,

[42]LW 46:65.
[43]Ibid., 69ff.
[44]Ibid., 70.
[45]Ibid., 71.
[46]Ibid., 74.
[47]Ibid., 84.

But these furious, raving, senseless tyrants, who even after the battle cannot get their fill of blood, and in all their lives ask scarcely a question about Christ—these I did not undertake to instruct. It makes no difference to these bloody dogs whether they slay the guilty or the innocent, whether they please God or the devil....I had two fears. If the peasants became lords, the devil would become abbot; but if these tyrants became lords, the devil's mother would become abbess. Therefore, I wanted to do two things: quiet the peasants, and instruct the pious lords. The peasants were unwilling to listen, and now they have their reward; the lords, too, will not hear, and they shall have their reward also. However, it would have been a shame if they had been killed by the peasants; that would have been too easy a punishment for them. Hell-fire, trembling, and gnashing of teeth in hell will be their reward eternally, unless they repent.[48]

The attitude of Luther here expressed at the very moment the princes had been victorious hardly qualifies him as a sycophant. Neither does the remark which he made a year later when overcome by the thought of the cruelty of some of the noble Junkers against the defenseless peasants; he exclaimed bitterly, "We Germans are and remain Germans, that is, swine and senseless beasts."[49]

Even in the great and bitter struggle of the Peasant War Luther's political utterances were guided by his consistent adherence to the distinction between the two ways of ruling which God has ordained for the world, the spiritual, which under Christ makes Christians, and the secular, which restrains the un-Christian and evil people so that they are compelled to keep peace, even against their will. To Luther the Peasant War illustrated the disaster which must result when these two kingdoms are confounded. Far from being the result of his preaching, as some of his enemies claimed, he felt that the conflict was evidence how very few had really listened to what he had to say.

If we now try to ask what, if anything, in Luther's views on domestic politics is of lasting significance, the answer is not easy. The territorial princes, the noble knights, the wealthy burghers, and the poor peasants to whom he spoke have long since disappeared. We live in a democracy which is based on a successful revolution and most of us are glad that "under God the people rule" and that the revolution did succeed. What in Luther's political teachings, addressed to an entirely different situation, can possibly have any meaning for us?

There are at least four such teachings which seem to speak as clearly and accurately to our time as they did to sixteenth-century Saxony. First of all, the proper concern of government is the earthly welfare of all. We must insist, with Luther, that the government trespasses demonically if it meddles with a person's faith, whether that be in Spain, promoting one particular form of Christianity, in the Soviet world, interfering with all religion, or in the USA, encouraging a religion of democracy in the schools of the land. Luther said, "The temporal government has laws which extend no further than to life and property and external affairs on earth, for God cannot and will not permit anyone but himself to rule over the

---

[48]Ibid.
[49]*Whether Soldiers, Too, Can Be Saved*, LW 46:101.

soul."[50] In an age when the power of government to influence the popular mind has reached proportions unthinkable in Luther's time, it becomes even more essential that every effort of political government to regulate the faith of its citizens be immediately and radically opposed.

Secondly, Christians as Christian citizens are called to support the government in its proper work, the promotion of the earthly welfare of all, to the best of their ability. Luther said, "If you find that you are qualified, you should offer your services...that the essential governmental authority may not be despised and become enfeebled or perish. For the world cannot and dare not dispense with it."[51] If this exhortation was justified in the patriarchal society of Luther's time it is infinitely more urgent in a democracy. Unless people who want to serve the neighbor through their participation in the work of the government volunteer for such offices they will of necessity fall into the hands of those who will use political power for personal gain. Political participation is not optional for Christians, it is their God-given duty. Not, to be sure, in order to make the world Christian, but rather to serve the neighbor in love. The neglect of the duty of active political participation by so many Lutherans in America is not only a reflection on their loyalty to Luther, but what is far more important, it is a sad reflection on their loyalty to Christ. As it is the duty of Christians to feed the hungry and to visit the sick, it is their duty to do everything in their power to contribute to the earthly welfare of all by political means. Especially in a democracy this responsibility is obvious. And the Lord will hold us no less responsible for our failure to use our political opportunities to serve the neighbor than for our failures to serve him in the neighbor in the more obvious forms of service mentioned in Matthew 25: "I was hungry and you gave me food, I was thirsty and you gave me drink, I was a stranger and you welcomed me, I was naked and you clothed me, I was sick and you visited me. I was in prison and you came to me." This description covers practically every constructive political activity in which we might engage. It implies concern with slums and education, health and immigration, food surpluses and prison-reform.

Thirdly, in order to accomplish these ends the government needs competent and well-educated people. Luther insisted that Christians ought to see to it that their children receive the education which will qualify them for competent government service. It is not enough to know how to complain about the failures of government; one must learn how to help. With the complexity of modern government the need for qualified civil servants has greatly increased. Government still needs lawyers and soldiers as in Luther's time, but now in addition it needs thousands of other specialists. Christians have the duty to help train and furnish them. Good intentions and sincerity are not enough. People are needed who have technical training and skill. We ought to do our share to supply and to elect such people.

[50]*Temporal Authority*, LW 45:105.
[51]Ibid., 95.

Fourthly, Luther never tired of teaching the ultimate mercy of strict law-enforcement. Against all the sentimental drivel which advocated easy-going law-enforcement as an especially Christian attitude on the part of government Luther insisted that such an approach will only lead to great bloodshed and eventual disaster.

He felt that if the princes had enforced the law justly and firmly at the very beginning of the Peasant War much suffering could have been avoided and the situation of princes and peasants would have been far better than it was after the disastrous revolt. In the USA, where in some of our big cities law-enforcement has become a cruel joke and gangsters help select judges and openly consort with police officials, we should take Luther more seriously. When a parole-board paroles habitual criminals, loses track of them for months, and only recovers them after they have been arrested for murder, then the alleged mercy of the parole-board is a horrible kind of cruelty. Luther knew that fair and firm law-enforcement is the basis of good government. In American cities where people are afraid to go out after dark, Luther's views have certainly not become obsolete. They should be taken seriously.

And finally, Luther claimed that people tend to have the government they deserve. Such a claim might have been debatable in Luther's time, it is self-evident in our age. Every criticism of our government should be understood as an implicit criticism of ourselves. We have the government we deserve. God has a way of punishing us through our own choices. This should teach us to begin the critical national self-examination with ourselves and work our way up, rather than to start with our leaders and never critically examine ourselves. Luther said that God let the knave rule because of the sins of the people. Especially in a democracy we can never disassociate ourselves from political corruption, for in a very real sense you and I are the basic cause of the corruption. Once we have understood this, a great deal more realism will enter our political thinking. Here, too, Luther is still a helpful guide.

Luther once claimed that since the time of the apostles the secular sword and secular government had never been so clearly described or highly exalted as by him.[52] Our examination has tended to bear out this claim. In his political writings he did not only speak to his time but also developed certain principles which may help Christians in our time to come to a clearer understanding of their political duties.

---

[52]*Whether Soldiers, Too, Can Be Saved*, LW 46:95.

Word & World
Supplement Series 2
1994

Luther and the
War against the Turks

MODERN PSYCHOANALYSIS TELLS US THAT DISEASE IS THE TOUCHSTONE OF THE healthy mind. What is true in the realm of psychology is not less true in the realm of ethics. The most terrible disease in the realm of human relations is war, and so we can say that war is the touchstone of a healthy ethical system. In its attitude toward war the weakness of an ethical system is revealed. In the war situation an ethical system is revealed as basically unrealistic if it proves unwilling to face the actual situation and therefore uses the escape of absolute pacifism. It is revealed as basically immoral if it condones any war to such an extent that it loses sight of sin and injustice and makes of that war a holy war or a crusade.

Because the attitude toward war growing out of an ethical system has peculiar significance, it is of considerable value to study Luther's attitude toward the war against the Turks. His attitude as expressed here will throw some light upon his theological presuppositions and will serve to illustrate his ethical system.

However, little has been written in regard to Luther's position in the war against the Turks. There are few studies of the subject and not one in English.[1] Yet the war against the Turks formed the colorful background of the reformation.

In the early years of the reformation, the Turkish danger had constantly increased. Large parts of southeastern Europe were under Turkish rule. After the sudden death of Selim I in 1520, Suleiman II became his successor. Some had

---

[1]During the recent war [World War II. Ed.], a German, Helmut Lamparter, in *Luthers Stellung zum Türkenkrieg* (Munich: Evangelischer Verlag Albert Lempp, 1940), has examined Luther's position in the war against the Turk. He is especially interested to prove Luther's absolute disavowal of military crusades.

Forell wrote this essay while working on a masters degree at Princeton. It first appeared in Church History *14 (1945) 256-271. This piece explores Luther's attitude toward Christian social ethics, war, and vocation. On this basis, Forell analyzes why Luther approved of the imperial call to arms, even though it was against Lutheran self-interest to do so.*

hoped that he would rest on the laurels of his predecessor, but such hopes failed to materialize. On the contrary, while Selim I had fought his major battles against Egypt in Africa, Suleiman had his hands free to attack Hungary, the southeastern bulwark of christendom. In 1521 he captured Belgrade, and in the battle of Mohacz of 1526, he routed the Hungarian army. King Louis II was killed and all Europe lay open to the victorious Turkish armies.

Ferdinand of Austria suddenly realized that his country was the next objective of the advancing enemy. He tried to appease the sultan with diplomacy. Sending ambassadors to the Turks, he offered peace and a "good neighbor policy." But the ambassadors returned with the disquieting message that Suleiman expected to discuss the matter personally with the Archduke of Austria—and in Vienna.

Small wonder that not only Austria, but Christian Europe in general, were terror-stricken. It was at that time that Luther published his first major statement in regard to the Turkish danger. It appeared in 1529 under the title *On War against the Turk,* and was written to counteract the prevalent opinion that Luther considered the war against the Turks a war against God. This impression of Luther's position had been fostered by the notorious papal bull, *Exsurge Domine,* in which Pope Leo X had condemned Luther's theses as heretical. In his fifth thesis, Luther had said that the pope cannot remit any other punishments than those which he or canon law had imposed.[2] He had claimed that the pope cannot remit God's punishments. And in his defense of the *Ninety-five Theses* of 1518, he had tried to make his point even more emphatic and had added that if the pope was as well able to remit divine punishment as he claimed, he should stop the advance of the Turk.[3] Luther said that everyone must indeed be a poor Christian who does not know that the Turks are a punishment from God, and invited the pope to stop that punishment.[4]

The pope had countered by condemning as heretical the following sentence of Luther: "To fight against the Turks is to fight against God's visitation upon our iniquities."[5] In this misleading form, Luther's attitude toward the war against the Turks had been widely publicized. This had given the general impression that Luther considered a war against the Turks sinful and preferred the rule of the Turks to the rule of the emperor.

Luther had to answer this accusation. He did that in a detailed reassertion of all the articles condemned by Pope Leo X.[6] In regard to the Turks, he said that unless the pope were put in his place, all attempts to defeat the Turks would prove futile. The wrath of the Lord would continue to be upon all christendom as long as

[2]LW 31:26.
[3]*Explanations of the Ninety-five Theses,* LW 31:77-252.
[4]Ibid.
[5]*Bulla Exsurge Domine,* June 15, 1520: "Proeliari adversus Turcas est repugnare Deo visitanti iniquitates nostras."
[6]*Assertio omnium articulorum M. Lutheri per Bullam Leonis X novissimam damnatorum* (1520), WA 7:94.

Christian nations continued to honor those most Turkish of all Turks, even the Romanists.[7]

But this answer merely showed that Luther's pronouncements in regard to the Turks were not a defense of the Turks but an attack against the pope. It had not clarified his own attitude toward the increasing Turkish danger. Luther did not want the pope to lead christendom in a war against the sultan, but did that mean that he felt that such a war in itself should not be waged? Such an attitude was not uncommon.[8] Was it also Luther's attitude?

Realizing the importance of Luther's position in this matter, friends urged him for years to write somewhat extensively on the subject. Finally, in January of 1529, he published the above-mentioned book *On War against the Turk.*[9] It could not have appeared at a more opportune moment. On October 9, 1528, Luther had written the introduction to the book and dedicated it to Philip, Landgrave of Hesse. Here he wrote the almost prophetic words: "And now that the Turk is actually approaching." It was not half a year later, May, 1529, that Suleiman actually left Constantinople. In the autumn of the same year, the Turkish army reached the outskirts of Vienna and encircled the city. It seemed that Vienna was doomed. Luther heard of the siege of Vienna on his way home from the Marburg colloquy. It was in Marburg that his attention had been called by Myconius to certain sayings of a Franciscan monk. This monk, Johannes Hilten, had predicted the Turkish danger on the basis of certain prophecies in the book of Daniel.[10] Luther was impressed and worried. He now began to believe that the book of Daniel might throw some light on the contemporary trials of christendom. It was under the impact of this information and of the siege of Vienna that he decided to write another book dealing with the Turkish danger. Before this plan could be executed, Luther heard with relief that Suleiman and his army had retreated from Vienna. Yet he felt that the repetition of a Turkish advance had to be avoided. In order to do his part in calling the attention of all people to the Turkish danger, he wrote his *Call to War against the Turk.*[11] Basing his position upon an investigation of Daniel 7, Luther tried to explain to his German countrymen the Turkish danger in all its seriousness.

But Luther's writings of the year 1529 were not his only writings that dealt with the Turkish danger. Many years later, in 1541, when the Turks were again threatening the empire, the Elector of Saxony asked Luther to write to all the

---

[7]Ibid., *WA* 7:141, line 24: "Qui habet aures audiendi, audiat et Bello Turchico abstineat, donec Papae nomen sub caelo valet" [He who has ears for hearing, let him hear and let him avoid the Turkish War as long as the name of Pope is strong under heaven]; see also, *WA* 7:141, line 7: "Et in iis omnibus non est aversus furor domini, nec dum intelligimus manum dei, percutientis nos in corpore et anima per hos Romanos Turcissimos Turcas" [And in all these matters the anger of the Lord is not remote, not as long as we understand that the hand of God is smiting us in body and spirit through these Romanists, these most Turkish of Turks].

[8]*Luther to Jacob Probst* (November 10, 1529), *WA, Br* 5:175, line 7.

[9]*LW* 46:155-205.

[10]*Friedrich Myconius to Luther* (December 2, 1529), *WA, Br* 5:191.

[11]*Eine Heerpredigt widder den Türcken* (1529), *WA* 30/2:160-197.

ministers in his domain to exhort them and their people to constant prayer because of the imminent danger threatening from the Turks. Luther did that in his *Appeal for Prayer against the Turks*.[12]

Besides these three major works, there are numerous references to the war against the Turks all through Luther's writings. He was so concerned with the Turkish problem that in 1530 he wrote a preface to a little book by a Dominican monk who had spent more than twenty years in a Turkish prison. This book dealt with the religion and customs of the Muslims and was Luther's main source of information on the subject.[13]

All these writings of Luther indicate quite clearly his grave concern with the danger that threatened Christianity from the Muslim world. More than most of his contemporaries, Luther realized what was involved in war or in pacifistic non-resistance against the Turks.

This is the more remarkable in the light of the actual historical situation. Instead of fearing the Turks, Luther had every reason to be grateful to them. It was the constant danger of a Turkish invasion that had kept the emperor from taking severe measures against Luther's reformation. The empire needed the help of the Evangelical princes in the war against the Turks and therefore had to postpone its plans to destroy Luther. From the point of view of realistic power politics, the safety of the reformation depended upon the strength of the Turkish armies. From many points of view the sultan and Luther might have been political allies.

That Luther was aware of this fact is best illustrated by a little episode reported in the *Table Talk*. At one time, Luther was informed by a member of an imperial mission to the Turkish sultan that Suleiman had been very much interested in Luther and his movement and had asked the ambassadors Luther's age. When they had told him that Luther was forty-eight years old, he had said, "I wish he were even younger; he would find in me a gracious protector." But hearing that report, Luther, not being a realistic politician, made the sign of the cross and said, "May God protect me from such a gracious protector."[14]

Although by all rules of strategy and power politics Luther and the Turks should have been allies, Luther urged war against the Turks. What was the reason?

I. THE DANGER

Luther's position concerning the Turks was determined by study of the Bible. It was Luther's intention to instruct the consciences of Christians on the basis of a study of scripture. He wanted them to learn "what we must know about the Turk and who he is according to Scripture."[15] According to scripture, the Turks were dangerous. Luther's attitude was not based upon political speculation in regard to a balance of powers. It was not based upon his desire to preserve a so-called

[12]*LW* 43:213-241.

[13]*Vorwort zu dem Libellus de ritu et moribus Turcorum* (1530), WA 30/2:205.

[14]*WA, TR* 2:508, line 22.

[15]*Eine Heerpredigt widder den Türcken*, WA 30/2:161, line 31.

Christian civilization. He thought very little of the Christian civilization of his time. Luther's position in regard to the Turks was the result of a thorough study of scripture and especially of those passages that seemed to point to the Turkish danger. Before Luther spoke about the Turks, he had first obediently listened to the word of God.

What was the message of scripture in regard to the Turks? First of all, they were the rod of punishment that God was sending. In his *Explanations of the Ninety-five Theses*,[16] Luther had called the Turk the rod of punishment of the wrath of God. He had said that, by means of the Turks, God punishes christendom for its contempt of the gospel. Pope Leo and his courtiers had tried to use this statement to imply that Luther lacked patriotism and claimed divine sanction for the Turkish sword. In spite of this misrepresentation, Luther repeated in 1529 what he had said before: "Because Germany is so full of evil and blasphemy, nothing else can be expected. We must suffer punishment if we do not repent and stop the persecution of the Gospel."[17] And he reiterated later that as long as the Christian world refuses to repent, it will not be successful in its wars, for the Lord fights against it.[18] Here Luther stood courageously in the prophetic tradition. With the prophets, he realized that God can and does use heathen nations in order to punish the so-called Christian nations for their unfaithfulness.

But Luther looked at the Turks from still another point of view. For him, they were not only the rod of punishment of the wrath of God, but also the servants and saints of the devil.[19] What did he mean by that? This combination of the rod of punishment of the wrath of God with the servants and saints of the devil throws some light upon Luther's peculiar conception of the devil. For Luther the devil was always God's devil, i.e., in attempting to counteract God the devil ultimately serves God. The Turks were the servants and saints of this devil. Why did Luther call them saints?

Luther had read a number of books concerning Islam, and he was aware of the fact that in many respects the Muslims lived a morally upright life. Luther thought that, compared with the sincerity of Muslim life and Muslim asceticism, the Roman asceticism seemed ridiculous. And in this context, he reminded his readers that "the devil also can make a sour face and fast and perform false miracles and present his servants with mystical raptures."[20] Such practices and experiences are the common property of all religions; they do not demonstrate a religion as true. Even the devil's own religion can be accompanied by such experiences and practices. In this sense, the Turks are the saints and servants of the devil: their religious exercises do not disprove it but rather prove it. Luther wanted all soldiers who had to fight the Turks to know their peculiar relationship to the

---

[16]*LW* 31:77-252.

[17]*Eine Heerpredigt widder den Türcken, WA* 30/2:180, line 19.

[18]*Sermons on the Gospel of St. John 1-4* (1537-1540), *LW* 22:85. See also, *Appeal for Prayer against the Turks* (1541), *LW* 43:224.

[19]For this division, see Lamparter, *Luthers Stellung zum Türkenkrieg.*

[20]*Eine Heerpredigt widder den Türcken, WA* 30/2:187, line 10.

powers of evil. He said, "Now when you go into battle against the Turks, be sure of this and never doubt it: what you are fighting is not flesh and blood, or just human beings...for the army of the Turks is really Satan's army."[21]

The Turk's peculiar relationship to the realm of the devil explained for Luther the renewed vigor of the Muslim armies at the time of the reformation. He felt that the devil was worried that the rediscovery of the gospel might endanger his empire and therefore made these powerful attempts to conquer all Europe.

As saints of the devil, the Turks were also destroyers of Christian faith and morals. The worth of their religion could not be measured by their religious exercises or their more or less moral legislation. Luther knew only one criterion by which all religion, and therefore also Islam, had to be judged. His all important criterion for the truth of religion was its attitude toward Jesus Christ as the Son of God.[22] He applied this criterion to Islam and found it wanting.

Luther realized that, measured by a purely moralistic standard, the religion of the Turks would come out fairly well. However, he considered such a criterion invalid. Only the faith expressed in the second article of the Apostles' Creed is a valid standard for the truth of religion. Luther had declared in *The Schmalkald Articles*,

> We cannot yield or concede anything in this article, even if heaven and earth, or whatever, do not remain....On this article stands all that we teach and practice against the pope, the devil, and the world. Therefore, we must be quite certain and not doubt. Otherwise everything is lost, and pope and devil and everything against us will gain victory and dominance.[23]

Now he claimed against the Turkish religion,

> Everything depends upon this second article; because of it we are called Christians and through the Gospel we have been called to it and baptized upon it and have been counted as Christians. And through it we receive the Holy Spirit and forgiveness of sins, the resurrection of the dead, and eternal life. For this article makes us children of God and brothers of Christ, so that we may become eternally like him and be his co-heirs.[24]

The second article of the Apostles' Creed judges all religion. It is the only valid criterion for Christians. It must be considered in judging the religion of the Turks and is far more important than any possible religious habits and experiences associated with Turkish religion. From this position, Luther came to the conclusion that the Koran is a "foul and shameful book."[25] Indeed, it is "merely human reason, and without the word of God and his Spirit."[26] Its teachings are collected together

---

[21]*Appeal for Prayer Against the Turks* (1541), LW 43:237.

[22]*Eine Heerpredigt widder den Türcken*, WA 30/2:186, line 15.

[23]WA 50:199, line 22 (quoted from *The Schmalkald Articles* [Part II, Article 1,5], trans. by William R. Russell [Minneapolis: Fortress Press, 1994]).

[24]*Eine Heerpredigt widder den Türcken*, WA 30/2:186, line 8.

[25]*On War against the Turk* (1529), LW 46:176.

[26]*Eine Heerpredigt widder den Türcken*, WA 30/2:168, line 15.

from Jewish, Christian, and heathen beliefs.[27] And since Mohammed denies that Christ is the Son of God and the Savior of the world, he must be considered an enemy and destroyer of the Lord Jesus and His Kingdom.

> If anyone denies the articles concerning Christ, that he is God's Son, that he died for us and still lives and reigns at the right hand of God, what has he left of Christ? Father, Son, Holy Ghost, baptism, the sacrament, gospel, faith, and all Christian doctrine and life are gone.[28]

Because of their denial of the divinity of Jesus Christ, the Turks are destroyers and enemies of the Christian faith.

But the Turks are also destroyers of Christian morals. In spite of all their ascetic rules and religious practices, Luther considered them murderers[29] and philanderers.[30] According to Luther, the Turks do not fight wars from necessity or to protect their lands. Like thieves, they seek to rob and damage other lands, whose people are doing and have done nothing to them. Luther thought that this was done because Islam saw it as a good work to attack and murder "unbelievers." Held in highest esteem are those Turks who are most diligent in increasing the Turkish kingdom through murder and robbery.

Furthermore, the Turk is the enemy of the institution of marriage. Luther knew that it was customary among the Turks for a man to have any number of wives. He had heard that Muslims bought and sold women like cattle.[31] This made the Turks polygomists, which was contrary to all true Christian morality.

Luther saw in the Turks the punishment of God and the servants and saints of the devil. He discerned their odd combination of purity and depravity. He found them possessed by a spirit of lies and of murder. All this could lead Luther to only one conclusion: the Turk is the Antichrist.

Luther's identification of the Turk with the Antichrist sounds confusing in view of his frequent claims that it is the pope in Rome who is the real Antichrist. But for Luther two Antichrists presented no problem. He said,

> The person of the Antichrist is at the same time the pope and the Turk. Every person consists of a body and a soul. So the spirit of the Antichrist is the pope, his flesh is the Turk. The one has infested the church spiritually, the other bodily. However, both come from the same lord, even the devil.[32]

This conclusion determined Luther's recommendations for the defense against this enemy.

II. THE DEFENSE

It is not sufficient to state that Luther saw the danger that threatened Europe

---

[27]*On War against the Turk* (1529), LW 46:177.
[28]Ibid.
[29]Ibid., *LW* 46:181.
[30]Ibid.
[31]Ibid.
[32]*WA, TR* 3:158, line 31.

because of the advance of the Turks. He also realized that he had to suggest means for the defense of christendom against the approaching danger. It would not have been very helpful if Luther had been satisfied merely to point out the evil confronting christendom without adding suggestions for its removal. What could be done in the face of such a great peril? What was the duty of the Christian in regard to the Turkish danger?

As usual, Luther separated the duties of a person as a Christian from the duties of a person as a citizen. He felt that as Christians all people were called to repentance and prayer. Luther was aware of the guilt of the so-called Christian nations. He knew also that sin and guilt were not limited to the German territories under the rule of Rome and of Roman Catholic princes. They were guilty of grave sins, for they had persecuted the word of God openly.[33] But the Evangelicals also had lacked the necessary respect for the word of God. Often they had used it to serve their own lusts and desires.[34] Therefore, both Romans and Evangelicals had deserved the punishment of God.

In his *Appeal for Prayer against the Turks*, Luther went into detail enumerating the manifold sins and transgressions of the so-called Christian nations. It was because of this general depravity that one should not be surprised that God had sent Turks to punish Germany. Luther felt that Germany received her deserts. In order, therefore, to assure a successful defense against the Turk it was necessary for all to repent and acknowledge their transgressions. Luther said, "The fight must be begun with repentance, and we must reform our lives, or we shall fight in vain."[35] And later:

> If we really want help and guidance, let us repent and change those evil ways which I described before. Princes and rulers are to see that justice prevails in the land. They will have to curb the money-lenders and protect us from the avarice of the nobles, burghers, and peasants. Above all, they will have to honor God's word, support, protect, and further schools and churches, preachers and teachers.[36]

Luther felt that the people needed to learn that only through faithful prayer could the Turkish danger be banished. He said, "Pray! For hope no longer lies in arms but in God. If anyone defends us against the Turk, the poor children who pray the Our Father will."[37]

But just as repentance and prayer are the tasks of all Christians, so these same Christians have an additional task as citizens. And here again Luther presented the task of the Christian from two different standpoints: the Christian as ruler and Christian as citizen.[38]

---

[33]*Appeal for Prayer Against the Turks*, LW 43:219.

[34]Ibid., LW 43:220.

[35]*On War against the Turk*, LW 46:171.

[36]*Appeal for Prayer Against the Turks*, LW 43:224.

[37]LW 54:419.

[38]Cf. Lamparter, *Luthers Stellung zum Türkenkrieg*, 68ff.

The Christian as ruler has the duty to resist the Turks. After the amazing victories of the Turkish armies, many voices could be heard all over Germany proclaiming that the time for fighting the enemy had passed and that the time for appeasement had come. What's the difference, they said, Germany is doomed, Islam is the wave of the future. Resistance is hopeless. Many people were resigned to become subjects of the sultan. Some even hoped for an improvement of their position once the Turks should take over. Against these appeasers Luther said, "Without any doubt, God is displeased and angry with those who will not put their trust in him but surrender to fear and despair."[39] Luther made it quite plain that it would show utter irresponsibility if the emperor and the princes should give in to the Turk without a fight. It is the task of the princes and rulers to protect their citizens against all enemies. That is the reason that God has given them power. If they fail in their task, they sin against God.[40]

But the duty to fight the Turks in defense of Germany and Europe does not mean that the war against the Turk is a crusade or a holy war. Luther knew the desires of the papacy to promote crusades. But he considered the very idea of a crusade utter blasphemy. The champions of crusades always implied that they were defending Christ against the devil. The spirit of the crusade was therefore a spirit of pride. Luther considered such a spirit contrary to Christ's spirit of humility and love. The war against the Turks could never be called a crusade of Christians against the enemies of Christ. Luther said:

> This is absolutely contrary to Christ's doctrine and name. It is against his doctrine because he says that Christians shall not resist evil, fight, or quarrel, nor take revenge or insist on rights [Matt. 5:39]. It is against his name because there are scarcely five Christians in such an army, and perhaps there are worse people in the eyes of God in that army than are the Turks; and yet they all want to bear the name of Christ. This is the greatest of all sins and is one that no Turk commits, for Christ's name is used for sin and shame and thus dishonored.[41]

Luther ridiculed the idea that the emperor had to fight a war against the Turks as a protector of the Christian faith and the Christian church. Only stupid pride and conceit could possibly produce such an idea. Luther said quite plainly,

> The emperor is not the head of Christendom or defender of the gospel or the faith. The church and the faith must have a defender other than emperor and kings. They are usually the worst enemies of Christ and the faith.[42]

Indeed, Luther said, we would be in a serious predicament if the Christian church had no other protector than some worldly prince. Monarchs are not sure of their own lives for the space of even one hour. Therefore, Luther considered the idea of a human defender of the faith an utterly stupid perversion of the truth. He said,

---

[39]*Appeal for Prayer Against the Turks, LW* 43:224.
[40]*On War against the Turk, LW* 46:184.
[41]Ibid., *LW* 46:165.
[42]Ibid., *LW* 46:185.

Here you can see how a poor mortal, a future victim of worms, like the Emperor, who is not sure of his life for even one moment, glorifies himself as the true protector of the Christian faith. Scripture says that Christian faith is a rock, too solid to be overthrown by the might of the devil, by death and all powers, that this faith is a divine power (Rom. 1:16). Should such a power be protected by a child of death who can be put to death by any kind of disease? Help us God, the world is crazy....Well, soon we shall have a king or prince who will protect Christ and then somebody else will protect the Holy Ghost, and then of course the Holy Trinity and Christ and Faith will be in a fine shape![43]

It is not the task of the princes and of the emperor to play the defender of the Holy Trinity and of the Christian faith, but it is their task to see to it that their subjects are safe from attack. The emperor is not the protector of the church and of the faith, but he is the protector of Germany and of its freedom. Let him be satisfied with that and do his duty.

Now what of the duty of the Christian citizen in the war against the Turks?[44] First of all, as subjects, they owe obedience to their rulers. They must help the ruler in the task of preserving law and order. Luther had explained before his position in regard to the powers that be. He had spoken of the duty of the citizen as soldier and assured his followers that the professional soldier could also be saved. But now he warned even the subject against participation in a crusade. He said, "And, too, if I were a soldier and saw a priest's banner in the field, or a banner of the cross, even though it was a crucifix, I should run as though the devil were chasing me."[45] Luther felt that what was true for the rulers was no less true for the ruled. Crusades were not only useless but actually blasphemous. No Christian could possibly participate in a crusade. And in this connection, Luther added that soldiers who serve under an emperor or prince should never let themselves be used in a war against the gospel, fought under the guise of a crusade but actually persecuting Christians. There is a limit to the obedience which the subject owes to the established order.

However, soldiers who fight for law and order and are Christians can rest assured of their salvation.[46] The fact that they are soldiers does not exclude them from Christ, as some of the enthusiasts had held. For soldiers do not fight for their own pleasure, but in the service of the ordinances of God. If they are aware of this fact, no one can harm them. Then the fear of death is overcome. If soldiers die, believing in Christ, then their death on the battlefield is merely the beginning of eternal life. And Luther considered such a death on the battlefield preferable to the slow death on the sickbed.[47]

If war is fought in defense of law and order and of home and family, then a Christian ought to go to war unafraid. Luther said that the war against the Turks is

---

[43]*Zwei Kaiserliche uneinige und widerwärtige Gebote den Luther betreffend* (1524), WA 15:278, line 1.

[44]Cf. Lamparter, *Luthers Stellung zum Türkenkrieg*, 97ff.

[45]*On War against the Turk*, LW 46:168.

[46]*Eine Heerpredigt widder den Türcken* , WA 30/2:180, line 7.

[47]Ibid., 30/2:175, line 28.

not our business as Christians but it is very much our business as citizens. As Christian citizens, we must face all dangers without flinching, for as Christians we know, "And who is he that will harm you, if ye be followers of that which is good."[48]

Luther's attitude toward the war against the Turks is an integral part of his entire theology. It is especially important because of his persistent denial of the right to proclaim a war, even a religious war, or a crusade.

But we cannot fully understand Luther's position on the war against the Turks unless we realize that, for Luther, there was also an eschatological element involved in this war. Luther had tried to understand the Turkish danger in the light of the book of Daniel. On the basis of his exegesis of Daniel, the Turk was for him an indication of the proximity of the parousia. The raging of the Antichrist in Turk and pope made Luther hope that the day of the Lord was at hand. The troubles of his time represented the birthpangs of the coming kingdom. This confident hope was the reason that Luther left the ultimate defeat of Turk and pope to the day of Jesus Christ that was soon to dawn. He said,

> Our self-confidence will not defeat Gog[49]....But thunder and lightning and the fire of hell will defeat him, as it once happened to Sanherib. That will be his judgment and his end. For this judgment Christians must work with humble prayer....If they don't do it, no one else will.[50]

To encourage Christians in their prayers and devotions, the gospel had appeared again in its clarity. This gospel and prayer were the weapons in the hands of Christian people. The end was at hand. Soon Christ would bring his judgment upon both the pope and the Turk, rid the world of the Antichrist, and save us all with his glorious future. And Luther added that for this day of Christ we wait daily.[51]

Luther knew that finally Antichrist, in whatever form he might appear, would be judged. But he knew also that this judgment would be God's judgment.[52] It is our task to do what we can to hasten this day of Jesus Christ. We can do it only with repentance and prayer and a life according to his word.

This is the core of Luther's teachings about the Turks. He was concerned with the Turkish danger most of his life. The Turks played a part in his first teachings as well as in his last. But with an amazing consistency Luther never changed his basic attitude. The Turks were God's punishment of a proud and sinful Germany in 1541, as in 1517. Never did the political exigencies of the time change Luther's statements concerning these enemies.

[48]*Eine Heerpredigt widder den Türcken,* WA 30/2:177, line 2.

[49]For Luther the Turk is Gog. He developed this idea in his preface to tbe 38th and 39th chapter of Ezekiel. Cf. *WA* 30/2:223ff.

[50]*Vorrhede Martini Luthers auff das XXXVIII. und XXXIX. Capitel Hesechiel vom Gog* (1530), *WA* 30/2:226, line 1.

[51]Ibid., WA 30/2:226, line 7.

[52]*Eine Heerpredigt widder den Türcken,* WA 30/2:172, line 9.

Because Luther knew that the hope of the Christian is based solely upon the power of the Lord Jesus Christ, he concluded his booklet *On War Against the Turk* with these words:

> I know that this book will not make the Turk a gracious lord to me should it come to his attention; nevertheless, I have wished to tell my Germans the truth, so far as I know it, and to give faithful counsel and service to the grateful and the ungrateful alike. If it helps, it helps; if it does not, then may our dear Lord Jesus Christ help, and come down from heaven with the Last Judgment and strike down both Turk and pope, together with all tyrants and the godless, and deliver us from all sins and from all evil. Amen.[53]

---

[53]*On War Against the Turk*, LW 46:205.

Word & World
Supplement Series 2
1994

Luther's View concerning the Imperial Foreign Policy

T HE STUDY OF LUTHER AND THE REFORMATION HAS ALWAYS BEEN PARTICULARLY subject to the changes of fashion. The enlightenment, the romantic movement, pietism and rationalism, Marxism and Nazism all have given us their own peculiar interpretation of reformation history. It is therefore with hesitation that I suggest that it would be possible to interpret the development of the reformation in terms of the successes and failures of the foreign policy of Emperor Charles V. Though Charles and the empire had little or no influence upon the ideological development of the reformation, considerations determined largely by foreign policy dominated the emperor's dealings with the reformer and his followers. There can be no doubt that had it been in the emperor's power and, had political considerations not interfered, Charles would have exterminated Luther and Lutheranism with all the power at his command. His statement to the princes at Worms makes his personal views abundantly clear. There he said:

> My predecessors the most Christian emperors of German race, the Austrian archdukes, and dukes of Burgundy, were until death the truest sons of the Catholic church, defending and extending their belief to the glory of God, the propagation of the faith, the salvation of their souls. They have left behind them the holy Catholic rites, that I should live and die therein, and so until now, with God's aid, I have lived, as becomes a Christian Emperor. What my forefathers established at Constance and other councils, it is my privilege to uphold. A single monk, led astray by private judgment, has set himself against the faith held by all Christians for a thousand years and more, and impudently concludes that all

---

This essay first appeared in Lutheran Quarterly 4 (1952), 153-169. *Here Dr. Forell continues a discussion that he began with "Luther and the War against the Turks" (Church History 14 [1945] 256-271). The issue here is how Luther interpreted the historical reality that the survival of the reformation was largely the result of the efforts of Francis I, Clement VII, and Suleiman the Magnificent to interfere with the plans of Emperor Charles V.*

> Christians up till now have erred. I have therefore resolved to stake upon this cause all my dominions, my friends, my body, and my blood, my life and soul.[1]

And turning to the assembled princes he continued,

> For myself and you, sprung from the holy German nation, appointed by peculiar privilege defenders of the faith, it would be a grievous disgrace, an eternal stain upon ourselves and our posterity, if in this our day, not only heresy, but its very suspicion, were due to our neglect. After Luther's stiff-necked reply in my presence yesterday, I now repent that I have so long delayed proceedings against him and his false doctrines. I have now resolved never again, under any circumstances to hear him. Under protection of his safe conduct he shall be escorted home, but forbidden to preach and to seduce others with his evil doctrines and incite them to rebellion. I warn you to give witness to your opinion as good Christians and in accordance with your vows.[2]

There were many political reasons which would have made a less outspoken condemnation of Luther desirable. Charles V's ambassador in Rome, Juan Manuel, suggested in a letter of May 2, 1520, that the emperor would do well to show some favor to Luther.[3] Luther was giving the pope trouble and thus made it possible for the emperor to bargain with the papacy for political advantage. However, Luther attacked all the spiritual values which Charles cherished, the unity of the church and the continuity of her rites. The only possible policy which Charles could follow in view of his own religious convictions was the extermination of Luther and all he stood for. That Charles was never able to accomplish this goal was largely the result of very mundane considerations of foreign policy.

Francis I, the French king who had failed to win the imperial crown in spite of the support of Pope Leo X and a number of German princes, was making sure that Charles would not enjoy the crown which Francis had desired. Immediately upon the end of the Diet of Worms there began the conflict between Charles V and Francis I which made any effective enforcement of the edict of Worms impossible. Dependent upon help from the Germans,[4] Charles was in no position to alienate large and powerful sections of the German people. Furthermore, the existence of the evangelical movement gave him a strong argument which could be used to keep Leo X from following his natural inclinations towards an alliance with France. The temporary alliance of pope and emperor, though the result of many considerations, was aided by the hope of some of the papal advisers—if not the pope himself—that cooperation with Charles would make him more eager to stamp out the Lutheran heresy.[5]

---

[1]Edward Armstrong, *The Emperor Charles V*, 2 vols. (London: Macmillan, 1902). See also Karl Brandi, *Kaiser Karl V*, 2nd ed. (Munich: F. Bruckmann, 1938) 112 [for English transl., see Karl Brandi, *The Emperor Charles V: The Growth and Destiny of a Man and of a World Empire* (London: Jonathan Cape, 1939)].

[2]Peter Rassow, *Die Kaiser-Idee Karls V* (Berlin: Emil Eberling, 1932) 26ff.

[3]Leopold von Ranke, *History of the Reformation in Germany* (London: Routledge, 1905) 234.

[4]E.g., Franz von Sickingen, one of Luther's early sympathizers, was instrumental in defeating Robert de la Mark, who attacked Charles V's possessions in the Netherlands. See Armstrong, *The Emperor Charles V*, 1:129-130.

[5]Leopold von Ranke, *Deutsche Geschichte im Zeitalter der Reformation* (Vienna: Phaidon) 239. This exchange is omitted in the English translation.

Against all expectations, Charles V defeated the French king decisively. The Peace of Madrid gave the emperor hope that he would now be able to deal with the enemies of the Christian faith, the Turks and "the heretics who have torn themselves from the bosom of the Holy Church."[6] A prolonged peace would have enabled him to enforce the Edict of Worms. But by now the papal throne was occupied by Clement VII who allied himself openly with the king of France in opposition to the emperor. Again Charles became involved in lengthy warfare which drove him to the side of the German Lutherans against the papacy. When the German princes and cities met at Speier in 1526 they felt free to disregard the anti-Evangelical proclamation which the emperor had sent from Seville. In his proclamation the emperor had defended the cause of the papacy. But in view of the fact that when these instructions arrived emperor and pope were engaged in battle against each other, the "Protestants" at the Diet chose to ignore the imperial instructions. They were convinced that the political events in Italy must have changed the emperor's mind. Under those circumstances the Diet of Speyer decided that everybody should act in "such wise as he could answer it to God and the emperor."[7]

Again the reformation was saved by the international political situation. The pope's alliance against the emperor made it necessary for Charles to hire German Lutherans to fight his battle against Rome. It was of some significance that many of these German soldiers felt that in fighting the enemy of the emperor they were also fighting the Antichrist who had perverted the church of God. When finally Rome itself fell into their hands without any significant resistance, these soldiers were convinced that God himself had led them to victory.[8] The war ended two years later.

Now it seemed as if the emperor would finally be able to enforce the Edict of Worms. In the treaty of Barcelona, Charles and Ferdinand promised the pope that they would subdue the heretics.[9] But by now this task, which might have been simple in 1521, seemed almost impossible without a great deal of bloodshed. At Worms Luther had not had a single prince openly taking his side. His own elector seemed more interested in the defense of the reputation of the university of Wittenberg than in Luther's contemplated reformation of the church. The eight years between the Diet of Worms and the second Diet of Speyer gave the reformation the necessary time to consolidate its gains and to organize its adherents.[10] Although it seemed obvious that the anti-reformation forces far outnumbered the Protestants, foreign political considerations made inadvisable an all-out effort to stamp out Protestantism. The danger which threatened Christendom from the Turks and which was highlighted by the siege of Vienna in 1529 forced Charles to

---

[6]Ranke, *History*, 417.

[7]Ibid., 428.

[8]Brandi, *Kaiser Karl V*, 218; Ranke, *History*, 442.

[9]Brandi, *Kaiser Karl V*, 239; Armstrong, *The Emperor Charles V*, 1:188.

[10]Hermann Baumgarten, *Karl V und die deutsche Reformation* (Halle: Verein für Reformationsgeschichte, 1889) 45; Brandi, *Kaiser Karl V*, 262.

seek the support of the Lutheran princes. Under these circumstances it was understandable that Charles V agreed to the truce of Nürnberg which granted the Protestants freedom of religion until a general council could meet and decide the matters at issue. It is noteworthy that even Alexander, one of the reformation's oldest and most intelligent enemies, suggested that concessions to the Lutherans were the only means of keeping their support against the Turks.[11] And Loayasa, the emperor's confessor, advised him in 1532 to tolerate the Lutherans if they would help him against the common enemy. He wrote, "Let your Majesty have no scruples in making use of them, heretics as they may be, for if your heart is free from sin, their errors will not disturb your own good fortune."[12]

From then on, until the death of Luther and the Schmalkald war, the imperial policy was largely dominated by a desire for peace, and no real effort was made to enforce the Edict of Worms in the Protestant states. For even when the acute danger from the Turks temporarily receded, there was always danger that the alliance between Francis I and Suleiman might attempt to draw in the disaffected Lutheran princes of Germany. Furthermore, the emperor's personal disappointments with the spiritual leadership of the church, whose defender he had believed himself to be, made the course of toleration the only feasible one.[13] Even though Charles V eventually defeated the League of Schmalkald he did not use his victory for the reintroduction of the Roman religion. By that time the reformation was an accomplished fact. It seems that Armstrong is justified in saying:

> Lutheranism owed its political existence as much to Clement VII as to the French and the Turks. His weak and crooked policy, strong and consistent only in opposition to ecclesiastical reform, had given it time, and time is the requisite of revolution. The German Reformation had not only both extended and consolidated its political forces, but had defined its doctrines and moderated them into a working possibility, shaking off the odium of violent extremes, socialist or anarchist. More than this—Clement had lamed the enterprise and perhaps injured the character of the most honorable champion of the Church. Charles had been at first straightforward in his attitude towards the religious revolution. He had given Luther a hearing and then frankly declared war in defense of the Church. But the later hostility of Clement, combining with that of Francis I, had driven him into subterfuge and concession—into an attitude of toleration inconsistent with his real convictions.[14]

It seems to be the judgment of history that the survival of the reformation in

[11]Armstrong, *The Emperor Charles V*, 1:254.

[12]Ibid., 1:255; Brandi, *Kaiser Karl V*, 272.

[13]Walter Rosenberg, *Der Kaiser und die Protestanten in den Jahren 1537-1539* (Halle: Verein für Reformationsgeschichte, 1903); Armstrong, *The Emperor Charles V*, 2:162.

[14]Armstrong, *The Emperor Charles V*, 1:266f. Cf., Baumgarten, *Karl V*, 13. In the last addition to his last will and testament (Sept. 9, 1558), Charles counselled his heirs to liquidate the Lutherans. See Karl Brandi, *Berichte und Studien zur Geschichte Karl V* (Göttingen: Nachrichten von der Gesellschaft der Wissenschaften zu Göttingen aus dem Jahre 1930, Philologisch-Historische Klasse) 269, 275. See also Brandi, *Kaiser Karl V*, 427, where Don Diego Mendoza, the ambassador at Venice is quoted as follows: "All the world knows that the pope alone has brought all previous and present difficulties to you. What prince has hurt you more than he? The blind are able to see that everything goes back to him—what the French have done and, consequently, every misdeed of the Turks" [editor's translation].

the critical stages of its infancy was the direct result of the difficulties which Emperor Charles V had in his relations with the papacy, France, and the Turks. How far did Luther, the champion of the reformation, comprehend the significance of the international events for his movement? Was he ever aware of the fact that its survival was largely the result of the efforts of Francis I, Clement VII, and Suleiman the Magnificent to interfere with the plans of Emperor Charles V?

In order to understand Luther's personal reaction to the foreign policy of Charles V, which proved so important for his life and work, it is essential to remember that Luther did not approach history as the result of the manipulation of power by individual leaders, or the natural process of rise and decline of nations according to their racial vitality, or even as the struggle for market and the control of the means of production, but history was for him the place where a sovereign God is at work punishing nation and rulers for their sins and disobedience. Like an Old Testament prophet Luther saw all history as the direct expression of the divine will. It is for this reason that he advocated the study of history. History teaches that God always fulfills his threats and promises. Thus the study of history nourishes faith and puts the fear of God into human hearts.[15] He said, "Therefore, it would be of the greatest value to the ruling class if from their youth up they were to read, or have read to them, history books, both sacred and secular."[16] Historical records are memorials to God's works and judgments. They show how he preserves the world and humankind in particular, and they reveal how he rules, hindering and helping, punishing and honoring.[17] Emperors and kings are therefore under an obligation to have the history of their time recorded and preserved in libraries. And the historians are "the most useful people and the best teachers, so that one can never honor, praise, and thank them enough."[18]

Luther believed that his own personal fate was part of this divine plan at work in history. God had protected him against the pope and all tyrants because God wanted him to proclaim the gospel.[19] It was God's plan which was at work in his life and in the history of his time. Charles V, Francis I, Clement VII, and Suleiman the Magnificent were all tools in the hands of God. Though they all might be personally evil people and destined for eternal damnation, God could use them and even their most evil efforts to show his power and glory. Thus Luther explained the 124th Psalm, verses 4 and 5, "Then the waters had overwhelmed us, the stream had gone over our souls. Then the proud waters had gone over our souls," with the following words:

> The Roman Pope Clement had moved all oceans, as if to devour all churches and the devil had risked everything and sent many thousand devils to Augsburg which were to goad the princes into suppressing us. There were floods of water

---

[15]*WA* 25:141, line 37.
[16]*Treatise on Good Works*, LW 44:95.
[17]*Preface to Galeatius Capella's History*, LW 34:275-276.
[18]Ibid., 276.
[19]*Admonition to Peace*, LW 46:31.

but He who is Lord over pope and devil desired that their godless thoughts be in vain.[20]

Luther's faith in the sovereignty of God made him look at history with a great deal of detachment. Historical decisions could not affect the divine plan, they could affect only the place of nations and individuals within this divine plan. The imperial attitude towards the gospel did not decide the fate of the gospel, but it did decide the fate of the empire. This is the perspective from which Luther views the policies of Charles V and his contemporaries.[21]

Personally Luther liked the emperor. One could almost consider Luther's attitude towards Charles V as the great political illusion of his life. We know that Charles immediately disliked Luther. He is supposed to have said about him: "This man will never make a heretic out of me."[22] Yet Luther's reaction to Charles was quite positive. He spoke of him as a "true father of Germany."[23] He appreciated his real concern for the unity of the church[24] and his modesty and consideration.[25] He also had some rather exaggerated notions of Charles' chastity.[26] Luther made it a point to praise Charles in comparison with his brother Ferdinand,[27] a man whom he intensely disliked and called the "pestilence of Germany."[28] All Christians should intercede in prayer for Charles[29] particularly since Luther considered him surrounded by evil priests who advised him badly. Luther said, "Dear Emperor Charles is surrounded by so many devils, evil priests, godless bishops and princes that they drive him into decisions which are not his own."[30] "What can this godly emperor do among so many rogues and villains, especially against that arch-villain, Pope Clement."[31] Yet Luther appreciated that the emperor had prevented bloodshed in Germany by his restrained actions.[32] And he praised his behavior at Augsburg.[33] With evident satisfaction he quoted alleged sayings of the emperor which made him appear favorable to Luther's cause. The emperor was supposed to have said that Luther's teaching could not be so evil "since so many great, exalted, learned, and honest people accept it."[34] And also, "If the priests were godly, they would not need a Luther."[35]

[20]WA 40/3:144, line 34.

[21]To the Councilmen of Germany, LW 45:352. Cf. also WA, TR 2:217, no. 1796.

[22]Ranke, History, 242.

[23]WA, TR 2:645, no. 2768.

[24]WA, TR 3:31-32, no. 2860b.

[25]WA, TR 4:15, no. 3927; 4:631, no. 5042.

[26]WA, TR 5:598, no. 6313.

[27]WA, TR 2:599, no. 2677b.

[28]WA, TR 3:596, no. 3764; 3:679, no. 3876.

[29]WA, TR 2:645, no. 2768; 2:570, no. 2639a.

[30]WA 32:182, line 17.

[31]Luther's Warning to His Dear German People, LW 47:34.

[32]WA 38:119, line 14.

[33]Luther's Warning, LW 47:30-31.

[34]Ibid., 31.

[35]Ibid., 32.

But at the same time Luther could not close his eyes to the obvious efforts of the emperor on behalf of the Roman church. Especially his promise to the pope to restore all losses to him[36] confused and annoyed Luther. He attributed this tendency to bad counsel from his clerical advisers, calling him "a lamb among sows, dogs, and devils."[37] He also blamed the influence of Spain and a congenital tendency to be overly deliberate and somewhat dull. But even in this tendency he saw some good. He said, "We have a pious emperor. He is pious and quiet. I take it that he doesn't talk as much in one year as I talk in one day."[38] Yet it was this hesitancy which led Luther to criticize him most severely. Charles hesitated against the Turks before Vienna and did not make the most of his military opportunities. Similarly Luther felt that he did not exploit his advantage after his victory at the Ticino.[39] And Luther was most critical of his peace and treaty with the king of France.[40]

In the conflict with France, Luther was impartial in his sympathy. He felt that the emperor should be strong and make his will felt among the other princes of Christendom. With approval he quoted the statement of Fabian von Feilizsch who had said to Frederick the Wise after the election of Charles V, "The ravens need a vulture."[41] Furthermore he intensely disliked the French king. The reasons were numerous. He considered him personally immoral[42]—and indeed compared with him Charles was a model of chastity. Furthermore, Francis was allied with the enemies of the Christian world, the Turks, and Luther felt that it would be fair to call him *"Turcissimus"* ("His Most Turkish Majesty").[43] He was violent in his persecution of the adherents of the reformation, and Luther claimed that Francis personally set fire to the stake when evangelicals were murdered.[44] And last, but not least, he was an ally of Clement VII. Luther said that soldiers had told him that the catastrophe that befell Francis at the battle of Pavia was the direct result of the fact that he had the troops of the pope with him.[45] All this fitted perfectly into Luther's general conception of history. And he would say that we can see in the story of the king of France that trust in arms is vain indeed.[46] For Francis was defeated in spite of his superiority in soldiers and armor, in spite of his tremendous expenditures for espionage.[47]

Luther never changed his view of Francis and his policies in spite of the

---

[36]WA 30/2:409, line 34.

[37]WA 30/3:196, line 29; 40/3:148, line 17.

[38]WA, TR 2:182, no. 1687; 3:233, no. 3245.

[39]WA 41:181, line 12.

[40]*Table Talk*, LW 54:421, no. 5416.

[41]WA, TR 6:49, no. 6571.

[42]WA, TR 4:151, no. 4124.

[43]*Table Talk*, LW 54:421, no. 5416.

[44]WA, TR 6:12, no. 6516.

[45]*On War against the Turk*, LW 46:168.

[46]LW 17/1:325, line 2.

[47]WA, TR 3:121, no. 2964b.

approaches of the king in the direction of the Schmalkald League. When in 1535 the king of France asked Melanchthon to come to his country to help settle the affairs of the church, Luther heartily endorsed the trip, not because he had changed his mind concerning the French king, but rather because he hoped that such a visit by Melanchthon might alleviate the hard lot of the evangelicals in France.[48] Of Francis and Henry VIII, Luther said that they were Lutherans in "taking" but not in giving. "They only seek their own, not what is God's."[49] There is good reason to believe that it was Luther's influence which prevented the Schmalkald League from following a policy which would have allied them completely with France and Turkey against the German emperor. Through this attitude, as Armstrong says, "Luther's conservative common sense and his German patriotism saved the emperor's cause and perhaps that of Christianity."[50]

It is even less surprising that Luther sided wholeheartedly with the emperor in his conflict with Clement VII and the papacy. Luther did not attack all popes with equal bitterness. Of Leo X he said that he was an example of how a person could be corrupted by his election to the papacy.[51] He believed that Adrian VI had been elevated because of his personal friendship with the emperor and in order to utilize his influence over Charles V against the evangelicals.[52] Luther was convinced that the election of this pope was very largely the result of the fear of the consequences of his attacks against the institution of the papacy. Adrian was not the target that Leo had been and that Clement was going to be. Though he attacked him bitterly for his hypocrisy,[53] he also reported a rumor that Adrian had been murdered because he confessed himself an adherent of the gospel.[54]

But there was no doubt in Luther's mind that Clement VII was an arch-criminal.[55] With scorn he reported how the pope had sent help to France against the emperor,[56] and he attempted to explain this Francophile policy by mentioning the marriage of Clement's daughter to a French prince.[57] Politically he considered him anti-German and claimed that Clement desired to wade in German blood.[58] Luther quoted him as having said that rather than stop persecuting the evangelicals, he would send the Turks into Germany.[59] Analyzing the pope's foreign policy in a letter to the archbishop of Mainz, Luther found in Clement an additional example

[48]*WA, Br* 7:229, no. 2221.
[49]*WA, TR* 3:112, no. 2947b.
[50]Armstrong, *The Emperor Charles V,* 1:252.
[51]*WA, TR* 2:237, line 10.
[52]*WA, TR* 5:513, no. 6150.
[53]*WA* 15:184, line 14.
[54]*WA* 39/2:382, line 18; *WA, Br* 2:247, line 31.
[55]*Luther's Warning, LW* 47:34; cf. *WA, TR* 2:184, no. 1694; 3:234, no. 3250.
[56]*WA* 52:232, line 17.
[57]*WA, TR* 3:556, no. 3713.
[58]*Luther's Warning, LW* 47:34.
[59]*WA, TR* 2:482, no. 2485.

of God's power over history.[60] His loss of Rome[61] and his eventual downfall[62] were welcomed with much satisfaction. Indicative of his sympathies in the conflict between Charles V and Clement VII were Luther's laudatory references to Georg von Frundsberg, the German leader of the imperial forces who was instrumental in bringing about the humiliation of the papacy.[63]

As far as Pope Paul III was concerned, Luther claimed that he had induced the Turks to war against Germany,[64] and he commented scornfully on the pope's Bull of Indulgence for the war against the Turks.[65] But while Luther's opinions concerning the political strife between the emperor and the king of France and the emperor and the various popes were the rather inconsequential views of a Wittenberg professor of theology on the international situation, his views on Charles V's duties and responsibilities in relation to the Turks were of the greatest significance. For in this realm Luther was in a position to influence important powers within the German empire in their policies, especially his own elector and the Schmalkald League. It is through his views of the Turks and the imperial foreign policy towards the Turks that his opinions on foreign affairs became of the greatest importance.

There had been early efforts by Luther's enemies to claim that he favored a Turkish victory and advocated a pacifist attitude towards this enemy of christendom. Pope Leo X in his bull *Exsurge Domini* of June 15, 1520, had implied that since Luther considered the Turks a punishment from God over an apostate christendom, he was opposing the defense of the western world against the Turkish danger.[66] Fortunately for christendom, this allegation was unjustified. Quite on the contrary, Luther advocated the military defense of the empire against the Turks, in three major writings: *On War against the Turk, Call to War against the Turk,* and *Exhortation to Prayer against the Turk.*[67] However, he insisted that such a defense would have to be directed by the emperor as the rightful ruler of Germany.[68] It was bound to fail if the emperor should attempt to fight against the Turks as a protector of the Christian faith and the Christian church, or if the just war in the defense of the empire should degenerate into a religious crusade under clerical leadership. On the first point Luther said, "The emperor is not the head of Christendom or defender of the gospel or the faith. The church and the faith must have a defender other than emperor and kings."[69] He ridiculed the notion that the emperor is needed as a protector of the Christian faith by saying,

[60]*WA* 30/2:411.

[61]*On War against the Turk, LW* 46:169.

[62]*WA, TR* 2:621, no. 2733a.

[63]*A Sermon on Keeping Children in School, LW* 46:247; cf. *WA, TR* 2:652, no. 2775; 5:31, no. 5256.

[64]*WA, TR* 2:233, line 25.

[65]*WA* 50:111.

[66]See George W. Forell, "Luther and the War Against the Turks," *Church History* 14/4; reprinted in this volume, pp. 123-134.

[67]*LW* 46:155ff.; *WA* 30/2:160ff.; *WA* 51:577ff.

[68]*On War against the Turk, LW* 46:184.

[69]Ibid., 185.

Here you can see how a poor mortal, a future victim of worms, like the emperor, who is not sure of his life for even one moment, glorifies himself as the true protector of the Christian faith. Scripture says that the Christian faith is a rock, too solid to be overthrown by the might of the devil, by death and all powers; that this faith is a divine power. Such a power should be protected by a child of death who can be put to death by any kind of disease? Help us God, the world is crazy...well, soon we shall have a king or prince who will protect Christ and then somebody else will protect the Holy Ghost and then of course the Holy Trinity and Christ and faith will be in fine shape.[70]

And he was similarly revolted by the notion of a crusade, since this would imply that there would be an army of Christians fighting against the enemies of Christ. Luther said,

This is absolutely contrary to Christ's doctrine and name. It is against his doctrine because he says that Christians shall not resist evil, fight, or quarrel, nor take revenge or insist on rights [Matt. 5:39]. It is against his name because there are scarcely five Christians in such an army, and perhaps there are worse people in the eyes of God in that army than are the Turks; and yet they all want to bear the name of Christ. This is the greatest of all sins and is one that no Turk commits, for Christ's name is used for sin and shame and thus dishonored.[71]

And Luther warned all soldiers against participation in a crusade. "And, too, if I were a soldier," he said, "and saw a priest's banner in the field, or a banner of the cross, even though it was a crucifix, I should run as though the devil were chasing me."[72] But while he disapproved of a crusade or holy war against the Turks in defense of Christ and the Christian faith, Luther called to war against the Turks in defense of the German empire, of law and order and of home and family.[73] And from this point of view Luther made some very constructive suggestions for the defense of the empire. He called for unity among the rulers, since the sultan is so very powerful that no king or country can withstand him in isolation.[74] And he reminded them that the Turkish empire is greater and more powerful than Spain, France, England, Germany, Italy, Bohemia, Hungary, Poland, and Denmark all taken together.[75] He criticized those princes severely who put the special tax for the war against the Turks into their own pockets and did not supply the needed help.[76]

He also encouraged the individual citizens to fight to the last breath, and he hoped that even the smallest village would not let itself be captured without a fight. Everybody should help in the defense, young and old alike.[77] All this willingness to cooperate with the emperor is the more surprising in view of the fact that Luther was rightfully suspicious about the manner in which the war was being

---

[70]WA 15:278, line 1.

[71]On War against the Turk, LW 46:165.

[72]Ibid., 168.

[73]WA 30/2:180, line 7.

[74]On War against the Turk, LW 46:184, 203.

[75]Ibid., 202.

[76]WA 53:558, line 11.

[77]WA 30/2:183, line 18.

fought. The fact that the pope considered the war against the Turks his personal affair constantly annoyed Luther. Before he had any specific damaging evidence, he had claimed that the princes could not succeed in their war against the Turks because they were dominated by the pope.[78] But later he expressed the suspicion that seemingly only Lutherans were being sent into the war against the Turks and that the entire war might be another piece of papal treachery.[79] Luther was aware of the political alliances which often included Venice, Florence, France, the Turks, and the pope against Charles V and the empire.[80] And he reported that this conspiracy was paying for the services of the army of the Turks with 300,000 gold gulden per month.[81] The money which the papacy was collecting all over the world for the war against the Turks was actually being used to supply the Turks against the Christians.[82] And he said with indignation that such a monstrous treason as the alliance of the "most Christian king of France" and the "most holy pope of Rome" with the Turks against the emperor had not been equalled in many centuries.[83] And in view of his own loyalty to the empire which had condemned him and the emperor, who had made every effort to destroy him, Luther's indignation seems understandable.

Luther had also had the opportunity to use the Turks against his enemies in Europe. This possibility was presented to him through the report of a German member of an imperial mission to Suleiman. This man, by the name of Schmaltz, told Luther that the sultan had personally asked him about Luther and his age. When Schmaltz had told Suleiman that Luther was forty-eight years old, the sultan had said, "I wish he were even younger, he would find in me a gracious protector."[84] When Luther heard this report he crossed himself and said, "May God protect me from such a gracious protector."

His reaction was similar when he was approached by the landgrave of Hesse who wanted him to use his influence with the elector of Saxony against granting the emperor any aid for the war against the Turks, in view of the emperor's treatment of the evangelical ambassadors who had been sent to him.[85] Luther answered evasively, saying that the elector had not asked him for any advice and that he would advise him when the opportunity would present itself to the best of his ability and as his conscience would permit. And again Luther indicated that the priests rather than the emperor were responsible for this tyrannical treatment of the ambassadors.[86] Nine years later, when again asked for his advice with respect to the war against the Turks, he wrote to John Frederick,

[78]*WA, TR* 2:320, no. 2093; cf. 1:448, no. 904.
[79]*WA, Br* 10:230, no. 3852.
[80]*Luther to Wenceslas Link, LW* 49:219-221.
[81]*WA, Br* 10:524, no. 3966; 10:526, no. 3967.
[82]*WA, Br* 10:541, no. 3974.
[83]*WA, Br* 10:553, no. 3982.
[84]*WA, TR* 2:508, no. 2537b.
[85]*Luther to Landgrave Philip of Hesse, LW* 49:250-253.
[86]Ibid.

> Since in this great emergency not only Ferdinand and our enemies will have to suffer but also our fatherland and many good and honest people, I believe that your electoral grace should rightly and with a clear conscience help to comfort and aid this poor group (though not the tyrants). Thus the conscience will not have to sigh after the damage has been done and accuse itself and say, "why didn't you help protect the poor people when you were able to do so and let the unimportant matter of the strife among tyrants prevent you from helping?"[87]

It was Luther's confidence that history is at all times God's history which often enabled him to gain perspective with respect to a contemporary situation. It was his eschatology which led him to believe that rulers should at all times be guided by a clean conscience. In his *Warning to His Dear German People* he wrote,

> You will fare as we Germans did when we ventured to break the peace with St. John Huss and fought against the Bohemians. On that occasion the pope also handed us over to the slaughter, so that we had to satisfy his pleasure with our blood and heads, and we fought against truth and justice.[88]

From this somewhat detached point of view Luther considered Charles V an honest person and a peacemaker surrounded by enemies who were evil and wanted war rather than peace. This belief placed Luther in all questions of foreign policy squarely behind Charles. The anti-evangelical stand of Charles, Luther attributed to his advisers, and he tried his very best to explain it away. Luther used his personal influence to strengthen the emperor's hand against his enemies, often disregarding the immediate political advantages which an anti-imperial policy would have offered. Not many of the Lutheran princes followed his leadership. But perhaps Napoleon was not so far wrong when he said that Charles by embracing Lutheranism could have conquered Europe at the head of a united Germany.[89] The tragedy of Charles V's foreign policy was that those who might have politically agreed with him opposed him for religious reasons—and that those whose religious cause he defended stabbed him in the back for reasons of politics.

---

[87]*WA, Br* 8:232, no. 3236.

[88]*LW* 47:17.

[89]Armstrong, *The Emperor Charles V,* 1:47.

Word & World
Supplement Series 2
1994

Luther Today

MARK TWAIN'S FAMOUS STORY ABOUT HIS EXPERIENCE WITH CROOKED WATCH-makers ends with the speculative remark: "And he used to wonder what became of all the unsuccessful tinkers, and gunsmiths, and shoemakers, and engineers, and blacksmiths; but nobody could ever tell him."

If people today should wonder what became of all the retired Plato scholars, aging refugee novelists, and ministerial experts on the rural church, they would only have to look at the recent writings of Dean Inge, Thomas Mann, and Martin Schroeder.[1] They have all become "Luther scholars" and are discovering Luther's responsibility for the social and political ills of our day.

It seems to meet a general human need to find a scapegoat for the ethical anarchy of our time, and all amateur historians seem to agree that this scapegoat is Martin Luther.

However, virtually the only writings of Luther used and quoted by his present-day critics are his pamphlets on the Peasant War. Such a procedure compares in fairness with an attempt to develop the ethics of the Bible solely on the basis of the book of Esther, but it is generally accepted.

Attacks against Luther are nothing new. From the day in 1517 when he nailed his *Ninety-five Theses* on the door of a church in Wittenberg he has been in the center of bitter controversy. Luther has been called an enlightened genius and a mentally deformed pervert, a herald of progress and a slave of reaction.

Generally Luther's critics come from two diametrically opposed camps. They are either Roman Catholics or Marxists. The one side claims that Luther was the

[1]See the recent statements of these writers in *Time, The Churchman, The Christian Century*.

This essay first appeared in The Augustana Quarterly 25 (1946) 291-296. *In this essay Dr. Forell proposes the thesis that was to appear later in his doctoral dissertation and subsequently in his first major book,* Faith Active in Love. *Here he relates that thesis to various interpretations of Luther at the close of World War II. Forell's words here also respond to some enduring misinterpretations of Luther fifty years later.*

father of modernism, the other that he was merely a tool of reaction. From John Eck to Denifle and Maritain, Roman Catholics blame Luther for the so-called modern world view. As Denifle said: "The [modern world view] is not the same as Lutheranism...but it was partly derived from Lutheranism and partly flowed from the same sources."[2] They see in the theory of evolution, agnosticism, immanentism, relativism, subjectivism, the Kantian ideas of autonomy, communism, and national socialism linear descendants of Luther and Lutheranism.

The others, from Thomas Munzer to Kautsky and Schroeder, see in Luther a befuddled reactionary. Kautsky, the well known Marxist historian, wrote: "From the very first, the only determined stand that (Luther) took was against the communistic enthusiasts. He resisted every attempt of the lower classes to derive material benefit from the Reformation."[3]

This basic disagreement among Luther's critics is further complicated by their willingness to quote each other to score a point against Luther. For example, Schroeder, who wants to prove that Luther was a reactionary intent on protecting the ruling class, quotes Dean Inge, although the dean claims that Luther was a "coarse and foul mouthed leader of a revolution."

In view of this contradiction and confusion among the critics of Luther, is it not quite possible that they all missed the main concern in Luther's work? Perhaps this was neither "modernistic" nor "reactionary." (It is impossible to analyze here his position in regard to all the social, political, and economic questions of his time. Detailed studies have been made, of which many are available in English. May it suffice here to say that Troeltsch's analysis is today no longer considered authoritative by most Luther scholars.) What was Luther's ethical concern?

Luther's ethics was profoundly and fundamentally religious. For a time which considers religion almost purely a means to an end, this religious character of Luther's ethics makes it difficult to understand.

For modern protestants, Christianity is generally the means to achieve the perfect society. For clerical Roman Catholics, Christianity is the means to establish the Roman Catholic Church and its vicar of Christ. For many sincere Christians, it is the means to get into heaven. For Luther, Christianity was an end in itself. It was heaven. To have a gracious God, that is, to be Christian in the deepest sense of this word, was Luther's ultimate concern. God, not humanity or the perfect society, was in the center of his religious thinking. This could not but influence his ethics.

Roman Catholic ethics as well as all non-Christian ethics is eudaimonistic and ultimately human-centered. Luther claimed that Christian ethics is God-centered. For him the key concept for all Christian ethics was love, excluding self-love and the human striving for happiness. This contradicted the church fathers and discredited "justified self-love" and the religious profit-motive basic for the ethical system of the Roman Catholic Church. Roman Catholic theologians, as Holl and

---

[2]P. Heinrich Denifle, *Luther und Lutherthum in der ersten Entwicklung*, 2 vols. (Mainz: F. Kirchheim, 1904-1909) 2:494.

[3]Karl Kautsky, *Communism in Central Europe in the Time of the Reformation* (London, 1897) 128.

Nygren have shown, speak of love in very general terms and distinguish between right love and wrong love on the basis of the object being loved. For them all love is acquisitive. It is good if it desires the good, and evil if it desires the evil. For Luther, Christian love is never acquisitive, but after the example of the love of Christ, "self-giving love." It is a love that does not consider the own self, is in fact the judgment of God over all self-love.

Luther was aware of the fact that, following Augustine and Peter Lombard, official Roman theology claimed that the commandment to love meant that first God is to be loved, then our soul, next our neighbor's soul, and lastly our body. Luther knew this doctrine of ordered love and that it included self-love. But he openly opposed what had been considered Christian love for more than a thousand years.

According to Luther, the commandment, "Love your neighbor as yourself," did not encourage self-love, but rather exposed the vicious love wherewith people love themselves. And breaking all precedent and destroying a very comfortable and practical interpretation, he said, concerning this commandment:

> "Love your neighbor as yourself," but not in the sense that you should love yourself; otherwise that would have been commanded....Thus you do wrong if you love yourself, an evil from which you will not be free unless you love your neighbor in the same way, that is, by ceasing to love yourself.[4]

It is important to recognize the complete change in the accepted definition of love made by Luther. All through the middle ages, love had been interpreted in essentially egocentric and eudaimonistic terms, even if these concepts were used in a sublimated sense. Love had been acquisitive; now it was defined as self-giving. Luther spoke of spontaneous overflowing love, which must be similar to the spontaneous overflowing love of God. This love does not ask about the worthiness of the object, it is not concerned with the inherent value of that which it loves, but "makes [the] sun rise on the evil and on the good, and sends rain on the righteous and on the unrighteous."

It is on the basis of this definition of love as overflowing and spontaneous that Luther's ethics must be understood. Such love cannot precede faith, it can only be the result of faith. For Roman Catholic ethics, faith was formed by love; for Luther faith is active in love (cf. Gal 5:6). Ethics is not the method to achieve faith, rather faith is a free gift, and Christian ethics is the result of the Christian faith. And if love is formed by faith, then this love must be more than the prudential desire for the highest good. Love must be a part of the divine love given to us by God to be passed on to the neighbor.

For Luther, ethics was faith in action. Human beings are merely the tube or channel through which God's love flows to the neighbor. While even Augustine spoke of "using one's neighbor in order to enjoy God," Luther spoke of

> faith and love by which a person is placed between God and the neighbor as a

---

[4]*Lectures on Romans,* LW 25:513-514. See also Anders Nygren, *Agape and Eros* 2/2 (London: S.P.C.K., 1939) 294.

medium which receives from above and gives out again below and is like a vessel or tube through which the stream of divine blessings must flow without intermission to other people. See, those are then truly god-like people who receive from God all that he has in Christ and in turn show themselves also by their well-doing to be, as it were, the gods of their neighbors.[5]

Here Luther explained what he meant by faith working through love. In faith we receive God's love and passes it on to our neighbor. In Luther's simple sentence, "To love God is to love one's neighbor," we have the key to his system of ethics.[6]

In the church which Luther had known since childhood, selfishness had been the driving force behind all ethical action. People were mainly concerned with their own salvation, and used everybody else and also the church only to achieve this goal.

Luther denounced this selfish striving for merits as a basis for Christian ethics. He believed that Christian ethics is always the ethics of Christian people. Its motive is faith that finds its expression in love. Nothing less can be Christian ethics. He said: "'Good works do not make a good man, but a good man does good works'....Consequently it is always necessary that the substance or person himself be good before there can be any good works."[7] Now ethical action could no longer be measured in legalistic terms and by fixed norms. It was the action of Christians.

The institution which has based its ethical system upon a legal code and upon a businesslike transfer of merits to those who need them could not possibly accept Luther's position. The Roman Catholic Church has good reason to attack Luther and his ethics.

And the Marxists who consider ethics merely the means to an end are justified in condemning Luther's ethics. Lenin said: "Our morality is wholly subordinated to the interests of the class struggle of the proletariat. We deduce our morality from the facts and needs of the class struggle of the proletariat."[8] Marxists cannot be expected to adopt Christian ethics as understood by Luther.

But for Christians in general Luther may prove a guide to a more biblical understanding of the ethical duties of the Christian.

Luther wrote more than almost any other human in history. Much that he wrote about contemporary politics and economics is dated, and some of it is quite obviously wrong. But Luther was neither a politician nor an economist; he was a sincere and profound Christian. Four hundred years after his death his theological insights are just as true as they ever were, because they were derived from the word of God.

For a Christian world which so frequently has made Christ merely the means to an end, it is well to remember Martin Luther, to whom Christ was the "alpha and omega, the beginning and the end, the first and the last."

[5]*WA* 10/1/1:100, lines 9ff. (author's translation); see also Nygren, *Agape*, 2/2:517.
[6]Nygren, *Agape*, 2/2:515ff.
[7]*The Freedom of a Christian*, LW 31:361.
[8]See *Politics* (March 1946) 81.

Part II

ON CHURCH AND THEOLOGY

Word & World
Supplement Series 2
1994

The Future of Theology in the Church

I F WE ARE TO LOOK TO THE FUTURE OF THEOLOGY IN THE CHURCH, A FEW REMARKS about our recent past are in order. Theology has played an important part in the life of the Lutheran church in the twentieth century. It was a theological revival in response to the National-Socialist movement in Germany that produced a world-wide effect which dominated Christian thought from 1934 (*The Theological Declaration of Barmen*)[1] into the sixties. It forced the church to oppose the worship of nature associated with the mythology of *Blut und Boden* [blood and soil] which characterized the racism of the Nazi movement. While some of the most important theologians giving leadership to the *Bekennende Kirche* [confessing church] were "Reformed," especially Karl Barth, Lutherans like Dietrich Bonhoeffer, Hans Asmussen, and hundreds of ordinary parish pastors participated in the opposition to the so-called *Deutsche Christen* [German Christians]. This confrontation with Nazism meant the end of the quietistic interpretation of Luther's so-called *Zwei Reiche Lehre* [two kingdom doctrine] and forced Lutherans to engage political issues on the basis of their faith. The Lutheran theologians who came as refugees to the United States, people like Paul Tillich (who always considered himself a Lutheran), Otto Piper,[2] and Bertha Paulssen, contributed to an understanding of the

---

[1]For a text of the Barmen Declaration, see George W. Forell, *The Protestant Faith* (Philadelphia: Fortress, 1975) 286-290.

[2]For the profound influence of Otto Piper on American Lutheranism, see *God and Caesar, A Christian Approach to Social Ethics*, ed. Warren A. Quanbeck (Minneapolis: Augsburg, 1959). This volume was the product of the Lutheran Social Ethics Seminar at Valparaiso University which met under the chairmanship of President O. P. Kretzmann and was guided throughout its life by Prof. Otto Piper of Princeton Theological Seminary, who served as moderator.

This essay first appeared in Lutheran Quarterly *NS 4/1 (Spring 1990) 1-9. Here Dr. Forell explicates the distinctive theological contributions that Lutheran theology has to offer the church and the world. This essay pointedly shows Dr. Forell's great ability to integrate the historical and confessional priorities of Luther and the Lutheran confessional writings with contemporary issues.*

social ethical implications of the Christian faith in a Lutheran mode very different from the customary one. Through their students they made a fundamental difference reflected for example in the social statements of the Lutheran Church in America (LCA)[3] and the American Lutheran Church (ALC).

While critical of the social gospel and what they considered its far too optimistic anthropology, these theologians articulated the need for social and political responsibility not independent from Lutheran theology but based upon it. They claimed that theology was not irrelevant to social action but actually supplied the basis for it. Only a social ethics rooted in theology would enable Christians to make a lasting contribution to a world where the people of God were to demonstrate their faith active in love.

It has become apparent that one aspect of this theological revolution succeeded. Today few if any people in responsible positions in the Evangelical Lutheran Church in America (ELCA) would dare assert that the church should not deal with questions of social policy. Love must become active in justice, and every agency of the ELCA is committed to this goal. The constitution of the ELCA proclaims in its statement of purpose: "To participate in God's mission, this church shall:...c. Serve in response to God's love to meet human needs, caring for the sick and the aged, advocating dignity and justice for all people, working for peace and reconciliation among the nations, and standing with the poor and powerless and committing itself to their needs."[4] But this constitutional commitment is also reflected in the articles printed in the national magazine of the ELCA and to a considerable degree in the preaching and activities in the local congregations.

While this is obvious to everybody, to the annoyance of some, the question arises, "How deeply is this social activism rooted in the theology of the Lutheran church?" It could be easily demonstrated that the social statements of the LCA, for example, reflected Lutheran theology quite self-consciously. Is this true of the mindset of the ELCA, and will it be reflected in its policy and proclamation in the future? To return to our initial question, "What is the future of theology in the church?"

First of all, one should be aware of the fact that it is possible to have a religious organization which does not have any theology. Individual members of the organization may have a personal ideology or philosophy of religion in the absence of a unifying faith that integrates the organization. It might be invidious to be too specific at this point, but I am prepared to assert that what is commonly called "main-line protestantism" has no clearly defined theology. In these denominations, theology or its absence is a matter of personal choice. What holds these groups together is a common history and certain sociological similarities. This is nothing particularly new. It has been noted by competent observers as early as H. R. Niebuhr in his *Social Sources of Denominationalism*. Such organizations are char-

---

[3]For a helpful analysis of the LCA statements see Christa R. Klein with Christian D. von Dehsen, *Politics and Policy* (Minneapolis: Fortress, 1989).

[4]*Constitution of the Evangelical Lutheran Church in America* (April 30,1987) 4.02.C.

acterized by a certain moral stance which stays very close to the conventional wisdom of the moment. They adjust their position on ethical and theological issues with the shift in public opinion which they do not shape, but emulate. Their slogan is "theological pluralism," which in an indubitably pluralistic world sounds most attractive.

It is my opinion that this may very well be the future of theology in the ELCA. Professional theologians—people who have done graduate work in theology—would be segregated in theological seminaries, where they would do what theologians are supposed to do. They could disagree with each other to their heart's content, within the limits of common courtesy (Martin Luther would certainly not qualify for such an appointment) but would be only marginally involved in policy-making in the church. The seminaries of the church would become increasingly "non-denominational," following the example of university graduate schools of religious studies and, for that matter, the religion departments of the church-related colleges of the ELCA. The notion that a theological consensus is desirable and should be developed, as expressed repeatedly in the *Book of Concord*,[5] would then seem quaint and obsolete. In fact, so would the notion of heresy or false belief. It would not matter what you believe as long as you are sincere.

Why do I consider this a possible scenario for the role of theology? Two reasons seem obvious. (1) The ELCA has not provided a structure for the interaction between theology and the organized church. There is nothing like a commission on faith and order. When a theological issue must be addressed it is turned over to a special commission which certainly and rightly will be inclusive (race, sex, age, language other than English, etc.) but may very well not include a theologian. There is no constitutional or other provision to guarantee that experts in theology will be included in committees making far-reaching theological decisions. Inclusivity does not go that far.

(2) The second obvious reason is largely the fault of the theological community itself. Many leaders and ordinary members of Lutheran churches consider theology irrelevant to the basic needs and tasks of the church. Professional theologians have the reputation of writing and speaking in a jargon which is practically incomprehensible to the average pastor, not to mention parishioners. One example from a recent textbook on Christian dogmatics, published by Fortress Press in 1984, must suffice as an illustration. The author, a professor at one of the seminaries of the ELCA writes: "The Christian faith confesses the epistemic priority of the kairotic event of Jesus for the knowledge of God."[6] The sentence is quite true. It

---

[5]See for example the conclusion to *BC*, 636: "Therefore in the presence of God and of all Christendom among both our contemporaries and our posterity, we wish to have testified that the present explanation of all the foregoing controverted articles here explained, and none other, is our teaching, belief, and confession, in which by God's grace we shall appear before the judgment seat of Jesus Christ and for which we shall give an account. Nor shall we speak or write anything privately or publicly, contrary to this confession, but we intend through God's grace to abide by it."

[6]*Christian Dogmatics*, ed. Carl E. Braaten and Robert W. Jenson, 2 vols. (Philadelphia: Fortress, 1984) 1:207.

means in the language of Jesus: "Anyone who has seen me has seen the Father" (John 14:19). But the very formulation of this sentence reveals a need to mystify, to obfuscate, rather than to teach and explain. As long as theologians see themselves apart from their function of serving God among the people of God they will play games which may be of interest to other theologians, but remove them and their craft from the life of the church.

Let us briefly return to the *Barmen Declaration* of 1934. It dealt with a situation in many ways similar to ours and with a theological establishment even further removed from the life of the people. It declared in the face of its version of what we might call a "new-age religion," the neo-paganism of the Nazis:

> Jesus Christ, as he is attested for us in Holy Scripture, is the one Word of God which we have to hear and which we have to trust and obey in life and death. We reject the false doctrine, as though the Church could and would have to acknowledge as a source of its proclamation, apart from and besides this one Word of God, still other events and powers, figures and truths, as God's revelation.[7]

While the Nazis are long gone, the problem here addressed is as acute as it has ever been. Modern religiosity in the United States, inside and outside the organized church, consists largely of the worship of "other events and powers, figures and truths" apart from and besides this one word of God. Many of the religious and theological movements of the day are precisely the worship of the self, the spiritual power in every individual claiming that every human being is god; or the worship of the elemental spirits—be that the power of the stars or the impersonal process undergirding the universe.

Even theologians who want to stay in touch with the trinitarian Christian tradition appear to have great difficulty with the second article of the Apostles' Creed and John 14:6, "I am the way and the truth, and the life; no one comes to the Father but by me." This scriptural claim is found offensive by many theologians. Willing to accept a creator God and equally willing to "share the spirit," they are offended by the scandal of christology. But if church history teaches us anything, it tells us that there is no Christianity without Christ. Our whiteness or blackness, our masculinity or femininity, our wealth or poverty, our liberal or conservative politics, or even the voice of our blood cannot substitute for this one word of God. Yet under the aegis of pluralism they do substitute and become sources of the proclamation of the church, often to the virtual exclusion of the gospel.

The *Barmen Declaration* continued: "We reject the false doctrine, as though there were areas of our life in which we would not belong to Jesus Christ, but to other lords—areas in which we would not need justification and sanctification through him."[8] Related to the embarrassment over the exclusiveness of christology then and now is the discomfiture with the doctrine of justification by faith as the article with which the church stands or falls. Luther claimed, "We cannot yield or

---

[7]*Barmen Declaration*, II.1; in Forell, *The Protestant Faith*, 288.
[8]*Barmen Declaration*, II.2; in Forell, *The Protestant Faith*, 288.

concede anything in this article, even if heaven and earth, or whatever, do not remain."[9]

It appears that mainline protestantism lacks the willingness to make such an uncompromising statement on justification and sanctification. If the Lutheran church joins this movement, as some signs indicate, the church as an institution will continue, though not necessarily as the Lutheran church. In the past its existence in America depended on two factors: the homogeneous ethnic fellow-ship, or "Teutonic alumni association" in Bishop Lazareth's felicitous phrase, which is rapidly disappearing, and a clear theological position articulated in the Lutheran confessions, which is threatened by the developments described above. Many people see no need for the preservation of a specifically Lutheran theology. Without such a theology and with the rapid disappearance of the ethnic club there would really be no need for the Lutheran church. The mainstream protestant church will become increasingly the advocate of the social and cultural consensus of its professional leadership, both clerical and lay (though many of these profes-sional lay-people will be paid employees of the ecclesiastical establishment serving as *pro forma* laity in its councils, while actually on the payroll of the ecclesiastical institution). It will promote culture religion, what H. R. Niebuhr called the "Christ of Culture." But since we live in a culturally pluralistic society, various denomina-tions will express the respective cultural consensus of this leadership elite (to the chagrin of those members who have another agenda and who will gradually stop making contributions and drift into denominations which better express their religious tastes). We shall have right-wing protestantism, left-wing protestantism and middle-of-the-road protestantism. Some will rely heavily on the authority of Adam Smith, others on Karl Marx, and some on Dale Carnegie. Worship will continue and may even become ever more colorful. In spite of the absence of Christian theology people will still be saved through word and sacrament as long as these continue. But as far as the interaction with culture and society is concerned the church will merely follow the crowd.

While this scenario is possible (and the stuff my nightmares are made of) it is not the only one conceivable for the future of theology in the church. It is imagin-able that the ELCA would take theology seriously, steering away from least-com-mon-denominator ecumenism and building its proclamation on the exposition of the Holy Scriptures with the help of the great trinitarian creeds and the confessions of the Lutheran church. The ELCA constitution certainly makes this possible. Chapter two could not be more emphatic, whatever ill-informed critics may say. But there are other reasons besides this part of the document (inadequately sup-ported by the structures described later in the constitution) which may supply reasons for hope. I shall mention four, though there may be more.

First of all, there is the hunger and thirst of all kinds of people for the good news of Jesus, the Christ. We live in an age in search of faith. This is a world-wide phenomenon. The frauds that make the headlines bear witness to the fact that

[9]Schmalkald Articles II. 1,5 (*The Schmalkald Articles*, translated by William R. Russell [Minneapolis: Fortress Press] 1994).

people in America are seeking and not finding. In Luther's time, when people were paying good money to Tetzel for his indulgences, it was a real need for salvation that was met with fraudulent pieces of paper. From the billion dollar business of the TV evangelists to Shirley MacLaine, from the late Ron Hubbard and Scientology to the purple Guru of Oregon, we see our Tetzels selling space-age indulgences. The only thing the church of the reformation has to offer is the gospel of justification by grace through faith, or Tillich's famous rephrasing: You must accept your acceptance in spite of the fact that you are not acceptable. Feeling good about yourself is not enough. We must believe that we are accepted even when we do not feel good about ourselves. Salvation by little moral rules does not work, but neither does salvation by embracing various political causes, be they ever so righteous. This does not mean that morality or political action are useless—they just don't save. The works-righteousness of the political left is just as hopeless as that of the legalists of the right. Because people are increasingly aware of it, they hunger and thirst for *the* gospel. To have a future the theology of the church must address this issue in language ordinary people can understand.

Second, there is a developing consensus among Lutheran theologians in this country on this basic issue of the gospel. I quoted earlier from a two-volume text on Christian dogmatics, written by a committee of Lutheran theologians. When I reviewed this book I was annoyed by some of the jargon, but much more importantly, I was struck by the consensus on the main issue reflected in this committee report.[10] I claimed then and am prepared to state now, that since the days of the repristinated Lutheran orthodoxy in nineteenth-century America there has not been a similar consensus. It is reflected in *dialog, Lutheran Quarterly,* and *Word & World.* (The very existence of three independent Lutheran theological magazines is in itself significant.) I repeat what I wrote then:

> It was encouraging to see such extensive basic agreement among the teachers who will introduce the majority of the pastors of the new Lutheran church into theology. In view of the prevailing chaos in theology, such agreement is both astonishing and encouraging! It may be the first time since the decline of orthodoxy in America that something like a rough consensus has been achieved, sufficient to sustain the kind of debate, within a universe of discourse which is essential for theology.[11]

But what about the third reason for optimism? The following assertion is not based on the reading of documents or the analysis of statistics but merely on personal observation, and thus anecdotal. The men and women preparing for the ministry in our Lutheran seminaries are different from those of a generation ago, and this difference may bode well for the future. It is clear that many are second-career people and a high percentage are women. The second-career people have a very clear idea why they want to be pastors. Some do not even come from Lutheran backgrounds but become convinced that the Lutheran tradition, which

---

[10]See Braaten and Jenson, *Christian Dogmatics.*

[11]George W. Forell, review of *Christian Dogmatics,* ed. Carl E. Braaten and Robert W. Jenson, *LCA Partners* 6/5 (October/November 1984) 26-28.

they value highly, would enable them to serve the triune God in our time. They have given up money and position and are going into debt, threatening the security of their families, because they want to be servants of God through the ministry of word and sacrament. They are an impressive lot—former lawyers and journalists, stockbrokers and engineers. The list is long. But they are not interested in the superficial aspects of the ministry. They had lessons in salesmanship before. They have come for that which is at the center of theology, the service of word and sacrament. It is a joy to teach them, in spite of their limited knowledge of the classical languages and their lack of philosophical background. The women bring a dimension to the ministry which may help us overcome the image of the pastor as judge, so colorfully described in Updike's *Rabbit Run*. They are open to the theology of the cross, if it is offered to them. And they are beginning to do theology on their own which may serve the church well.

But now to the last point: the significance of the intentional inclusiveness of the ELCA for the future of theology. Anybody who has participated in worship in those Lutheran congregations which are largely black or Hispanic will have observed the vitality with which the heritage of the reformation, the gospel of justification and forgiveness, has been appropriated. It is apparently easier to understand the gospel as "good news" in the inner city than in the suburbs. As Jesus observed: "Those who are well have no need of a physician, but those who are sick" (Matt 9:12). There are few of the oppressed and the poor who think that they are god or even feel particularly good about themselves. Without cross and resurrection the church has no real message for them. When they sing their hymns they sing about law and gospel, even if they have never heard about Lutheran theology. Thus they bring a theological realism about the human situation to the "Teutonic alumni association," which may have a profound effect on our theology. The same is true of our sisters and brothers in Africa and Asia. Having people from Namibia or Korea among the students in our colleges and seminaries gives a new perspective to our theologizing. It is obvious that inclusiveness is not generosity on the part of the traditional Lutherans to "lesser breeds without the law," rather it gives us a new perspective on the nature of God's word to humanity, on law and gospel. Thus, the success or failure of our outreach may indeed affect the future of theology in the church.

We have considered the future of theology in the church. The result of this brief investigation has been complex. Other alternatives may exist than the two here explored. In view of the euphoria of some over the establishment of the ELCA one should be aware of the flaws in its structure, especially in regard to theology. In view of the pessimists who suggest that the amalgamation of the Lutheran tradition into the mainstream of American civil religion is irreversible, one should be aware of the potential of the Lutheran movement because of the place of the word of God in its life. Indeed, as so often before in the history of the Christian church we may be at a moment of decision, a kairotic moment as some theologians would say. At this moment the proper stance for us may be the prayer *Veni Creator Spiritus*.

Word & World
Supplement Series 2
1994

A Neglected Aspect of St. Paul's Doctrine of the Church

IN EVERY DISCUSSION OF THE NATURE AND DOCTRINE OF THE CHURCH, THE influence of the Apostle Paul can be felt. No other individual has contributed more to the development of the doctrine of the church. His definition of the church as the "body of Christ" and as the "bride of Christ" has influenced all later dogmatic theologians. His understanding of the church as the *corpus Christi mysticum* ["the mystical body of Christ"] has been the basis of the evangelical doctrine of the *ecclesia abscondita*, the hidden church. All theologians who have tried to define the nature of the church have had to refer to St. Paul as a basic source.

However, while investigating St. Paul's theology most scholars have thought to find the key to his doctrine of the church in the conceptions "body of Christ" and "bride of Christ." But besides these two expressions, St. Paul uses another conception which is equally important for the doctrine of the church which has been somewhat neglected. According to St. Paul the church is not only the "body of Christ" or the "bride of Christ," but also the "true Israel."

In the following pages the attempt is made to sketch the background for this conception and to examine its importance for the Christian doctrine of the church. For if we understand St. Paul's conception of the "true Israel," we shall be one step closer to an understanding of the essential nature of the church of Christ.

We shall see that according to St. Paul the church is more than a society of

---

This essay stems from Dr. Forell's studies at the Lutheran Theological Seminary at Philadelphia (Mt. Airy) and is his first published work. This piece represents a watershed in the life and career of Dr. Forell, because through his work on ecclesiology, he began to read Luther with renewed seriousness. The essay first appeared in Lutheran Church Quarterly 17 (1944), 48-60. *Those interested in a fuller explication of this theme will want to investigate Dr. Forell's Master's thesis from Princeton, which was published as* The Reality of the Church as the Communion of Saints, A Study of Luther's Doctrine of the Church *(Wenonah, New Jersey: by the author, 1943).*

individuals who voluntarily come together for the purpose of worship. According to St. Paul, the church is the "true Israel," the divine collectivity, the legitimate successor of the *qahal* ["congregation"] of the Old Testament. And if that is the case, the old slogan, *extra ecclesiam nulla salus* ["outside of the church, there is no salvation"] receives new meaning.

Outside this divine collectivity, outside this "true Israel," there is no salvation. The acceptance of this fundamental principle must necessarily reform the protestant conception of the nature of the church. St. Paul's doctrine of the "true Israel" could form the basis of an evangelical doctrine of the church that avoids simultaneously the individualism of papal dictatorship and the individualism of liberal protestant anarchy. A study of St. Paul's doctrine of the "true Israel" may help us to rediscover the true source of all authority in and for the church of Christ. This source is not the will of the pope or bishop, nor the will of the individual members, but the will of God as revealed in the word of God.

ST. PAUL, THE JEWS, AND THE GENTILES

In order to understand St. Paul's doctrine of the church we must first examine the actual situation in which it was developed. St. Paul was born into a world of hatred and tension. The Roman Empire connected superficially and loosely a great multitude of contradictory institutions and movements. It had won its victory over all serious opponents. Rome had no longer to fight constantly for its existence. Now its task was merely to police established conquests. Under such circumstances, moral disintegration set in. The tensions increased within the Roman Empire and below the thin veneer of Roman political power and order. A catastrophe was approaching and seemed to be unavoidable.

One of the most critical of these dissensions within the realm of Rome was the gap that existed between the Greco-Roman civilization on the one hand and Jewish religion on the other. Educated gentiles and religious Jews hated and despised one another. They completely lacked mutual understanding. Into the midst of this tension St. Paul was thrown by his birth at Tarsus. In this hellenistic city, which had a large number of Jewish inhabitants, St. Paul spent the formative years of his boyhood and received his first critical impressions. Both Jewish religion and gentile civilization influenced his development and contributed to his education. If, therefore, any of the early Christian leaders had the qualifications to become the mediator between Judaism and Hellenism and take the gospel from the Jews to the gentiles, Paul of Tarsus was the one. Although born in the diaspora and surrounded by the culture of Hellenism, he received an orthodox Jewish education, and as a youth he was sent to Jerusalem to be taught by Gamaliel, the outstanding Jewish teacher of the time (cf. Acts 22:3; 22:5; 23:6). St. Paul, like no other apostle, was able to be a Jew to the Jews, and a Greek to the Greeks, because he could actually understand both Jews and Greeks.

Most certainly St. Paul was a Jew. There have been scholars who denied the influence of his Jewish culture and who claimed that St. Paul had hellenized Christianity. According to them a hellenistic education was the main influence which shaped St. Paul's theology. They claim that since he used the Greek language, he must have thought as a Greek.[1] But they forget that St. Paul was a Pharisee; he was proud to be a Jew. As a matter of fact, we know that he had been a fanatical Jew and as such had persecuted the church of Christ before his conversion (cf. Gal 1:13; Acts 22:4). But even after his conversion, St. Paul remained a Jew, as far as nationality is concerned. He repeatedly called himself a Hebrew (2 Cor 11:22; Phil 3:5; etc.), an Israelite (2 Cor 11:22; Rom 11:1; etc.), and of the seed of Abraham (2 Cor 11:22; Rom 11:1). He used the rabbinical method of exegesis and counted by the Jewish calendar (1 Cor 16:8; Acts 27:9). Aramaic was probably his mother tongue and his use of *abba* seems to indicate that he used Aramaic in his prayers.[2] If we consider these facts, we understand how he could be a Jew to the Jews.

But in how far was St. Paul a Greek? He had a Greek name besides his Jewish name. He wrote his letters in the Greek language, and he used the Greek Bible, the Septuagint, for his quotations. But was his use of the Greek language an indication of his inner relation to hellenism? Did he use Greek like a foreigner, or did he have complete mastery of the language? An examination of his vocabulary shows that he used the language of the hellenistic middle class and used it well.[3] He did not write a literary Greek, but at the same time he avoided the vulgar language of the proletariat as it was used in many of the contemporary papyri. He used his surroundings, the Mediterranean cities, to supply him with illustrations for the proclamation of his message. Jesus had used the language of the craftsfolk and peasants of Palestine to proclaim his gospel. St. Paul made use of the language of his environment to spread the same message to the people in the cities and towns on the shores of the Mediterranean Sea. He used the vocabulary of the stadium (1 Cor 9:24, 25; Phil 3:14), the language of the army (1 Thess 5:8; Eph 6:10 ff.; Philemon 2; 1 Cor 9:7, 14:8; 2 Cor 10:3 ff.; etc.), the familiar conceptions of slavery, and frequently the language of the court. He did not refuse to use the expressions of the building trade, of the craftsfolk, of the merchant, and of the sailor. St. Paul was indeed acquainted with the language and the world of ideas of the Greeks.

St. Paul lived in a time of seemingly insurmountable contrasts between gentiles and Jews. Gentile civilization and Jewish religion stood in absolute opposition to each other. But in St. Paul the Christian church had a person who could overcome both Jewish and gentile national and cultural limitations. Although he was himself a Jew, he could think of a church of Jews and gentiles which was the valid continuation of the *qahal* of the Old Testament. St. Paul, knowing Jews and gentiles, their pride and prejudice, developed a new idea of the church which made the growth of the church of Christ possible. Because of his peculiar background he saw in the church the "true Israel," not because her members were all

---

[1]So Richard Reitzenstein, *Die hellenistischen Mysterienreligionen nach ihren Grundgedanken und Wirkungen* (Leipzig: B. G. Teubner, 1927).

[2]Paul Feine, *Der Apostel Paulus* (Gütersloh: Bertelsmann, 1927) 525.

[3]Theodor Naegeli, *Der Wortschatz des Apostels Paulus* (Göttingen: Vandenhoeck & Ruprecht, 1905).

racially Jews, but because they were heirs to the faith of Abraham. By this interpretation, St. Paul opened the way for a new understanding of the church.

ST. PAUL'S CONCEPTION OF ISRAEL

The importance of St. Paul in the history of the church is based upon the fact that he became the great apostle to the gentiles. We have seen how his background and education qualified him for his task. Now the question arises, How could St. Paul, the Jew, justify in his own mind the proclamation of the gospel among the gentiles?

There can be no doubt that he considered Israel the chosen people of God, but by his missionary activities he proved that the gentiles too were possible objects of missionary work. This attitude of St. Paul toward the gentiles seems the more remarkable in the light of his pharisaic education. Jewish leaders generally despised and feared the gentiles and considered them second-rate human beings because of their idolatry.[4] How could St. Paul justify his proclamation of the gospel among these idolaters? That this is a real problem can be proved by the fact that St. Paul has been accused of anti-semitism and of a heartless indifference to the fate of his own nation. Passages like 1 Thess 2:15 have been used to prove this charge. However, the accusation of anti-semitism can easily be refuted on the basis of many passages that show St. Paul's burning love for his people according to the flesh. Nothing else could have made him write: "For I could wish that I myself were accursed and cut off from Christ for sake of my own people, my kindred according to the flesh" (Rom 9:3). He lived in ceaseless sorrow because of the fall of Israel, and his proud proclamation in 2 Corinthians testifies that he was not an anti-semite. No anti-semite would have written: "Are they Hebrews? So am I. Are they Israelites? So am I. Are they the seed of Abraham? So am I" (2 Cor 11:22). But how could a person, so proud of national heritage, go out and invite gentiles, non-members of this Hebrew nation, into the church of Christ? How could St. Paul ever believe that God's covenant with Israel included the gentiles? We find the answer to this question in St. Paul's particular conception of the "true Israel."

According to St. Paul there exist two Israels, an Israel according to the flesh and an Israel according to the spirit. It would be the ideal state if these two groups were identical, i.e., if membership in the Israel according to the flesh would necessitate membership in the Israel according to the spirit. But that is not the case. The refusal of the majority of the Hebrews to accept Jesus of Nazareth as their Messiah excludes them from the Israel according to the spirit. However, they still remain members of the Israel according to the flesh. They remain the racial descendants of the patriarchs. Even unbelieving Jews have the indisputable right to call themselves Israelites. But their highest distinction consists in the fact that Jesus Christ, according to the flesh, was a member of their nation. In this very fact the

---

[4]Hermann Strack and Paul Billerbeck, *Kommentar zum Neuen Testament aus Talmud und Midrasch*, 6 vols. (Munich: Beck, 1922-1961) 4:356, 359, 385, etc.

tragedy of the Jewish fate becomes obvious. The Jews refused to accept their highest mark of distinction. "Salvation is from the Jews" (John 4:22), but these very Jews did not want to accept this salvation. The majority of the Israel according to the flesh is therefore worse off than the rest of the world, in spite of the promises, in spite of the adoption and the covenant and the patriarchs. Does that mean that the promises of God have become invalid? Does that mean that the word of God loses its reliability? Does that mean that God changed his mind concerning Israel? St. Paul answers that it does not mean any of these things. In fact, such an interpretation would destroy the basis of our faith. If God did not keep his promise in regard to Israel, we cannot be sure that he is going to keep his promise in regard to the church. The word of God and the revelation of God are an inseparable and indivisible entity. If the word of God loses its validity in any of its parts, it loses its validity in respect to all matters. If the revelation of God's will in regard to Israel is not true, then faith in the revelation of God, and even in God himself, is destroyed. St. Paul realized that and explained the situation by saying: "For they are not all Israel that are of Israel" (Rom 9:6). Besides the Israel according to the flesh, there is an Israel according to the spirit, the Israel of God (Gal 6:16). The membership in the racial group called Israel does not, and never did, necessitate membership in the Israel of God. On the other hand, membership in the Israel of God does not, and never did, depend upon any blood relationship to Abraham.

> For a person is not a Jew who is one outwardly; nor is true circumcision something external and physical. Rather, a person is a Jew who is one inwardly, and real circumcision is a matter of the heart—it is spiritual and not literal. Such a person receives praise not from others but from God. (Rom 2:28-29)

This distinction between the two Israels is as old as the nation. Abraham had two children. Ishmael was his son according to the flesh; Isaac was the son according to God's promise. And we read: "In Isaac shall thy seed be called" (Gen 21:12). Although Ishmael was a real descendant of Abraham, he was excluded from the promise because only in God's call did the promise receive validity. The promises as received by Israel as a nation were always valid only for those who were called by God. The Israel of God is a product of God's will. Later, when Rebecca gave birth to twins, their distinction was not racial or by the laws of primogeniture; the difference between Esau and Jacob was "that God loved Jacob and hated Esau" (Mal 1:2-3). Membership in the Israel of God was at that time, and ever since, dependent upon nothing else but God's calling. The "true Israel," the Israel of God, is, according to St. Paul, the group of men and women whom God called and set apart in the *qahal* of the old covenant and later in the *ecclesia* ["church"] of the new covenant. Therefore, Abraham, as the father of faith, is the father of the gentile Christians, as well as the father of the Jewish Christians (cf. Romans 4). Membership in this Israel is dependent upon nothing else but the call of God's grace, and this call can go out to gentiles as well as Jews. Since the Israel of God is a church composed of Jews and gentiles that comes into existence and is kept in existence by an act of God's grace, it is not up to human beings to criticize God's selection. St. Paul's conception of Israel can be summed up in these words: The true Israel is not a racial or national group and is not dependent upon the number of its members. It is a product of God's will; the true Israel is the church.

Jesus had left with the apostles the idea of the world mission of Christianity. He had shown by his teachings, his life, his death, and his resurrection that Christianity is the absolute religion. In comparison with this revelation of God in Christ, all other religions became unbelief, the blasphemous human attempt to get hold of God. St. Paul had understood better than anyone else this ecumenical mission of Christianity. He realized that the call of the Holy Spirit was not limited by any racial, national, or social barriers. St. Paul believed in the one, holy, universal church, whose Head is the risen Christ (Col 1:18, 1:24; Eph 1:22ff.; Rom 12:4ff.; 1 Cor 12:12ff.; Rom 10:12).

THE IMPORTANCE OF ST. PAUL'S IDENTIFICATION OF THE TRUE ISRAEL WITH THE CHURCH FOR THE DOCTRINE OF THE CHURCH

We have now examined St. Paul's use of the word "Israel" and have found that, according to St. Paul, the "true Israel" is a synonym for the church, that the *Israel tou theou* ["Israel of God"] is identical with the *ecclesia tou theou* ["church of God"]. It is obvious that the application of a word with such an evident national connotation to the church must shed some light upon St. Paul's doctrine of the church and the doctrine of the early church generally. In fact, it must necessarily jeopardize the conception of the early church as held by liberal protestantism. What is this commonly accepted liberal view of the church? Liberal protestantism considers the church a fraternal organization. Membership in this organization has little or no bearing upon the salvation of the individual. Individual Christians organized the church because they desired communion with others who were like-minded. The church is a religious society. The office of the ministry is an administrative office. Schleiermacher expressed this commonly accepted view by saying: "The Christian Church takes shape through the coming together of regenerate individuals to form a system of mutual interaction and co-operation."[5] The church follows after the Christian individual. This view of the church influenced the liberal protestant scholars to understand the conception of the church held in the early days of Christianity in the light of these preconceived opinions. As in the field of exegesis and textual criticism, they used their own opinion on the subject as a measure of the genuineness of the tradition. Everything that did not fit into their conception of the church was considered a later addition or falsification. According to liberal protestantism the early church was a democratic federation of autonomous congregations. There was no spiritual ministry, but the officers of the congregation were only administrators.[6] The congregation was a confederation or

---

[5]F. Schleiermacher, *The Christian Faith* (Philadelphia: Fortress, 1976) 532.

[6]Albrecht Ritschl, *Die Entstehung der altkatholischen Kirche* (Bonn: Marcus, 1857) 356-358; Carl von Weizsäcker, *The Apostolic Age of the Christian Church*, vol. 2 (New York: Putnam, 1895) 291-337, 351-352; Emil Friedberg, *Lehrbuch des katholischen und evangelischen Kirchenrechts* (Leipzig: Tauchnitz, 1909).

association of autonomous individuals, its officials were secular officials, and the spiritual ministry, the service of the word of God, was up to each member of the congregation according to his or her charisma and had nothing whatsoever to do with the administration. The church had come into existence through the voluntary federation of congregations, as the congregation had come into existence through the voluntary federation of individuals. This commonly accepted view of the early church was based mainly upon St. Paul's letters to the Corinthians. The congregation at Corinth was considered the typical Christian congregation. Here liberal protestantism thought to find this democratic, individualistic congregation. Moreover, there was a tendency to trace back the constitution of the Christian congregation to Jewish or hellenistic antecedents. Many claimed that the Christian congregation copied the constitution of the Jewish synagogue. In the synagogue everybody had the same rights, and even the laity could preach to the assembled congregation, and such a procedure agreed with their preconceived opinion of the church.[7] Others again insisted that the Christian congregations had taken their administrative system from the contemporary pagan societies of the Roman Empire.[8] But whatever the differences in detail, the view of the atomistic structure and secondary origin of the early church was generally accepted.

Not even otherwise conservative scholars were in disagreement with these views. These conservative scholars were mostly pietists, and as such considered the church the confederation of the true and pious Christians. They also believed that the Christian existed before the church. Their piety was individualistic and their doctrine of the church was congregationalistic.[9] The only opposition to these generally accepted opinions came from certain Lutherans who instinctively realized the weakness of this entire conception. Kliefoth complained: "The conception of the congregation, which is only a part of the conception of the church, replaces the conception of the entire church."[10] And Wilhelm Loehe wrote:

> No assertion is less tenable than the assertion that the officers of the New Testament received their office from the congregation. Not the congregation transmits the office—where is there a passage in the New Testament to justify such an assertion? On the contrary, the office originates in him who called his congregation through His holy office and who created the office of the ministry for the creation and education of the congregation.[11]

But these people were voices crying in the wilderness and they could not

---

[7]Campegius Vitringa, *De synagoga vetere* (Leucopetra: Wehrmannum, 1726); Richard Rothe, *Die Anfänge der christlichen Kirche und ihrer Verfassung* (Wittenberg: Zimmermann, 1837); Ferdinand Christian Baur, *Das Christentum und die christliche Kirche der drei ersten Jahrhunderte*, 2nd ed. (Tübingen: Fues, 1860).

[8]Giovanni Battista de Rossi, *Roma Sotteranea; or, An Account of the Christian Catacombs* (London: Longmans, 1879); Ernest Renan, *The Apostles* (New York: Carelton, 1866); Paul François Foucart, *Des Associations Religieuses chez les Grecs* (Paris: Klincksieck, 1873).

[9]Olof Linton, *Das Problem der Urkirche in der neueren Forschung* (Uppsala: Almqvist & Wiksells, 1932) 24 ff.

[10]Theodor Kliefoth, *Acht Bücher von der Kirche* (Schwerin: Stiller, 1854) 219.

[11]Wilhelm Loehe, *Aphorismen über die neutestamentlichen Ämter und ihr Verhältnis zur Gemeinde* (Nürnberg: Raw, 1849).

claim any great scientific or historical competence. For a while there was nobody to challenge the congregationalistic individualistic conception of the church.

However, in more recent years the picture has somewhat changed. Through the increased understanding of the eschatological motives of the early church, scholars were led to a deeper appreciation of the conception of the church as held by the early Christians (cf. A. Schweitzer, J. Weiss). Simultaneously there came a clearer understanding of the conception of the Holy Spirit in the early church and the discovery that the charismatic gift of the early Christian had very little in common with the personal and individualistic religiosity of the theologians of the end of the nineteenth century. Theologians began to differentiate between the religious life of the early church and the religious life of the nineteenth century, and so opened the way for a new understanding of the early church. Moreover, investigations into the meaning and background of the word *ecclesia* have shaken the formerly generally accepted view. *Ecclesia* was found to define the totality of the people of God, and one discovered that it originally meant the whole church and was used in this sense prior to its use for the local church.[12]

In the view of these latest investigations, let us now remember St. Paul's identification of the church with the "true Israel." What is the importance of this idea for the understanding of the doctrine of the church? Nothing else would make the inadequacy of the "confederation conception" of the church more obvious than this identification of St. Paul. We saw that St. Paul's idea of the church as the people of God was derived directly from the Old Testament conception of the people of God. In the Old Testament, God acted with and through his people. Israel was the agent of God, Israel was God's servant. But this Israel is not a racial but a spiritual group. Only insofar as Israel is the church, is Israel the nation of God. St. Paul claimed that the church of the New Testament is this "true Israel." He did not see the synagogue and the church as two different religions. According to St. Paul, one did not leave Judaism and join Christianity, but the church was a creation of God that put an end to Judaism and the old covenant. With Christ, the Messiah, a new era had come upon the world, and this era was manifest in the church. This church is heavenly and earthly at the same time. She is the ark that swims on the sea of this corrupted world. Here, in the church, Christ's victory over the prince of this world, which is to become obvious to all the world on the day of judgment, had already become obvious. In the church, eschatology has become contemporaneous. The "true Israel" are those who know that the new era has begun, those who know that the prince of this world has been defeated.[13] To become a Christian is to be saved into this "true Israel." Out of the world, out of the power of the devil, Christians are saved into the church. Out of isolation and alienation from God, individuals are, through an act of God's grace, placed in the communion of the "true Israel," they are made members of the people of God. The

---

[12]Rudolf Sohn, *Kirchenrecht*, 2 vols. (Leipzig: Duncker & Humbolt, 1892-1923); Arthur Headlam, *The Doctrine of the Church and Christian Reunion* (London: John Murray, 1921).

[13]Linton, *Das Problem der Urkirche*, 150.

application of St. Paul's conception of the "true Israel" as the church to the doctrine of the church makes it quite clear that before the individual there was the church, that the church as a collectivity is the "bride of Christ," and that the Holy Spirit is active within that church. Furthermore, the correct understanding of St. Paul's identification of the "true Israel" with the church should make it obvious that it is as impossible to join the church as it is impossible to join a nation. The individual is made a member of the nation by birth, regardless of one's own desires. In the same manner it is an act of God's sovereign grace to make an individual a part of the "true Israel," the church of God. Therefore the individual's race (Jew or gentile), social position (slave or free), sex (male or female), etc., do not matter at all. All that matters is God's love and grace. From St. Paul's conception of the "true Israel" we learn that the church is not created by the voluntary confederation of individuals, but by a sovereign act of God.

This conception of the church, which we base upon our investigation of St. Paul's understanding of Israel, must influence the entire evangelical doctrine of the church. The doctrine of the church has been neglected by pietistic and modernistic individualism; it must be restudied and redefined. Radical individualism is a thing of the past. It is foreign to the evangelical church and had entered into the church by way of the enlightenment. We must rediscover the truth that we are not autonomous personalities, complete in ourselves, but that we need to be made complete by being made members of the body of Christ. The importance of St. Paul's doctrine of the "true Israel" lies in the fact that it can help us to rediscover an evangelical doctrine of the church, a church that is more than the fraternal organization of dubious merits of modern protestantism, a church that is again the communion of saints of the New Testament and the reformation. Outside of this church there is no salvation.

Word & World
Supplement Series 2
1994

Eucharistic Presence as the Key to Theological Understanding

THE ISSUE WHICH FINALLY AND PERMANENTLY DIVIDED THE TWO MAJOR BRANCHES of the Protestant reformation in the sixteenth century was the understanding of the Lord's supper. Because of the profound disagreement on this subject, four cities of the empire, Strassburg, Memmingen, Constance, and Lindau, submitted at Augsburg in 1530 the so-called *Confessio Tetrapolitana* while Zwingli presented his *Ratio Fidei*. All were unable to subscribe to the *Augsburg Confession*.

The reason was made clear by Zwingli. In his *Ratio Fidei* he wrote:

> I believe that in the holy Eucharist—i.e., the supper of thanksgiving—the true body of Christ is present by the contemplation of faith; i.e., that they who thank the Lord for the kindness conferred on us in his Son acknowledge that he assumed true flesh, in it truly suffered, truly washed away our sins in his own blood; and thus everything done by Christ becomes present to them by the contemplation of faith. But that the body of Christ in essence or really—i.e., the natural body itself—is either present in the supper or masticated with our mouth or teeth, as the Papists and some who long for the flesh-pots of Egypt assert, we not only deny, but firmly maintain is an error opposed to God's Word.[1]

---

[1]"Zwingli's Reckoning of his Faith," in *The Book of Concord*, ed. Henry E. Jacobs, 2 vols. (Philadelphia: General Council Publication Board, 1908) 2:170.

This essay was originally published in Vierhundertfünfzig Jahre lutherische Reformation 1517-1967. Festschrift für Franz Lau zum 60. Geburtstag *(Berlin: Evangelische Verlagsanstalt, 1967)* ed. Helmar Junghans, 145-156. Here Dr. Forell follows the implications of Luther's (and Lutherans') understanding of the Lord's Supper to analyze a number of important contemporary theological problems: the doctrines of the human person, the church, and the word.

Zwingli stated the one position opposing the eucharistic teaching of the *Augsburg Confession*. He denied the real and bodily presence of Christ in the sacrament most plainly. The other opposing position was stated in the formal *Confutation of the Augsburg Confession* submitted to the emperor by the Roman Catholic theologians. Here it was observed that the "very necessary article," namely, "that by the almighty Word of God in the consecration of the Eucharist the substance of the bread is changed into the body of Christ" was missing.[2] As over against the *Augsburg Confession* and its statement, "It is taught among us that the true body and blood of Christ are really present in the Supper of our Lord under the form of bread and wine and are there distributed and received,"[3] the Roman theologians in line with the doctrine of transubstantiation denied the presence of the substance of bread and wine in the sacrament. In the ensuing discussion, Luther's own theological understanding of the real presence became decisive for the Lutheran formulations. This is clearly shown in the *Formula of Concord*, where Luther's *Confession Concerning Christ's Supper* is quoted at length.[4] It is this book of the Reformer which furnishes the key to the understanding of the "real presence" by the Church of the Augsburg Confession. The *Formula of Concord* states it as follows:

> The grounds on which we stand in this controversy with the Sacramentarians are those which Dr. Luther proposed in his *Great Confession*:
> "The first ground is this article of our Christian faith: Jesus Christ is true, essential, natural, complete God and man in one person, inseparable and undivided.
> "The second ground is: God's right hand is everywhere. [Christ, really and truly sits at this right hand of God according to his human nature, rules presently and has in his hands and under his feet everything in heaven and on earth. No other human being, no angel, but only Mary's Son, is so sat down at the right hand of God whence he is able to do these things.][5]
> "The third ground is that God's Word is not false nor does it lie.
> "The fourth ground is that God has and knows various modes of being at a given place, and not only the single mode which the philosophers call *local* or spatial."[6]

The influence of Luther is significant because it resulted in a christological emphasis in the discussion. The presence of Christ with the bread and wine is part of the presence of Christ in all things as the eternal Logos, the second person of the Holy Trinity. This analogy is explicitly stated in the *Solid Declaration*:

> In addition to the words of Christ and of St. Paul (the bread in the Lord's Supper "is true body of Christ" or "a participation in the body of Christ"), we at times also use the formulas "*under* the bread, *with* the bread, *in* the bread." We do this to reject the papistic transubstantiation and to indicate the sacramental union between the untransformed substance of the bread and the body of Christ. The

---

[2]"Confutation of the Augsburg Confession," in *The Book of Concord*, ed. Jacobs, 2:214-215.

[3]*AC* 10, in *BC*, 34.

[4]*FC, Ep*, 7:10, in *BC*, 483.

[5]The material in brackets is an interpolation in *FC* not found in Luther's Confession; cf. *LW* 37:214.

[6]*FC, Ep* 7:10-14, in *BC*, 483.

> Scriptures do the same thing when they reproduce and explain the statement, "The Word became flesh," with such equivalent phrases as, "The Word dwelt in us" or "In Christ the whole fullness of the deity dwells bodily," or "God was with him," or "God was in Christ," and similar expressions. Thus the Scriptures explain that the divine essence has not been transformed into the human nature but that both untransformed natures are personally united...For as in Christ two distinct and untransformed natures are indivisibly united, so in the Holy Supper the two essences, the natural bread and the true, natural body of Christ, are present together here on earth in the ordered action of the sacrament, though the union of the body and blood of Christ with the bread and wine is not a personal union, like that of the two natures of Christ, but a sacramental union.[7]

It is this analogy which determines the Lutheran understanding of the "real presence" "in, with, and under" the elements of bread and wine and makes it suggestive for the understanding of a number of problems which face the Christian church in our time.

The Lutheran interpretation of the real presence in the sacrament is an attempt to avoid the real absence of the divine in the things of this earth suspected in the Zwinglian position as well as the real absence of the earthly in the elements of the eucharist suspected in transubstantiation. Quite apart from the adequacy of these formulations for a definitive contemporary theology of the eucharist, the Lutheran insistence upon the presence of the divine in the earthly may be a helpful clue to a number of contemporary theological issues. To state these implications clearly and offer them for open discussion may be part of the ecumenical responsibility of Lutheran theology.

THE DOCTRINE OF THE HUMAN PERSON

Contemporary theology is confronted by the loss of a doctrine of the human person. Pan-biological thinking reduces people to primates whose difference from other animals is only marginal and a quantitative rather than a qualitative factor. This situation is new. For the two streams whose influence constituted western culture—the Hebraic and the Greek—were firmly convinced of the qualitative uniqueness of human beings. They are to "have dominion over the fish of the sea, and over the birds of the air, and over the cattle, and over all the earth, and over every creeping thing that creeps upon the earth", according to Genesis 1. Even the most agnostic Greek thinkers like the Sophist Protagoras saw in humanity "the measure of all things,"[8] while the Stoic Epictetus was prepared to say: "If one could only take to heart this judgment, as one ought, that we are all, before anything else, children of God and that God is the Father of gods and humans, I think that one will never harbour a mean or ignoble thought about one's self."[9] This confidence in

---

[7]*FC, SD* 7:36-38, in *BC*, 575-576.

[8]Diogenes Laertius, *The Lives of Eminent Philosophers* 9:51, ed. R. D. Hicks, 2 vols. (London: W. Heinemann; Cambridge, MA: Harvard University, 1965-66) 2:463.

[9]*The Stoic and Epicurean Philosophers*, ed. W. J. Oates (New York: Random House, 1940) 229. [Translation altered.]

humanity's uniqueness was not shaken in the west even by the liberal movements of renaissance and enlightenment. They rather tended to reenforce it. It was left to our age to experience the death of the human being. While it would take us too far afield to discuss this development in detail, it could be said that Erich Fromm is right when he says, "In the nineteenth century the problem was that God is dead; in the twentieth century the problem is that *man is dead.*"[10] Thus, those theologians who have recently stumbled upon Nietsche and who constantly advertise their "new" discovery of the death of God are actually addressing a nineteenth-century problem.

The twentieth-century problem is the death of the human being. This is revealed in much of our contemporary literature which is characterized by its loss of humanity, but is perhaps most effectively symbolized in the comparison between Daniel Defoe's *Robinson Crusoe*[11] and William Golding's *Lord of the Flies.*[12] Both books deal with humans confronted by the jungle. But Defoe's Englishman is the person of the eighteenth century. Robinson Crusoe conquers the jungle for civilization. He is enabled, with God's help, to make the wilderness into paradise, and to live up to the promise and call of Genesis 1. The English boys who are stranded without adults on Golding's desert island in the second half of the twentieth century are refugees from an atomic holocaust. They have brought the remnants of civilization with them, consisting apparently of something like *Robert's Rules of Order* in the back of their mind and the vestigial remains of law and discipline. Yet Golding describes eloquently how rapidly the jungle conquers civilization. The symbols of law and order are soon crushed and the boys become wild animals, the "beast" conquers.

As this comparison and the development of a new art form—the "futopia," the colorful description of a terribly futile and inhuman future society—show, we no longer seem to believe in our ability to retain our humanity. The human being, as a human being, appears to be doomed.

What is the proclamation of the Christian faith in this situation? The answer of the theologians is ambiguous. We have had a liberal and a conservative Christian anthropology and both have failed to do full justice to the nature of the human predicament as reflected in our literature. Both, indeed, have quoted scripture, but both have tended to do so selectively.

The liberals have quoted Gen 1:27, the so-called P source. They have been satisfied to say that "God created humankind in his image, in the image of God he created them; male and female he created them." The story of humanity's fall was understood as meaningless mythology of no relevance to our enlightened age. The result has been an essentially sentimental view which has made liberal Christianity

---

[10]Erich Fromm, *The Sane Society* (New York: Rinehart, 1955) 360.

[11]Daniel Defoe, *The Life and Surprising Adventures of Robinson Crusoe* (1719; many reprints).

[12]William Golding, *Lord of the Flies* (London: Faber & Faber, 1954).

irrelevant to the self-understanding of modern people as we encounter it today. Those who honestly believe in the innate goodness of people, their moral freedom and ability to love unselfishly, simply have no access to the people described in the political or social history of the twentieth century or in their most sensitive and honest literary creations. A sentimental anthropology has made the theological liberals seem sadly obsolete.

But conservative theology has served us not much better. Here theologians, following the authority of the early church, have quoted Genesis 3, the so called J source, and described the reality and significance of the fall, but at the same time relegated Gen 1:27 and its proclamation of the image of God in people to ancient history. According to conservative theology, the *imago dei* since the fall is no longer relevant to us—and only an archaeological curiosity. If they talk about the modern human being, the historical human being, the conservatives think and write as if only the fall were germane to the nature and destiny of humanity. The result of this one-sided view of the amplitude of the scriptural witness has been a pessimistic fatalism, which, while more realistic according to the self-evaluation of moderns, has hardly been more helpful.

Thus Christian theology has vacillated between unrealistic sentimentalism and fatalistic legalism in its view of humankind because it has not taken the complementary character of the varying Biblical views of humanity seriously.

It seems that here the understanding of the real presence of Christ in the Eucharist can throw some light on the Christian understanding of humanity. As the elements are not once bread, now body, once wine, now blood, but, through the power of Christ, the living word, body and blood in, with and under the bread and wine, so people can be suffused and empowered by the presence of Christ.

The same Christ who is really present in the bread and wine can be really present in the men and women of our time. This does not mean that their humanity is abolished but rather that the ordinary person, even without halo or Ph.D., can become an instrument of the living Lord. This is the message expressed by Luther in his phrase that humans are *simul justus et peccator*, righteous and sinners at the same time. And this implies the rejection of the sequential thinking which sees the process of becoming Christian as a human accomplishment and the saint as a moral or mystical athlete. The real presence of Christ in us is not something we contemplate as real only in heaven, nor does it involve some transubstantiation, the abolition of our earthly human nature. It is rather real presence in, with, and under the bodily, biochemical, metabolic humanity which constitutes our human existence and is the only humanity we know.

THE DOCTRINE OF THE CHURCH

But how relevant is this insight to some of the other theological issues debated in our time? There can be little doubt that the doctrine of the church is one of these controversial issues in the second half of the twentieth century. Hardly a month goes by without the publication of a new book attacking the established church and its ministry. We have all heard a great deal about the "suburban captivity of the churches" and "the noise of solemn assemblies."[13] There is doubtlessly a deep malaise which affects the contemporary understanding of the doctrine of the church. On the one hand people see the church in completely inclusive terms. It is the political community at worship. From this point of view it includes Protestant, Catholic, and Jew and even the agnostic or atheist in so far as they participate in these all-pervasive socio-religious functions like invocations, benedictions, hymns, and readings from scripture at all possible and impossible occasions of our life together. Everybody who is a member of the socio-political community is also a member of the church in this broad and inclusive sense. It makes little difference whether they are Protestant, Catholic, or Jew—and the denomination to which they belong is more of a status symbol, in line with the car they drive, than of any theological significance. Successful ministers of this church are those who support the prevailing value system, the conventional wisdom, with their sermons, and who by means of pastoral counseling enable individuals who may have difficulties adjusting to the prevailing climate to learn to like it.

This function of the religious community is well known and has been ably described by so many competent observers that it can be considered common knowledge. The biblical motto for this inclusive view of the church might be Jesus' word, "Whoever is not against us is for us" (Mark 9:40), and the parable of the kingdom of heaven being like a net which was thrown into the sea and gathered fish of every kind (Matt 13:47).

But this is by no means the only view of the church prevalent in our time. Simultaneous with this inclusive view, there is an exclusive view which sees in the church a voluntary association of God's elect. Menno Simon's definition of the church has found many supporters in our time. He said,

> Christ's church consists of the chosen of God, His saints and beloved who have washed their robes in the blood of the Lamb, who are born of God and led by Christ's Spirit, who are in Christ and Christ in them, who hear and believe His word, live in their weakness according to His commandments and in patience and meekness follow in His footsteps.[14]

Friedrich Schleiermacher says something very similar in the nineteenth century when he states, "The Christian Church takes shape through the coming together of regenerate individuals to form a system of mutual interaction and co-operation."[15] Most criticisms of the institutional church in our time are made in the light of such pietistic, individualistic, and legalistic definitions, which have become the normative theological concept of the church in Protestantism across the entire theological spectrum from extreme conservatism to extreme liberalism. While the various critics of the church may make one or the other exclusive

---

[13][See Gibson Winter, *The Suburban Captivity of the Churches* (Garden City: Doubleday, 1961) and Peter Berger, *The Noise of Solemn Assemblies* (Garden City: Doubleday, 1961). Ed.]

[14]Henry Fosdick, ed., *Great Voices of the Reformation* (New York: Random House, 1952) 316.

[15]Friedrich Schleiermacher, *The Christian Faith* (Edinburgh: T. & T. Clark, 1928) 532.

position the perch from which to hurl their thunderbolts—they are always hurled from some pietistic-individualistic-legalistic perch.

Some may emphasize their exclusive intellectual superiority—and put advertisements in the newspaper appealing to those who have "outgrown supernaturalism." Others, again, may emphasize their exclusive moral superiority and disdain the eating and drinking habits of the rest of christendom. Still others may emphasize their exclusive spiritual superiority and rejoice in their mystical gifts and their speaking in tongues. All have in common their pride and exclusiveness, based on some achievement or other, and the biblical motto for this exclusive view of the church might very well be: "Whoever is not with me is against me, and whoever does not gather with me scatters" (Luke 11:23). And their favorite saying, "For the gate is narrow and the way is hard, that leads to life, and those who find it are few" (Matt 7:14).

But both the inclusive and the exclusive view have one great weakness in common. Neither view says anything to the world in which we live. The speech of the inclusive church is so much like the politics and the sociology, the morality and the spirituality of the "conventional wisdom" that they cannot be distinguished. It is all the same sad combination of Fourth-of-July oratory and "Dear Abby" counseling that is heard everywhere else. A newspaper advice column could teach many a lesson to a pastor—especially if the pastor's approach is essentially that of a newspaper columnist.

On the other hand, the speech of the exclusive church is so esoteric that it is incomprehensible. Whether because it has borrowed the irrelevant language of contemporary linguistic analysis in a vain effort to be relevant or because it uses the historical language of Canaan, the pious vocabulary of christendom, without any effort at translation, or even literally talks in tongues; whatever it says is simply not heard.

This could be illustrated by the image of the church reflected in contemporary American literature. It is apparent that many of our contemporary authors are interested in God. This is as true for John Updike[16] as for J.D. Salinger.[17] Even that chronicler of soulless humanity, Hubert Selby, in his *Last Exit to Brooklyn*[18] uses biblical sayings to set the mood for each of his soul-shrivelling chapters. But the church, either in its inclusive or exclusive version, does not occur to them as having anything to say to the human situation they attempt to interpret. The inclusive church is simply not distinctive enough in its message to come to their attention. It does not say anything that is not said better by politicians, sociologists, or businesspeople. The exclusive church is buried beneath its ecclesiastical jargon, and this jargon is no more meaningful when it is translated from early Aristotle to late Heidegger. The fact is, nobody is listening to either.

[16]E.g., John Updike , *Rabbit Run* (New York: Knopf, 1960), and *Pigeon Feathers and Other Stories* (Greenwich, Ct: Fawcett, 1962).

[17]E.g., J. D. Salinger, *The Catcher in the Rye* (Boston: Modern Library, 1951), and *Franny and Zooey* (Boston:Little, Brown, 1961).

[18]Hubert Selby, *Last Exit to Brooklyn* (New York: Grove, 1964).

Perhaps here, too, the doctrine of the real presence of Christ in, with, and under the bread and wine, can serve as a clue in the search for the recovery of the meaning of the church. As he is present in the bread and wine, he is potentially present for all people. They may awaken to this fact when they hear the "good news" of their acceptance and the meaningfulness of their life in whatever form it may be proclaimed to them. If we trust in this presence in, with, and under all the varied institutional forms that surround us, we may abandon our vain search for the perfect institution—or even the perfect absence of institution—and use what is at hand, confident that he who made out of water wine may use our totally inadequate institutional means to make his presence felt, and that he who once spoke by Balaam's ass (Num 22:28) may speak in our time persuasively through speakers whom we in our wisdom consider not much better.

Thus the proclamation of the real presence may *free us from* the ecclesiological impasse, the search for the perfect institution, the perfect minister, the perfect member, *for the service* of the perfect Lord in failing institutions with failing members under failing ministers. To point to this possibility may be part of the ecumenical responsibility of Lutheran theology in our time.

THE DOCTRINE OF THE WORD

A third area of theological conflict, apparent even to the most superficial observer, is the doctrine of the word. Is the doctrine of the real presence in the eucharist of any help here? The Holy Scriptures and their interpretation were not a serious problem to christendom until the reformation. The reason is obvious. As long as the church used the allegorical interpretation of scripture, no serious problems could arise. The allegorical method supplied such a latitude of interpretation as to make questions of scriptural authority irrelevant.

We are familiar with the Latin jingle which served as the hermeneutical key: *Littera gesta docet, quid credas allegoria, moralis quid agas; sed quid speres anagoge* (The letter lets you know what happened, and allegory what you must believe; the moral sense which you must do, the anagogical what you may hope for). Thus, for example, "Jerusalem" meant literally the "city in Palestine," allegorically it meant "the church," morally it meant "the human soul," and anagogically it meant "heaven." Similarly, the story of Ishmael and Isaac was subject to a multitude of legitimate interpretations. Literally one could speak about the two sons of Abraham. Allegorically it was supposed to mean the Old and the New Testaments, or the synagogue and the church, or law and grace. The moral sense of this story had to do with the conflict between flesh and spirit. Anagogically the story told about hell and heaven and humankind's eschatological destiny.

It is easy to see how the problem of the "word" could not come up as long as the allegorical method held sway. Since almost anything could be meant by any passage of scripture the real issue was that of the teaching authority of the church. Only an authoritative, even infallible, *magisterium* could decide between the unlimited possibilities which the allegorical method presented.

It was the protestant reformation which, in its conflict with Rome, appealed to the historical and literal sense of scripture and more and more abandoned the allegorical method of the past.[19] This, however, tended to place the Christian faith increasingly at the mercy of the exegete. In the course of history, exegesis became more and more independent of the faith of the church, until exegetical concerns and pastoral concerns became totally separated towards the end of the nineteenth century. While the one tried to discover the "Jesus of history," the other tried to proclaim the "Christ of faith." It was of little help that the so-called "Jesus of history" turned out to be a most elusive figure, so that Albert Schweitzer could say as early as 1906,

> The Jesus of Nazareth who came forward publicly as the Messiah, who preached the ethic of the Kingdom of God, who founded the Kingdom of Heaven upon earth, and died to give His work its final consecration, never had any existence. He is a figure designed by rationalism, endowed with life by liberalism, and clothed by modern theology in an historical garb.[20]

In spite of all the refinements of this "quest" in the last sixty years, Schweitzer's observation still holds. The issue is not really between the "Jesus of history" and the "Christ of faith," but rather between various faiths who each use the complexities and refinements of exegesis to support their respective views. In this development, Holy Scripture has become the object of much debate. It is considered totally and exclusively a human word by modernists and liberals, and totally and exclusively God's word by fundamentalists and conservatives. In support of their respective faith, these theological parties interpret the Bible naturalistically or supernaturalistically as merely a fallible human document or as an inerrant divine record. This polarization of attitudes towards Holy Scripture has gone so far in our day that communication between the contending groups seems no longer possible. The disdain for the obscurantism of the "fundamentalists" by the "liberals" is only equalled by the contempt for the apostasy of the "liberals" by the "fundamentalists."

The bitterness of the conflict affects to some degree most American denominations and is exported by them to the younger churches all over the world. It frequently divides congregations and even individual Christian families in the same congregation.

Does the doctrine of the real presence of Christ in the eucharist offer any help towards reconciliation? Indeed, if the doctrine of the word is seen in the light of the eucharistic presence, a number of difficulties should immediately disappear. It becomes apparent that the statements "the Bible is a human word" and "the Bible is the word of God" are no more mutually exclusive than the statement that in the sacrament bread and wine as well as body and blood are present. It is in, with, and under the human words of an Amos or a Paul that through the power of the Holy Spirit the living word of God reaches us. To deny the humanity of the Bible is

[19]For Luther's development, see the detailed analysis in Gerhard Ebeling, *Evangelische Evangelienauslegung* (Munich: Albert Lempp, 1942) 44-89.
[20]Albert Schweitzer, *The Quest of the Historical Jesus* (London: A. & C. Black, 1931) 396.

biblical transubstantiation and particularly inappropriate for Lutherans. To deny the presence of the divine word is Zwingli's doctrine of the "real absence" and equally inappropriate.

If Christ deigns to be present to us in the very earthly bread and wine of holy communion so he also is present for us in the very human words of prophets and apostles as they are proclaimed ever anew as the *viva vox evangelii*, the living voice of the gospel.

Thus the doctrine of the real presence in the eucharist could free theology from the false alternatives of a contemporary theological debate. It could free exegesis to do the job of understanding the scriptures in all their human variety, complexity, and color without being burdened with the task of producing a definitive systematic theology on the side. Lutheran exegetes should be willing to face the theologies of the Old and New Testament, and hesitate to suppress any one of them in order to support their own particular "biblical" theologies.

Similarly, the systematic theologian should be free to express the faith of the Christian Church in language adequate to the questions of our time, without trying to produce some final, infallible, inerrant system, as "irrefutable as scripture itself," as was said foolishly not so long ago about the dogmatic theology of the late Franz Pieper.[21] This may produce a number of different systematic theologies for our time; none of them perfect. None of them making the ridiculous claim that they represent "The Secular Meaning of the Gospel"[22] or "The New Essence of Christianity"[23] or "Christ Without Myth"[24] or whatever the pretentious titles of our contemporary theologians may claim. In the light of the real presence of God the Son in, with, and under the human word of witness, we may learn through the power of God the Spirit to worship and adore in thought, word, and deed God the Father, who with the Son and the Spirit lives and reigns, ever one God, world without end.

[21]Edward Plass, "Appendix D," in *What Luther Says*, vol. 3 (St. Louis: Concordia, 1959) 1634.

[22]P. van Buren, *The Secular Meaning of the Gospel* (New York: Macmillan, 1963) 205.

[23]W. Hamilton, *The New Essence of Christianity* (New York: Association, 1961) 159.

[24]Schubert Ogden, *Christ Without Myth: A Study Based on the Theology of Rudolf Bultmann* (New York: Harper, 1961) 189.

Word & World
Supplement Series 2
1994

The Formula of Concord and the Teaching Ministry

IN SPITE OF THE MUCH PUBLICIZED EFFORTS OF THE PSYCHO-HISTORIANS, IT should be apparent by now that the clue to the Lutheran reformation was the University of Wittenberg and Luther's activities as a university professor. The reformation resulted from the teaching ministry of Luther, whatever the much discussed tower was and whenever the so-called tower-experience occurred.

Luther and his colleagues managed to change a university completely in line with the general medieval scholastic tradition into a powerful instrument of reform. The reformation can be understood more easily by means of the academic changes which took place in Wittenberg after 1512 and the influence which the professors and students of this university exerted upon their age by means of their academic activities than by any of the subjective experiences in Luther's life, such as the thunderstorm near Stotternheim, the alleged seizure during his first mass, the nailing or mailing of the *Ninety-five Theses*, or the somewhat dubious "Here I Stand" episode at Worms.

Luther used the university's adversary system in theology, as practiced by means of the disputation, as a teaching device in order to present his ideas to his colleagues and students—not only at Wittenberg, but also in Heidelberg and Leipzig. It was by the full and competent utilization of an existing teaching method, the academic disputation, that he created the Wittenberg university theology which carried the reformation from Saxony across the entire world.

It is against this background that we want to look at the *Formula of Concord.* Here, too, it would be possible to discuss at length the psychological problems and traumas of the architects of this document. Jakob Andreae was the son of a

---

This essay was first published as part of the 400th anniversary edition of The Sixteenth Century Journal *(VIII/4 [1977] 39-47), dedicated to investigations of the* Formula of Concord. *Dr. Forell here provides a lucid example of historical theology, which demonstrates the continuing relevance of the formula to contemporary issues facing the teaching ministry of the church.*

blacksmith and because of his humble background apparently suffered from a massive inferiority complex in a class-conscious age. His jealousy of Martin Chemnitz and other theologians seemed at times to border on the paranoid.[1] Martin Chemnitz could also be described by psycho-historians on the basis of his stuttering and sleepwalking while a child, his life-long obsessions with astrology,[2] and perhaps even his autodidactic theology. David Chytraeus was born just after his father, a Lutheran pastor, was attacked in the pulpit by an imperial official with drawn sword. As a result, David's mother was in complete shock for about an hour before she gave birth to her son.[3] Even Nikolaus Selnecker had a traumatic experience in his youth. On his way to the University of Wittenberg he was ambushed, shot, and so severely wounded that he was bedridden for months and had to postpone his studies for a year. As one observer stated: "The incident seemed permanently to have weakened his body, he was frequently ill thereafter. Psychologically his self-assurance was shaken."[4]

But we shall leave the pursuit of this path of investigation into the *Formula of Concord* to the Erik Eriksons and Norman O. Browns of the world and rather ask, what, in fact, was different in the changes which Luther and his colleagues had brought about and which the *Formula of Concord* accomplished some fifty years later? The date and the event which makes the difference between the two developments is the Peace of Augsburg of 1555 and the establishment of the principle *cuius regio eius religio*, that whoever rules the land determines its religion. As a result the *Formula* is a thoroughly political event, unthinkable without the active and decisive participation of the princes, who, in order to make progress, occasionally met without their theologians, as for example at the Frankfurt Recess of 1558 and the Convention of Naumburg of 1561. Because of the power and theological involvement of the princes, if there was to be concord at all, it had to be the work of house-theologians. A free general Lutheran council, as desired by the Gnesio-Lutherans, seemed the road to the utter fragmentation of the Lutheran movement.

But house-theologians were a special breed, then as now. Andreae's childhood had been burdened by poverty. He had to leave Latin school at the age of ten and begin an apprenticeship as a carpenter, from which a dual scholarship rescued him. His education continued to be dependent on the duke, and his career reflected this political dependence. From preparatory school to university to the doctorate he experienced the good will and support of Ulrich and Christoph of Württemberg. His appointments to high ecclesiastical and academic office were made by the duke. As Robert Kolb has stated it,

> By bestowing on Andreae the variety of assignments and duties which came to

[1]See Selnecker's diary on Andreae's behavior in Theodore R. Jungkuntz, *Formulators of the Formula of Concord* (St. Louis: Concordia, 1977) 146-154.

[2]In his difficulties with Duke Albrecht of Prussia, resulting from his conflict in Königsberg with the duke's favorite, Andreas Osiander, Chemnitz observed, "Next to God I had my one protection in my astrology, without which the duke would not do." Ibid., 50.

[3]Ibid., 69.

[4]Ibid., 9.

him before he was even thirty-five years old, Duke Christoph demonstrated his great confidence in the judgment and capability of the smith's son who would not have gone on to university study had not Christoph's father been willing to subsidize his education. That investment was rewarded with loyal service because Andreae stood ready to provide it and because Christoph regarded him highly enough to command and use it.[5]

But the involvement of Chemnitz, Chytraeus, and Selnecker was also thoroughly political. The entire effort toward unifying the Lutherans was motivated as much by political as theological reasons. The result was a compromise between the two extreme positions in the Lutheran movement: gnesio-Lutheranism led by the technically most competent theologian of the age, Flacius, and Philippism, named after Philip Melanchthon, which attempted to compromise the Lutheran position in all directions.

The *Formula of Concord* is an effort to avoid both extremes, as its affirmative theses as well as the different antitheses clearly indicate. Thus, for example, the affirmative theses in regard to original sin insist both on the seriousness of sin and "that it is so deep a corruption that nothing sound or uncorrupted has survived in man's body or soul, in his inward or outward powers,"[6] while they make a clear distinction between a human being's nature and original sin: "The distinction between our nature and original sin is as great as the difference between God's work and the devil's work."[7] Again, in regard to free will, the effort is made to avoid "the mad dream of the so-called Stoic philosophers and of Manichaeans, who taught that whatever happens must so happen and could not happen otherwise,"[8] as well as the teaching of the "crass Pelagians" that people can convert themselves to God by their own powers, without the grace of the Holy Spirit,[9] and that of the Semi-Pelagians "that man by virtue of his own powers could make a beginning of his conversion but could not complete it without the grace of the Holy Spirit."[10]

In this manner all the controverted issues are dealt with,[11] in effect causing the "exclusion of the extremists by means of antitheses with accompanying condemnations."[12] But regardless of the people who wrote the *Formula* and the manner in which the final document was produced and approved, questions of

---

[5]Robert Kolb, *Andreae and the Formula of Concord* (St. Louis: Concordia, 1977) 14.

[6]*BC*, 467.

[7]Ibid., 466.

[8]Ibid., 470-471.

[9]Ibid, 471.

[10]Ibid.

[11]In view of this effort to avoid polarization it is ironic that Eugene F. Klug, in his recent book, *Getting into the Formula of Concord* (St. Louis: Concordia, 1977) 13, tries to pin the label "moderate," used frequently in the present debate in the Lutheran Church–Missouri Synod, on the Philippists. But it is obvious that the authors of the *Formula* attempt to choose a moderate way between the extremes perceived by them.

[12]Jungkuntz, *Formula of Concord*, 41.

considerable historical interest, what is the significance the *Formula* for the teaching ministry of the church today?

First of all, we must appreciate that the *Formula* is a historical document that speaks specifically to the problems and conflicts of an age which is not ours. The very success of the *Formula* was the direct result of the precision with which it addressed the controversies of its time. To revive the debates about the effects of garlic juice smeared on a magnet held by Victorin Strigel[13] would not be helpful today. And to become exercised about Matthias Flacius' claim that since the fall no distinctions can be made between human nature itself and original sin[14] would still not contribute meaningfully to the proclamation of the gospel in our world. We do not think in terms of substance and accidents, and to reintroduce this terminology into contemporary theological speech would not seem to help anybody.[15] The very fact that the *Formula* states that "the prophetic and apostolic writings of the Old and New Testaments are the *only rule and norm* according to which all doctrines and teachers alike must be appraised and judged,"[16] precludes using this document and any other document besides the scriptures as "rule" and "norm" today. The function of the *Formula* as well as of all other Lutheran confessions is to be a responsible exposition of scripture, which obligates the teaching ministry to take them seriously as such. But like all exposition of scripture this particular and binding exposition did not take place in a historical and cultural vacuum. To read the *Formula* out of its historical and cultural context is not taking it seriously and represents a form of gnostic unfaithfulness which can appear only superficially as a superior form of loyalty and is, in fact, ultimate disloyalty.[17]

Second, we must observe the *odi errorem, amo errantes* (["hate the sin, love the sinner"] Augustine) which characterizes the *Formula*. Every opportunity existed to name names. Modern editions in their footnotes enlighten us concerning the persons whose errors the *Formula* condemns. Yet the *Formula* itself avoids name-calling, at least concerning the followers of Luther whose errors are being rejected. The old heretics are mentioned by name, such as Marcion and Manes, Arius and Eutyches, and there is an occasional swipe at Zwingli and Erasmus. But by and large the *Formula* is free from personal invective. Even though the description of the pope as Antichrist is taken over from the Smalcald Articles,[18] individual popes are cited with approval as "ancient teachers" of the church, as for example Leo I and Gelasius I, or Gregory the Great.[19] This is particularly astonishing in view of the fact that it was, after all, Gelasius I who had asserted that "the pope is to be judged by no one" as early as the end of the fifth century. Apparently the *Formula*

---

[13]*BC*, 468.

[14]Ibid.

[15]Ibid., 508.

[16]Ibid., 464 (my italics).

[17]See also, Edmund Schlink, *Theology of the Lutheran Confessions* (Philadelphia: Muhlenberg, 1961) xvii-xxix.

[18]*BC*, 614, line 22.

[19]Ibid., 575; cf. 483, 606.

is able to make distinctions which later Lutherans claiming loyalty to it were no longer able to make.

The implications are obvious for the teaching ministry of the church. It is important to oppose error and to show love and compassion for those who err. The *Formula* was able to reunite the quarreling Lutheran factions because of its amazing restraint, especially admirable in a time when restraint was hardly customary and all sides were skilled in the use of personal invective.

Third, we must look at the *Formula* with some care in an effort to distinguish the doctrinal intention and the doctrinal form without taking the form lightly and jumping too easily and superficially from the actual form to the assumed intention.[20] Friedrich Brunstäd suggested that one must begin with the existing and traditional form of the teaching (*Lehrgestalt*) in order to grasp and examine within it the intention of the teaching (*Lehrintention*).

> The doctrinal intention is testimony to the truth of the gospel which has been opened up in a new way in the reformation witness. Doctrinal form is the manner in which this testimony was articulated in the context of the history of ideas of a particular time. In this process the available thought forms were used and perhaps sovereignly changed and fused, but they were also negatively affected by that time so as to be hindered, broken, and twisted out of shape so that the expression might become inadequate.[21]

The task of the teaching ministry is to fix clearly on the intention in order to modify the form by utilizing the instruments made available by the contemporary situation in the history of ideas.

I have tried to illustrate this procedure in another context in relation to the development from Paul's position expressed in Romans 13 to the position taken in the *Augsburg Confession* Article XVI:

> There is a profound difference in mood between the position of the Christian citizen in the sixteenth century and the position of this citizen in the time of St. Paul. The difference between Romans 13 and Article XVI of the *Augsburg Confession* is dramatic. Paul writes to the Roman Christians, in the first century: "Every person must submit to the supreme authorities" (Rom. 13:1). The *Augsburg Confession* calls Christians to act as authorities. It is written for people and signed by people who have great political and social responsibility. It recognizes the changes that have taken place in the intervening fifteen centuries.[22]

But the changes since the sixteenth century are equally if not more dramatic, so that if we are to be faithful to the confessions, we must now extrapolate from Romans 13 through *Augustana* XVI to our present situation as citizens of a "powerful democracy which has awesome responsibilities for the future of the world."[23]

---

[20]See Friedrich Brunstäd, *Theologie der lutherischen Bekenntnisschriften* (Gütersloh: Bertelsmann, 1951) 8-12.

[21]Ibid., 9 (author's translation).

[22]G. W. Forell, "The Augsburg Confession: Article XVI, Civil Affairs," *Bulletin*, Lutheran Theological Seminary, Gettysburg, Pennsylvania, 49/3 (Fall 1969) 28-29.

[23]Ibid., 29.

But what is true about *Augustana* XVI is equally true in regard to the *Formula of Concord*. Here too a process of extrapolation has to take place in order to proclaim the gospel in our time faithfully in line with the "prophetic and apostolic writings of the Old and New Testaments" as "the only rule and norm," and with the testimony of the *Formula of Concord* as a faithful summary of this proclamation made four hundred years ago. But when the line is drawn from apostolic times through the sixteenth century to our own age, certain shifts in emphasis may become not only possible, but imperative if the scriptures and the confessions are taken seriously.

Two examples may indicate how a responsible teaching ministry may have to speak out in our age. It is clear that there is a superficial similarity between what the *Formula* calls "the mad dream of the so-called Stoic philosophers and of Manichaeans who taught that whatever happens and could not happen otherwise, that man always acts only under compulsion, even in his external acts,"[24] and the present eloquent advocates of the abolition of freedom and dignity. Yet the abolition of the "human being" advocated by certain behavioral scientists, such as B. F. Skinner, is a far cry from the relatively harmless—since utterly individualistic—withdrawal from society advocated by the Stoics of old. After all, behavioral scientists have access to incredible power not only in the world of Skinner but also in the world of Pavlov, and they do not hesitate to exercise it. Skinner wrote, "As the science of behavior adopts the strategy of physics and biology, the autonomous agent to which behavior has traditionally been attributed [the human being] is replaced by the environment."[25] The result will be the obsolescence of what we have been accustomed to call art and literature. As Skinner puts it,

> We shall not only have no reason to admire people who endure suffering, face danger, or struggle to be good; it is possible that we shall have little interest in pictures or books about them. The art and literature of the new culture will be about other things.[26]

What a relief this will be not only to Skinner and his friends but also for people who have been plagued by people like Solzhenitsyn.

It seems that it would be an essential exercise of the teaching ministry of the church to apply the insights of the *Formula* in the context of the threats to human beings as they confront us in our age. In view of this situation and the anthropology of the Bible and the confessions one must wonder if it can be described as faithfulness to the reformation heritage when a book written in America dealing with the *Formula* in 1977 can discuss Article I without a single reference to the "mad dream" of the determinists so clearly described in these confessions.[27] Faithfulness to the Lutheran confessions means to apply them with imagination and

---

[24]BC, 470-471.

[25]B. F. Skinner, *Beyond Freedom and Dignity* (New York: Knopf, 1971) 175.

[26]Ibid., 156.

[27]Klug, *Getting into the Formula of Concord*, 29-33.

precision to the present-day attack against the humanity of human beings in their relationship to God.

And this involves simultaneously a new look at the Pelagianism and semi-Pelagianism described in Article II. Even more sinister than the false prophets listed in the antitheses of the *Formula* are our contemporary false prophets described by Peter Marin as the "new narcissists" who practice the "deification of the isolated self" and assert selfishness and moral blindness as enlightenment and moral health. Marin attributes their success to what he calls "the growing solipsism and desperation of a beleaguered class, the world view emerging among us centered solely on the self and with individual survival as its sole good."[28] And while the followers of the man who calls himself Werner Erhard are probably the most extreme new Pelagians, Ron Hubbard's Scientology comes a close second, and many other outgrowths of the so-called "human potential movement" do not follow very far behind. To utilize the *Formula of Concord* for the teaching ministry of the church today would seem to mean to see the "enthusiasts" in our day "who imagine that God draws men to himself, enlightens them, justifies them, and saves them without means, without the hearing of God's Word and without the use of the holy sacraments,"[29] or who even assert that they are indeed God.[30] In view of the profound effect the new enthusiasts have had outside and inside of the Christian church, not to extrapolate from the scriptures and the confessions to witness against them would appear to be unfaithfulness to the *Formula of Concord*.

The other example I would like to take from Article IX, which deals with Christ's "Descent Into Hell." No other article would seem at first more unfruitful for the teaching ministry of the church today. Many Christian denominations have actually removed the clause dealing with the descent into hell from their version of the creed, and it is common knowledge that this particular clause is a relatively late addition to the so-called Apostles' Creed. Nevertheless, the way the *Formula* handles this somewhat obscure controversy may prove to be of special significance for the teaching ministry in our age.

At the time the issue was, does the descent into hell "belong to Christ's suffering or to his glorious victory and triumph?" The *Epitome* asserts, "It is enough to know that Christ went to hell, destroyed hell for all believers, and has redeemed them from the power of death, of the devil, and of the eternal damnation

---

[28]Peter Marin, "The New Narcissism," *Harper's Magazine* (October 1975) 45-56.

[29]*BC*, 471.

[30]Marin reports the following encounter with a woman who had just been through a weekend of Erhard Seminar Training. In the course of an evening at home she assured him: "(1) that the individual will is all powerful and totally determines one's fate; (2) that she felt neither guilt nor shame about anyone's fate and that those who were poor and hungry must have willed it on themselves; (3) that the North Vietnamese must have wanted to be bombed, or else it could not have happened to them; (4) that a friend of hers who had been raped and murdered in San Francisco was to be pitied for having willed it to occur; (5) that in her weekend at EST she had attained full enlightenment; (6) that she was God; (7) that whatever one thought to be true was true beyond all argument; (8) that I was also God, and that my ideas were also true, but not as true as hers because I had not had the training; and (9) that my use of logic to criticize her beliefs was unfair because reason was 'irrational' though she could not tell me why." Marin, "The New Narcissism," 46.

of the hellish jaws." And the *Formula* continues, "How this took place is something that we should postpone until the other world, where there will be revealed to us not only this point, but many others as well, which our blind reason cannot comprehend in this life but which we simply accept."[31] Similarly the Solid Declaration states that "with our reason and five senses this article cannot be comprehended any more than the preceding one, how Christ has been made to sit at the right hand of the almighty power and majesty of God."[32] Both documents refer to one of Luther's sermons dealing with this topic for further clarification, a sermon he preached in Torgau in 1533.[33] Here Luther addresses a problem which has troubled the church, namely the relationship of "how" questions to "who" questions. For Luther the important point is: "Christ conquered the devil and took away all his power; that is the true and Christian way to think about it; it exactly hits the real truth and the meaning of this article although not strictly describing the fact or expressing it just as it occurred." And he observed, "We should let well enough alone, and not worry ourselves with profound and curious questions as to how it may have taken place, since it surely did not occur physically, for he remained those three days in the grave."[34]

Luther enjoys referring to the fresco paintings found in the churches of the time depicting

> how Christ went down, clad in priestly robe and with a banner in his hand—how he reaches hell and with his banner beats and drives out the devil, takes hell by storm and delivers his followers....And I am glad to see it thus set before the simple minded in paintings and plays and songs.

Paintings, poetry, drama are all means for him to proclaim an important aspect of the gospel. They help people focus on the "who" question and enable them to ignore the "how" question. Or as Luther puts it, "otherwise, if I wanted to be as smart as some who carry their heads very high and make fun of our simplicity, I too could joke about it and ask what kind of banner he had, whether it was made of cloth or of paper, and how it happened that it was not burned in hell."[35] And he continued,

> For we are, thank God, not so dumb as to believe or say that this took place physically or with a standard of wood or cloth, or that hell is a wooden or iron building. But we have nothing to do with such questions, cavils, and explanations, simply saying that one may form an idea from such rude (*grobe*) pictures of what this article means; just as other doctrines concerning divine things are represented by rude outward images as Christ himself everywhere in the gospel exhibits to the people the mystery of the kingdom of heaven by visible images and by parables.[36]

---

[31]*BC*, 492.

[32]Ibid., 610.

[33]*D. Martin Luthers Werke: Kritische Gesamtausgabe* (Weimar: Böhlau, 1883-) 37:62-67, translated in H. E. Jacobs, *Book of Concord* (Philadelphia: United Lutheran Publication House, 1908) 2:279-280.

[34]Ibid., 279.

[35]Ibid., 280.

[36]Ibid.

Luther was a strangely unliteralistic literalist. Paintings, plays, songs, poetry were for him all means to point to the Christ who conquered hell and bound the devil. We must form our ideas of such cosmic events by means of images.

> God may decide whether the banner, portal, gate and chain were of wood or iron or whether there were none at all: no matter about that, if I only hold on to that which I am to believe concerning Christ, and which is represented by such images. This is the principal matter, the benefit and the power that we derive from it, that neither hell nor devil can capture or harm me or any who believe on him.[37]

To be sure Luther's sermons are not Lutheran confessions. But in this instance the *Formula* makes a particular sermon confessional. In view of the history of a tortured literalism which has plagued the Lutheran churches through the generations and is still troubling them today, it would be well for a teaching ministry faithful to the scriptures and the confessions to take Luther's emphasis in his Torgau sermon utterly seriously: "If I only hold on to that which I am to believe concerning Christ," all other questions fall into their proper place.

Today we are confronted by a rationalistic reductionism ill at ease with the particularity of Christ, which tries to reduce the gospel to optimistic trivialities concerning the inexorable progress of humanity. It is embarrassed by the crude symbols of the Christian faith and tries to confine the gospel to pleasant platitudes. It avoids cross and resurrection either by a triumph without a cross or a cross without a victory. On the other hand, we observe an equally rationalistic obscurantism which assumes that salvation is deserved by those who assent to the largest number of theological propositions having the lowest degree of plausibility or credibility. The power of the Holy Spirit using the authority of the scriptures and their responsible summation and interpretation by the confessions, including the *Formula of Concord*, for the teaching ministry of the church should enable the Evangelical Lutheran churches to stand firm against present dangers as the Spirit enabled them to stand firm in the past.

[37]Ibid., 282-283.

Word & World
Supplement Series 2
1994

The Place of Theology
in the Church

A FEW MONTHS AGO I PUBLISHED AN ARTICLE IN THE *LUTHERAN QUARTERLY* WITH the title, "The Future of Theology in the Church."[1] In it, I claimed that the Evangelical Lutheran Church in America was confronted by two obvious possibilities:

(1) It could join the other mainline Protestants in sanctioning, in the literal sense of the word,[2] the prevailing culture without any reference to the gospel, producing church growth with the help of entertainment evangelism and the tried and true methods of the expert communicators and promoters of our age. Actually, the Lutheran church's separate existence would no longer be necessary and it could readily be absorbed within an even more United Church of Christ, following its cousin, the Evangelical Church, descendant of the very same Prussian Union to which so many Lutherans who came from Germany in the nineteenth century had once belonged.

Or (2) the ELCA could take its own classic theology, summarized in the constitution, seriously and steer away from least-common-denominator ecumenism and the promotion of the theological fad of the month, and build its proclamation on a christocentric exposition of the Holy Scriptures with the help of the great trinitarian creeds and the confessions of the Lutheran church in the context of the turn of the century and in the church's North American setting. There may be other options which are not apparent to me. I said, moreover, that the secret of our past

---

[1]*Lutheran Quarterly* 4/1 (Spring, 1990) 1-9. [This essay is reproduced in the present volume, pages 153-159. Ed.]

[2]According to Webster from the French *sancire*, to render sacred or inviolable.

This essay was originally published in Lutheran Forum *25/1 (February, 1991) 34-38, under the title, "The Place of Theology in the ELCA." However, because Dr. Forell here writes to articulate the distinctive contribution of Lutheran theology to the whole church, the title has been altered for the purposes of this volume.*

evangelical success, dependence on waves of northern European immigrants who found support and shelter against an alien environment within the walls of Lutheran churches, is no longer available. Our kind of immigrants are no longer coming.

Thus it seems apparent to me that theology, which for so long has been considered by some leaders and members of our church a luxury pursued by theologians hidden away in theological seminaries, is no longer a frill but the very basis for the legitimacy of the continued existence of the Church of the Augsburg Confession. The good causes described in the Statement of Purpose in the Constitution of the ELCA[3] can never be realized unless they are based on faith which motivates and sanctions their implementation.

I would now like to ask: What are the distinctive elements of such a faith which teaching theologians within the ELCA would have to articulate and make comprehensible to themselves as well as to their students, the world-wide church, and all men and women with whom they are called to live in this pluralistic age? Indeed, is there any reason to perpetuate a theological tradition, to enunciate a special version of the Christian faith, that has become associated with the name Lutheran? There are many people inside and outside the ELCA who would not hesitate to answer No! to this question. We see in Europe and the so-called third world persistent efforts to amalgamate all those who are loosely described as protestants into united churches. Polls in this country indicate that whatever teaching theologians may teach, the constituency of the ELCA seems to hold religious views indistinguishable from others of similar sociological background. What, then, is the reason for being for a Lutheran church in the twenty-first century?

In this brief article, I can only indicate where such justification might be found. While I make no claim to originality, I hope to describe some specific aspects of the faith which must be articulated in our context and would likely be lost if there were no Lutheran church. I would like to show the relevance of these Lutheran emphases to the life and proclamation of the ecumenical church at the turn of this century and their importance for the encounter of the Christian church with the non-Christian world. One might want to add that it is precisely the disappearance of a cultural support system in America, which still upholds Lutheran churches in Europe even when theology and the life of the church have been totally separated, which raises the question for us. It is the intrinsically different situation in North America which makes theology essential for the survival of the ELCA. And it is precisely Lutheran theology which makes the survival of a Lutheran tradition important for the ecumenical church and for the proclamation of the gospel in a pluralistic world. If one were to compare the Christian church to a choir, it would be my claim that Lutherans are responsible for singing certain parts or perhaps certain notes which would be missed if they were not

[3]ELCA Constitution, 4.02.a - 4.03.q.

sung. It is my claim that their absence might lead to serious distortion of the music. Let me list a few of these notes. I shall try to show that some of them make the Christian message more comprehensible to our contemporaries while others tend to add to the difficulties modern women and men have in hearing the gospel.

The presentation so far has not engaged the important question raised by Professor George A. Lindbeck in his book *The Nature of Doctrine*[4] and their relevance to my analysis. The reason for this neglect is that the theological theories of religion and doctrine examined in this book are, for the purpose of evaluation, artificially disassociated. I consider them, and others omitted in the book, important and inescapable dimensions of the religious reality. None can be made exclusive if one wants to understand the complexity of religion. They affect all religions and all expressions of the Christian faith.

But let us return to my specifically Lutheran aspects of Christian theology, always aware of the fact that this is not the only way in which the Christian faith can be articulated, but that if these elements are missing, the legitimacy of the continued existence of a Lutheran church at least on this continent is called into question.

THE DISTINCTION BETWEEN LAW AND GOSPEL

Lutherans have always insisted that God deals with human beings through law and gospel. It is a cliché of classic Lutheran preaching that one must preach the bad news of the accusing law in order to prepare people for the good news of the liberating gospel. While this may be true, I am concerned that in our stress on the homiletical significance of the distinction we have lost track of the first use of the law, the political use, and its value for our anomic society. Besides the law as a tutor leading people to Christ, it is a resource for life in this world and the basis for human liberty. Please note, I am not talking about the freedom of the Christian. This, indeed, is solely the gift of the gospel, the justification of the godless by grace alone. But the law, if you will, the Ten Commandments and the Golden Rule, should enable us to live together in relative peace in a pluralistic world.

There are theologians who are prepared to jettison the gospel of salvation through Christ and his cross in order to be open to our pluralistic age, which deeply resents the exclusive christological claims of our faith. Is it possible to accept the pluralistic age without jeopardizing the second article of the creed? It is precisely the distinction between law and gospel which should enable Christians to work together with all people for the earthly welfare of all human beings and to appreciate the moral and social contributions of non-Christians to the common good on the basis of the general accessibility of the law to humanity.

It is not necessary to make all people into anonymous Christians or include them in some hidden church against their will and best judgment. Once one could escape the Inquisition by dying at the stake; today, confronted by this pretended

---

[4]George A. Lindbeck, *The Nature of Doctrine: Religion and Theology in a Postliberal Age* (Philadelphia: Westminster, 1984).

Christian openness to the world, the non-Christian is manipulated into the fold without any recourse whatsoever.

By using the law as described in the scriptures and in the Christian tradition as a bridge between Christians and non-Christians, one is able to collaborate without forcing the issue of "salvation and other faiths."[5] The global concern for peace and justice can and should be recognized and appreciated wherever it is found and form the basis for cooperation among all men and women of good will. In the New Testament, Paul told the Philippians to think and appreciate "whatever is true, whatever is honorable, whatever is just, whatever is pure, whatever is lovely, whatever is gracious; if there is any excellence, if there is anything worthy of praise, think about these things."[6] As I have observed in another place, "the rapid success of Christianity in the hellenistic world was partially the result of the willingness of a majority of Christians to accept from the prevailing cultural tradition whatever was true, honorable, just, pure, gracious, etc."[7]

The recognition of the law in its political use, as bond between Christians and all other human beings who have had the law inscribed in their hearts, allows for wide ranging cooperation in this pluralistic age. By utilizing the distinction between the law and gospel, this cooperation can be achieved without surrendering the gospel of justification by faith. It avoids the false alternatives of a theology of relevancy, which endorses the various agendas of the world, be they the Christian Marxism of elements of liberation theology or the neo-conservativism of theologians like Richard John Neuhaus and Michael Novak. At the same time, it escapes the other extreme, the new sectarianism illustrated by Stanley Hauerwas and William Willimon,[8] which in order to evade endorsing the constantly shifting agenda of the world withdraws into a Christian ghetto content to let the world go by.

The utilization of the political use of the law enables Lutherans to assert simultaneously the gospel of salvation by Christ alone and by grace alone without any compromise. There is no other gospel than the *justificatio impii*. Luther stated it clearly in the *Schmalkald Articles* (II, 1).[9] This remains the article with which the church stands or falls, not because Luther wrote it, but because it is the word in which God must keep us steadfast and the little word that subdues this world's tyrant. This word cannot be replaced by any ever so well meaning program or project, by proper piety or proper politics. They all have their place, but they are not the gospel.

---

[5]Ibid., 55ff.

[6]Phil 4:8.

[7]See Forell, *History of Christian Ethics*, vol. 1 (Minneapolis: Augsburg, 1979) 28.

[8]Stanley Hauerwas and William H. Willimon, "Embarrassed by God's Presence," *The Christian Century* 101/4 (January 30, 1985) 98-100.

[9]"Here is the First and Chief Article: That Jesus Christ, our God and Lord, "was handed over to death for our trespasses and was raised for our justification" (Rom. 4); and he alone is "the Lamb of God, who takes away the sin of the world" (John 1); and "the LORD has laid upon him the iniquity of us all" (Isa. 53); furthermore, "All have sinned," and "they are now justified without merit by his grace, through the redemption which is in Christ Jesus...by his blood" (Rom. 3)." Translation from *The Schmalkald Articles by Martin Luther*, edited and translated by William R. Russell (Minneapolis: Fortress Press, 1994).

We are surrounded by a multitude of good causes which happen to be false gospels. Some are more attractive than others. Race and gender, poverty and riches, choice of lifestyle, nationalism and internationalism, science and spirituality all have their eloquent prophets. We must evaluate them carefully with the help of the law and ask which may contribute most to the earthly welfare of the human race. But only the gospel of Jesus Christ can save. It must not be confused or mixed with any of the other causes. To make this very clear seems to be a major task of the teaching theologians of the ELCA. It is a formidable mission amidst the confusion of spirits that surrounds us but it is an inescapable assignment.

SINNER AND RIGHTEOUS AT THE SAME TIME

A second note that must be sounded is the proclamation that as long as we live in this world, Christians remain sinners and righteous at the same time. We live in a time when even psychoanalysts wonder, "Whatever became of sin?"[10] The word has disappeared from the language of enlightened men and women. They make mistakes, are sick, had incompetent parents, a burdensome environment, poor genes, have been inadequately socialized, suffer from cognitive dissonance, etc. The list of reasons for the malfunctioning of people who live in a realm praised by distinguished psychologists as "beyond freedom and dignity" is endless. Why did sin disappear? Partly because the people who in our culture talked most about it described it in such a trivial and culturally determined way that it seemed simply irrelevant in a pluralistic world. Sin was often what other people did, "the lesser breeds without the law," in Rudyard Kipling's memorable phrase.

In the Lutheran tradition, sin is primarily idolatry, having other gods, *Abgötter* as Luther would say, instead of the one true God. All other sins are the result of this idolatry. Nobody is without sin. This is not the invention of Luther or Augustine or even St. Paul; it is the same basic human predicament observed and addressed by these theologians with particular clarity, the predicament which results in the chaos which we notice all about us. As long as we live on this earth, we are afflicted by sin and the devil. Luther writes: "For original sin is a root and inborn evil, which only comes to an end when this body has been entirely mortified, purged by fire and reformed. Meanwhile, however, it is not imputed to the godly."[11] Righteousness, on the other hand, is life under the shadow of God's grace. In Luther's *Commentary on Galatians* he writes: "Both things are true; that I am righteous here with an incipient righteousness; and that in hope I am strengthened against sin and look for the consummation of perfect righteousness in heaven."[12] Thus the believer is sinner and righteous at the same time, and goes on to perfection only in an eschatological sense. As Luther said on his deathbed, "In this world we are always beggars."

In a theological atmosphere where righteousness is often understood as

---

[10]Karl Menninger, *Whatever Became of Sin?* (New York: Hawthorne, 1975).

[11]*The Disputations Concerning Justification* (1536), LW 34:165.

[12]*Lectures on Galatians* (1535), LW 27:22.

enthusiastic support for the right causes, be they conservative or revolutionary, theologians have the assignment to proclaim that the righteousness Christians talk about is always alien, not the result of our actions but of God's deed for us. In some ways the mention of sin tends to aggravate the view that Christianity deals with dead symbols, with language that does not contribute to communication, but rather fosters misunderstanding. Is there any way in which this talk about sin and righteousness may help us to relate to our pluralistic world? For one thing, it removes a major handicap in our human relations, the pervasive perception that Christians consider themselves superior to other mortals, that they think of themselves as being the moral majority, who because of their virtue are saved from poverty, disease, confusion, and inner turmoil. Because God is on their side, they do not experience the slings and arrows of outrageous fortune. The most profoundly alienating element of Christianity in the eyes of a non-Christian world is the impression Christians—whether Quaker or Roman Catholics, fundamentalists or modernists—convey, of a superiority that is apparently not affected by the doubts and questions which afflict the rest of the human race. Most human beings in our age sympathize with the question raised by Shakespeare's Macbeth whether the entire human enterprise may not, indeed, be "a tale, told by an idiot, full of sound and fury, signifying nothing."[13]

A lifestyle or a theology which ignores this issue is hard to comprehend for most of our contemporaries, and especially the cultured among the despisers of Christianity.

The insistence that Christians are righteous and sinners at the same time describes the predicament that is experienced as *Anfechtung* [temptation] by Christians. This is radically different from the notion that one was a sinner once upon a time, but is now righteous, the message found on many a bumper sticker. It is not something that sets Christians apart from other human beings, but places them in their very midst. *Anfechtung* is an inescapable part of the Christian life as it was part of the life of Christ. It obviates the notion of Christians as moral superstars who have the answers to all the perplexing questions which trouble their neighbors. It empowers the very humility which *ex cathedra* pronouncements on the issues of the day tend to obscure. It enables us to say side by side with our non-Christian sister and brother: "Woe unto me!" as well as "Lord, have mercy!" It is a note which must be sung loudly if the Christian message is to be heard in a non-Christian world.

THE FINITE AS THE BEARER OF THE INFINITE

There is still another particularly Lutheran note that we are called to sound at this time, the message that the infinite and eternal God deals with humanity through very finite, temporal means. Anybody who talks seriously about God in our age is amazed by the overwhelming majesty of God, the *mysterium tremendum*. This is the reason why the very notion of the identification of God with humanity,

[13]Shakespeare, *Macbeth*, V.v.17

not to mention an individual human being, is so offensive to many. The God of the spiral nebulae and of the quanta does not fit our language of personal piety. In this setting, we are called to assert that God is known in the ordinary events of life. This is the *scandalon* of christology as well as the reason for the discomfort that confession of the real presence in the sacrament creates for many. It may be easier to handle the miracle of transubstantiation as something appropriate to God Almighty, as part of the *apotheosis* of the human race, the evolution toward the omega point which explains the universe. Or, on the other hand, the total absence of any involvement of this prodigious being in the world, the belief that the sacrament is a memorial in which we think devotionally of this omnipotent God, may be plausible. But the insistence on the sacramental presence in, with, and under the elements of bread and wine staggers the imagination. This presence of God for us and with us is too simple, too ordinary, too unspectacular.

In addition to the offense caused by christology and the Lutheran understanding of the Lord's supper, there is the way Lutherans deal with the Holy Scriptures which strikes others as odd. Among people who either insist on the transubstantiation of human words into an inerrant divine document or claim that the scriptures are ancient or more recent mythical accounts, our insistence on the real presence of God's word in human words of the scripture is seen as saying at the same time too much and too little. And yet, may this not be of help to those contemporaries who are bewildered by the strident and conflicting claims made about the nature and authority of the Holy Scriptures? Again, the conviction that the finite can be the bearer of the infinite may help solve one of the controversial issues among Christians.

Perhaps nowhere is this Lutheran note insisting on the finite as the bearer of the infinite more helpful than in its application to the notion of Christian vocation. This concept has often been interpreted as the transformation of ordinary mortals into something extraordinary, even superhuman. The notion of the Christian saint as generally understood in our culture comes to mind. It is assumed that God reveals himself in people who are very different from other human beings. They are by their own choice chaste, obedient, and poor, to use the standard example. Even in the typical protestant understanding of saintliness, the much-maligned Sunday school literature caricatured by Mark Twain, the true Christian is supposed to be very different from the rest of humanity, immediately and obviously distinguishable—indeed, extraordinary. Where vocation no longer means that one abandons ordinary life, it may mean that one is extraordinarily successful. This is interpreted as a sign of God's election. Here the Lutheran insistence of salvation *in vocatione* [in vocation], rather than *per vocationem* [through vocation], is an important aspect of the Christian message as it relates to the understanding that God uses ordinary people to accomplish his extraordinary purposes. Even their selection may not be accompanied by extraordinary events. One may not be called by hearing voices or seeing signs in the sky, but in the course of an uneventful career as a tax collector, fisherman, or college student.

What is extraordinary is what God can do with such ordinary material. As

Luther observed in his *The Freedom of a Christian*, through God's vocation we may, indeed, becomes Christs to each other. He wrote: "Hence, as our heavenly Father has in Christ freely come to our aid, we also ought freely to help our neighbor through our body and its works, and one should become, as it were, a Christ to the other, that we may be Christs to one another, and Christ may be the same in all, that is, that we may be truly Christians."[14] We may not even be aware of the use God is making of us. When we retrace the way God came to us in the course of our life, we will hardly recall a list of spectacular events, but rather many ordinary events God used to enter our lives and take us by surprise. In an age of so much religious pretension, it may help the proclamation of the gospel if the claims of Christians are reduced in order to emphasize the claim of Christ.

THE THEOLOGY OF THE CROSS

Now for a final note Lutherans ought to sound, the proclamation of the theology of the cross. In a sense, the theology of the cross summarizes everything we have said so far. God makes himself known by going into hiding. He heals by suffering for us. He shows us power by becoming utterly powerless. He bestows eternal life by dying. This message is difficult to accept, especially in our time and in our land. Power, fame, and success are worshiped by practically everybody. The immense popularity of the lottery and hope for instant fame and success it engenders show the basic need for triumph in our culture. Promising instant glory, without any effort, it represents the ultimate materialistic indulgence sale. It offers immediate release from the purgatory of poverty and want for the tiny faction that are the elect of this powerful symbol of the religion of materialism.

Against this background, we must insist on the transvaluation of values implicit in the theology of the cross. This is not easy since the church seems to have bought into the notion of success measured by statistics. If you read an article on ten successful churches, you may be sure that the success will be measured statistically. To insist in this context that the story of the cross tells God's way to victory is offensive. Few can follow Simone Weil's observation:

> Christ healing the sick, raising the dead, etc., that is the humble, human, almost low part of His mission. The supernatural part is the sweat of blood, the unsatisfied longing for human consolation, the supplication that he might be spared, the sense of being abandoned by God. The abandonment at the supreme moment of the crucifixion, what an abyss of love on both sides! "My God, My God, why hast thou forsaken Me?" There we have the real proof that Christianity is something divine.[15]

To most contemporaries this seems absurd. But it is precisely this apparent absurdity which must be proclaimed even at the cost of offending our success-oriented contemporaries.

---

[14]*The Freedom of a Christian* (1520), LW 31:367-368.

[15]Simone Weil, *Gravity and Grace* (New York: Putnam, 1952) 139; as quoted in Forell, *The Protestant Faith* (Philadelphia: Fortress, 1975) 167.

In the past, Lutherans have made many compromises with the prevailing culture. European examples abound. They practically invented *Kulturprotestantismus* [cultural protestantism]. On this continent, Lutherans were protected for a while from a wholesale endorsement of a theology of glory by their ethnic alienation from the mainstream. In their rush towards approval, they have succeeded. This could be illustrated by the hymns they sing, by the disappearance of the crucifix from their altars as too depressing, by the absorption of the Advent season into Christmas, and Lent into Easter. These are all apparently trivial accommodations to a theology of glory. The big adjustments are the acceptance of political and sociological changes as forerunners of the reign of God. Just as some wanted to identify socialism with God's coming realm, so now that the victory of capitalism seems assured this dubious achievement is seen by many as the triumph of Christianity over the prince of this world. Whatever side one chooses in the ideological conflicts of our age, the simple identification of a particular political agenda with the victory of God is theology of glory. It is the ongoing responsibility of the Lutheran church to say No! to such theologies, especially if they appear in forms that appeal to us. I am convinced that the next century will bring even greater temptations. Perhaps we shall be told that the solution to all our problems is offered by biochemistry. Eternal life by hormone injection is just around the corner. It may be the task of the theology of the cross to insist that this version of eternal life is just another word for hell.

We asked at the beginning whether there is any reason for the continued existence of a Lutheran church apart from inertia and nostalgia. It has been my claim that specifically Lutheran theological emphases within the context of the Christian proclamation are necessary for the proclamation of the gospel. I have tried to list some that seem to be of particular importance. There may be others that I have missed. Some may contend that those listed are asserted equally clearly by other Christian traditions. If this is the case, the Lutheran church may, indeed, be expendable. But it seems clear that the emphases listed are theological rather than sociological. They can only be maintained if theology is taken seriously. If this does not happen, there is no future for the ELCA and frankly, there is no reason why there should be. For the first time in the history of the Lutheran church, theology is in the very center of its ability and right to survive. Should it not survive, God will find other servants to proclaim the theology of the cross and all it implies in an age committed to a theology of glory.

Word & World
Supplement Series **2**
1994

Law and Gospel

THE DISTINCTION BETWEEN LAW AND GOSPEL AND THE RELATIONSHIP OF CREATION and redemption has become one of the central problems in contemporary theological discussion. It relates to questions ranging from nature and grace to science and religion, reason and revelation, and Bonhoeffer's distinction between the penultimate and the ultimate.

In view of the centrality of the problem, it is of interest that some years ago Professor Gustaf Wingren claimed that the major difficulty with the theological system of three of the most prominent theologians of this century was their confusion of law and gospel. He accuses Nygren, Barth, and Bultmann of speaking about God apart from concrete revelation in which God has spoken and of which the scriptures are the record. Among his own teachers, the Lundensians and especially Anders Nygren, he says that agape-love was developed as a dominant motif in which all other aspects of revelation are dissolved.

> The Christian message of God as forgiving agape is in reality an answer to a pregnant question, viz., the question of guilt. This message is meaningless unless the man who hears it is standing under the claim of God even before he hears the gospel. There is a continual danger that in Nygren's theology the center of the Christian faith, the gospel, becomes erroneously interpreted, since the gospel is divorced from the question of guilt and tied to a formal philosophical question.[1]

Here the essence of God, namely the "motif," is abstracted from the concrete

---

[1]Gustaf Wingren, *Theology in Conflict* (Philadelphia: Muhlenberg, 1958) 16-17.

In the 1960s, Forell served as a Lutheran Church in America representative to the "Lutheran-Reformed Dialogue," a series of meetings "to explore the theological relations between the Lutheran and Reformed churches." Papers which served as the basis for discussions were collected and published. This essay first appeared in Marburg Revisited: A Reexamination of Lutheran and Reformed Traditions, *ed. Paul Empie and James McCord (Minneapolis: Augsburg, 1966) 128-152. Here Forell explores Lutheranism's distinctive theological theme and its continuing relevance for the church's preaching and teaching.*

revelation. But when law and gospel are only apparent contradictions, the biblical theology of the cross has been surrendered in favor of a theology of glory.

In criticizing Karl Barth, Wingren points out that the *knowledge* of God is the central concern of Barth's theological system.

> The main question with Luther is the question of righteousness. But with Barth the main question is whether we have knowledge of God, or whether, in ourselves, we lack such knowledge and must receive it from the outside....Luther holds that natural law compels us to do works; there is no encroachment on the gospel which deals with an entirely different righteousness....Barth cannot bear to hear about a natural law, because in that case the will of God would be known independently of the incarnation, and the revelation in Christ would only complement something natural, that is, something human.[2]

Because of this epistemological emphasis (rather than the soteriological emphasis of the New Testament) Barth has no use for the law as our enemy. Here, too, law and gospel are not distinguished. This expresses itself in Barth's famous reversal of law and gospel into gospel and law: "The law is nothing but the necessary form of the gospel, whose content is grace."[3] For Barth, the law has lost its terror; it does not bring wrath as St. Paul says (Rom 4:15). And if the law is only the form of the gospel, what shall we do with St. Paul's words, "Likewise, my brethren, you have died to the law through the body of Christ, so that you may belong to another, to him who has been raised from the dead in order that we may bear fruit for God" (Rom 7:4)?

The confusion of law and gospel in Barth's theology results in a situation described by Wingren as follows:

> There is in Barth's theology no active power of sin, no tyrannical, demonic power that subjects man to slavery and which God destroys in His work of redemption. There is no devil in Barth's theology. This is a constant feature in his theological production.[4]

Or, as Thielicke puts it, "Through this doctrine of law and gospel, the abstract monism comes into theology and is made into a gracious worldview."[5]

In Bultmann, Wingren claims that the New Testament message which tells of God's becoming human, living with people, dying for all, and rising from the dead is dissolved in an essentially philosophical concern. However, Bultmann does not ignore humankind's guilt. In fact, this guilt is the basic presupposition of his theology. However, it is a guilt which is significantly different from the guilt of which the Scriptures speak. In the Bible, we are guilty before God (Rom 3:19). In Bultmann, guilt is lack of self-realization. Again quoting Wingren, "Human life

---

[2]Ibid., 26.

[3]Karl Barth, *Evangelium und Gesetz*, Theologische Existenz Heute, n. F., 50 (1935; reprint, Munich: Chr. Kaiser, 1956) 13.

[4]Wingren, *Theology*, 25.

[5]Helmut Thielicke, *Theologische Ethik*, vol. 1 (Tübingen: J. C. B. Mohr [Paul Siebeck], 1951) 193, §569 [editor's translation].

(*Dasein*) has fallen, but it has fallen exclusively from itself."[6] Bultmann himself says to his critics,

> Some critics have objected that I am borrowing Heidegger's categories and forcing them upon the New Testament. I am afraid that this only shows that they are blinding their eyes to the real problem, which is that the philosophers are saying the same thing as the New Testament and saying it quite independently.[7]

However, they are saying it without reference to Jesus Christ. Bultmann would like to retain what he calls "the act of God through which man becomes capable of self-commitment, capable of faith and love, of his authentic life."[8] In order to do so, he dispenses with all the concrete statements of the New Testament concerning this Christ. He discards the pre-existent Son of God, the virgin birth, miracles, resurrection, etc., and he adds,

> We are compelled to ask whether all this mythological language is not simply an attempt to express the meaning of the historical figure of Jesus and the events of his life; in other words, significance of these as a figure and event of salvation. If that be so, we can dispense with the objective form in which they are cast.[9]

What is left when the New Testament is thus demythologized is a philosophy of existence which, for some illogical subjective and emotional reason, attributes extraordinary significance to a certain Jew who was killed in Palestine a long time ago. Or perhaps the reason is not quite so illogical. Actually, psychologically, this Jesus does help people. Bultmann makes again and again statements like these: "*Hilft er mir weil er der Sohn Gottes ist, oder ist er der Sohn Gottes weil er mir hilft?*"[10] The saving efficacy of the cross is not derived from the fact that it is the cross of Christ: it is the cross of Christ because it has this saving efficacy.[11]

The key sentence which may give a clue to the peculiar attachment to the demythologized Jesus—though he represents philosophically an acute embarrassment—is, "Does Christ help me because he is the Son of God or is he the Son of God because he helps me?" (see above). For Bultmann, he is the Son of God because he helps me. The concern is now *only* what this faith does for the hearer. In this theology, there is no room for the distinction between law and gospel; the law has been egocentrically spiritualized and the gospel has been demythologized, the distinction between the two has been abolished.

While the scope of Wingren's interpretation has been severely criticized[12]

---

[6]Wingren, *Theology*, 131.

[7]W. Bartsch, ed., *Kerygma and Myth* (London, S.P.C.K., 1957) 25.

[8]Bartsch, *Kerygma*, 33.

[9]Ibid., 35.

[10]"Does he help me because he is the Son of God, or is he the Son of God because helps me?" [editor's translation]. Rudolf Bultmann, *Glauben und Verstehen: Gesammelte Aufsätze*, vol. 2 (Tübingen: J. C. B. Mohr, 1952) 252.

[11]Bartsch, *Kerygma*, 41.

[12]E.g., the important correction of the analysis of Barth in Robert W. Jenson, *Alpha and Omega: A Study in the Theology of Karl Barth* (New York: Thomas Nelson and Sons, 1963), especially 138, note 11.

(with special bitterness in Sweden), the significance of the Wingren analysis has not been questioned.

It is against the background of this admitted importance of the law-gospel dichotomy that its significance for the ecumenical engagement of the Lutheran church should be discussed.

THE NATURE OF THE LAW IN THEOLOGICAL DISCOURSE

According to *Webster's New Collegiate Dictionary*, law is "the binding custom or practice of a community; rules of conduct enforced by a controlling authority; also any single rule of conduct so enforced." Paul Lehmann in the *Handbook of Christian Theology* says,

> Law is the principle and operation of order in the world. As principle, law is expressed in the form of prescriptive statements. As operation, law expresses the fact that diverse and changing relations unfold in a dependable and an intelligible pattern.[13]

This is law in general, in all its cosmic, social, moral, and religious forms.

In theological discourse, law is a personal demand of God. The controlling authority which makes it binding is God. In the law, we are confronted by God who establishes a relationship with us. This God is the almighty maker of heaven and earth. And God confronts *all people* in the divine law; it is the personal demand of God's almighty authority. Within the context of the Christian proclamation the law is not a propositional code (doctrine) but a personal (existential) demand. It is the claim of God upon us and all people. It confronts us quite independently of our familiarity with one or the other legal code—which may more or less adequately express these demands at a certain time and in a certain place. Human beings experience the law even if they have no formal knowledge of it. They may experience it differently at different periods of history, or different individuals may experience it in different ways. Nevertheless all people everywhere and at all times are confronted by the law.[14]

1. Old Testament

In the Old Testament, we find the record of this personal confrontation of human beings by God, which expresses itself in law.

Covenant and Law—The law in the Old Testament is not independent of the covenant, or contrary to it, but rather its byproduct. The covenant fact is always associated with the covenant law. But a covenant is a relationship, and in the Old Testament this relationship, true to the nature of all personal relationships, implies obligation. For example, Noah is given certain obligations when God establishes the covenant with him (Genesis 9). This obligation is central in the Sinaitic cove-

---

[13]M. Halverson and A. Cohen, eds., *A Handbook of Christian Theology* (New York: Meridian, 1958) 203f.

[14]Here lies the significance of Tillich's analysis of anxiety in his *Courage to Be* (New Haven: Yale University, 1952). Fate and death, guilt and condemnation, emptiness and meaninglessness are different ways in which the reality of law is experienced in different times by different people.

nant: "Now therefore, if you will obey my voice and keep my covenant, you shall be my own possession among all peoples; for all the earth is mine, and you shall be to me a kingdom of priests and a holy nation" (Exod 19:5)

Law and Legalism—The perversion of the law which always threatens to reduce it to mere legalism is the reduction of the personal demand into a propositional code. This personal demand is at the center of passages such as Isa 1:11: "'What to me is the multitude of your sacrifices?' says the Lord; 'I have had enough of burnt offerings of rams and the fat of fed beasts....Wash yourselves, make yourselves clean; remove the evil of your doings from before my eyes; cease to do evil, learn to do good; seek justice, correct oppression; defend the fatherless, plead for the widow.'"[15] The development of legal skill for the purpose of circumventing the personal demand of God is a deviation characteristic of later Jewish casuistry.[16]

New Covenant—Because humankind abuses the law in legalism as the prophets complained, and reduces the personal demand of God to a propositional code, the prophets see the need for a new covenant which reestablishes the personal relationship: "I will put my law within them, and I will write upon their hearts; and I will be their God and they shall be my people."[17] In the Old Testament, law is the divine demand expressing a personal relationship between God and His people. Because humankind breaks this relationship, the law condemns and the hope is a new law.

2. New Testament

The New Testament does not abolish God's personal demands. In the New Testament the law as confrontation with God's personal demand is emphasized and focused through Jesus Christ and his law of love ("A new commandment I give to you, that you love one another even as I have loved you, that you also love one another" [John 13:34]). Everywhere in the New Testament we are summoned to this love: "Truly I say to you, as you did it to one of the least of these my brethren, you did it to me" (Matt 25:40). Love is the fulfillment of the law (Rom 13:10).

The New Testament proclamation of the law is not immune to legalism. The perversion of personal demand into a propositional code results in a highly developed legalistic casuistry and the domination of christendom for centuries by lawyers.

The New Testament law accuses humankind. And the efforts to reduce the demands of the New Testament law of love to counsels of perfection for the elect

---

[15]Cf. Psalm 50; Jeremiah 7.

[16]Abraham Heschel, *God in Search of Man* (New York: Meridian, 1959) 328: "The outstanding expression of the anti-agadic is contained in a classical rabbinic question with which Rashi opens his famous commentary on the Book of Genisis." Rabbi Isaac said: The Torah (which is the law book of Israel) should have commenced with chapter 12 of Exodus, "since prior to that chapter hardly any laws are set forth." See also page 329: "In justification of their view, exponents of religious behaviorism cite the passage in which the Rabbis paraphrased the words of Jeremiah (16:11), 'They have forsaken Me and have not kept My Torah' in the following way: 'Would that they had forsaken Me and kept My Torah.'"

[17]Jer 31:31; cf. Exod 34:25, Isaiah 55.

tends to obscure the function of the law as taskmaster, *paidagogos*, driving us to Christ (Gal 3:24).

Both in Old and New Testament God addresses us by means of the law. We are confronted by God's holy will and by God's willingness to meet us to deal with us. If anything, the demands of God's law are more personal and more total in the New Testament. In both Old and New Testaments, people are guilty because they have broken the relationship which God has offered them. They are separated from God through their own fault. And because this relationship to God is in fact broken, the law always accuses.

3. The Lutheran Church

In the Church of the Augsburg Confession, the distinction between law and gospel has been methodologically central. As early as 1518, Luther used it in his *Explanations of the Ninety-five Theses.* Luther commented on Thesis 62, "The true treasure of the Church is the most holy gospel of the glory and grace of God," as follows:

> The gospel is a preaching of the incarnate Son of God, given to us without any merit on our part for salvation and peace. It is a word of salvation, a word of grace, a word of comfort, a word of joy, a voice of the bridegroom and the bride, a good word, a word of peace.[18]

And he describes the law as follows: *Lex vero est verbum perditionis, verbum irae, verbum tristitiae, verbum doloris, vox iudicis et rei, verbum inquietudinis, verbum maledicti* ("The law is a word of destruction, a word of wrath, a word of sadness, a word of grief, a voice of the judge and the defendant, a word of restlessness, a word of curse"). And he refers to 1 Cor 15:56, Rom 4:15 and 7:5 and then continues, *Ex lege enim nihil habemus nisi malam conscientiam, inquietum cor, pavidum pectus a facie peccatorum nostrorum, quae lex ostendit nec tollit nec nos tollere possumus* ("Through the law we have nothing except an evil conscience, a restless heart, a troubled breast, because of our sins, which the law points out but does not take away. And we ourselves cannot take it away").[19]

This distinction between law and gospel is a consistent feature of Luther's theology throughout his entire life. We find it developed in detail in his commentaries on Galatians and in his sermons. Though he considers the distinction crucial, he is also convinced that it is impossible to accomplish it consistently. The tendency is always either to become what he calls an "unbelieving worker" or a "workless believer."[20] His awareness of the difficulty of making the right distinction is perhaps most clearly expressed in a remark at table in 1531 reported by Johannes Schlaginhaufen:

> There's no man living on earth who knows how to distinguish between the law and the gospel. We many think we understand it when we are listening to a

---

[18]LW 31:231.
[19]Ibid. (for Latin, cf. WA 1:616).
[20]*The Gospel of John, 14-16,* LW 24:249 [editor's translation].

sermon, but we're far from it. Only the Holy Spirit knows this. Even the man Christ was so wanting in understanding when he was in the vineyard that an angel had to console him; though he was a doctor from heaven he was strengthened by the angel. Because I've been writing so much and so long about it, you'd think I'd know the distinction, but when a crisis comes I recognize very well that I am far, far from understanding. So God alone should and must be our holy master.[21]

But while the distinction is difficult, it has to be made. Out of the confusion of law and gospel grow both legalism and antinomianism, which obscure and pervert the Christian proclamation. Once the distinction has been made, Luther insists that the law has two purposes: the civil and the theological uses of the law.[22] This he summarizes in the second disputation against the Antinomians: "It is declared that there are two uses of the law: the first restrains faults and the second displays faults."[23] This means that all Christians are under the law. As the Formula of Concord later put it in regard to the believers,

> For although they are indeed reborn and have been renewed in the spirit of their mind, such regeneration and renewal is incomplete in this world. In fact, it has only begun....On account of this Old Adam, who inheres in people's intellect, will, and all their powers, it is necessary for the law of God constantly to light their way.[24]

This, by the way, is the controversial "third use of the law" in the *Formula of Concord*. However, if one keeps in mind the description of the human situation as *simul justus et peccator* [simultaneously saint and sinner] it appears that this third use could easily be subsumed under the two uses as proposed by Luther. Luther's position has been the object of a number of significant studies since Werner Elert rejected this "third use" as attributable to Luther.[25]

The significant result is not so much a precise number of "uses of the law" as the undeniable and profound relationship between faith and works in Luther's theology which was somewhat obscured by the more Kantian-idealistic interpretations. The fourfold use of the law suggested by later Lutheran dogmaticians (the political [preservation of external discipline], the elenchtical [manifestation and reproof of sins], the pedagogic [indirectly compelling the sinner to go to Christ], and the didactic [moral instruction and direction],[26] is dubious not only as far as its

---

[21]*LW* 54:127.

[22]*Lectures on Galatians 1–4* (1535), *LW* 26:308ff.

[23]*WA* 39/1:441, "Scitis duplicem esse usum legis, primum coercendi delicta, et diende ostendendi delicta" [editor's translation].

[24]FC, Ep 6:3, in *BC*, 480.

[25]W. Elert, *The Christian Ethos* (Philadelphia: Muhlenberg, 1957) 294ff. See also Wilfried Joest, *Gesetz und Freiheit, das Problem des tertius usus legis bei Luther und die neutestamentliche Parainese* (Göttingen: Vandenhoeck and Ruprecht, 1951); Albrecht Peters, *Glaube und Werk* (Berlin/Hamburg: Lutherisches Verlagshaus, 1962); O. Modalsli, *Das Gericht nach den Werken* (Göttingen: Vandenhoeck and Ruprecht, 1963).

[26]David Hollazius (d. 1713), *Examen Theologicum Acroamaticum* (1707), quoted in Heinrich Schmid, *The Doctrinal Theology of the Evangelical Lutheran Church*, 3rd ed., revised (1875; reprint, Minneapolis: Augsburg, 1961) 515f.

biblical basis is concerned, but also tends to confuse the boundary lines between the law and the gospel.

For our discussion, two insights of the Lutheran theologians ought to be retained: (1) the twofold use of the law, its political or civil use, conducive to a modicum of civil righteousness, and its theological use, driving us to Christ, basic for an understanding of the law; (2) *lex enim semper accusat conscientias et perterrefacit*—"The law always accuses and terrifies consciences."[27] Because and as long as human beings live in a broken relationship with God the law must always accuse them. Whenever this accusing demand of the law is obscured, the human situation is misunderstood and aggravated and the only remedy made unavailable.

The Nature of the Gospel in Theological Discourse

The gospel is the good news of God's saving deed in Jesus Christ. This is a personal deed, reestablishing through the cross the relationship humankind has broken. It is anticipated in the Old Testament, recorded in the New Testament, and remembered and proclaimed in the church.

1. Old Testament

The distinction between law and gospel is not identical with the distinction between Old and New Testament, for as the New Testament proclaims gospel and law, so the Old Testament proclaims law and gospel.

Covenant and Gospel—While the covenant is certainly and properly associated with the law, the same covenant is quite as properly associated with the gospel. It is God's gracious election which brings about the establishment of the covenant with Israel. This election is good news pointing in the direction of Jesus Christ, the author and finisher of our faith. For the Christian church and according to its inner history, the Old Testament bears witness to the good news in Christ. The covenant must be seen in the context of the gospel as well as the law.

Universalism—But the gospel in the Old Testament points beyond the election of Israel to the saving deed of God for all people. "Behold, I make him a witness to the peoples, a leader and commander for the peoples. Behold, you shall call nations that you know not, and nations that knew you not shall run to you because of the Lord your God, and the Holy One of Israel" (Isa 55:4-5). This is the message of Jonah: not only Israel but also Nineveh is within the realm of God's care. "God repented of the evil which he had said he would do to them; and he did not do it" (Jonah 3:10)."

The Messianic Vision—The gospel appears clearly in the Old Testament in the anticipation of the Messiah, whether this Messiah be the Davidic king or the apocalyptic figure of Daniel or the suffering servant of Deutero-Isaiah. All three anticipatory types—and there may actually be even more—are fulfilled and transcended in Jesus Christ.

---

[27]*Ap* 4:38, in *BC*, 112.

2. New Testament

The New Testament proclaims this gospel as its central message.

Gospel and Covenant—The New Testament proclaims this gospel in continuity with the Old Testament, fulfilling, not rejecting, it. The New Testament is the new covenant, meaningful only in the context and against the background of the old covenant. Once separated from the Old Testament, the New Testament message deteriorates into religious gnosticism or philosophical idealism.

Gospel and Kerygma—The New Testament presents this gospel as a kerygma, i.e., a proclamation. It is not a series of logical propositions here recorded in a particularly brilliant or reliable manner; rather we are confronted by an urgent message which may appear illogical, even shocking, but which tells about God's deeds for us. Its value depends neither on the logical coherence of this message, nor on its incoherence (though it may appear to exhibit both); neither on its conformity to what could have been expected nor on its nonconformity; but rather on the deed which it proclaims, God's deed in Jesus Christ.

Gospel and Discipleship—This New Testament proclamation of the gospel does make a difference. It works a change. If God's deed in Jesus Christ is proclaimed and believed, something will happen. This is the new life in Christ, it is the discipleship which is always the result of faith in the deed of God in Christ. Where there is no new life there is no faith. This message, if believed, makes all the difference in life. To use Wingren's illustration of the check:

> A person who receives a check in the mail certainly gains some knowledge when he takes the check and reads it. But if this is the main point, that before he read the check he lacked a certain knowledge which now has been given to him, he has a false conception of at least three realities. He has a false conception of his own situation before the check came, as if the absence of knowledge was the important part. He has a false conception of the function of a check, as if its primary function were to convey knowledge. And he has a false picture of the sender, as if he who was previously unknown now had made himself known.[28]

If we carry this illustration a little bit further, if someone accepts this check, believes that it is good, it will make all the difference in that person's life. If a person acts as if nothing had happened, does not cash the check—frames it, worships it, but does not work with it—that person does not really accept it. Discipleship means to work with what God has given, to take God at his word, the God who acts in Jesus Christ.

THE CONFUSION OF LAW AND GOSPEL

The present situation in theology is characterized by the confusion of law and gospel as distinguished in the discussion up to this point. The distinction is not being made, not even by Lutherans. And when they make it they do it in such a mechanical fashion, that it contributes more to the confusion. Ignoring the distinction or making it inadequately results in certain detrimental tendencies in the life of the church.

[28]Wingren, *Theology*, 42f.

Theological Legalism—Theological legalism is the denial of God's love. The Christian message is homogenized into law, i.e., into demands ranging in their character from the sublime to the ridiculous. This law is understood as the message of the Christian church and thus interpreted as the gospel. The difference between Christianity and other religions is then merely the difference in laws. One religion may demand one kind of behavior pattern; another religion may demand the exact opposite—but if religion is merely the demand of conformity to a certain pattern it is always legalism.

Another form in which this legalism may appear is that of reducing the very gospel into a law. Here the uniqueness of the gospel is formally recognized; the centrality of the person and work of Jesus Christ is emphasized. However, the relationship to this Christ is construed as a legal relationship. Christianity is now the acceptance of statements about this Jesus and his work. The good work which saves is not loving the enemy or wearing hooks instead of buttons, but rather accepting theological propositions about this Jesus Christ. The more these propositions run counter to logic and common sense, the more meritorious the faith. The sacrifice of the intellect is here the saving deed, and whoever sacrifices the intellect with the greatest abandon is considered the most holy. This sacrifice of the intellect is then a substitute for all other good works which other legalists are prepared to do. Since these other good works, e.g., loving the enemy, giving alms, not getting drunk, etc., have definitely positive social aspects (civil use of the law), the intellectual legalism, which often disparages these deeds, is actually socially less useful than the other forms of legalism.

Theological Antinomianism—Another result of the confusion of law and gospel is an antinomianism which denies the relevance of the law for the Christian, either because of an unduly optimistic view of the human situation or because of a radical pessimism concerning humankind's predicament.

Since the time of the gnostic conflict which had threatened the survival of the early church, there have always been some who claimed that Christians should sin so that grace might abound. Because of a peculiar metaphysics which resulted in an inability to associate the order of this world in any way with the God and Father of our Lord Jesus Christ, they felt that breaking this natural order was not only excusable but indeed advisable. Similar views have appeared again and again in the course of Christian history. They threatened the great reformation of the Christian Church in the sixteenth century and were the reason for Luther's writings against the antinomians. Today there are also those who because of the superficial view of the nature of sin discard the significance of the law and speak and act as if obedience to the law were not part of the Christian life, indeed were beneath the dignity of the Christian.

Strangely enough, a complete pessimism concerning the human predicament leads to very similar conclusions to those of the contemporary optimistic antinomians. Some contemporaries see sin as so serious a deficiency and people so utterly perverted by it that the very effort to oppose it is considered vainglory and pride. The total depravity of humankind is made the basic Christian assertion and the ambiguity of all human action so clearly discerned that all sensitivity to the shades of grey in human action has been lost. Here we find those whose advice in ethics to moderns is a counsel of desperation. It is not entirely comforting that Luther's *pecca fortiter* [sin boldly] is their favorite saying, quoted frequently and always out of context.

Whether antinomianism has its roots in an unjustified optimism concerning the human situation or a radical pessimism, the denial of the law in either case results eventually in the denial of the gospel. For the message of liberation cannot be taken seriously if either the slavery to sin and law is not understood radically enough or if the proclamation of this slavery usurps the place of the proclamation of the liberation. The gospel is not gospel if the law does not exist. But neither is the gospel good news if it cannot free us from the bondage of sin, if its proclamation makes absolutely no difference.

In contemporary Christian thought, law and gospel are confused in so many and subtle ways that almost any corrective statement is in danger of aggravating the confusion by encouraging either legalism or antinomianism, the denial of God's love or the denial of God's justice.

THE CONTEMPORARY TASK

Within the framework of this presentation it is not possible to offer a solution to the problem, even if such a solution were available. Our task was to attempt a description and analysis of the problem. Yet a few hints indicating where the solution might possibly lie may be in order.

While the Lutheran distinction between law and gospel often appears hackneyed and has assumed the character of a theological panacea with which the Lutheran theologian can solve any and all problems, the basic concern expressed in this formulation is sound and must be recovered if the Christian message is not to be obscured and falsified.

It is the same God who deals with humanity through the law as well as the gospel, who confronts us as the God of justice and of love. The work of the law may indeed be God's strange work while the work of the gospel is his proper work, but both are God's. Thus the church has a responsibility to both. Unless it responsibly proclaims law and gospel, demand and gift, the power of God's justice and the power of God's love, its message becomes inept and confused sentimentality or harsh and self-righteous condemnation. Both dangers are clear and present today. Both are the direct result of the theological confusion of law and gospel.

But law and gospel are not the same thing. If they are identified and one is made merely the appendix of the other, neither the seriousness of the human predicament nor the glory of the divine salvation is described with precision. It is the task of the church to make this distinction in its proclamation in order not to jeopardize the truth of the message. Only if the law is proclaimed as law in all its demanding seriousness does it produce its beneficial results for the social life of humanity. Simultaneously, only if the law is thus proclaimed is there any chance that it will accomplish its pedagogical work as a taskmaster driving us to Christ. A law not taken seriously contributes nothing to the preservation of society or to the growth of the body of Christ.

And only if the gospel is proclaimed as God's gracious deed for humankind does it free us from sin and death. A gospel which is merely a new and different law, a heavier burden for humankind, a greater demand, is not "gospel" at all. The fact that the message of the church has become associated in the minds of most people with irrelevant restrictions, often applicable only to other times and climes, seems a sad reflection of the fact that the good news of salvation has not been proclaimed with perception and passion.

This situation is not helped by those contemporary advocates of a "new morality" who act as if an ethic of love were a simple human possibility.

When the Bishop of Woolwich writes, "Love alone, as it were, because it has a built in moral compass, enabling it to 'home' intuitively upon the deepest need of the other, can allow itself to be directed completely by the situation...it is able to embrace an ethic of radical responsiveness, meeting every situation on its own merits, with no prescriptive laws,"[29] he is really begging the question. He and his more sophisticated associates in the call for a "new morality" never tell us how the human beings the Bible knows, the human beings contemporary literature knows, the human beings we know—you and I—become enabled to love. Indeed, the much-touted new morality seems only to be a new romantic and sentimental legalism.

Law and gospel are a problem to contemporary theology, partly because both are misunderstood, partly because both are confused. If the distinction between law and gospel is as crucial as Luther and our forbears believed, it is high time that we address ourselves to the problem of defining them both more accurately, distinguishing them more clearly, and relating them more positively.

[29]John A. T. Robinson, *Honest to God* (Philadelphia: Westminster, 1963) 115.

Word & World
Supplement Series 2
1994

Justification and Justice

FIRST, I WOULD LIKE TO NOTE THAT THE WORD *"RECHT,"* FOR A PERSON WHO thinks in English, is ambiguous. My dictionary translates it as "right, privilege, claim, title, law, justice, administration of justice," and that is only the beginning of the list. It is for us a word of many colors, encompassing the great tension between *"Recht"* as law and *"Recht"* as justice. For this reason, and because I was asked to deliver my lecture in German, I would like to begin the investigation of this theme with Karl Barth's well-known discussion of this question.

In the first installment of his series, *Theologische Studien,* he published an essay entitled, *"Rechtfertigung und Recht."* In it we read,

> Is there a connection between the reality of the one-time, complete justification [*"Rechtfertigung"*] of the sinner through faith alone, which is accomplished by God in Jesus Christ, and the problem of human justice [*"Recht"*]? Is there an internal, necessary connection through which God's justification of the sinner and human justice become in some sense the object of Christian faith, Christian responsibility, and Christian confession?[1]

Then Barth makes the interesting observation that, in the working out of this connection, not only Luther (as one might expect from Barth) but also Calvin and Zwingli have abandoned us.[2] He writes:

> One will not be able easily either to overlook or accept this gap in the instruction we have received from our church's forbears—the lack of an evangelical (by

---

[1]Karl Barth, *Rechtfertigung und Recht* (1938) , 4th ed. (Zürich: EVZ, 1970) 5.
[2]Ibid., 5-6.

This essay was first presented as a lecture, "Rechtfertigung und Recht," at the September 9-12, 1991, international consultation, "Rechtfertigung und Weltverantwortung" ("Justification and Responsibility for the World"). The proceedings were held at Neuendettelsau, Germany, and published under the conference name (Neuendettelsau, 1991). This essay appears on pages 221-235. The translation here is by the editor.

which I mean, in the strict sense, christological) basis for this part of their confession.[3]

Barth attempts to fill this gap, in distinction from the reformers, by demanding a christological basis for the state. Speaking of the state, he says that for Paul,

> *within* the christological realm (though *outside* the sphere normally designated by the word justification) there was, embodied in the world of angelic powers, *another* sphere connecting the church with the cosmos—one that might be called a secondary-christological sphere.[4]

And this means for him that precisely the preaching of justification as the preaching of the kingdom of God already here and now forms the basis of the true law ["*Recht*"], the true state.[5]

All of these ideas are expressed by Barth rather cautiously. Human law and the human state should make the proclamation of justification possible. The proclamation of the gospel is central for him, and it is very important that the state fulfill its responsibility to facilitate the proclamation of that gospel. Barth describes the failure of the state when he points to the condemnation of Christ by Pontius Pilate. Pilate did not fulfill his duty as the bearer of lawful responsibility. For all that, however, Barth opens a path to a fundamental confusion of justice and justification by founding human law and the political order in the preaching of justification—which, in my opinion, has often led in our present situation to turning Barth's position upside down.

The connection of justification and justice, i.e., the christological foundation of politics, which Barth required, has been widely accepted. However, Barth's emphasis, that the state's main purpose is to guarantee the proclamation of justification, has been hardly accepted at all. We live in a time when many theologians assert that the church only exists in order to further the realization of particular human rights. The state does not exist in order to make the proclamation of the gospel possible—as Barth intended—but rather the church exists in order to fight for the rights of certain people and special groups who are described as victims of the ruling system.

But in this struggle for particular human rights, which is in many cases completely appropriate, the gospel of the justification of the sinner by faith is now pushed into the background. The institutional church and its individual members have the duty to compel the so-called "liberation" of those who for various reasons do not want to accept the political program of these theologians. This "liberation" is understood politically and has nothing to do with the "Freedom of the Christian."[6] Every means available may be employed in this struggle. As the American theologian Joseph Fletcher says quite openly: "The end justifies the means."[7] A

[3]Ibid., 7.
[4]Ibid., 22.
[5]Ibid., 28.
[6][Here Dr. Forell refers to Luther's famous 1520 tract by the same name. Ed.]
[7]Joseph Fletcher, *Situation Ethics: The New Morality* (Philadelphia: Westminster, 1966) 120ff.

characteristic slogan, though today already largely outdated, would be: "God is not dead—God is red."

In distinction from Barth, classical christology is here completely excluded. Jesus is the son of God only in the sense that we are all daughters and sons of God. He is just another struggler for human rights, unfortunately a white male (even-though he is a Jew), which hinders his ability to act as a role model. Justification in its classical sense, which—whether we follow Anselm or Irenaeus—had something to do with atonement, must be dropped. At best, one could simply employ the interpretation of Abelard and the liberal theology of the nineteenth century.

I see the reason for this break with classical christology in the fact that the uniqueness of Christ's incarnation includes an exclusive and universal claim for the gospel. It is now said, however, that one can no longer justify this exclusivity in a pluralistic world. It is a scandal, because it appears to call human rights into question. The second article is wrenched out of the creed. A creator-god—especially if he can be completely identified with the creation—might be retained as part of the proclamation. Also, a spirit, who exists in every person and in whom everyone can participate in one another (exemplified in, "Come Share the Spirit," the motto of the ELCA in the U.S.A.), is still possible. However, there is no longer any place for Jesus Christ, "God from God, Light from Light, True God from True God...who for us and our salvation came down from heaven."

All of this could be documented with specifics, but to do so would lead us too far afield. A few quotations should suffice to indicate the direction of this tendency. Already in 1902 Alfred Loisy wrote: "Jesus announced the kingdom of God, and what came forth was the church."[8] Theology then becomes, "the religious production of the dominating classes, whose function it is to sacralize and secure their privileges."[9] The new theology:

> consciously and radically excludes everything described in the categories of atonement, vicarious death...and the bloody satisfaction of a retribution-demanding God whose honor has been offended....The miracle that this counter-theology celebrates is that the murdered liberator continually produces emulation—revolutionary praxis, perpetual hope, and the readiness to lay one's life on the line in behalf of other comrades, whatever the cost. The liberator's selfless life continues to kindle opposition to the gods and the powers of death.[10]

But Paul is also brought into this new theology. José Porfirio Miranda writes:

> Paul wants a world without law. Exegesis which avoids this fact makes an understanding of the Pauline message impossible. Neither Kropotkin nor Bakunin nor Marx nor Engels made assertions against the law more powerful and subversive than those which Paul makes. Paul is convinced not only that the

[8]Alfred Loisy, *L'Evangile et l'Eglise* (Paris, 1902). Quoted from *Die Bibel als politisches Buch*, ed. Dietrich Schirmer (Stuttgart: Kohlhammer 1982) 47.

[9]Georges Casalis, "Der ermordete Befreier," in Schirmer, 47.

[10]Ibid., 55.

law has failed in human history in its attempt to acheive justice, but that justice cannot be achieved in the world as long as law exists.[11]

Neither law nor gospel make it in this so-called "counter-theology."

In this situation, the word from the article upon which the church stands or falls must be spoken:

> Here is the First and Chief Article: That Jesus Christ, our God and Lord, "was handed over to death for our trespasses and was raised for our justification" (Rom. 4); and he alone is "the Lamb of God, who takes away the sin of the world" (John 1); and "the LORD has laid upon him the iniquity of us all" (Isa. 53); furthermore, "All have sinned," and "they are now justified without merit by his grace, through the redemption which is in Christ Jesus...by his blood" (Rom. 3). Now because this must be believed and may not be obtained or grasped otherwise with any work, law, or merit, it is clear and certain that faith alone justifies us. In Romans 3, St. Paul says: "For we hold that a person is justified by faith apart from works prescribed by the law"; and also, "that God alone is righteous and justifies the one who has faith in Jesus." We cannot yield or concede anything in this article, even if heaven and earth, or whatever, do not remain. As St. Peter says in Acts 4: "There is no other name given among mortals by which we must be saved." "And with his bruises we are healed" (Isaiah 53).[12]

How can we understand the relationship of justice and justification in the light of this fundamental assertion of the evangelical Lutheran church? How do we respond to Karl Barth's question: "Is there a connection between the reality of the one-time, complete justification of the sinner through faith alone, which is accomplished by God in Jesus Christ, and the problem of human justice?" We see the key to a right understanding in the distinction between law and gospel. As the creator of heaven and earth, God gives us the law. It is available to all people, for as Paul says, all people "show that what the law requires is written on their hearts, to which their own conscience also bears witness; and their conflicting thoughts will accuse or perhaps excuse them" (Rom 2:15). Thus Paul can assert that all people know that sinners (whose sins Paul has precisely described), "according to God's law, deserve to die" (Rom 1:32).

Justice, in this sense, is the basis of all just human laws, and all human laws, which are themselves deeply entangled in sin, must be evaluated by God's law. Paul shows that this is possible by naming the lawlessness in verses 29 and 30 without hesitation. He assumes that all people are aware of these things.

What does this mean in a pluralistic age? We are tied to those who do not share our faith in Jesus Christ and justification through our common obligation to the law, as it is described here by Paul. We may and can work together with them against all the evil named here. As the *Formula of Concord* says, "We believe, teach, and confess that the preaching of the law is to be diligently applied not only to

---

[11]José Porfirio Miranda, *Marx and the Bible: A Critique of the Philosophy of Opression* (Maryknoll, NY: Orbis, 1974) 187.

[12]*Schmalkald Articles* 2/1. Translation from *The Schmalkald Articles by Martin Luther*, edited and translated by William R. Russell (Minneapolis: Fortress Press, 1994).

unbelievers and the impenitent but also to people who are genuinely believing, truly converted, regenerated, and justified through faith."[13] What our forbears called the "usus legis politicus" ["the political use of the law"] serves as the basis for us to make commom cause with all people who with us see the danger posed by the flood of antinomianism.

In order to fulfill this task, we do not need to wait for the whole world to be converted to justification by faith in Jesus Christ before we can work together with our non-Christian friends for earthly justice against hunger, homelessness, oppression, exploitation, racism, sexism, and other evils. We do not first need to make these people members of the church against their will, through subtle theological manipulation, calling them "anonymous Christians." We do pious Jews or Moslems no favors by labeling them "anonymous Christians." We must be willing to work together on the basis of law, about which they are also concerned, without placing before them the pre-condition of a christological confession. As the former Lutheran Bishop of New York, William Lazareth, once said:

> This means that reasonable men, even apart from faith in Christ, are capable of a high degree of social justice in the building of a peaceful and humane society. It is wholly unevangelical to deny that God has written his law on the hearts of all men created in his image. Moreover, the moral zeal of a humanitarian, however motivated, often exceeds that of an apathetic Christian. Especially in our kind of pluralistic society, the church's social minstry will often take the form of working together for human justice under the law with other civic minded groups, both voluntary and governmental.[14]

The question here is the question of the standards used to evaluate our actions and those of our non-Christian friends. At this point, the history of Christian ethics has had much to say about natural law. In the nineteenth century, however, the suspicion arose that natural law was really only the mores of the ruling group of a specific culture. Justice, it was said, was always whatever a particular civilization or ideology said it was. In the notorious idiom of the time, it was said, "Justice is what serves the people." In the American context, the first Chief Justice of the Supreme Court said in 1821, "The people made the Constitution, and the people can unmake it. It is the creature of their own will, and lives only by their will."[15] And 100 years later, one of his successors said, "We are under a Constitution, but the Constitution is what the judges say it is."[16]

This positivistic understanding of law probably reached its highpoint in the twentieth century. The crimes which have been committed in its name in our time, however, have seriously called it into question. Can we, in our pluralistic world, return to natural law? If this concept is modestly defined, then it can help us define more clearly the political justice that God has given to all people (whether they

---

[13]FC, Ep 6, in BC, 480, §3.

[14]William Lazareth, *Social Ministry: Biblical and Theological Perspectives*. Quoted in Christa Klein and Christian von Dehsen, *Politics and Policy* (Minneapolis: Fortress, 1989) 65.

[15]John Marshall (1755-1835), *Cohens vs. Virginia*, 6 Wheaton (19 US) 264, 389 (1821).

[16]Charles Evans Hughes (1862-1948), Lecture in Elmira, New York, 1907.

know it or not). It is the attempt to come closer to a world-wide understanding of justice based on the "Golden Rule" (Matt 7:12), which is known to all world religions. This could sound very much like Immanuel Kant's "categorical imperative"; but we must free ourselves from the ban on reason that has become theologically fashionable. Because in the realm of human cooperation, the only alternative is the tyranny of irrationality. We have seen in this century where that leads.

We know that human reason has no ability to lead us to God, the Father of our Lord Jesus Christ. But as Melanchthon writes in the *Apology to the Augsburg Confession*:

> We are not denying freedom to the human will. The human will has freedom to choose among the works and things which reason by itself can grasp. To some extent it can achieve civil righteousness or the righteousness of works. It can talk about God and express its worship of him in outward works. It can obey rulers and parents. Externally, it can choose to keep the hands from murder, adultery, or theft. Since human nature still has reason and judgment about the things that the senses can grasp, it also retains a choice in these things, as well as the liberty and ability to achieve civil righteousness. The righteousness which the carnal nature—that is, the reason—can achieve on its own without the Holy Spirit, Scripture calls the righteousness of the flesh.[17]

Even if human reason is insufficient in these things because of the great "power of concupiscence,"[18] all people have the ability to use this limited free will in this world to set certain limits on injustice and evil. In this important task we may, for quite pragmatic reasons, count on the cooperation of many people who otherwise do not know (or even want to know) anything about the church and the gospel.

But if it is possible for people who, viewed theologically, are "unjustified" to live responsibly together, then what does justification do with respect to justice? We know what Luther said in *The Schmalkald Articles*. What does the view of justification described there have to do with justice?

Every Christian who has made an attempt to cooperate with others who care about law and justice in the practical and political struggle against injustice and evil, discovers very quickly how deeply all humans are entangled in unrighteousness and oppression. Even if we realize an occasional success, we learn quickly the truth of Lord Acton's observation: "Power corrupts and absolute power corrupts absolutely."[19]

As long as we live only for our individual piety, protecting our religious life from the concerns and victims of the everyday world, with its mean-spirited rulers, then this talk about justification sounds old-fashioned and unimportant. For those who have in this struggle lost faith in themselves and others because they have discovered what Luther's observation about sin as *incurvatus in se* means—what

---

[17]*Ap* 18/4, in *BC*, 225.

[18]Ibid.

[19]John Emerich Edward Dalberg-Acton (1634-1902); Letter to Bishop Mandell Creighton (April 5, 1887).

difficulties it produces in this struggle for justice—there is no hope without justification. Justification does not give us a political program, but helps us to hold the goal and target of our actions in view—not like those whose programs and plans have failed and who are in danger either of giving up in despair or of cynically and bureaucratically continuing on without hope. Without the daily new start that Luther describes in his explanation of baptism in *The Small Catechism*, this is impossible.

We return once again to Barth's question:

> Is there a connection between the reality of the one-time, complete justification of the sinner through faith alone, which is accomplished by God in Jesus Christ, and the problem of human justice?

Our answer is that justification enables the Christian to follow Jesus the Christ in the real world in which we live, as people who are simultaneously sinful and righteous. Without illusion or despair, we may work together on the problems which are before all people in this time between the times.

In this task, we cannot rely on a supposed "biblical" political, social, or economic program. Neither socialism nor capitalism nor any political system is "Christian." The choice between the various means to human justice which stand before us must be made with the help of the God-given reason that has been bestowed on all people.

We must be thankful that God still today has servants like the Persian King Cyrus long ago (Isa 45:1), who, without theological understanding, still often play leading roles in the common work for law and justice. Our particular activities as Christians in service to the world, regardless of what motivates those who work with us, are made possible only by the forgiveness of sins, by justification through faith alone. The connection between the justification of the sinner through faith alone and the problem of human justice lies in the heart of the person who has been accepted by God in Christ.

Christ and Culture:
Reflections and Questions

T HE RELATIONSHIP BETWEEN CHRIST AND CULTURE IS A PERMANENT AND INES-
capable problem in the life and history of the church militant. It is reflected in
Jesus' conflict with the religious establishment of his time and is recorded in the
gospels. It is also apparent in the tension between Jewish and gentile Christians
described in a somewhat mediating way in the Acts of the Apostles and more
acrimoniously in Paul's epistle to the Galatians. In post-biblical times the problem
recurs regularly as Christianity encounters the Hellenistic world and later the
Latin culture of the western empire as well as the indigenous cultures of Asia and
North Africa. Some of the most creative movements within Christianity as, e.g., the
monastic movement from the hermits in the Egyptian desert to the Franciscans and
Jesuits are responses to the problems raised by proclaiming Christ in a variety of
cultural contexts.

The reports presented to this consultation in Jerusalem are further evidence
of the permanent and profound tension between Christ and culture.

If one looks at the conflict from a historical and systematic perspective a
number of reflections may be conducive to further debate and may even contribute
to the correlation of our results:

First of all, we should see culture as the enemy of Christ and the gospel. This
adversary relationship seems to be a permanent aspect of this complex engage-

---

*In the late 1970s and early 1980s, Dr. Forell served as a consultant to the Lutheran World
Federation's Department of Studies. In this capacity, he participated in conferences and meetings of a
worldwide scope, as he brought to bear on the issues before these groups his conviction that Luther
was indeed a theologian of the church. This short piece was originally published in a collection of
papers from an LWF International Consultation in Jerusalem (March 23-27, 1981),* Confessing
Christ in Cultural Contexts, *vol. I, Lectures, Reports, Recommendations, ed. Maren Matthiesen (Geneva: Lutheran World Federation Department of Studies, 1981). Here Dr. Forell uses the
distinction between law and gospel to analyze culture and the church's participation in it, from both
a theological and historical perspective.*

ment. The apostle Paul addressed this feature when he referred to the gospel as a "stumbling block" to the Jews and "foolishness" to the Greeks. Indeed, the persecution of the Christians in the Roman Empire was based much more on the perspective on the non-Christians that Christians were culturally subversive than on any awareness of or interest in Christian theological or christological dogmas. If Christians had participated even minimally in the emperor cult their assertion that Jesus is the Christ could have been ignored in the religiously pluralistic Roman empire. Culture as the enemy of Christ may have been one reason—though not the only one—for the rise of monasticism at the very moment when culture adopted and embraced Christ. We can safely assert that the tension with culture is a permanent feature of the Christian movement. It is against this background that the phenomenon of culture as the enemy of Christ must be observed in contemporary Germany and Indonesia, Tanzania and Sweden, Japan and the U.S.A.

In each of these settings the gospel has to be proclaimed against redemptive pretensions on the part of culture. The German saying, "*Es wird am deutschen Wesen noch die Welt genesen*" ("The world will yet be restored by the German character") predates Hitler and in its obvious conceit is not particularly German. It is only one of the many such brazen assertions of the redemptive character of culture that could be duplicated in practically every human language. Salvatory claims are made by most if not all human cultures, as derogatory descriptions of members of other cultures in most human languages demonstrate (e.g., "barbarians," "goyim," "infidels," "foreign devils," etc.). The inscriptions on the American dollar bill furnish a "small catechism" of the cultural pretension of American culture: "Annuit Coeptis," "Novo Ordo Seculorum," "In God We Trust." No discussion of "Confessing Christ in Cultural Context" would be adequate if this idolatrous aspect of human culture, its pretension to offer ultimate meaning, were not taken seriously.

Not unrelated to the enmity between Christ and culture as observed throughout the history of Christianity is the equally problematic tendency to use Christianity specifically and not some general civil religion as the means to endorse the prevailing culture and its mores. Especially in the west since the days of Emperor Constantine, an obvious effort has been made to use Christianity as a means of endorsing and legitimizing the prevailing culture. The king as "defender of the faith," as "most Christian," the close relationship of throne and altar, may be observed everywhere. Religious leaders supported by the government have been expected to uphold and endorse the value system of the culture and refrain from any prophetic criticism. Thus the church, which once had been the refuge of the downtrodden and outcasts, became identified with the ruling class of the culture while engaged in worship. As a nineteenth-century English observer expressed it, "The Anglican Church is the Conservative Party at prayer." Similar observations could be made in other western countries. In the United States, church membership is highly correlated to income, and the lowest percentage of the church membership is found among the very poor. But the most terrible result of this symbiotic relationship between culture and Christianity has been the endorsement of a multitude of wars by the Christian community for allegedly Christian reasons. From the crusades of the middle ages to the christological justification for war of Karl Barth in his letter to Josef Hromadka and the anti-Communist crusades sponsored by Christians in Europe and America, the list is long and depressing. This attitude is also implicit in the effort on the part of some theologians to give Christian endorsement to certain economic or political systems as specifically approved by God, be that capitalism, or as they would prefer to call it, "the free enterprise system," as God's economic system for the world, or be it Marxism as endorsed with equal vigor by another group of theologians. Especially where Christianity represents a majority of the population, the tendency to identify Christ with the values of the culture is common. Culture is indeed baptized but with idolatrous results for church and state. One must be very careful to speak of "Christian" as an adjective modifying anything but human beings. If the term is used in relation to other objects, like churches, colleges, art, and culture, not to mention political parties or economic systems, it can only be justified because of the Christian people involved. The term is then applied by extension rather than strictly speaking. In the latter sense only a human being, a woman or man or child, can be called "Christian."

But there is a third way in which culture functions in relationship to the confession of Christ. It is simply observable that culture identified by insiders and outsiders as "Christian," however problematic this identification might be, has functioned as a missionary device. Christianity, associated in the minds of many with modern education and technology, has been perceived by outsiders as a means to achieve identification with western culture. In the nineteenth century the German poet Heinrich Heine, himself of Jewish background, noted that baptism was the entrance ticket to western civilization. This same pattern can be observed in other contexts. In certain areas of the world the term "Christian" is associated or identified with "educated person." While in and of itself a serious problem compromising the integrity of the Christian gospel, the perceived identification of Christianity and western culture has indeed offered openings for the proclamation of the gospel, from the English lessons to corporation executives in Japan, to the Christian school with overwhelmingly non-Christian students in Hong Kong, to Madras Christian College and the many church-operated school systems in Africa. The attraction of culture has frequently offered an opening for the gospel. One ought to be aware of the fact that confessing Christ in this cultural context raises a great many obvious and subtle questions which deserve to be addressed.

But aware of the complexity of the relationship of Christ and culture what, if anything, can we say as Lutherans about confessing Christ in the cultural context? If we keep in mind the basic theological distinction between law and gospel, God's demand and God's gift, and try to apply this distinction to our assignment, it becomes clear that culture is in the realm of the law. It always raises questions about our human situation. It is our culture, as we heard in various presentations, which addresses the problems of marriage and family, death and dying, meaning and meaninglessness. No culture can escape these issues, as was apparent in our discussion. But culture also raises the questions of justice, whether that be in Brazil or Sweden, Tanzania or West Germany. Sensitivity to the cultural context should help us to become aware of the real issues which confront us in our time, to hear the actual questions that our particular period in history poses. Theology has a deplorable tendency to answer questions nobody is asking. It frequently offers salvation to people who have no idea that they need to be saved. Attention to our cultural context might enable us to hear the real questions of our moment in history to which the gospel of Jesus Christ is the precise answer. A careful analysis of our culture, taking our culture seriously, might teach us to see why people in our time feel that they are sitting in darkness and are in need of the light. It is significant that the poets and novelists, the painters and musicians, the makers of motion pictures and television plays in our various cultures, seem to be able to describe our situation so much better than the theologians. But gospel responses that are not answers to law questions will always miss their mark. And the help we have to offer to the men and women in our time does not come from the law but from the gospel. Confessing Christ is not confessing a new law-giver, but the Messiah, the anointed one, the Savior, who has reconciled the human race and the suffering world with God.

I promised some reflections and some questions. You have heard my reflections, my questions are very simple:

The law always accuses as the *Apology of the Augsburg Confession* states plainly. Where do we find ourselves accused in our various cultures? Why are people in the USA and Tanzania, in Sweden and Indonesia, in Japan and Germany, Brazil and South Africa people who sit in darkness? There can be little doubt that they all perceive themselves as people who sit in darkness. We can only talk meaningfully about the light if we define our darkness with some precision. We must answer questions that are being asked. Cultural context means to listen carefully to these questions. What are the questions that West Germans are asking which drive them by the thousands to Hindu ashrams? What are the questions Americans are asking that drive them by the millions into the arms of peddlers of fundamentalistic legalism? What is the appeal of Islam in Tanzania? Why does a brilliant Japanese author like Mishima commit ritual suicide? Why does Ingmar Bergman, a Swedish Lutheran pastor's son, make the kind of movies he does? Before we can confess Christ, i.e., proclaim the gospel with precision to our culture, we must first try to understand the questions implicit in our culture. The gospel is good news; it will be received when we understand the bad news which our culture reveals. We might use our studies as a background to specify briefly and precisely the questions which we believe our cultural context raises so that we may be empowered by the Holy Spirit to confess Christ.

Such reflection might help us to assist the member churches of the LWF to confess Christ in the cultural context.

GENERAL DISCUSSION

Questions: If the gospel is always the enemy of culture, does not the gospel also demand a cultural expression? Does not the gospel also give answers to questions which are never asked? Does the gospel not also transform or does it simply oppose culture?

Dr. Forell: Law also has a civil use, but it is always threatened by the claim of culture to become redemptive. The finite can be the bearer of the infinite in a multitude of ways. God becomes operative in our lives in many ways, but one should not use incarnational language for this. Incarnation is not a principle but an event.

Questions: Is it possible to distinguish so clearly between text and context or does not the gospel itself participate in ambiguity?

Dr. Forell: It is impossible to translate the gospel unless one listens very carefully to the law and the questions it poses. There are no universal solutions to proclaiming the gospel, since each situation is peculiar. We are always living from the notion of justification throughout our lives.

Questions: To what extent is there an incarnational response to the sacraments? What is the significance of works for the justified? If culture is human self-expression, do Christians express themselves differently than non-Christians?

Dr. Forell: One must be totally open to the people and the needs which they express. Transformation of culture indeed takes place, but as soon as it happens it participates in sin. The worst thing in the pretension of a Christian culture is that it is Christian. Lutheran talk is peculiarly paradoxical in talking about the new creation. We have to insist on a theology of the cross in the face of a variety of theologies of glory. We live in a perfectionist world and we get much less discouraged than others if we recognize our limitations. We should be faithful to the end, not successful.

Questions: Is the Christian life not static but in movement? Do we need a substitute for the term 'progress' to show a forward movement in terms of sanctification?

Dr. Forell: We run around in circles a lot. Tomorrow our situation may be worse, since we have no assurance of continuously becoming better. There is no evolutionary progress, but much more an up-and-down.

Questions: Are the theology of cross and theology of glory both acceptable, since they are victory signs of God? Is it legitimate to say that there is some progress as long as we do not perceive it as ultimate?

Dr. Forell: We always have a choice between good and bad, as well as between good and better. But not everything we perceive as good turns out to be good. All our efforts are of penultimate character.

Questions: Must we not see the theology of cross and the theology of glory in their context? Do we not need justification and sanctification? Should not Luther too be used with discernment? Is there a plan in God's world? Is not an anti-progress thesis culturally conditioned?

Dr. Forell: There is a principle of faith active in love. But such faith is rather open-ended and has not a definite pre-established programme. Jerusalem shows that even God's marvellous deeds can be perverted and denigrated by human sinfulness.

Word & World
Supplement Series **2**
1994

The Significance of
Being Human:
A Lutheran Perspective

IN HIS SEMINAL WORK *GOD IN SEARCH OF MAN*, THE LATE ABRAHAM JOSHUA HESCHEL wrote:

> Freedom is an event. The reality of freedom, of the ability to think, to will, or to make decisions beyond physiological and psychological causation is only conceivable if we assume that human life embraces both *process and event*. If man is treated as a process, if his future determinations are regarded as calculable, then freedom must be denied. Freedom means that a man is capable of expressing himself in events beyond his being involved in the natural processes of living. To believe in freedom is to believe in events, namely to maintain that man is able to escape the bonds of the processes in which he is involved and to act in a way not necessitated by antecedent factors. Freedom is the state of going out of the self, an act of *spiritual ecstacy*, in the original sense of the term.[1]

This point of view is in stark contrast to the prevailing mood of our time. For example, one highly regarded American psychologist, B. F. Skinner, has asserted: "As a science of behaviour adopts the strategy of physics and biology, the autonomous agent to which behaviour has traditionally been attributed is replaced by the environment."[2]

To the critics of this development, like C. S. Lewis who spoke of the *Abolition of Man* and the replacement of humankind by what he called "the trousered ape," or Joseph Wood Krutch, who wrote,

---

[1]A. J. Heschel, *God in Search of Man* (New York: Farrar, Straus, and Cudahy, 1955) 410.
[2]B. F. Skinner, *Beyond Freedom and Dignity* (New York: Knopf, 1971) 184.

This essay first appeared in a journal entitled Christian-Jewish Relations *(15/2 [1982] 17-27). Here Dr. Forell speaks with a classically Lutheran voice as he engages modern understandings of what it means to be a human being.*

> For at least one hundred years we have been prejudiced in every theory, including economic determinism, mechanistic behaviourism, and relativism, that reduces the stature of man until he ceases to be man at all in any sense that the humanists of an earlier generation would recognize (quoted in Skinner, 200)

or Abraham H. Maslow who asserted, "What is now under attack is the 'being' of man" (cf. Skinner, 200), Professor Skinner replies: "What is being abolished is autonomous man—the inner man, the homunculus, the possessing demon, the man defended by the literature of freedom and dignity," and he continues,

> His abolition has long been overdue....To man *qua* man we readily say good riddance. Only by dispossessing him can we turn to the real causes of human behaviour. Only then can we turn from the inferred to the observed, from the miraculous to the natural, from the inaccessible to the manipulable. (200-201)

With disarming frankness B. F. Skinner tells us that in order to reach his utopia, a humankind manipulated by behavioral scientists, we must get rid of the outworn notions of human freedom and human dignity. And he says about this utopia,

> We shall not only have no reason to admire people who endure suffering, face danger, or struggle to be good; it is possible that we shall have little interest in pictures or books about them. The art and literature of the new culture will be about other things. (163-164)

Since he has just relegated to irrelevance Homer and all Greek tragedies, the Bhagavadgita and the Bible, Shakespeare and Goethe, Dostoevsky and Solzhenitzin, not to mention every opera and every great piece of religious music ever written, the art of Michelangelo and Leonardo da Vinci, Grünwald and Dürer, Van Gogh and Picasso, he mercifully spares us the subjects the art and literature of his new culture will be about. No wonder Arthur Koestler has referred to behaviorism as "a monumental triviality" and Peter Gay has spoken of the "innate naïveté, intellectual bankruptcy, and half-deliberate cruelty of behaviorism" (cf. Skinner, 165).

It would hardly be worth our while to spend much time with B. F. Skinner, called by one critic "a marvellous animal trainer and a terrible philosopher," if what he advocated were not a threat to the survival of a humane humanity. We do live in an age when, again in the words of Heschel, the "term 'humane' has become ambiguous. It has the connotation of weakness. ('He is only human.' 'Adam was but human.' 'To err is human')" (Heschel, 26).

And modern literature does not particularly stress the humane in the human being. Professor Fitch's description of the writing of Tennessee Williams may serve as one illustration:

> Since [Tennessee] Williams frankly declares himself to be an evangelist, we may inquire what is the gospel, the good news which he has to offer. Man is a beast. The only difference between man and the other beasts is that man is a beast that knows he will die. The only honest man is the unabashed egotist. This honest man pours contempt upon the mendacity, the lies, the hypocrisy of others, who will not acknowledge their egotism. The one irreducible value is pleasure and power. The specific ends of life are sex and money. The great passions are lust

and rapacity. So the human comedy is an outrageous medley of lechery, alcoholism, homosexuality, blasphemy, greed, brutality, hatred, obscenity. It is not a tragedy because it has not the dignity of a tragedy. The man who plays his role in it has on himself the marks of a total depravity. And as for the ultimate and irreducible value, life, that in the end is also a lie. (quoted in Heschel, 26-27)

Perhaps the eclipse of freedom and dignity is illustrated most clearly if one compares two books dealing essentially with the same subject, humanity on the desert island, one written by Daniel Defoe, an English writer who lived from 1661-1731, the other by William Golding, an English writer who lives in our own time. *Robinson Crusoe* shows the humanity of the human person. Crusoe and his friend Friday conquer the wilderness and make it into a paradise. It is a book which celebrates the triumph of human freedom and dignity. Golding's *Lord of the Flies* describes the disintegration of a group of civilized boys who come to the desert island, believing in the dignity and freedom of human beings, to order their society in a humane manner. Bringing along the principles underlying *Robert's Rules of Order*, they learn fast that the human being has been abolished, freedom and dignity are destroyed, and the "beast" triumphs.

That this is a very real scenario for the future of the human race must now be obvious even to the most sanguine contemporary. The animal trainers who are threatening to take over have not told us what gives them the right to run the circus. They have not told us why they should determine the nature and destiny of humanity. To say as they do, "a scientific view of man offers exciting possibilities. We have not yet seen what man can make of man" (Skinner, 215), is not encouraging to those who have seen the motion picture of Frederick Wiseman, called *Primate*, which shows only too convincingly what this kind of person can make of monkeys. We need a better model for humanity than the behavior-modified animal and a more promising guardian of our destiny than the animal experimenter.

For such models I shall without apology turn to the books which have inspired our view of man and woman, their freedom, their dignity, and their destiny, more profoundly than any other in our culture—namely the Bible, and particularly the book of Genesis. (As an aside I would suggest that were I to give this lecture in New Delhi and as a philosopher trained in Hindu rather than Christian thought, I think I should have little difficulty finding adequate models in the Bhagavadgita. I suspect that the teachings of the Buddha and of Mohammed would also serve us better than B. F. Skinner. But I am speaking as a person coming from a particular culture and to people who, like me, are heirs to this culture.)

We are all people whose worldview has been shaped by the notion that human beings are addressed by God; furthermore, that these humans are to respond to this address, i. e., that they are responsible. In our tradition the very source of our humanity is our relationship to our Creator. It is true, of course, that the view of the creation of which we experience ourselves to be a part has changed dramatically in the course of history, never more strikingly than in the centuries since Copernicus. But while our new understanding of the vastness and complexity of the created universe has changed, this change has if anything made God greater and the human being smaller. The replacement of a geocentric by a helio-centric universe may have diminished the stature of the human being; it has not affected God—as thoughtful observers from Newton to Whitehead and Heisenberg have frequently pointed out. Similarly, Darwin and Freud have done much to affect our human self-image, but nothing to the greatness of God.

The result has been a very serious problem with human self-understanding which the late Erich Fromm called "the death of man." In his book *The Sane Society*, he wrote:

> The nineteenth century problem was that *God is dead*; in the twentieth century the problem is that *man is dead*. In the nineteenth century inhumanity meant cruelty; in the twentieth century it means schizoid self-alienation. The danger of the past was that men became slaves, the danger of the future is that men become robots. But given man's nature, robots cannot live and remain sane, they become "Golems," they will destroy their world and themselves because they cannot stand any longer the boredom of a meaningless life.[3]

B. F. Skinner's insistence that freedom and dignity are dangerous and anti-scientific illusions is part of this development—robots are indeed without freedom and dignity and as any thoughtful observer will note, a threat to themselves and the world.

The question now arises: In this situation what can be done? What in fact does the Bible teach about human beings and their relationship to God?

As Ludwig Köhler has pointed out in his *Old Testament Theology*, neither the individual nor humankind as a concept are Old Testament words. The Hebrew word *Adam* means the human race and becomes only slowly and later a concept which might describe an individual. Actually *Adam* as an individual male occurs only rarely. This explains the seeming confusion in Gen 1:26: "Let us make man in our image, after our likeness; and let them have dominion," etc. The theological significance of this fact is threefold:[4]

(a) The Old Testament does not operate with an abstract concept of humanity. It always deals with a concrete human being in a specific or, if you will, existential relationship with God, the neighbor, and the world.

(b) The Old Testament knows the human person only in relationship to other human beings. In fact, this relationship to other human beings is part of one's humanity. "*Ein Mensch ist kein Mensch*" ["One human is no human"]. One is human only in encounter and dialogue with others.

(c) The Old Testament does not know the "individualist." The human person always stands before God in relationship to other human beings. The individual, the being separated from the community, is the odd, the peculiar situation. It is cause for complaint when God so isolates the prophet. "I did not sit in the company of the merry-makers, nor did I rejoice; I sat alone because thy hand was upon me, for thou hadst filled me with indignation" (Jer 14:17).

---

[3]Erich Fromm, *The Sane Society* (New York: Rinehart, 1955)360.
[4]Ludwig Köhler, *Old Testament Theology* (Philadelphia: Westminster, 1957) 129.

Or Job complains: "He has put my brethren far from me, and my acquaintances are wholly estranged from me. My kinsfolk and my close friends have failed me; the guests in my house have forgotten me; my maidservants count me as a stranger, I have become an alien in their eyes. I call to my servant, but he gives me no answer; I must beseech him with my mouth. I am repulsive to my wife, loathsome to the sons of my own mother. Even young children despise me; when I rise they talk against me. All my intimate friends abhor me, and those whom I love have turned against me" (Job 19:13-19). This is not the normal situation. Generally, even before God, the human being in the Old Testament is always member and organ of the community of human beings. Any separation from the community is seen as a profound problem.

However, of theologically crucial importance is the claim of Old Testament scholars that the Old Testament submits two entirely different reports concerning the origin of humankind, namely Gen 1:26-31 and 2:4-7, 18-22. If we try to understand what the fact of the two reports in their difference means to our understanding of humanity—influenced so profoundly by this biblical tradition—we must add that, while the earlier report speaks of a stay in paradise, a fall, and an expulsion from paradise, the later report ignores all this. Here life is opportunity, not punishment. The relationship to God is seen as unbroken.

What does all this mean for our understanding of the human situation? People are created in the image of God and at the same time formed of dust from the ground. The earth has been given to them so that they might subdue it. Yet the earth is cursed because of Adam; in toil shall he eat of it all the days of his life. "Thorns and thistles it shall bring forth to you....In the sweat of your face you shall eat bread till you return to the ground from which you were taken: you are dust and to dust you shall return" [Gen 3:18-19]. The sexes are equal, mutually dependent upon each other, created to have dominion over all the things of the earth *together*. Yet woman is subordinated to man and man is led astray by woman. Be fruitful and multiply is the will of God for humankind, yet in living according to this will, there is pain and toil.

In the Lutheran tradition one way of handling this seemingly contradictory picture of the human being in the Old Testament is to use one view of the human being as a description of humanity before the fall, the other of humanity after the fall. In other words, to conceive of the "J" story as relevant to the human situation today, the "P" story as relevant only to the *status integritatis*, the state of original purity, the stay in paradise. This is in fact the way in which the Old Testament has generally been interpreted by the Christian tradition. The human being has been seen as passing through two succeeding stages, the state of integrity and the state of corruption. "The state of integrity is the original condition of man created after the image of God, in goodness and rectitude" (Quenstedt II/2).[5]

Human beings in the original condition possessed, according to the orthodox

---

5John Andrew Quenstedt, *Theologia Didactico-Polemica* (1685); quoted in H. Schmid, *Doctrinal Theology of the Evangelical Lutheran Church* (1875; reprint, Minneapolis: Augsburg, 1961)217.

Lutheran dogmaticians (cf. Schmid, 218): (1) wisdom and the power to understand perfectly, according to the measure of their necessities, things divine, human and natural; (2) holiness and freedom of the will according to which humans loved God and that which is good, and possessed the power to live in all respects in conformity with the will of God; (3) purity of the natural affections, and the perfect harmony of all their powers and impulses.

This then is the human being before the fall. It is humanity as it no longer exists. In other words, the description here offered is not relevant to *our* situation. It says nothing about us, but describes only a possible ancestor of ours. To use the creation narrative as P submits it, in this manner, seems to reduce this part of scripture to mere ancient history, or even prehistorical history. And the use of the word "history" would certainly be considered debatable. The narrative does not speak to our situation, but only to the situation of Adam and Eve. Actually, Gen 1:26-31 does not affect us. It is not our concern. It is a story about a real or mythical ancestor, but even if taken as describing a real ancestor, it is certainly no more interesting than what happened to one's great-great-grandfather—may he have been ever so real, as he certainly was.

Our actual human situation, my situation and your situation, is not described in Gen 1:26-31, but rather in Genesis 3ff. Here we have the Old Testament anthropology as far as the "real" human beings are concerned. And this "real" man and woman are only known in what the ancient dogmaticians call the state of corruption: "The state of corruption is that condition into which man voluntarily precipitated himself by his own departure from the chief good, thus becoming both wicked and miserable" (Quenstedt II/48; Schmid, 231).

Everything that is said about humanity is said in view of this corruption. Human beings now completely lack spiritual light so that they cannot know God. They are prone to false judgements, impotent in the knowledge of God and the government of life. The will is inclined to evil acts.

If we understand the Old Testament message with its two descriptions of the human situation as descriptions of two periods of time—the time before the fall and the time after the fall—then only the J report is relevant to us. For we are the people who live in the time after the fall. Then the other report is not really our business at all, it is either ancient mythology or ancient history, but in neither case does it speak to us. This exactly is the danger of the Old Testament understanding of Lutheran orthodoxy (and fundamentalism). It is a particular danger in our time because it tends to give support to all those who depreciate the freedom and dignity of human persons and supports their cynicism.

Another possible solution would ignore the J report on the ground that it is sheer mythology, that its view of the human being reflects a low state in the development of Hebrew religion which makes it irrelevant to us. We can therefore adopt the P narrative as the more adequate Old Testament anthropology. The human being is God's creature, created in his image, profoundly and permanently dependent upon the Creator. This dependence is not affected by any fundamental corruption. To maintain the relationship to God expressed in the concept of the image of God is with God's help a human possibility. It is the task of humanity to live on earth, for which they were created, not to live as "expellees" from paradise; to accept life on earth as a divine opportunity for service and not as punishment for an offense of mythical ancestors. Work is not cursed but there is the opportunity to obey God and subdue the earth and to exercise the dominion God has granted to people. Humanity's task is to create and maintain culture and to accept this responsibility gladly. "And God saw everything that he had made, and behold it was very good" (Gen 1:31).

This interpretation of Old Testament anthropology allows for ever greater progress. It is life-asserting and optimistic. But the question arises, does it give an accurate picture of human beings as we find them described in the Old Testament? Or does this anthropology, since it discards half of the Old Testament witness, describe the human situation at all? It may be cheerful and optimistic, but is it true? This is the danger of the Old Testament understanding of protestant modernism, and a certain kind of Roman Catholic triumphalism. Because of its obvious inability to account for the situation in which we actually find ourselves in the 1980s, it tends by its extreme and moralistic optimism about the human situation to undermine all confidence in its credibility and thus in the possibilities of humanity. Indirectly it supports again the attack against freedom and dignity.

It may now be possible to suggest that both anthropologies of the Old Testament belong together, that they are not merely historical or mythical, but the description of the human relationship to God, then, now, and until the end of time. Both descriptions are true. Only in the light of the biblical witness concerning a humanity created in the image of God can we take seriously the biblical witness concerning a humanity which is corrupt. Both descriptions, P and J, report a relationship to God, and not a quality of the human being. The *imago dei* is not a static quality of the human person, but rather a dynamic relationship to God. Similarly, the human being expelled from God's presence, "sent forth from the Garden of Eden," does not possess a certain quality, but is rather in a certain relationship to God. And these two relationships belong together. Without the reality of the image the corruption is mere fate; without the reality of the expulsion of the image it is mere illusion.

If we try to understand the biblical view of humanity in this fashion, a number of other relationships will take on a different form—for example, the problem of the relationship of the sexes. Without the reality of the equality (Gen 1:27), the actual relationship of coordination between man and woman (Gen 2:18) is merely fate (biology, sociology). Without the coordination of man and woman the equality is merely illusion. Or, without the dominion over the earth (Gen 1:28), the toil of humankind (3:17ff.) is merely fate (humans are a part of nature). Without the toil of humankind, the dominion is merely illusion (the soul as unrelated to nature) (see the *animal laborans* vs. *homo faber*, in Hannah Arendt, *The Human Condition*). The creation narratives of P and J belong together, but perhaps not as an historical sequel, where the one is suppressed in favor of the other, be it that the assertion of the image of God be suppressed in order to assert a static condition of human corruption and bondage, as a quality of the human being; be it that the expulsion from God's presence be suppressed in order to assert an equally static condition of human integrity and freedom as a quality in humanity. The creation narratives belong together in order to show that the Bible knows human beings in their relationship to God. This relationship is as profound as it is ambiguous, and is falsified if the ambiguity which according to the Bible is inherent in it is removed in favour of a "pessimistic" or "optimistic" anthropology. Because the Lutheran tradition rejects both a naive optimism that would ignore the human potential for evil and a cynical pessimism that would ignore the human potential for good, it should be able to defend human freedom and dignity realistically.

Perhaps no one has stated the resulting potential for freedom and dignity more clearly than Martin Luther in his book *The Freedom of a Christian* (*De Libertate Christiana*, 1520). He wrote: "A Christian is a perfectly free lord of all, subject to none. A Christian is a perfectly dutiful servant of all, subject to all."[6]

Both these insights must be proclaimed simultaneously in defence of freedom and dignity. They are important for our time as well. It is apparent that what is proclaimed today is the dutiful servant who is never a free lord on the one hand, and the free lord who is never a dutiful servant on the other.

What behaviorists describe is the dutiful servant determined by an environment which is "responsible both for the evolution of the species and for the repertoire acquired by each member" (Skinner,214). While he applauds this development, Aldous Huxley in *Brave New World*, George Orwell, Kurt Vonnegut, and many others have described it with a mixture of horror and fascination. In the minds of many, this is the inescapable destiny of the human race, and Skinner suggests we might as well like it since we cannot leave it.

However, there are others who see human beings, or at least some elite, as lords of everything and subject to nothing. With William Ernest Henley, they say, "It matters not how strait the gate, how charged with punishments the scroll; I am the master of my fate. I am the captain of my soul!" This is the conviction of a journalist and philosopher of Jewish origin, Ayn Rand, and her cult of devoted followers, among whom we find today many men and women of influence in the circles of government. It is also the conviction of all those who believe that they have no responsibility for anybody or anything, the devotees of the joyless hedonism and narcissism that threatens to engulf us.

Its adherents trample human dignity underfoot and are content to see the enslavement of the poor serve the self-indulgence of the rich. Their advice to the hungry is "eat less." In the United States this is true of the so-called libertarians who attack the graduated income tax, as well as of the men and women who claim that the rich have a God-given right to the resources of the world and will assert it with military power if need be, but the world has no right to the resources which God has given them. Only by rejecting this stance and being dutiful servants to our neighbor can we work towards the dignity of all human beings.

[6]*LW* 31:344.

But perhaps some of us might say with Skinner: It does not matter what we believe about human beings since "no theory changes what it is a theory about; man remains what he has always been" (p. 206). I would counter with Ernst Bloch, that the clue to the future of the human race may be its hopes today. In his monumental study *The Principle of Hope*, Bloch has asserted that Freud was wrong. In his *Interpretation of Dreams*, Freud had claimed that the clue to a person is what one dreams at night about one's past. Bloch asserts that the clue is rather what we dream during the day about our future.

We are determined by our hope. But we are free to hope that there will be a time when we will use our freedom to serve God by serving human beings and, as perfectly free lords subject to nobody, become perfectly dutiful servants of everybody who needs our help, and thus rejecting slavery and alienation, vindicate human freedom and human dignity.

Word & World
Supplement Series 2
1994

Make Church Politics Ethical!

IN ALL THE DISCUSSION ABOUT THE CHURCH'S DUTY IN RELATION TO POLITICS, ONE important aspect of the problem has been entirely neglected; namely, her own internal politics—"church politics," as it is depreciatively referred to whenever church people meet. Yet the church, being a social structure, can carry on and direct its business only by way of politics. The great studies by social scientists of the control of political power are thoroughly relevant to the church as an institution.

Because this major technical problem has never been openly faced, political patterns in the church do not develop according to any discernible plan, but seem to grow like weeds. Apparently most Christians hope that "church politics," like the communist state, will wither away if only it is steadfastly ignored. Even church people who are highly realistic about problems of world and national politics appear to believe that frank discussion of problems having to do with ecclesiastical politics is somehow indecent.

This attitude is particularly dangerous in view of the tremendous political problems of a purely technical nature which have to be overcome to make a complex body such as the National Council of Churches work effectively. Similarly, the attempts to unite various denominations into larger and more meaningful groupings would seem far more unambiguously right if the technical political problems of large-scale organizations were faced openly rather than only in the ecclesiastical counterpart of the smoke-filled room.

AN UNDEMOCRATIC SITUATION

From some reports on the recent meeting of the N.C.C. in Denver it seems fair to say that it did not represent the democratic process at its best. A distinguished

This essay, which appeared first in The Christian Century *70/11 (March 18, 1953) 317-318, takes a rather pragmatic approach to the analysis of how the church makes decisions. Dr. Forell recommends that the church squarely admit its political and social dynamics so that it can apply its own ethical standards in a self-conscious and responsible manner.*

group of Christian people listened to distinguished Christian leaders who made distinguished speeches. If the reports are correct, there was little of the frank facing of facts that might lead eventually to greater mutual understanding and effective cooperation.

In a sense the problem of Denver is the problem of all the denominations that have to do their work with the help of delegates representing clergy and parishioners and are not small enough to have all pastors and interested laity attend their conventions. "Representation" is indeed one of the crucial problems in church politics. Who are the people that represent the church when it assembles in convention? They are outstanding clergy and outstanding laypeople. How do we know they are outstanding? Why, they are the ministers of the largest congregations and the secretaries of the church boards and agencies, and those layfolks who are interested enough to attend and can afford to take time off from their work to do so. It is not unfair to say that the church in convention assembled is in the main represented by the pastors of the biggest congregations and by the representatives of successful businesses.

ONE-SIDED REPRESENTATION

This situation is aggravated when it comes to the boards and agencies of the denominations. To be elected to any of these, it is almost essential that one have a top-level white-collar job. For example, in one of our larger Protestant denominations the people named for the various boards by the nominating committee were 35 businesspeople, 13 educators, 9 publishers and editors, 8 lawyers, 5 government officials, and 3 scientists. Nobody not nominated by the nominating committee was elected. However, in this particular church the overwhelming majority of the members are farmers, craftsfolk or skilled workers. No member of any of these groups was so much as placed in nomination.

This incident typifies one of the major political weaknesses of the church—inadequate and one-sided representation. The results of such unbalanced representation are dangerous. The church as a political structure becomes insensitive to the problems of the vast majority of its constituency. This insensitivity contributes to organizational schizophrenia, the people at the top acting without any real awareness of the internal problems that beset the people they are chosen to represent. And so the well known sociological stratification of American protestantism is further strengthened.

POWER IS A FACT

Another major political problem is the unwillingness of the church as a social structure to face the fact of power and the balance of power. Through sheer lack of political imagination, protestantism concentrates an immense amount of power in the hands of executive secretaries who are accountable to boards which in turn are practically self-perpetuating and absolutely sovereign. Executive, legislative and political functions are exercised by the same board and often by the same board secretary. But unchecked power corrupts not only people in the "world"; it also corrupts people in the church. And it is almost demonic naiveté to assume that Christian people in executive positions in the church are not subject to corruption by power.

This danger is best illustrated when the clear interest of the church as a whole conflicts with the vested interest of the agency or institution from which the executive derives power. The interest of the agency will invariably be safe-guarded—not because the executives are unusually wicked but because they are human and will rationalize their desires to maintain power. However, since they are working for the church, any criticism of their attitudes will be understood as a criticism of Christ and his church, and the critics will soon learn that such open criticism is not "loyal." So either they will never criticize again or they will be made to feel the despotic power of the executive within the seemingly democratic pattern of protestant church life.

In such a framework, all criticism tends to become petty and personal. Since there is no machinery for debating the issues openly, discussion becomes discussion of personalities. And so a strange spectacle emerges: while in some of our great secular political bodies people may oppose each other violently on basic issues yet remain personally friends, in the church criticism tends to become personal, and controversies revolve largely around personalities rather than around issues.

No Room for Prophets?

This situation promotes a type of leadership which is somewhat vague on issues (since they are not important anyway) but strong on building the personal relationships and personal power basic for success within the political structure of the church. Of necessity the leadership will pass to people who are kind and friendly, who are fairly good orators and do not disagree violently with other people who have power. For prophets in the tradition of Isaiah and Amos or even Luther and Wesley, there can be no room in such a structure. We do not want religious issues; we want administrative compromises. To attain this objective we put our trust in those who are most able to bring it about—people whose personalities are above reproach, who do not feel too strongly on any issue (which would give rise to unnecessary conflict), and who are willing to administer for the sheer joy of administering.

The immediate practical consequences are revealed in the statistics of every major protestant denomination. Since administration is the chief interest of the people who are actually in power, the number of administrators and assistant administrators increases steadily, quite out of proportion to the number of people that have to be administered.

All these are technical political problems which have grown out of and become aggravated by the political naiveté of protestantism. It might be well to look at some of the possibilities for improvement.

One obvious need is some sort of two-party system through which constructive criticism can be carried on openly within the church and not merely between denominations. The Roman Church, much maligned because of its totalitarianism, nevertheless allows relative independence to the various monastic orders so that through them the necessary self-criticism can be carried on. In some ways the Roman Church is actually less monolithic than the administrative machinery of some protestant denominations which allows for no organized centers of criticism and opposition. If this situation is to be changed, the church papers, which are often merely "house-organs" extolling virtue and attacking sin, must become avenues for vital debate of those central issues on which the church is in disagreement. If that cannot be done with one all-embracing magazine, the idol of uniformity and bigness should be openly attacked and publications should be encouraged which would forcefully express the differing points of view of the contending parties, while remaining loyal to the church which includes all parties.

VIEWS COUNT, NOT SOCIAL PRESTIGE

The problem of representation should be studied. Perhaps a system of rotating representation, such as is used by some denominations even now, would make the delegates more representative. Perhaps the prospective delegates from the various local churches should take sides on the issues and be elected on the basis of their views rather than their names and social prestige. There can be no doubt that a more effective method of choosing representatives can be found once the problem is honestly faced. But as long as it is ignored, the councils of the church will rarely debate issues; they will listen to speeches and rubber-stamp the decisions of the various executive committees.

In national politics we have discovered that democracy operates best with a two-party system. Here criticism is made responsible by occasionally giving the critic power to put plans into action and placing the executive into the position of the critic. Two parties, we have found, are not necessarily bodies holding diametrically opposed views but rather a technical means of controlling power in the framework of a democratic system.

In view of the great challenge of ever greater federation of churches, denominations and other bodies might do well to study the technical problems of politics as they apply to the church, before the pattern of government by executive committee and board secretary is transferred from the denominations, where it has been annoying, to the larger federations, where it would be tyrannical and fatal. As a political structure the church is in politics to stay, whether we like it or not.

Word & World
Supplement Series 2
1994

How to Speak about God in a Pluralistic World

PERHAPS THE MOST DRAMATIC DIFFERENCE BETWEEN, ON THE ONE HAND, THE writers of the Hebrew Bible and the Lutheran pastor-theologians who wrote the confessions and later constructed the baroque edifice of Lutheran orthodoxy, and on the other, modern Jews and Lutherans and their twentieth-century contemporaries, is the different way in which they and we speak about God. It is obvious to the psalmist that "the heavens declare the glory of God; and the firmament showeth his handiwork" (Ps 19:1). And to question God's existence is a demonstration of self-evident, empty-headed foolishness: "Fools say in their hearts, 'There is no God'" (Ps 14:1; cf. Ps 53:1), and "Foolish people have blasphemed thy name" (Ps 74:18). Therefore: "Arise, O God, plead thine own cause: remember how the impious scoff at you all day long" (Ps 74:22).

The orthodox Lutherans could speak of "innate" and "acquired" knowledge of God, and John Quenstedt claimed that

> the natural knowledge of God is that by which man, without any special revelation, may know of himself, though very imperfectly, by the light of Nature and from the Book of Nature, that there is some supreme Divinity, and that He, by His own wisdom and power, controls this whole universe, and that He has brought all things into being.[1]

---

[1]John Quenstedt, *Theologia Didactico-Polemica* (1685) 1:251, quoted in Heinrich Schmid, *Doctrinal Theology of the Evangelical Lutheran Church*, 3rd rev. ed. (1899; reprint, Minneapolis: Augsburg, 1961) 105.

This essay was first delivered at one of a series of colloquia, sponsored jointly by the Interreligious Affairs Department of the American Jewish Committee and the Division of Theological Studies of the Lutheran Council in the U.S.A., and published in Speaking of God Today, *ed. Paul Opsahl and Marc Tannenbaum (Philadelphia: Fortress, 1974) 99-107. These meetings, held between 1969 and 1973, were intended to further Jewish-Lutheran dialogue. Here Dr. Forell uses a multi-dimensional definition of religion, with special reference to Judaism and Christianity, in order to indicate how different religions can communicate with one another in a world where no single religion predominates.*

John Gerhard says, "Innate knowledge is that common conception concerning God engraved and impressed upon the mind of every man by Nature."[2]

It is part of our common experience as twentieth-century people that the denial of the existence of God does not demonstrate either the foolishness or the inhumanity of a person. Indeed some very intelligent and humane contemporaries, some of them self-consciously Jewish, others self-consciously Christian, have felt it incumbent upon them to claim, "There is no God," or even more dramatically, "God is dead!"

It is this obvious change in our situation which raises the question, "How can we speak about God in our pluralistic world?" Perhaps Peter Berger's common-sense definition of pluralism offers a helpful beginning for our discussion. He describes the contemporary situation with the following words:

> Subjectively, the man in the street tends to be uncertain about religious matters. Objectively, the man in the street is confronted with a wide variety of religious and other reality-defining agencies that compete for his allegiance or at least attention, and none of which is in a position to coerce him into allegiance. In other words, the phenomenon called 'pluralism' is a social-structural correlate of the secularization of consciousness.[3]

Both Jews and Christians have reacted negatively to the reality of pluralism in their past history. The preferred solution for both traditions was a land in which there would be no adherents of false gods to lead the followers of the true God astray. About the Hivites, the Canaanites, and the Hittites, we read: "You shall make no covenant with them and their gods. They shall not stay in your land for fear they make you sin against me, for then you would worship their gods, and in this way you would be ensnared" (Exod 23:32, 33). The religion of the true God did not tolerate competing "reality-defining agencies." Similarly, Luther wrote in the preface to his most popular and widely read and studied work, *The Small Catechism* of 1529, to "all faithful and godly pastors and preachers":

> If any refuse to receive your instructions, tell them that they deny Christ and are no Christians....Parents and employers should refuse to furnish them with food and drink and notify them that the prince is disposed to banish such rude people from his land.[4]

And Luther continued, "Although we cannot and should not compel anyone to believe, we should nevertheless insist that the people learn to know how to distinguish right and wrong according to the standards of those among whom they live and make their living."[5] As late as the sixteenth century it seemed obvious to almost everybody that the moral and religious standards of a community were both knowable and unequivocal—*almost* everybody, for by then the Jewish experience was significantly different. The days of the religiously homogeneous Jewish king-

---

[2]John Gerhard, *Loci Theologici* (1621) 1:93, quoted in Schmid, *Doctrinal Theology*, 105.

[3]Peter L. Berger, *The Sacred Canopy* (New York: Doubleday, 1967) 127.

[4]Martin Luther, *The Small Catechism,* in *BC,* 339.

[5]Ibid.

dom were long gone, if they ever existed anywhere but in the pious imagination, and Jews had to pioneer the arduous experience which characterizes the modern person, namely, to be a cognitive minority, to be people with a discrete perspective among an alien majority. What set the Jews apart in Europe since the beginning of the Constantinian era is now the common experience of all men and women of faith. They are all cognitive minorities who look at the world from a perspective which is not shared by the majority. It would be my claim that we must learn from our Jewish neighbors how to maintain our idiosyncratic perspective in a pluralistic world. No longer supported by *cuius regio eius religio* ("whoever rules the land, determines the religion") or even a *consensus gentium* ("agreement of nations"), we must learn to maintain our faith in a world whose dominant plausibility structures are not supportive of our faith, but are either neutral or inimical.

In order to speak of God in this kind of world, the complexity of the religious reality must be kept in mind.

(1) There is more to being a Christian than intellectual assent to certain Christian propositions. Jews always knew that there is more to being a Jew than making a Jewish confession of faith. In a pluralistic world all must learn as much. Christians in general, and American Lutherans in particular, have frequently over-emphasized the cognitive aspect of faith, as if the symbols we use to speak about God were the reality itself. Some of the controversies among Christians about the nature of God seem to assume the accessibility of information about him that is simply not available to mortals. Not satisfied to see through a mirror dimly, we claim to see face to face. Eastern and western Christians, for example, were divided by the *filioque* phrase in the Nicene Creed, claiming to know definitively that the Spirit proceeds from the Father or from the Father and the Son, as the case might be. The cognitive aspect of our religion is important and inescapable. One cannot be a Christian without the assent to certain propositions, as for example, "God was in Christ, reconciling the world to himself" (2 Cor 5:19). Whether there are such minimal propositions for all people who accept themselves as Jews, I cannot judge. But Christianity is far more than such assent, and in the kind of world in which we live, we must be careful not to speak about God in such a manner that he merely becomes a proposition to which we assent.

(2) But there is also more to being a Christian than the adoption of and adherence to a moral code. Religion has indeed a moral dimension. It implies a way of life, a style of life. Christianity has frequently been understood by those on the inside as well as those on the outside as a life lived according to certain moral precepts. They may be as detailed and specific as those governing the everyday existence of an Amish farmer. They may be as vague as the exhortation of the follower of "situation ethics" to do the most loving thing.[6] In either case those who see religious reality in general and the Christian faith in particular as obedience to one, few, or many commandments, also fail to see the complexity of the Christian faith. The reality of the threat of legalism will not be denied by anyone who has

---

[6][Dr. Forell here refers to Joseph Fletcher's *Situation Ethics* (Philadelphia: Westminster, 1966). Ed.]

studied protestant or Roman Catholic moral theology and is familiar with the example from one text, published in America in the last generation, which claims that masturbation is a greater sin than rape—since the former is basically counter to nature, while the latter is not. But it is really only a quantitative and not a qualitative difference between this monstrous type of legalism and the agapeic calculus advocated by the new morality, which allegedly enables us to determine with complete certainty in respect to every action whether it is "good" or "evil."

Again, our Jewish brothers and sisters are familiar with the problem of pan-halachism, "which regards *halacha* [law and tradition] as the only source of Jewish thinking and living."[7] As the late Professor Heschel writes:

> In justification of their view, exponents of religious behaviorism cite the passage in which the Rabbis paraphrased the words of Jeremiah (16:11), "They have forsaken Me and have not kept My Torah," in the following way: "Would that they had forsaken Me and kept My Torah."[8]

And Heschel continues,

> However, to regard this passage as a declaration of the primary if not exclusive importance of studying Torah over concern for God is to pervert the meaning of the passage. Such perversion is made possible by overlooking the second part of the passage, which reads as follows: "Since by occupying themselves with the Torah, the light which she contains would have led them back to Me."[9]

This warning against pan-halachism, whatever its status in the Jewish community, is of the greatest importance for Christians. Those who today say "There is no God, but Jesus is his Son," who would replace orthodoxy with their evolutional or revolutionary orthopraxis, do not help us to speak meaningfully to a pluralistic world. Indeed, what we do is important. As Luther put it succinctly,

> God threatens to punish all who transgress these commandments. We should therefore fear his wrath and not disobey these commandments. On the other hand, he promises grace and every blessing to all who keep them. We should therefore love him, trust in him, and cheerfully do what he has commanded.[10]

But this does not mean that we can speak of God today as the giver of eternal laws, as the great computer in the sky, if we lean in the direction of fundamentalism, or as the inexorable process of history through which justice works itself out with the help of dialectical materialism, as those who lean in the direction of neoliberalism, or the so-called radical theology would have it. The God of the Bible is a God in search of humankind, who desires that we accept our acceptance though we know ourselves to be unacceptable (Tillich).

(3) But there is also more to being a Christian than an emotional experience or the feeling that, "I am okay and you are okay." There can be no doubt that an overwhelming experience is at the heart of the Christian speech about God. If there

[7]Abraham Heschel, *God in Search of Man* (New York: Farrar, Strauss, & Cudahy, 1955) 328.
[8]Ibid., 329.
[9]Ibid., 329-330.
[10]Luther, *The Small Catechism*, in BC, 344.

is no experience there is no power. It is the experience of the disciples which makes them eloquent; it is the experience of Paul which compels him to speak. Again Luther says, "I believe that by my own reason or strength I cannot believe in Jesus Christ, my Lord, or come to him. But the Holy Spirit has called me through the Gospel."[11]

It is this awareness of a divine call, of an encounter or at least a "feeling of absolute dependence" (Schleiermacher) which enables the Christian to say "I believe," and not only "The church believes." But the Jewish experience seems not to be radically different. The Hebrew Bible is full of experiences of encounter with God which are decisive and determinative for those who are exposed to them. They have become models for Jews and Christians. And this prophetic experience is seen as transcending all knowledge, all philosophy, by Moses Maimonides:

> Prophecy is a different source and category of knowledge. Proof and examination are inapplicable to it. If prophecy is genuine then it cannot and need not depend on the validation of reason. The only test ever asked of a prophet in the Scriptures is concerning the genuineness of his claim to have prophecy, but no one ever asked for proofs or reasons or validations above prophecy itself.[12]

But for Christians and Jews experience is qualified. Not every powerful emotional experience is the encounter with the God of the Bible. Sincerity of emotion is not enough. We, who live in an age when unspeakable crimes are being committed by utterly sincere fanatics and where almost every day brings news from all over the world of deeds of vicious violence in the name of patriotic or religious emotions, or a horrible combination of the two, must be particularly insistent upon the content and result of religious experience. When Luther spoke about the work of the Holy Spirit in *The Large Catechism*, he said: "To this article, as I have said, I cannot give a better title than 'Sanctification.' In it is expressed and portrayed the Holy Spirit and his office, which is that he makes us holy."[13] Thus the experience is a sanctifying experience, or, again in Luther's words,

> We come to love and delight in all the commandments of God because we see that God gives himself completely to us, with all his gifts and his power, to help us keep the Ten Commandments: the Father gives us all creation, Christ all his works, the Holy Spirit all his gifts.[14]

Indeed there is such a thing as Christian experience, but it is sharply focused. It is not morally neutral, it helps us to live lives of love, that is, to obey the commandments.

It would appear to me that Rabbi Heschel speaks of a similarly qualified experience when he writes:

> What gave the prophets the certainty that they witnessed a divine event and not a figment of their own imagination? The mark of authority of the divine character

[11]Ibid., 345.

[12]Maimonides in a letter to Rabbi Hisdai, quoted in Heschel, *God in Search of Man*, 233.

[13]Martin Luther, *The Large Catechism*, in *BC*, 415.

[14]Ibid., 420.

of revelation was not in outward signs, visible or sonorous; revelation did not hinge upon a particular sense-perception, upon hearing a voice or seeing a light. A thunder out of a blue sky, a voice coming from nowhere, an effect without a visible cause, would not have been enough to identify a perception as a divine communication....This, it seems, was the mark of authenticity: the fact that prophetic revelation was not merely an act of experience but an act of *being experienced*, of being exposed to, called upon, overwhelmed and taken over by Him who seeks out those whom He sends to mankind. It is not God who is an experience of man; it is man who is an experience of God.[15]

Certainly experience is central to the speech about God in a pluralistic world. If we speak without reference to experience we will seem incredible to an experience-oriented age. But not every experience will do. False prophets are more common than prophets of the living God and religious experience can now be obtained in the drug store or in an encounter group. If we speak about God in terms of experience in our pluralistic world we must say that valid experience is not absolute but qualified by righteousness and holiness.

(4) And finally, there is more to being a Christian than the sense of belonging to the Christian community. In our pluralistic world the importance of religion as an aid to personal and sociological identification has assumed ever greater importance. In an age in which the reality of pluralism offers so many possibilities, the problem of identity has assumed increasing significance, especially for the young, who see these options more clearly and thus feel more threatened by what the existentialist would call a "dreadful freedom." Obviously it did not involve any great effort for Lutheran Swedes at the end of the nineteenth century to accept themselves as Lutherans. There was actually little else they could do. For their descendants living in America at the end of the twentieth century to do the same is something vastly different, because they now have a genuine choice. If they accepts themselves as Lutheran Christians, they identify themselves with a certain historical and cultural tradition, and this identification rather than any belief in certain theological propositions, a particular moral outlook, or specific emotional experiences may be the reason for their decision. Because of the human need for roots, the importance of the remembrance of things past in order to establish one's identity, the communal aspect of the Christian faith has assumed new significance. A person suffers from amnesia if he does not know who he is, and this happens when he cannot remember anything about his past. And such amnesia is ever more common. People do not know who they are because they do not know where they came from, because they have forgotten their pasts.

It is the increasing awareness of the resulting isolation and estrangement which makes speech about the God who calls people into a community meaningful to rootless and isolated human beings in a pluralistic world. Speaking about God to this world means to speak about him who calls the "solitary into families." Luther said:

I believe that there is on earth a little holy flock or community of pure saints

---

[15]Heschel, *God in Search of Man*, 229-30.

under one head, Christ. It is called together by the Holy Spirit in one faith, mind, and understanding. It possesses a variety of gifts, yet is united in love without sect or schism. Of this community I also am a part and member, a participant and a copartner in all the blessings it possesses.[16]

It is clear that, for Luther, belonging to this community is a great source of strength and that he sees the gifts of God coming to him and to all Christians as members in this community. To be a Christian means to belong to a community. Just as in the New Testament the term "saint" (*hagios*) does not occur in the singular but always in the plural, so it is impossible to be a Christian in splendid isolation. This notion, which may strike an individualistic and autistic age as primitive and perverse, should not seem surprising to Jews who have always said that "Jewish faith consists of attachment to God, attachment to Torah, and attachment to Israel."[17] Indeed the experience of Jews as a minority in an alien world has anticipated the pluralistic development where all religions experience themselves as minorities in a world in which the majority sees everything differently. Here we may learn both the opportunity and the danger of this situation.

Indeed, we are called to community but the community which God's call establishes is a community for the world. The church exists not for itself but for the service of the world. We belong to the church only if we lose ourselves in service to humankind. Again the similarities to the Jewish self-understanding are obvious.

> The future of all men depends upon their realizing that the sense of holiness is as vital as health. By following the Jewish way of life we maintain that sense and preserve the light for mankind's future visions. It is our destiny to live for what is more than ourselves.[18]

It isn't just any community Jews and Christians speak about but a community of service to the world. In order to speak about God in a pluralistic world in the light of the communal dimension of the Bible, it is not enough to speak about sociological and personal identity and identification. Any community, from the Boy Scouts to the Ku Klux Klan and from the Rotary Club to the John Birch Society, may supply some such meaning. Christians must be a disciplined community. When they speak about God they must speak about the God who wants a people to serve him. Community is qualified by holiness.

We spoke of the complexity of the religious reality. If we are to speak of God in a pluralistic world all aspects of the religious reality must be taken seriously— the cognitive dimension, the moral dimension, the emotional dimension, and the communal dimension. But none of them are enough in themselves. We have often been misunderstood because we have isolated one of these dimensions and emphasized it out of all proportion and made it dominate our speech. But they all belong together. When any of them is missing, our speech about God is falsified

---

[16]Luther, *The Large Catechism*, in *BC*, 417.
[17]Heschel, *God in Search of Man*, 425.
[18]Ibid., 424.

and thus misleading. In a pluralistic world all kinds of people will be attracted and repelled by various aspects of our speech. This is as it should be. Some who may be repelled by theology might find community helpful, some who abhor emotion may cherish the moral dimension. In the pluralistic world in which it is our destiny to live, we will do best to mention all the dimensions of God's reality as we see it. But because he is the God of reason as well as righteousness, of feeling as well as community, we will hope that these dimensions are not seen as mutually exclusive and thus falsified. We will also remember that even the most eloquent human speech about God remains *human* speech, subject to all the frailties to which humans are heir. It is only when God himself uses our speech for his purposes that he will speak so that people will be able to hear even in a pluralistic world. That God be heard in spite of and through our human speech is our hope and prayer.

Word & World
Supplement Series 2
1994

Reason, Relevance and a Radical Gospel: Hartford and the Future of Protestant Thought

S HORTLY AFTER THE HARTFORD APPEAL FOR THEOLOGICAL AFFIRMATION RECEIVED wide publicity, a former student and friend of mine who serves as pastor of a congregation in a small town in Iowa was returning with the local funeral director from a funeral he had conducted. It should be remembered that a mortician in a small town has the opportunity to listen regularly and frequently to sermons by clergy of all religious persuasions. No one who is at all interested in the subject has a better chance to evaluate the theological atmosphere in a community.

In the course of the conversation my friend learned that the undertaker had been much impressed by the Hartford Appeal. He exclaimed that he was grateful that some theologians were finally making sense and expressing beliefs to which he could assent. His curiosity aroused, my friend pursued the subject further only to discover that the mortician was enthusiastic about all the themes which the signers of the Hartford Appeal had described as false and debilitating. At least this one reader—superficial, to be sure—of the Hartford Appeal agreed wholeheartedly with every one of these themes.

Traveling about the country discussing the Appeal with individuals and groups across the west and midwest, I became aware that the themes do in fact describe a good deal of the "religious consensus" among many people superfi-

In the early 1970s Forell helped to draft the "Hartford Appeal for Theological Affirmation." This document called for a theological renewal of the Christian church, based on the affirmation of classical doctrines. It was signed by twenty-three scholars. This essay, which explicates the Hartford Appeal, appeared in the collection of essays, Against the World, for the World, *ed. Peter Berger and Richard Neuhaus (New York: Seabury, 1976) 63-77.*

cially attached to the religious establishment, at least in its protestant manifestation. Indeed, the angry reaction the Appeal elicited, especially among some of the clergy associated with colleges and universities, indicated that a sensitive spot had been touched. Later, talking to friends in Europe, especially in West Germany where the Appeal had been widely disseminated, I learned that there, too, it was seen as a document which addressed a pervasive religious mood.

The question arises: What went wrong with protestant thought—which has its roots in the Bible, stresses Pauline theology, depends on the seminal insights of an Augustine, and finds its classical articulation in the writings of Luther and Calvin—that made it so susceptible to the religious cant summarized in these thirteen themes?

The following pages are an attempt to offer one answer to this question. It is hoped that it will further the discussion and encourage others to suggest both modifications and new and better answers. It is written from a particular point of view, represented in the Hartford group but by no means the only or even the dominant one.

Preoccupied with Unreason

The claim that "religious statements are totally independent of reasonable discourse" pervades the religious atmosphere. One might try to derive it from Luther's tendency to depreciate reason and refer to it occasionally as "the devil's whore." But as any reader of the sources will remember, Luther's concern was to liberate theology from its fatal enslavement to philosophy,[1] and his critical statements about reason deal with it when used as a means to reach certainty about God. Such statements could easily be balanced by other utterances extolling reason as an essential tool in all human efforts, including religious communication. It was the utter irrationality of the enthusiasts of his time, the people he called *Schwärmer*, who depended for their authority on direct inspiration, which drove Luther to sarcastic remarks about people like Thomas Münzer, of whom he said that he sounded "as if he had swallowed the Holy Spirit, feathers and all."

Luther himself tried to reason with his opponents. His style was forceful and often sarcastic. He tended toward hyperbole, but he was trying to persuade. Even his frequent use of paradoxical formulations was for him a persuasive device, from the assertion of a theology of the cross in his Heidelberg Disputations of 1518 to the insistence, in his later writings, on the human being as righteous and sinner at the same time.

As far as Calvin is concerned, his effort to use reasonable persuasion so dominates his *Institutes of the Christian Religion* as to be exemplary. Thus, while the religious polemic of the period was often vicious and ready to use the cheap *ad hominem* argument, it remained an effort at reasonable discourse. The opponents were clearly aware of the other person's intent; they disagreed violently, but they

---

[1]Wilhelm Link, *Das Ringen Luthers um die Freiheit der Theologie von der Philosophie* (Munich: Chr. Kaiser, 1940).

tended to understand each other nevertheless. In fact, they not infrequently borrowed each other's best arguments and modified them for their own use in the ongoing controversy. Deplorable as the tenor of the religious debate was, it revealed a common universe of discourse.

It would take us too far afield to trace the development of the preoccupation with unreason in protestant thought and to attempt to identify the period when the respect for reason was lost to protestantism. But it would seem that the increasing preemption of reason by the rising modern science, especially in the nineteenth century, forced the protestant defenders of religion, in whose environment its new world view was advancing, into a defensive position which rejected reason in favor of feeling. This resulted in a bifurcation of the theological enterprise. There have always been and there are now academic theologians of protestant background who use reason with great skill and devotion in order to articulate their idiosyncratic theological perspective. Their efforts, however, proceed independently of the protestant movement. Their books are only read by a small elite and have no discernible effect on the life of the protestant churches.

Indeed, the striking feature of the contemporary religious situation which the Hartford Appeal addresses is the apparent absence of reasonable discourse. Not only are most religious arguments totally incomprehensible to the outsider, who simply ignores them (they have no "apologetic" significance), they are almost equally nonsensical to the committed member of the Christian movement who attends church regularly. This is as true of the statements of the mod-theologians as of the so-called fundamentalists. It has produced the reaction among churchgoers of "turning off" the sermon, since it is no longer a form of understandable communication. Indeed, thousands of regular attendants at protestant church services are in the habit of ignoring what goes on in the pulpit for twenty or thirty minutes and engaging instead in their own religious or secular meditations, since it is simply impossible to follow many sermons as a form of rational discourse. Among some protestants it is the frequent recurrence of some "approved" words which establishes the acceptability of the sermon. These words may be moralistic or biblical clichés among the so-called fundamentalists, or sociological, psychological, or political clichés among the mod-theologians. But it is the occurrence of the "approved" words rather than their reasonable connection which validates the address.

Perhaps the so-called "gospel of Christian atheism" may serve as an example of what is commonly called the religious "left." There the "good news" is that the human story is "a tale told by an idiot, full of sound and fury, signifying nothing." "Christian" means the denial of Jesus as the Messiah and the assertion that he was the paradigm of the ultimate loser, and "atheism" means "pantheism."

But the absence of reasonable discourse is not less striking, though perhaps less surprising, on the religious "right." Here faith becomes credulity and the "faithful" compete with each other in an effort to interpret the Bible in such a way as to demand assent to the largest number of statements having the least degree of credibility. If one of them claims that it is part of the Christian gospel that Jonah was literally swallowed by the big fish, then the other will insist, "If the Bible reported that Jonah swallowed the big fish, I would most certainly believe that, too." "Anything you believe I believe better" becomes the contest, and the good work which saves human beings is not charity or humility but simply the sacrifice of the intellect.

It is the resulting excommunication of reason which is described in Theme 2 of the Hartford Appeal. The task which now confronts theology is to begin again to try to help the Christian community express its message in such a way that participants as well as nonparticipants in this movement can honestly say "yes" or "no" to the Christian message because they have at least some idea of what is being proclaimed.

It is not the theologian's task to devise formulae describing the Christian faith so inclusively that nobody could possibly deny them, and thus to convert the world "by definition." This is an unfair game which does violence to reason and honesty, and it is not understood as a compliment by those who, for their own good reasons, prefer not to be Christians yet suddenly find themselves included "by definition." One could escape the forced conversion "by inquisition" by dying at the stake; the forced conversion "by definition" is simply inescapable. Thus terms like "anonymous Christians" should be used sparingly, if at all.

Neither is it the task of the theologian to devise formulae describing the Christian faith which are so exclusive that anybody with a shred of intellectual integrity and historical information must reject them immediately, since they demand the abject surrender of one's God-given reason not to God but to the authors of these unhappy formulations.

In the task of defining the Christian message for our time, clergy as well as academic advocates for the Christian faith should avoid standing in awe of what is called "modern thought" as if it could supply not only tools for the understandable expression of the Christian message, which it can, but also the final criteria for judging the validity of this message, which it cannot. At the same time they should take seriously the wealth of the Christian tradition inherited from the past, without attempting to repristinate the allegedly perfect theological vision of one period or the other.

The eschatological orientation of the Christian movement should protect theologians from illusions concerning the superiority or finality of any period of *human* history, past, present, or future. This same orientation should, however, inspire hope that human communication is possible and, while we hold this treasure of the gospel in earthen vessels, we hold, indeed, a treasure which may be so perceived by others if we do not let the earthen vessels obstruct the view. And while we may see the truth only dimly as in a very old-fashioned mirror, there is a truth to be seen which all the distortions of the inadequate mirror cannot ultimately obscure. This vision can and must be shared. It is the reality of this treasure and vision which is at stake whenever the attempt is being made to reduce theology to anthropology. This is the reason why the notion that "religious language refers to human experience and nothing else" must be categorically rejected.

Similarly, the preoccupation with subjective religious feelings and the various efforts at manipulating the supernatural carried on inside and outside of the Christian churches, which has become so popular, should be seen as idolatrous. Far from being hailed as harbingers of religious revival, they should be recognized as opposed to the God who spoke and it was, "and the Word [which] became flesh and dwelt among us, full of grace and truth."

OBSESSED BY RELEVANCE

If an uneasy relationship, if not enmity, to reason and reasonable discourse is one problem which plagues contemporary protestantism; a second, no less serious, is the almost obsessive quest for relevance. Again, it could be claimed that "concern for the matter at hand," which may be a definition of relevance, motivated the reformers of the sixteenth century. In whatever manner Luther's *Ninety-five Theses* were distributed, they dealt with a matter of considerable current interest; otherwise their incredibly rapid spread across Europe would be hard to explain. It is true that nothing of general interest in the sixteenth century escaped the attention of the reformers. Both Luther and Calvin made not very insightful observations regarding the new theories of Copernicus about the arrangement of the heavenly bodies, for example. On most important matters they commented at length. Luther's *Address to the Christian Nobility* of 1520 was an obvious effort to speak to the issues which troubled his fellow citizens at the time. Calvin's relevance to Geneva was so evident that the council of this city had to ask him back because, in their judgment, the city could not operate successfully without his leadership. It was Calvin's relevance to the solution of the problems of Geneva which led to the successful effort to urge him to return. But Calvin was relevant to the problems of Geneva; he was not simply trying to find some issue that would make him appear to be relevant.

This is the difference between the relevance of a Luther and Calvin to the central issues of their age and the frantic quest for relevance of contemporary protestantism. A number of themes of the Hartford Appeal attempt to describe this quest. "Jesus can only be understood in terms of contemporary models of humanity." Or, "The world must set the agenda for the Church. Social, political, and economic programs to improve the quality of life are ultimately normative for the Church's mission in the world."

Again it might appear that the problem is here addressed in its liberal expression. But the effort to make Jesus into a political agitator of the left, like the *Comrade Jesus* of the late Sarah Cleghorn, and all the succeeding attempts to see him as an early version of Ernesto "Che" Guevara, so popular in certain circles, are equaled in intensity by the even more bizarre attempts to make him the prototype of the successful businessman and the inspiration for the victorious defense of capitalism against socialism and communism. Here Bruce Barton's book *The Man Nobody Knows* must stand as the classical example of Jesus' alleged capitalist relevance.

The agenda is set by the world. And what is the agenda? For Americans it is

MARTIN LUTHER, THEOLOGIAN OF THE CHURCH

often "the religion of the Republic," appropriately enshrined on our money: "In God We Trust," "*Novus Ordo Seclorum*," "*Annuit coeptis*." The inscriptions on the dollar bill supply the catechism and politicians write the commentary:

> Ours is the most advanced, most productive, richest, and most powerful society that humanity has seen since the dawn of history. What were the key elements in the formula we have followed which allowed us—in the brief span of two centuries—to raise up on this continent a nation which is a model for the world and a credit to mankind? It was freedom—freedom to work and to worship—to learn—to choose—to fashion the best life attainable with individual initiative, imagination, and courage. It was an unfettered free enterprise economic system that delivered to each man and woman the rewards they earned.[2]

With this sort of drivel as the agenda, it becomes the task of religion to maintain the illusion. For that large part of the world scared to death by the changes that are occurring, the church and its Jesus are devices to tell the earth to stop turning and to guarantee that the status quo is frozen forever. It is fascinating to observe protestant sectarians who are unwilling to pray the Lord's Prayer with anybody who does not assent to their sectarian vision suddenly embrace every-body in the common cause of defending capitalism and what they like to call the "American way of life." Thus J. A. O. Preus, the fundamentalist leader of the right wing of the Lutheran Church–Missouri Synod and author of their official key to the scriptures, preached at the command performance chapel services in the Nixon White House. His entire effort, which apparently attempts to restore his denomi-nation to its nineteenth-century position, is actually a cover-up for a strange utilization of the language of nineteenth-century conservative Lutheranism in order to endorse a peculiarly reactionary variety of American culture religion.

But while the advocates of relevance on the right see the world's agenda as demanding a holding action by the church, even if this means "presenting arms" and using military force to stop the changes taking place in Asia, Africa, Latin America, and the United States—the advocates of relevance on the left endorse all revolutions and see every change as God's hand at work in the affairs of humanity. Here the agenda of the world suggests that religion endorse any and all leftist revolutions. Thus while the repression of a black majority by a white minority in Namibia is seen for what it is, hardly a word is said about Uganda and the efforts to exterminate a black majority by a black minority. OPEC oil sheiks become forces of liberation and democracy against "fascist" Israel, and following the world's agenda means to supply religious justification to whatever human beings happen to want at the moment. Nobody has presented this theology of "radical chic" more persuasively than Harvey Cox in a succession of books that have in common only a charming style and the effort to keep up with the rapidly changing agenda of the world. Nobody has criticized this approach more incisively than Jacques Ellul, who wrote in 1972 about one of Cox's books:

> The latest fabulous example of justification is Harvey Cox's celebrated book, *The*

[2]Senator James O. Eastland, as quoted in Arthur Herzog, *The B.S. Factor: The Theory and Technique of Faking in America* (New York: Penguin, 1974) 31.

Secular City. It is hard to believe that a book so feebly thought through, so loaded with historical error, so sociologically and theologically superficial, so ordinary, with its repetition of all the commonplaces about secularization and the profane, and lacking in any depth in the subject, that a book so dubious in its historical analyses and so generalized in its sociology—that such a book would enjoy such a success. Just one thing explains it: It offers the public a justification for what is going on in the world, for what man is in the process of doing. It is true that modern man in his most fallen aspect wants exactly above everything else that someone should come along to tell him that he is right in doing what he is doing. That was the springboard for all the propaganda. From the standpoint of ideology and publicity, *The Secular City* is a great book. It supplies precisely the "solemn complement" (that Marx rightly accuses religion of supplying). Urban anonymity? That is great. That is freedom. Urban mobility is admirable, the very condition of progress. Pragmatism conforms to God's way of acting. The profane accords with God's will. The secular city is the meeting place of man and God. Since man's technological power is constantly increasing, the Church's message consists in giving assurance that it is up to man to create his own destiny.

This is a tissue of commonplaces, all of which are entirely nonbiblical and are rooted in an imaginary factor in modern society. Here is where theology does indeed become a completely futile superstructure. Yet, as Marx rightly said time and again, no matter how futile and tasteless it might be, it nevertheless turns into a deadly poison, in that it prevents man from seeing things as they really are. It causes him to live an illusion and to turn his back on the real. *The Secular City* is the prime example, for our modern society, of the opiate of the people.[3]

It is this manner of following the agenda of the world, whether done by J. A. O. Preus or Harvey Cox, which the Hartford Appeal calls into question, especially when this effort at relevance defends the violence of undeclared wars or senseless revolutions. In a quest for relevance, preachers do not only present arms to the forces of the status quo but also to the often equally violent and destructive "rebels without a cause."

The Christian faith could act as one of the most powerful de-alienating forces if theologians would only abandon their obsession with a fraudulent relevance. But in order to do so, and to help people to "see things as they are," it must be proclaimed in such a way as to reveal the illusions of the right, about capitalism and the American way of life, with the same honesty as the illusions of the left, with their glorification of revolution and utopian expectations. It can do so only if it resists the efforts from both directions to co-opt Jesus, the Christ, into the ideologies of the right or the left. The best way to achieve this is to take seriously the authority of Jesus as the eternal word and the presence of God with us. This New Testament Jesus is hard to fit into the programs of the right or the left, of the advocates of salvation by some nostalgic faith in the past or some euphoric faith in the future. It is the gospel's concern with the ambiguity of the existence of women and men in their present predicaments which must be emphasized. Human beings who have to live in a world in which good and evil are strangely mixed in their environment and in each human heart must not be sacrificed either to the perfectionist illusions of an imaginary past or the equally perfectionist illusions about an

---

[3]Jacques Ellul, *Hope in a Time of Abandonment* (New York: Saber, 1973) 152f.

imaginary future. We have to live now in the midst of a world in which the saving message for me may well be: "Let him who is without sin cast the first stone." Our task is not to point to our glorious history and our past accomplishments or to an elusive future which we cannot foresee, but to try now to live courageously in spite of all the ambiguities of saints and sinners in which we fully share. When Jesus was confronted by the doubting disciples of John the Baptist he sent this message to John, "Go and tell John what you have seen and heard: the blind receive their sight, the lame walk, lepers are cleansed, and the deaf hear, the dead are raised up, the poor have good news preached to them. And blessed is the one who takes no offense at me" (Luke 7:22-23).

In some small way we may be empowered to share in these signs of God's coming kingdom if we find ways to sustain human beings in their life together now. All human answers to the problems of this world are penultimate. God's ultimate answer will be a surprise to believers and unbelievers alike; in the meantime we are allowed to care for each other, show concern for each human being. In the abstract ideologies of both the right and the left, human persons count for very little; only the ultimate outcome matters and the end justifies any means which allegedly will help achieve it. A truly Christian relevance means concern and action in order to prevent people from being sacrificed to abstractions, be they those of the free enterprise system, dialectical materialism, machismo, women's liberation, or whatever the current fashion demands. "The Sabbath was made for human beings and not human beings for the Sabbath" is the verdict over the ideologies which have so successfully co-opted the Christian movement. "The norms for the Church's activity derive from its own perception of God's will for the world."

THE SCANDAL OF BEING RADICAL

If relevance and following the agenda set by the world is not the answer, does this not undercut the radical character of the Christian gospel? Is not the emphasis on Jesus as the Christ, and on the biblical witness concerning him, an escape from the involvement in the world which the cross of Christ demonstrates and symbolizes? As Theme 11 formulates this claim: "An emphasis on God's transcendence is at least a hindrance to, and perhaps incompatible with, Christian concern and action."

What, indeed, is radical Christianity? Is it really the reductionism which tries to trim from the biblical witness all those elements that are not plausible to the "cultured despisers of religion"? Is it radical to say things in a way that will not give offense? To eliminate from your message all controversial elements so that you may sound like any other moderately educated person? Nothing has been less radically Christian than the attempts on the part of some protestant theologians to sound like well-meaning supporters of the "conventional wisdom" that prevails at the university faculty club. This is no better than the effort on the part of others to sound just like every racist, sexist, or chauvinistic flag-waver. Is it radical Christianity to proclaim geological opinions about the age of the earth or the extent of

Noah's flood as the mark of true orthodoxy? Such obsession with trivialities can hardly be classified as defense of the faith. Indeed, there are different conventional wisdoms that one can conform to. But conformity to the conventional wisdom of your subculture is not radicalism. The opposition to the culture religion of one group from the vantage point of the culture religion of another group does not help us to escape from the falsification of the gospel by culture religion. Both the right and the left glorify a culture which is radically challenged by the New Testament and the proclamation of Jesus as the Christ.

The Hartford Appeal points toward the radical (in the sense of "root") assertion of the Christian movement in its last theme, where it rejects the claim that "the question of hope beyond death is irrelevant or at best marginal to the Christian understanding of human fulfillment." In a death-obsessed age (in recent years the most popular religion courses in American colleges and universities have dealt with death and dying), an age when the finality of death is the certainty which supplies the somber background to western thought, both capitalist and Marxist, the radical Christian assertion of the ultimate triumph of the God of Abraham, Isaac, and Jacob, who has chosen to be a God of the living and not of the dead, is revolutionary.

It was always thus. As long as Paul discussed religion and morality at Athens everybody had a good time. When he asserted the resurrection of the dead, the mood changed: "Some mocked; but others said, 'We will hear you again about this.'" Don't call us. We'll call you.

Yet it is this insistence on the victory of life which gave the Christian movement the power to transvalue all values in the first century. Political powers whose final weapon was the ability to kill their opponents did not know what to do with people who believed that God had said "yes" to life in the paradigmatic death and resurrection of Jesus, the Christ.

This notion was as offensive at the end of the first century as it is at the end of the twentieth. It was radical. And it was a scandal then, as it is a scandal now. Yet there is not much point in talking about the Christian faith without coming to terms with this scandal of the cross and the resurrection. All the moralistic legalism of the defenders of the status quo or the champions of revolution and utopia has little to do with the New Testament proclamation of God's victory over the last enemy.

We live in an age of joyless hedonism. The political movements of the right and the left vie with each other in an effort to supply the greatest good for the greatest number and seem like rival deck stewards competing with each other about the arrangement of the deck chairs just before the Titanic hits the iceberg. The general awareness of this situation is the reason why our hedonism is so joyless. For Christians to get into this act of the deck stewards and to come up with an alternative arrangement seems ludicrous in view of the radical news which constitutes the gospel and which, if true, changes the human situation completely. It is quoted at the end of the Hartford Appeal. It is the articulation and application of this truly radical insight which is the task of Christians. Everything else is ultimately trivial.

> We believe that God raised Jesus from the dead and are "...convinced that there is nothing in death or life, in the realm of spirits or superhuman powers, in the world as it is or in the world as it shall be, in the forces of the universe, in heights or depths—nothing in all creation that can separate us from the love of God in Christ Jesus our Lord." (Theme 13)

A radical Christian theology for our time can be derived from this gospel, but only by people who believe it and take it seriously. In contemporary protestantism, the people on the right seem to believe this gospel but fail to take it seriously; otherwise they could not be so preoccupied by what they call "fundamentals" as to obscure the proclamation of God's victory for humankind by their legalistic and literalistic controversies.

The people on the left may indeed take this gospel seriously, but precisely for this reason they do not believe it. That is why they substitute human fulfillment, self-realization, and evolution (not as a biological theory but as a means of grace) for the radical gospel. The Hartford Appeal would seem to be a call to the radical center of the Christian proclamation, the *kerygma* of the New Testament.

By doing this, it transcends all denominational boundaries. After all, it is an appeal issued by Orthodox, Roman Catholic, and protestant Christians. Thus it demonstrates that ecumenism has come a long way. No longer do Christians have to be content with an occasional ecumenical meeting. They may now be able to do theology together, addressing common problems and attacking jointly the dangers they perceive. Even the fact that those who publicly expressed their disapproval of the Hartford Appeal came from various denominational camps, both Roman Catholic and protestant, is an indication that the point may have been reached where theological issues can be discussed without any narrow denominational uniformity. This, too, may contribute to a truly radical Christian theology. Perhaps the Hartford Appeal has been one modest step in this direction.

Word & World
Supplement Series 2
1994

The Importance of Law for Christian Sexual Ethics

IT IS A CENTRAL PROPOSITION OF LUTHERAN THEOLOGY THAT THE DISTINCTION BE-tween law (God's command) and gospel (God's gift) is fundamental for an understanding of the Christian faith. This is of special significance for ethics since the political use of the law establishes a bridge between Christian ethics and the ethics of non-Christians. Because it is assumed that God's law in its political use addresses all people—even atheists—it makes it possible to discuss and even agree on ethical issues even though a fundamental disagreement on the understanding of the nature and destiny of human beings exists. One does not have to be a Christian to be a moral person in the sense of knowing the difference between right and wrong and acting in a morally responsible manner, thus contributing to the earthly welfare of human beings. It is, of course, assumed that such relatively moral behavior, while desirable and beneficial to the agent and the society in which he or she acts, does not "save." But it does benefit humanity and makes for a more humane world. As Luther puts it in the *Large Catechism*, "In the sight of God it is really faith that makes a person holy; faith alone serves [God] while our works serve the people" (*BC*, 385, §147).

In the discussion of sex and marriage in the Lutheran confessions and in Luther's writings it is assumed that the papal rules concerning marriage and celibacy are not only un-Christian but are also unnatural:

> We cannot approve of the law of celibacy put forth by our opponents because it clashes with divine and natural law and conflicts with the very decrees of councils. It obviously endangers religion and morality, for it produces endless scandals, sins, and the corruption of public morals. (*Apology*, *BC*, 240, §6).

For the *Apology*, marriage is an ordinance which God has built into nature and

---

This short essay was presented to Evangelical Lutheran Church in America Consultation on Sexuality, at its August 28, 1992 meeting. "The Importance of Law for Christian Ethics" (its original title) provides a general ethical framework for the discussion of sexuality.

human regulations cannot abolish it (*BC*, 241, §9). In the *Large Catechism*, Luther calls it "the first of all institutions" (*BC*, 393, §207). He claims

> It is not an estate to be placed on a level with the others; it precedes and surpasses them all, whether that of emperor, princes, bishops or anyone else. Important as the spiritual and civil estates are, these must humble themselves and allow all people to enter the estate of marriage, as we shall hear. It is not an exceptional estate, but the most universal and the noblest, pervading all Christendom and even extending throughout all the world. (Ibid., 393, §209-210).

The importance of marriage is not limited to Christians but is known by all human beings, though some might organize it differently (as, for example, the patriarchs). The *Apology* is prepared to say, "There may be greater purity of heart in a married man like Abraham or Jacob than in many others who are truly continent" (*BC*, 244, §35). In fact the depreciation of marriage implies the degrading of women. For Melanchthon this is further evidence for his suspicion of the rule of the Antichrist in the papacy and he observes: "Daniel says that it is characteristic of Antichrist's kingdom to despise women" (ibid., 243, §25).

A second implication of the relationship of sex and marriage to law is that for Luther and the confessions the law always accuses. Since sex and marriage are under the law they will, indeed, contribute to the earthly welfare of humanity (the political use of the law) but at the same time reveal our forgiveness and grace (the theological use of the law). Thus the attempt to claim that sexual behavior—any sexual behavior—can be free from sin is counter to the understanding of the human situation as presented in the confessions. But it is precisely because of the power and prevalence of sin that marriage is needed. "Marriage is more necessary now than in the state of purity" (*Apology*, in *BC*, 241, §16).

One of the problems in the discussion of human sexuality is the tendency to see this aspect of human life in isolation from all others. All facets of human existence are involved in sin. Human communication is threatened by our tendency to bear false witness and to lie. Our basic and necessary quest for food and shelter and the resources to provide for those who are dependent upon us is threatened and perverted by greed and the desire to take what does not belong to us and covetously accumulate and squander our possessions. The Christian community is called to proclaim the law and the gospel in all these situations. The isolation of sexuality and the attempt to exonerate all sexual behavior, whether it supports the welfare and continuation of the human family or not, contributes to the very anomie threatening the survival of the human race. It threatens the earthly welfare of all people which the law is designed to promote.

It is apparent from the scriptures and reason that the standards for human behavior should not be derived from statistics and opinion polls but from the law available to all human beings through reason and conscience. The clarification of this law as well as obedience to its demands is the common task of all men and women of good will. In this task, Christians may learn from all who are engaged in this pursuit but they themselves will be guided not only by reason but by what they perceive to be the revelation of the divine purpose for human life in holy scriptures. The result may be considerable agreement on some issues, disagreement on others. Only where a majority of the body politic can be persuaded that a law does, indeed, contribute to the public good will it be adopted. When a basic conflict arises between the law of the state and what Christians believe to be the law of God they will obey God rather than human beings—and take the consequences.

Word & World
Supplement Series 2
1994

Why Recall Luther Today?

THERE ARE MANY REASONS WHY ONE MIGHT WANT TO REMEMBER AND DISCUSS a Christian theologian who has managed to excite politicians, psychologists, playwrights, and even preachers five hundred years after his birth. Most theologians are barely noticed while they are among us and completely forgotten once they are dead. What made Luther such a lasting presence not only in the Christian world but in western culture?

Some reasons for the attention given to Luther in the twentieth century are simply wrong. By now it is common knowledge that Luther was not a pioneer of capitalism or nationalism. He did not understand the economic changes caused by the explorations of his age which eventually (much later to be sure) produced modern capitalism. A rudimentary form of venture-capitalism had existed long before Luther and had facilitated both the discoveries of the explorers and the sale of indulgences. Nationalism, in the modern sense of the word, came into existence centuries after Luther's death. There was no German state in Luther's time. The emperor, who was also the king of Spain, spoke broken German; his Spanish was not much better, and he preferred to speak French. Soldiers in the sixteenth century were not nationalistic freedom fighters but more like professional football players or hired guns who fought for those employers who could afford their services.

Furthermore, Luther was not a forerunner of Hitler (who unlike Karl Marx was not even nominally "Lutheran") or even an anti-semite. He did express vicious and deplorable anti-Jewish sentiments, precisely because he took the Old Testament and its patriarchs and prophets so very seriously. He felt threatened in the very center of his theology by the rabbinic exegesis of the Hebrew Bible and by the hopes of his Jewish contemporaries that his critique of the established church

---

In 1983, Dr. Forell was asked to respond to this question by the editorial board of Word & World, *as a special issue was devoted to the occasion of the 500th anniversary of Luther's birth. This essay forms a fitting conclusion to this retrospective collection of Dr. Forell's work, because it ties together many of the themes found throughout the preceding pages.*

might lead to a reexamination of all Christian claims and thus presage the coming of the Messiah.

Thus it appears that some fashionable reasons to remember Luther are wrong. There are others which are at best dubious. The emphasis on Luther as a religious genius is beside the point, even if the various advocates of this view were more precise as to the exact meaning of the word "genius." Religious geniuses tend to be too idiosyncratic to be long remembered. Since their experience of the divine is so extraordinary, it cannot be replicated by ordinary people, and they are soon forgotten. Like comets they are spectacular to behold but hardly a source of light or aids to navigation.

Not much more can be said in support of "Luther, the German prophet." Most Germans are embarrassed by all the nonsense written on this topic. This title, indeed, was applied to him, even during his lifetime, but he observed then, "this haughty title I will henceforth have to assign to myself, to please and oblige my papists and asses,"[1] and promptly called himself something much less pretentious, "a faithful teacher." Even if the years 1933-1945 could be blotted from memory, the description "German prophet" tends to obscure our understanding of Luther. He was a German, but what makes him interesting today is the universal appeal of his understanding of the gospel. In fact, the somewhat surprising scope of the celebration of Luther's birthday by the government of the German Democratic Republic may be a combination of pride in their most famous native son (Marx, after all, was born in what is now the Federal Republic) and an understandable desire to attract western currency to their country from tourists interested in Luther's legacy. It is hardly "the German prophet" who attracts all this attention.

None of the significant sayings of Luther is limited in application to Germany. Even his frequent excoriation of German drunkenness might apply more generally than he thought. He did not translate the Bible into the German language because he thought German was more significant than other languages, but because the people he dealt with spoke it. The opinion that Luther's German Bible is superior to all other translations is a later development which did much to retard the indigenization of the Church of the Augsburg Confession in North America.

Thus it is my claim that the reasons why one might want to recall Luther today are essentially theological—even if they have social and political implications. I would like to mention three that are rather obvious.

I. LAW AND GOSPEL

Luther recognized and reiterated that the church is a creature of God's word. This is the message of his hymns and prayers: "Lord, keep us steadfast in thy word!" But this word is a very complex reality. Not only does the term describe the second person of the Trinity and the proclamation of his work and will, as well as the canon of the Bible; it is also both law and gospel, God's demand and God's gift. The ability to distinguish between the two makes the theologian. It is equally

---

[1]*Dr. Martin Luther's Warning to His Dear German People* (1531), LW 47:29.

disastrous to make the law into the gospel or to make the gospel into a new law. Both are God's word. Both have to be proclaimed by God's people. But if they are confused, the message is perverted and the church degenerates. It could be useful to the church and the world to apply Luther's clarifying distinction to our present situation.

Today fundamentalists and liberals, capitalists and Marxists vie with each other in propagating their particular laws as the liberating message for all people. If we only adopt their particular program, the kingdom of God or its secular equivalent is bound to come. It is faintly amusing to observe those who yesterday made redemptive claims for their religio-political legalism complain about those who today make similar claims for quite a different set of laws. Yesterday's proponents of religion in politics are today's opponents. What both groups have in common is their unjustified trust that their particular political program will save the human race.

There are, indeed, better and worse moral and political agendas. They deserve full and open debate. Luther would suggest the meticulous use of reason in these discussions. It was because he rejected the claims made by some of his contemporaries, the crusaders on the right and on the left—that gospel answers were available to law questions—that his solutions proved to be so nonideological. As long as this world lasts, human beings will have to be satisfied with provisional answers, subject to revision on the basis of better information. But since there are important differences between the proposed social, political, and cultural programs, one would hope that the agenda lending greater support to the earthly welfare of human beings would be adopted and implemented. To be sure, the kingdom of God will not be brought in by any of these efforts. It was not ushered in at Wittenberg, as Luther stated frequently, nor in Rome, Geneva, or Constantinople. It is not being realized in Washington or Moscow, Nicaragua or El Salvador, Johannesburg or Harare. This does not mean that there are no significant distinctions between these various efforts. Some are far closer than others to the divine law which all human political systems ought to reflect. But they are all pretentious and even idolatrous if they claim to solve the ultimate problems of human existence.

Luther is so useful to us because his distinction between law and gospel can help us to avoid making redemptive claims for whatever kind of law we cherish. In this sense he may be of service to all of us, Christians and non-Christians, whenever we are tempted to make ultimate claims for our penultimate insights. Since no law—moral, historical, scientific, aesthetic, or even religious—can save us, we will have to be satisfied with less ambitious achievements and leave salvation where Luther left it. It is not subject to manipulation—not even by charismatic personalities or ecclesiastical institutions.

II. THE *SIMUL* PRINCIPLE

Luther's second theological insight of significance for us today was his insistence that Christians are righteous and sinners at the same time. Righteous through faith in Christ (or as he sometimes said "in hope"), they are sinners in fact as long as they live in this world. This notion may be found as early as his commentary on Romans. He maintained it throughout his life. It gave him perspective on all the honors and adulation which came to him from his supporters so that he never forgot that before God we are all beggars. This insight tends to relativize all absolute claims human beings are apt to make. It reduces the differences which they establish between themselves to mere insignificance.

We live in an age when all sorts of small differences are being senselessly exaggerated and given metaphysical importance. Good and evil are associated with the distinctions between political and economic systems. The differences between the sexes and races are exalted to a point where virtue and vice depend on pigmentation or genitals. These distinctions are further exacerbated by loyalties to languages, lifestyles, tastes, and traditions. As a result, the human race has been divided into a multitude of camps, each claiming some kind of superiority and blaming their suffering and the suffering of the human race on the diabolic machinations of their opponents. While this attitude may not be new, it has become disruptive and destabilizing in an age when the sheer number of human beings resulting from the population explosion and their close proximity caused by advances in transportation technology make such sentiments more dangerous.

The realization that all human beings are sinners might help to reduce the barriers among us, which we have magnified and embroidered out of all proportion. This path, suggested by Luther, seems more promising than the proposal that we might accept each other as being really good people, or as the popular psychology would have it, as being "O.K." It is easier to admit that we are all sinners, since this assertion conforms to our experience, than that we are all "good." We might be willing to make such a claim for ourselves but not equally willing to grant this to others. Luther's negative approach is actually more promising because it is more credible.

The massive self-righteousness, the overweening pride and arrogance of our age make negotiations and compromise in politics and economics, in international and human relations so difficult. Luther's emphasis on the pervasiveness and profundity of sin may prove helpful to us, even if some other term has to be used by our anti-theological friends in order to describe the sickness unto death that Christians call sin, which threatens the survival of the race. It is hard to help anybody who is convinced that he or she does not need help. Luther described the bondage of men and women so colorfully because he wanted them to be ready to accept liberation. It was not a counsel of despair or some ingrained pessimism but in his language, "the proclamation of the law," which would prepare people for the gospel.

Even those who do not share Luther's confidence that there is a remedy to the sickness of the human race might have to grant that fighting among the patients in the ward that we call our world makes our situation even more desperate. The honest acceptance of our limitations, the reduction of vanity and self-deception is a valuable first step for everybody, whatever the cure, and even if one believes that such a cure is not available.

Of course, nowhere is this counsel more in order than among the religious communities who have often supplied the most perverse examples of self-righteousness and arrogance. Mere verbal affirmation of human sinfulness is not enough, lest the abject confession of sin becomes the most subtle form of pride.

III. FINITE AS BEARER OF THE INFINITE

But there is a third theological insight submitted by Luther which may help us understand our human predicament at the end of the twentieth century. It is the notion undergirding Luther's christology, his view of the scriptures, the eucharist, and vocation—namely, that the finite is the bearer of the infinite, that God deals with human beings not by some unmediated confrontation but through earthly means. The other side of this same insight is Luther's conviction that all human creatures are instruments of God's will.

The christological dimension is obvious. He sings:

> Den aller Weltkreis nie beschloss
> Der liegt in Marien's Schoss
> Er ist ein Kindlein worden klein
> Der alle Ding erhält allein.[2]

For Luther the incarnation, the atonement, and the resurrection are all seen as events in time and space, taking place in human history, revealing God's presence to his people. Luther pushed this emphasis to the barely orthodox extreme of proclaiming the death of God—on the cross. Even in the *Small Catechism*, written so that children might understand and memorize it, Luther says, "I believe that Jesus Christ, true God begotten of the Father from eternity, and also true man, born of the Virgin Mary...delivered me and freed me...with his innocent sufferings and death."[3] He insisted that Jesus Christ, who is true God, died on the cross. Thus Luther was a very special "death of God theologian." The implications of this emphasis upon the significance of the finite as a medium of God's revelation is clearly seen in the conviction that the bread and wine of holy communion are simultaneously the body and blood of Christ, and, perhaps not as clearly to many Lutherans, that the human words of Paul and Peter are the word of God. No transubstantiation of bread and wine or human word, no apotheosis of the finite, but real presence in, with, and under the human products of bread and wine, language, grammar, and worldview.

Indeed, Luther's view of the finite as bearer of the infinite explains his much debated understanding of vocation as well. The Christian is the means through which God works in the world. He writes:

---

[2]["He whom the world could not inwrap/Yonder lies in Mary's lap;/He is become an infant small,/who by His might upholdeth all" (Bernhard Pick, *Luther as a Hymnist* [Philadelphia: Lutheran Book Store, 1875] 43). Ed.]

[3]*BC*, 345.

> Surely we are named after Christ [Christians], not because he is absent from us,
> but because he dwells in us, that is, because we believe in him and are *Christs one*
> *to another* and do to our neighbors as Christ does to us.[4]

God uses human beings to accomplish his purpose. This is true not only in the more obvious area of service to the neighbor, but for Luther the entire world is a divine masquerade in which God's purpose is accomplished through the witting or unwitting cooperation of human beings. As he stated in *The Bondage of the Will*: "All things even including the ungodly cooperate with God" (*Omnia enim impia illi cooperantur*).[5]

> He does not work in us without us, because it is for this he has created and
> preserved us, that he might work in us and we might cooperate with him,
> whether outside his Kingdom through his general omnipotence, or inside his
> Kingdom by the special virtue of his Spirit.[6]

What can this possibly mean to us today? We live in a world plagued by the most ancient of all heresies called variously dualism, Manichaeism, or gnosticism. While sharply dividing reality into opposing realms—the realm of the spirit or the realm of matter—either one or the other is devalued if not denied. There are those who still follow their prophets Marx or Freud and reject religion and the realm of the spirit as the opiate of the people or hopeless illusion. Others who only yesterday proclaimed science the savior of the human race are today dreading it as a polluting demon destroying human life and all spiritual values and threatening the abolition of humanity. Theologians are at least marginally involved in this conflict. Some vacillate between the "death of God" and "the new polytheism." The rediscovery and positive evaluation of gnosticism is a symptom of our time. The veneration of the unfathomable processes of nature and history, though at first sight contradictory, is ultimately one in the denial of the specific and unique event of Exodus and Golgotha.

Thus Luther speaks to our age. He asks us to examine the much-heralded division of reality carefully and critically, for this theologian of the "two kingdoms" never forgot that both kingdoms had but one king, that the right hand and the left hand executed the will of the one head. Even for those who do not accept Luther's theological axioms, the reexamination of his insistence on the unity of reality might prove helpful. But for those who take his theology seriously, the insight that the finite is the bearer of the infinite is a somber warning against withdrawal, allowing participation and service to the world and its people as service to God.

There is hardly an issue confronting men and women today where Luther's insights have not some relevance. The distinction between God's law and gospel allows full cooperation with all men and women everywhere on behalf of their

---

[4]*The Freedom of a Christian* (1520), LW 31:368. Italics added.
[5]*The Bondage of the Will* (1525), LW 33:242.
[6]Ibid., 33:243.

earthly welfare, while at the same time insisting without compromise or reduction on the uniqueness of the gospel of God's participation in human life and history in the life, death, and resurrection of Jesus. Christians everywhere, but particularly in Africa and Asia, are confronted by the question, How is it possible for a Christian to relate openly and positively to a largely non-Christian world? The law allows not only tolerance, which is far too little, but appreciation and utilization of the insights given to all women and men everywhere.

Luther's insistence on the pervasiveness and persistence of sin warns Christians against an easy identification of themselves, their theologies (even Lutheran theologies), and their institutions with the cause of God and sees all people as equally in need of grace and forgiveness. Negotiation and reconciliation are not only possible but imperative because of our common failure to obey the law written in the hearts of all.

The finite as the bearer of the infinite applies not only to the classical Christian means of grace, the word and the sacraments. The awareness of this divine mode of operation could also enable us to see the presence of God in unexpected people and places. The God who, according to Luther, has created and preserved us in order that he might work in us, and we might cooperate with him, may then open our eyes to opportunities to see his works where we have never seen them before.

ACKNOWLEDGEMENTS

We gratefully acknowledge the original publication of the essays appearing in this book and, where applicable, thank the copyright holders for their kind permission to reprint this material.

"They Told What Had Happened on the Road," *dialog* 33/2 (1994) 129-134. Reprinted with permission.

"The Reformation and the Modern World," in *The Reformation and the Revolution* (Sioux Falls, SD: Augustana College, 1970) 57-67. Reprinted with permission of the author.

"Faith Active in Love," originally published as "The Meaning for Man of Luther's Concept of Faith," in *Reformation and Authority*, ed. Kyle Sessions (Lexington, MA: Heath, 1968) 83-94. Reprinted from FAITH ACTIVE IN LOVE by George Forell, copyright © 1954 Augsburg Publishing House. Used by permission of Augsburg Fortress.

"Justification and Eschatology in Luther's Thought," *Church History* 38/2 (1969) 164-174. Reprinted with permission from *Church History*.

"Luther and Christian Liberty," *The Bulletin* 68/1 (1988) 3-11. Reprinted with permission.

"Luther and Conscience," *The Bulletin* 55/1 (1975) 3-11. Reprinted with permission.

"Luther's Conception of 'Natural Orders,'" *Lutheran Church Quarterly* 18/2 (1945) 160-177. Reprinted with permission.

"The Political Use of the Law," "Luther's Theology and Foreign Policy," and "Luther's Theology and Domestic Politics," originally published as "Luther and Politics," in *Luther and Culture*, ed. George W. Forell, Harold Grimm, and Theodore Hoelty-Nickel (Decorah, IA: Luther College, 1960) 1-69. Reprinted with permission.

"Luther and the War against the Turks," *Church History* 14/4 (1945) 256-271. Reprinted with permission from *Church History*.

"Luther's View concerning the Imperial Foreign Policy," *Lutheran Quarterly* 4/2 (1952) 153-169. Reprinted with permission.

"Luther Today," *The Augustana Quarterly* 25/4 (1946) 291-296. Reprinted with permission.

"The Future of Theology in the Church," *Lutheran Quarterly*, New Series 4/1 (1990) 1-9. Reprinted with permission.

"A Neglected Aspect of St. Paul's Doctrine of the Church," *Lutheran Church Quarterly* 17/1 (1944) 48-60. Reprinted with permission.

"Eucharistic Presence as the Key to Theological Understanding," in *Vierhundertfünfzig Jahre lutherische Reformation 1517-1967: Festschrift für Franz Lau zum 60. Geburtstag*, ed. Helmar Junghans (Berlin: Evangelische Verlagsanstalt, 1967) 145-156. Reprinted with permission.

"The Formula of Concord and the Teaching Ministry," *The Sixteenth Century Journal* 8/4 (1977) 39-47. Reprinted with permission.

"The Place of Theology in the Church," originally published as "The Place of Theology in the ELCA," *Lutheran Forum* 25/1 (1991) 34-38. Reprinted with permission.

"Law and Gospel," in *Marburg Revisited: A Reexamination of Lutheran and Reformed Traditions*, ed. Paul C. Empie and James L. McCord (Minneapolis: Augsburg, 1966) 128-152. Reprinted from MARBURG REVISTED, edited by Paul C. Empie and James L. McCord, copyright © 1966 Augsburg Publishing House. Used by permission of Augsburg Fortress.

"Justification and Justice," translated from "Rechtfertingung und Recht," in *Rechtfertigung und Weltverantwortung: Internationale Konsultation Neuendettelsau 9. - 12. September 1991* (Neuendettelsau: Freimund-Verlag, 1993) 221-235. Translated and reprinted with permission.

"Christ and Culture: Reflections and Questions," in *Confessing Christ in Cultural Contexts: International Consultation, Jerusalem, March 23-27, 1981*, ed. Maren Matthiesen (Geneva: Lutheran World Federation, 1981) 64-68. Reprinted with permission.